Introduction to PLAY
in Early Childhood

This book is for Aubrey and Frank.
Play well little ones.

2nd Edition

Introduction to
PLAY
in Early Childhood

Edited by
Jane Waters-Davies

S Sage

S Sage

3rd Floor, HYLO
103-105 Bunhill Row
London, EC1Y 8LZ

2455 Teller Road
Thousand Oaks
California 91320

10th Floor, Emaar Capital Tower 2
MG Road, Sikanderpur, Sector 26
Gurugram, Haryana – 122002
India

8 Marina View Suite 43-053
Asia Square Tower 1
Singapore 018960

Library of Congress Control Number: 2025947185

British Library Cataloguing in Publication data

A catalogue record for this book is available from the British Library

ISBN 978-1-0362-0964-3
ISBN 978-1-0362-0963-6 (pbk)

Editor: James Clark
Editorial Assistant: Harry Dixon
Production editor: Nicola Marshall
Copyeditor: Raxshana Ravindraraj
Indexer: TNQ Tech Pvt. Ltd.
Marketing manager: Lorna Patkai
Cover design: Wendy Scott
Typeset by: TNQ Tech Pvt. Ltd.
Printed in the UK

Contents

List of Figures and Tables

Figures

Tables

About the Editor

Jane Waters-Davies is an Associate Professor in Early Childhood Education at the University of Wales Trinity Saint David. Originally a teacher in London, she has worked in higher education in Wales for over 25 years, leading programmes in Early Childhood Studies, Initial Teacher Education and Doctorate in Education. Jane is now involved in research, works with postgraduate research students in the field of education and sits on the Welsh Government advisory panel for early years. Her doctorate explored the affordances for interaction and child agency in the outdoor and indoor spaces of the early years at school. Her research interests lie in young children's participation, play and learning, outdoor play and early concept development and the professional education of those working with young children. She is passionate about the importance of early childhood educators understanding the complexities of their professional role, being able to advocate for playful learning on behalf of children and being respected for the tremendous work they do.

About the Authors

Tereza Aidonopoulou-Read is a Senior Lecturer in Inclusion and Special Educational Needs at the University of Northampton. Her research and practice focus on inclusive pedagogy, neuro-diversity and participatory approaches with children and families. Tereza leads international collaborations on inclusive education and has developed award-winning programmes supporting professionals in the United Kingdom and Thailand. She is especially interested in how play and creative assessment strategies can empower disabled learners and inform equitable educational practices.

Louise Atkins is an Associate Professor in Early Childhood at the University of Greenwich. Louise studied at the University of Greenwich and is an EYP. She has an MA in Education (Early Years) and an MA in Research and is studying towards a Doctorate in Education focusing on the impact of Early Years Teachers in the sector. She has worked and lead in settings for 10 years within the private, voluntary and independent sector. She is an ex Early Years Ofsted Inspector. Her areas of interests in research are the impact that graduate early years practitioners and teachers have in settings, quality practice and reflection and the importance of attachment and relationships.

Amanda Bateman is an Associate Professor in Early Childhood Education, University of Waikato. Her research involves collecting and analysing video footage of children's social interactions, and teacher–child pedagogical interactions. Recent publications include the books *Early Childhood Education: The Co-Production of Knowledge and Relationships* (Ashgate, 2015), and *Talking with children: A Handbook of Interaction in Early Childhood Education* (co-edited with Amelia Church; Cambridge University Press, 2022).

Karen Boardman has been working in the field of Early Childhood Education for 40+ years, particularly with under-threes and more recently, as a researcher over the last 10 years. Karen's research interests and publications are focused on under-threes, literacy, early reading, play, leadership and research circles. Karen is the Head of Department for Early Years Education at Edge Hill University, supporting undergraduate students, postgraduate students and colleagues with their research projects. Karen is also the Director of the new International Centre for Early Years Education (ICEYE) at Edge Hill University.

Natalie Canning is the Co-Director of the Children's Research Centre at the Open University, Professional Doctorate lead for Childhood and Youth and a Senior Lecturer in Early Childhood. Her research centres on children's empowerment in play, supporting children to explore personal, social and emotional development through play. She has published in the areas of professional development, children's play and creative spaces and taught across Early Childhood undergraduate and postgraduate programmes.

Sarah Chicken is a Senior Lecturer in Childhood and Education at the University of the West of England, with an interest in pedagogical practices which stem from a children's rights perspective. Her doctoral research explored interpretations of project approaches, including Reggio Emilia. As an adult with dyspraxia, she is also engaged with research related to inclusive pedagogy and neurodiversity.

Jennie Clement is a Lecturer in Teacher Education and Professional Learning at Cardiff Metropolitan University. Her research interests are underpinned by democratic and participatory constructions of teaching and learning with young children. They consider the pedagogical roles and relationships that are formed and supported through different constructions of space and spatial practice.

Linda Cooper is the Programme Coordinator for the family of Education Studies degree courses at the University of Chichester, having taught in education for 25 years. Before commencing her current post, she was a Lecturer in Early Childhood Studies at Portsmouth University and a member of the teacher training team at Bishop Grosseteste University. She has published in the fields of early years, technology and humanities education as well as education in crisis settings.

Giulia Cortellesi works at International Child Development Initiatives (ICDI), the Netherlands. She is a cultural anthropologist with more than ten years of experience as researcher and trainer in the field of ECEC and social inclusion. Since 2017, she has been overall coordinator of the TOY for Inclusion Project, which explores how intergenerational learning embedded in ECEC initiatives can support intercultural dialogue and social cohesion.

Charlotte Greenway is a Senior Lecturer in the School of Psychology and Counselling at the University of Wales Trinity Saint David. She has been the programme manager for the BSc Applied Psychology programme since 2011. Her recent research interests focus on children with ADHD and children's mental health.

Laura Hutchings is the Programme Director for the Education Studies programmes at University of Wales Trinity Saint David. She delivers on a range of modules that focus on curriculum, pedagogy and assessment, additional learning needs and creativity and well-being. She has supported adults, children and young people with additional learning needs in a range of education settings.

Carys Jennings is an Early Years Educator, working at the Open University. She taught in the primary sector for over ten years, before moving into teacher education. She has worked on many projects to support teachers' planning and pedagogy, and co-authored publications for use with young children. Carys remains passionate about the importance of ensuring play opportunities for children, and her doctoral studies involve exploring children's well-being and happiness in school.

Margaret Kernan has spent the last 30 years working in education and development. She is co-editor with Giulia Cortellesi of the 2020 book, *Intergenerational Learning in Practice: Together Old and Young* (Routledge). She was previously a Senior Programme Manager at International Child Development Initiatives, the Netherlands, and now is a Lecturer in Education at Hibernia College, Ireland.

Debra Laxton is a Senior Lecturer in Education and Early Childhood Lead at the University of Chichester. She has spent her career of over 30 years focused on the education of young children, and currently lectures on early years education across initial teaching and education programmes. Debra is studying for a PhD at De Montfort University, exploring how translational research can impact on educator practice to improve early childhood education for children both in crisis settings and in the United Kingdom.

Natalie MacDonald is the Programme Director for degree programmes in Early Years Education and Care at the University of Wales Trinity Saint David. Natalie is undertaking a Doctorate in Education, her thesis 'Exploring the visibility of Foucault's "governmentality" within early years practice; how do practitioners navigate conflicting "regimes of truth"?' is based on the influence of early years education and care policy in practice.

Mel McCree is a Senior Lecturer within Early Childhood Studies at Bath Spa University (BSU), teaching modules on play, justice and research with children. Mel's research focuses on environment–society relationships, for example the everyday eco-social in/justices in how children and families participate as citizens. Her interdisciplinary research communicates between more-than-human geographies, environmental humanities, nature connections and feminist new materialisms with childhood studies. She is currently exploring these questions as a Research Fellow for Creative Industries at BSU.

Pekka Mertala works as an Assistant Professor of Multiliteracies and Digital Literacies in the Faculty of Education and Psychology at the University of Jyväskylä. His research focuses mainly on young children's and early years teachers' relationships with digital technologies.

Alison Murphy is currently a Lecturer on the BA Education Studies: Primary at University of Wales Trinity Saint David, teaching a range of modules across the programme. She has previously worked in a number of HE settings and her research interests focus around children's perceptions of national identity, participatory research methods, children's rights and inclusion.

Sarah Ndlovu is the International Education Specialist at Children on the Edge, a UK-based iNGO which works to educate and protect marginalised children. With a Master's in Education and International Development from University College London (UCL), she specialises in implementing education in emergency contexts. Sarah is responsible for curriculum development and integrating play-based learning into global sustainable early childhood programmes for refugee and displaced children.

Introduction to Play in Early Childhood

Mariana Palazuelos works at International Child Development Initiatives (ICDI), the Netherlands. She is a social worker with more than five years of experience in project management, research and training. Her research interests include early childhood and child protection. Since 2018, Mariana has been working with Margaret Kernan and Giulia Cortellesi on the 'Making the first 1000 days count!' programme and was involved in the development of the 'Home Visiting Toolkit'.

Alison Rees-Edwards is a Senior Lecturer on the BA (Hons.) Early Years Education and Care degree programmes at University of Wales Trinity Saint David, and has interests in the importance of play, language development and additional needs. Her published research includes articles that focus on knowledge and attitudes of teachers and teaching assistants towards ADHD.

Angela Rekers is a Lecturer in Early Childhood Education at Saint Ambrose University, Davenport, Iowa, with a teaching background in English and Environmental Education. Her research interests include literacy, ecological literacy and children's use of outdoor space(s). Her doctoral research focused on children's participative experiences in reciprocity with the socio-material environments of the reception year classroom and at forest school. She recently co-edited *Outdoor Learning and Play: Pedagogical Practices and Children's Cultural Formation* with L.T. Grindheim and H.V. Sørensen (Springer, 2021).

Nanna Ryder is a former primary school teacher and is a Senior Lecturer in Initial Teacher Education at the University of Wales Trinity Saint David. She is currently studying for her Doctorate in Education and her main research interests include children's well-being, inclusion and additional learning needs. She edited an e-book, *Cefnogi Pob Plentyn* (*Supporting Every Child*), that was awarded runner-up for the best Welsh-medium resource in 2019.

Jennie Swift is a Senior Lecturer in the Department of Early Years Education at Edge Hill University. Jennie Leads the Year 1 Undergraduate BA (Hons) Primary Early Years Education with QTS, setting our new trainee teachers on their pathway to becoming a teacher on the 3-7 programme. Jennie also teaches across all programmes in the Early Years Education Department. Jennie is a strong advocate for play, communication, language and literacy. Her research interests are literacy, play and pedagogy. Jennie's passion is to get our trainee teachers 'playing'.

Saara Salomaa works as a Senior Advisor and Media Education Team Leader in the Finnish National Audiovisual Institute KAVI, a governmental agency legally obligated for promoting media education in Finland. She is also conducting her PhD research in Tampere University, focusing on media education in the context of early childhood education.

Glenda Tinney is a Senior Lecturer at the University of Wales Trinity Saint David interested in outdoor learning and young children's experiences of Education for Sustainable Development and Global Citizenship (ESDGC). She has a level 3 Forest School Leader qualification which supports her work with children and adults in the outdoors. She regularly volunteers in a local setting supporting outdoor learning.

Lauren Whale is a Senior Lecturer in Early Childhood at the University of Greenwich. Lauren has been working in the early years sector since 1995 and has a background in early years leadership and management. Lauren is passionate about the benefits of developing reflective practice and believes this strategy is a step towards bridging the gap between theory and practice.

Sarah Whitehouse is a Senior Lecturer in Childhood and Education at the University of the West of England, where she specialises in teaching the humanities subjects across a range of age phases. Her doctoral research explored the teaching of sensitive and controversial issues in history.

Acknowledgements

Thank you to all the wonderful authors who have contributed to this book. They have given their time and expertise, willingly and with care and attention, throughout the development of this second edition. As a part of our ongoing reflexive consideration, the contributing authors and I are mindful of the need to consider the origins of the theories and knowledges upon which we build our understanding of the world of play. As part of the collaborative effort to decolonise curricula, we are aware of discussions and questions being raised about the origins of theories and to whom they are attributed; for example, see the debate about Maslow's theory around the hierarchy of needs (Sidebottom 2019; Blackstock 2011). We are mindful that there may well be other theorists/theories that will, in due course, be subject to similar critique and appropriate scrutiny, and we are fully engaged with this ongoing exploration regarding the appropriation of ideas.

Blackstock, C. (2011) The emergence of the breath of life theory. *Journal of Social Work Values and Ethics* 8(1) [Online]. Available at: https://jswve.org/download/2011-1/spr11-blackstock-Emergence-breath-of-life-theory.pdf?

Sidebottom, K. (2019) *Whose knowledge, whose culture? Re-thinking theory through restorative approaches.* Leeds Becket Carnegie Education Blogs. Available at https://www.leedsbeckett.ac.uk/blogs/carnegie-education/2019/04/whose-knowledge/

Introduction to Play in Early Childhood

Jane Waters-Davies

Welcome to an *Introduction to Play in Early Childhood*

The second edition of this text remains unashamedly introductory in nature, intended primarily for students for whom an understanding of play forms part of their studies and practice, and also for their lecturers, and professionals who are interested in finding out about play and its importance for children's development, and within early years provision. Play is a contested concept; with three completely new chapters, as well as extensions and revisions to the original chapters, this edition provides engaging insight into critical ideas and practice in an accessible manner. The new chapters bring deeper consideration of inclusion in play practice, planning for play, observing play, and innovations in the field of play in Early Childhood Education and Care (ECEC).

The authors of each chapter are experts in their field, and have a deep understanding of play and its complexities, tensions and challenges. They have written each chapter in a manner that does not assume prior knowledge, but explains concepts, ideas, and theories in clear, concise, and accessible language. We deal with some complex ideas in this book, but intend to help you, as the reader, navigate these complexities and think critically about them, by signalling additional reading and links between one chapter and another, so that you can extend and deepen your knowledge and understanding as you wish.

In this text you will find descriptive chapters and discursive chapters. Established ways of thinking and working are set alongside new ideas being brought to this field of understanding, so that we think anew about established patterns. This text provides you with background information, as you would expect from a source text, and also challenges you to think about provision and practice critically and deeply. Each chapter is a stepping off point for your development as a critical thinker in the field of play.

In each chapter you will find a set of specific features. The objectives, set out at the start, establish what the chapter will enable you to know, understand, or consider as you read. Within the main text you will find reflection points; these are moments of reflection or action that support you to consider and take in what you have read, and can be undertaken when you read alone, or as part of a lecture or directed task; as part of your studies for a play module, for example. Each chapter also provides a case study; this is a real-world example of the ideas you have met, and offers a window through which to consider the implications of these ideas for early years practice. Towards the end of each chapter you will find a summary, this is a bulleted list of key ideas that are the main 'take-aways' from the chapter. This is followed by an annotated list of additional reading; here the chapter author has indicated some further material that would expand upon, or deepen, the content introduced in the main body of the chapter. Finally, there is a full reference list sitting at the end of each chapter – this allows you to follow up on any citations within the chapter directly.

As you read, you should expect different styles of writing throughout the book. Some chapters are more descriptive, providing information about the field of play, and some chapters provide critical consideration of tensions that arise when we think deeply about provision for our youngest children. Each chapter is intended as an *introduction* to the ideas it contains – each chapter is therefore a *launching-off pad* for your thinking and understanding, not a stand-alone source!

Finally, there are some central ideas that thread throughout this book. These ideas include the construction of the child as competent and capable, the role of the adult as partner in play and the importance of recognising our own cultural expectations in order to ensure we are inclusive of all the children with whom we work.

We sincerely hope that you enjoy this book and that it provides a starting point for your interest in, and exploration of, the phenomenon that is *PLAY*!

Overview of the Book

In Chapter 1, Natalie provides an insight into the complexity of defining play. She shows us how this complexity has been addressed across a range of literature and encourages us to recognise why this complexity exists, and the tensions that it raises for those working in early childhood education and care (ECEC).

Chapter 2 then positions play as a right, enabling us to understand the legal status of children's right to play. I explain the tensions that can arise when we try to support children to enact this right, and consider agency as a mechanism for thinking about children's enactment of their right to play.

Alison provides a thorough typology of play in Chapter 3, intended as a descriptive reference chapter. She includes early theory about stages of play, as well as traditional and more contemporary descriptions and categories of play behaviour.

Chapter 4 then provides an engaging overview of the lives and works of the thinkers who pioneered our current understandings of play. Alison brings to life influences and key experiences in the lives of the play pioneers, and outlines their legacy.

Next, in Chapter 5, Lauren and Louise explore provocations for play based on ideas of both contemporary and established pioneers. This new chapter for the second edition extends the coverage of play pioneers and includes contemporary innovations such as how a play-based curriculum can invoke science, technology, engineering, arts, and mathematics (STEAM).

Natalie and Angela ask you to think carefully in Chapter 6 about children's holistic development and what this means when we understand play as foundational. This chapter sets out the relationships between play and children's physical, social-emotional, and cognitive development and introduces the role of play in brain development.

Amanda then offers us a detailed insight into how young children communicate complex ideas through their play, in Chapter 7. We come to understand the high levels of competence that young children have in their early communication, and, as a result, to recognise the role of the adult as co-player in order to support learning.

In Chapter 8, Charlotte and Laura deftly lead us through a range of psychological constructs to understand the relationships between children's play, their well-being, and creativity. We come to realise the relationship between risk-taking, imagination and the development of resilience and coping.

In our next new chapter, Tereza challenges us to take the position of the child with autism when she explores observation and assessment of play in Chapter 9. She carefully and cleverly exposes the restrictive norms that can underpin ECEC and expands our view to include neuroatypical children when we observe and assess play.

In Chapter 10, the third new chapter for this edition, Karen and Jennie help us understand some of the underpinning principles of planning for play. They explain the role of the adult in the creation of enabling environments for playful learning indoors and outdoors, where the child, as an active learner, can explore their own ideas and interests in depth.

Jennie explains, in Chapter 11, that as early years professionals we are architects of the spaces we provide for young children. She helps us understand the messages that sit within these spaces and how they shape children's activity and their play.

Glenda describes a rich outdoor play environment in Chapter 12, and then takes us through the many aspects to consider when we make provision for outdoor play for young children. She highlights tensions that arise when we think about the implications of ethical and sustainable concerns and how these translate to our practice contexts.

In Chapter 13, Pekka and Saara provide a thoroughly accessible introduction to some complex ideas about children and the digital world. We are urged to analyse children's play in the digital sphere through the lens of media culture, and to consider our early childhood pedagogy from this perspective.

Carys walks us through the curricula of the four UK home nations in Chapter 14, and offers insight into processes for planning for playful learning for early years children in which the children have a voice and some agency over the content and direction of their playful learning experiences.

Following this, in Chapter 15, Angela and Mel set out clearly the decisions that we face as practitioners seeking to support children's play. Couched in terms of *joining in* or *stepping back* this chapter allows us to make explicit the intentions that we have when supporting play, and to recognise where we may be inadvertently interrupting children in their play.

Chapter 16 is all about inclusion. Nanna and Charlotte enable us to grasp the concept of inclusion in a manner that goes beyond a simple recognition of the varied learning or support needs of different children. This chapter helps us understand how to provide inclusive and accessible play spaces that support all children to thrive.

In Chapter 17, Margaret, Giulia and Mariana provide insight into how play can be a unifying language between generations. In unpacking the idea of intergenerational learning, the authors challenge us to think anew about the value of ensuring the older and the youngest members of our society have meaningful opportunities to play together.

Angela and I use Chapter 18 help us understand that cultural context informs 'taken for granted' practices including play. We demonstrate how different cultures embrace different understandings of ways of being, through worked examples exploring gender roles and approaches to risk.

Debra, Linda and Sarah set the play agenda in the context of 'extremis', that is, when communities are in a state of crisis and/or great turbulence, for example as a result of war, forced migration, or natural disaster. Chapter 19 offers insight into the value and importance of offering play opportunities for children living through such upheaval, and mechanisms by which knowledge about play provision and play practice can be brought to such communities are explained and exemplified.

In Chapter 20, Sarah and Sarah invite us to consider three powerful models of international play-based curriculum approaches to young children's learning. Detailed and accessible, this chapter provides an insightful introduction to Reggio Emilia, (Italy); HighScope, (USA); and Te Whāriki, (New Zealand), challenging us to consider the construction of the child underpinning each.

Collectively, the chapter authors and I would like to welcome you to the world of play. We sincerely hope that this introductory text supports you to make your way into it with ease, interest and an increasingly critical understanding of the opportunities, challenges, tensions, and rewards inherent in working with young children through play.

Part I
What is Play?

1
What is Play?

Natalie MacDonald

Chapter Objectives

This chapter will:

- Explore definitions of play illustrating the complexity of defining a varied and individual concept.
- Explore perceptions of play, how these may differ between adults and children, and the implications of this.
- Begin to evaluate practice based on understanding the importance of play.

Introduction: What is Play? Definitions and Perceptions

Play is predominantly associated with children and is essential for their holistic growth, learning and development (UN Committee on the Rights of the Child, 2013). The importance of play is recognised internationally through Article 31 of the United Nations Convention on the Rights of the Child, more commonly known as the UNCRC (UNICEF, 1990) (see Chapter 2). The UNCRC is the most widely ratified treaty by countries across the world including non-UN member states, highlighting international recognition of the fundamental need children have for play.

Through play children construct meaning about the world around them. The central pillars of play are children's autonomy and independence within it (Tovey, 2020). The power of play to support and deepen children's learning lies in their engagement in first-hand, authentic and purposeful experiences. The value of play in this respect forms the basis of many classical child development theories and modern approaches to children's learning. Adults have used *play* to underpin interventions, curricula and pedagogy in order to facilitate and enhance children's learning and development. However, adult understandings of what play *is* may not align with the perspective of the child.

The challenge in defining and utilising play to support children's development lies in the nature of play itself. If we understand that play is individual and unique for all children, we may wonder how play can be planned for children through curriculum structure, pedagogy, and provision. Within this chapter, the complexities and contradictions around defining play are discussed. Furthermore, differing perspectives about play are considered. This chapter concludes by highlighting the implications of the above for providing play opportunities for learning, growth and development, and recreation, and begins to explore the role of the adult.

Defining Play

Play is defined in general comment 17 on Article 31 of the UNCRC (see Chapter 2): 'Children's play is any behaviour, activity or process initiated, controlled and structured by children themselves; it takes place whenever and wherever opportunities arise'.

Academics have found it difficult to define 'play' and what characteristics a situation needs to have to be 'playful'. Also, what play is or is not as determined by a child and by an adult can differ widely (Howard & McInnes, 2013). Defining something that is individual, complex and means different things to different people is inherently difficult. Many definitions of play highlight what play *is* through describing what play *provides* or *should be* rather than through an explicit definition. We now go on to consider how play is explained elsewhere.

Eberle (2014, p. 214) suggests that to constitute play there must be six common elements in an activity: 'anticipation, surprise, pleasure, understanding, strength, and poise'. Eberle goes further to say that at its centre play must be 'fun'. Bottrill (2018, p. 26) discusses what play *is* and *should be* rather than providing a definition, stating that play is 'creativity, it is abandon... its meaning is infinite' and that play should be 'open ended... offer[ing] limitless possibilities and endless interpretations'. These statements resonate strongly with the UNCRC's definition of play, which is helpful, but they still leave us trying to define a slippery concept. Some may say that play, as a term, is impossible to define. This means that we must constantly consider what we mean in our practice when we plan for children's activity and their play. We might ask ourselves whether utilising 'play' to support children's education and learning within early years curricula is even possible, especially when curricula can be outcome-focused, with an emphasis on observable, measurable, and/or specific attainment.

Reflection Point 1.1

Consider what play means to you.

- How would you define it?
- What is required for 'play' to take place? (Things? People? Space?...)

Evidence of the benefits of play are wide-ranging and discussed across a range of sociological, psychological, and biological perspectives, as detailed later in this chapter, and indeed throughout this book. However, as we have seen, the definition of play is notoriously complex, conflicting and individual. A commonly agreed definition cites play as being *'freely chosen'*, *'personally directed'*, *'intrinsically motivated'*, and *'without external goal or reward'* (NHS, 2017); this definition has been adopted by a large number of organisations and governments (for example, Play Wales, 2020; Scottish Government, 2013). The key terms within this definition need to be unpicked in more detail to explore what is meant by each of these terms and how they can be enabled in practice.

Freely Chosen

The term 'freely chosen' means the children themselves choose when, how and what to play. It should not have steps that need to be completed or be part of any set programme. Similar to the term *child-led* this indicates complete control over the play by the child. These terms often form the basis of play-based pedagogy in curricula across the world (see Chapters 14 and 20). However, this term is at risk of being tokenistic if children are not truly allowed to engage in their own choice of play. The role and influence of the adult, through direct or indirect engagement in the play, can quickly alter the perception of the activity as *play* by the child through too much involvement, direction, or limitation (see Chapter 15).

Intrinsically Motivated Without External Goal or Reward

Children have an innate desire to play; it drives their growth and development. Motivation is a key component for promoting learning, enjoyment, persistence and performance. Enabling and supporting children's innate intrinsic motivation to engage in play enhances a child's natural learning and development. Children who are intrinsically motivated to play show more interest, excitement, fun and engagement in their play (Dumford, 2009). Intrinsic motivation stems from the pleasure and satisfaction gained from the knowledge or mastery that comes from the play and the feelings of excitement and enjoyment from taking part in the play itself. These contribute to feelings of positive self-esteem and well-being, which are essential components for children to realise their potential (Aubrey & Riley, 2019). If a child's motivation to engage in play is intrinsic, this means the play is undertaken for its own sake and not for any external reward or goal.

Once we understand the idea that play is intrinsically motivated then we realise there is a tension between this understanding and many modern practices in early education. For example, 'golden time' (rewards of free choice time), reward points systems or negative reinforcement consequences (such as reduced free time or breaks) create externally motivated play opportunities (see also Chapter 2). Lepper and Greene's (1975) classic study into the effect of external rewards on motivation for children aged 4–5 years demonstrated that children's interest in an activity dropped after receiving an external motivator and interest was more sustained where the motivation was intrinsic. Indeed, research into motivation has shown that the utilisation of rewards for outcomes undermines the intrinsic motivation to engage in the first instance (Dumford, 2009). This is where one of the greatest challenges lies for the role of the adult; play is undertaken for the process of the play itself, for the value and intrinsic reward of playing, not for the outcome or reward. It can be difficult for adults working with children to value this aspect, when they may feel under pressure to provide evidence of children's outcomes and developmental progression against assessments and regulatory measures. In a culture where education is often outcomes-driven and measured through external assessment, it can be difficult to focus on the child's intrinsic motivation as the driving factor for play. Key international curricula that focus on the process of play and learning rather than the product are renowned for their view of children as competent and capable (see Chapter 20), and central to this ethos is the knowledge that by valuing and supporting play, adults are also enabling children's development.

Personally Directed

This is where the children themselves have complete control over the context of the play; they decide the rules and roles they (and you) undertake within their play.

Key consideration for the adult here is that the choice, direction and level of engagement from the child (and the adult) remains in the child's control – not the adult's. Adults working with young children must accept that they are not the leaders, initiators or masters of play, and that control remains with the child. Developing an understanding of what play *is*, and also what play *is not*, can support adults to effectively enable children to engage in play that supports their learning and development.

Reflection Point 1.2

Think about a time when you have supported a child playing, or observed a child playing in a setting or at home.

- Consider how you could support children's play without taking control.
- What changes could be made or introduced to the environment you provide for the child to enable more opportunities for play, as defined above?

Play and Playwork

Playwork is a distinct and separate discipline from, for example, early years or education. When playworkers work with children and young people they are guided by a specific theoretical position, though there is some relationship with guidance in education and care provision. What resonates strongly between playwork theory and other theoretical discussions of play is the importance of the child's perspective and control of play. Part of the central ethos of playwork is that it is the role of the adult to enhance play spaces and enable children to extend and develop their own play through following the Principles of Playwork (e.g., Play Wales, 2021). The play cycle and play frame are distinct aspects of playwork and provide a practice model and theoretical framework for working with children and young people. There are specific playwork qualifications required to work in the field;

however, exploring the play cycle and play frame theories provides us with further insight into the complexities of defining play and the role of the adult in maintaining a 'child-led' approach with a focus on a child's intrinsic motivation to play.

Playwork principles are centred on the play cycle based on work by Sturrock and Else (1998) and further refined by King and Newstead (2020). The focus of playwork is on supporting and facilitating the play process; this is undertaken through creating and maintaining rich play environments for children, through removing barriers to play to enable children to choose, control, and engage in their own play. The role of the adult as an enabler is critical within playwork principles and requires playworkers to have an in-depth understanding of their own role in enabling play choice and play spaces for children, and not controlling or directing the play in any way. Playwork theories consider the role of the adult from two perspectives: enabling play and 'adulteration' (see also Chapter 15).

The play cycle consists of six components including 'play cues' and 'returns' within a 'play frame', leading to 'play flow' after which the frame is discarded or destroyed when it is no longer of use (Sturrock & Else, 1998). There is no defined length of time for a play cycle to last; the key aspect is that the child is in control. The end of a play cycle or the 'annihilation' (as termed in playwork theory) happens naturally for a number of reasons; however, where this happens due to the unwanted interference of an adult this is termed 'adulteration'. Where a play cycle ends naturally, this would be within the child's control and is an accepted feature of play. Where a play cycle ends as a result of an adult's interference, this could interrupt the flow and engagement that occurs within children's play – hindering rather than enhancing the play's potential for learning and development. There are a number of ways adults can end a play cycle inadvertently, and often the intentions of the adult are well-meaning. Adults often want to enhance or improve the play by making suggestions for changes, or may see that the play cycle is coming to a natural end and wish to try to 'rescue' the play to extend the cycle, or they may just want to join in the play without being invited in.

The most common adult interference that prematurely ends a play cycle is trying to 'educate' the children in their play. The role of practitioners is to support children's learning and development; often we will see opportunities to 'teach' children something or enhance their learning and development while they are at play. Although, as supported by learning theorists such as Vygotsky and Bruner, this is an effective way to enhance children's development, how this is done through play needs careful consideration and an appropriate approach. Ultimately, adults must find a way to balance their support for children's learning and development with maintaining the children's perceptions of the activity as play (see also Chapter 15).

Why is Play Important?

Classical child development theorists influence the pedagogy and practice of early years education and care settings today. Classical theorists such as Froebel, Vygotsky, and Piaget may differ in descriptions of how a child learns and develops (see Chapter 4 for more detail), however they all share one commonality – the importance of play. Play, within these theorists' work, has been identified as stages, types, and observable phenomena. Despite this, what is described are *aspects* of play rather than what play *is*. However, across classical learning theories, play is identified as central to a child's learning and development, and as an innate and natural drive to explore and understand the world around them.

During play children are shown to have higher levels of motivation, self-esteem, and engagement, showing higher levels of emotional well-being (McInnes et al., 2013; see also Chapter 8). Through play children are able to take control of themselves, explore their own limits and experience a sense of freedom. In play, children should have independence and autonomy, allowing them to engage in decision-making and problem-solving, building their self-esteem and confidence in their own capabilities.

Neurological research evidences the positive impact play can have on brain development (Harvard University, 2021). Play provides the opportunity for children to develop responsive relationships with the environment, adults and their peers alike. Through play children can engage in natural interactions with others and the world around them. These experiences and interactions through play build brain architecture, allowing children to make and strengthen connections between what they know and what they experience within the world around them. The neural connections in the brain establish a foundation for learning and an infrastructure for thinking, knowledge, behaviour, and life. Interactions with the environment and/or with others facilitate what is known as 'serve and return' interactions. Serve and return is when children engage with the environment or with others (the 'serve') and receive a response (the 'return') which deepens their understanding; this strengthens and develops connections within the brain. Children use these experiences to make sense of their world; the strengthening and development of the neural connections through rich experiences lead to the development of patterns of learning (Dowling, 2013). Therefore, the quality, diversity, and extent of a child's interactions with their world are critical to supporting their neurological development.

Play allows children to engage in testing out theories, taking risks and problem-solving in a safe space without the fear of failure, allowing for the development of resilience. The importance of resilience cannot be underestimated. Neurological research into the long-term impacts of remaining in high states of anxiety or 'toxic stress' have been documented to impact on neural development and have lifelong implications; resilience is a protective factor. Providing opportunities through play for children to engage in and develop self-regulation and problem-solving skills, and a sense of self control supported by positive and caring adult relationships, is a key factor in the development of resilience (Harvard University, 2021). Good experiences and happy events compensate for and balance the stressors and adversities children may face (Rutter, 1985). Play provides the opportunity and safe space to enable the development of these protective factors (see also Chapter 8). A recent study by Davis et al. (2025) exploring perceptions of 'flourishing' in the early years of life found that children identified play as one of the key themes that made them happy, helping them to flourish. The importance of play is addressed in greater detail across Chapters 5, 6, 7, and 8.

The Role of the Adult in Play

As we can see, defining play is not a straightforward task. We might suggest that this difficulty in definition reflects the individuality of play; that the value of play comes from the feelings and process of playing rather than an end product. Arguably this aspect is the most difficult for adults to support; as discussed above the role of the adult who supports play and learning *through* play is a complex one. For play to remain *play*, the adult cannot take control of, or direct, the play to meet their own agenda, or to meet a specific outcome. However, as outlined above, and throughout this book, play is an essential part of the process of development. For children to gain the most from play the role of the adult is crucial, this includes their understanding of how to develop and extend play as well as facilitate it. Such professional knowledge is fundamental to early years provision having long-term sustained impact on children's development (Siraj et al., 2002; Sylva et al., 2014).

The general comment on play within the UNCRC provided above indicates play as being 'any behaviour, activity or process; initiated, controlled and structured by the children themselves', and there is a legal requirement for member states to recognise, enact, and enable opportunities for children to engage in 'play' as defined. However, in monitoring this provision concerns have been raised about poor recognition of the significance of play within children's lives by member states, and too much focus being placed on structured and organised activities that fail to recognise the intrinsic and spontaneous nature of children's play required (see Chapter 2).

A significant theme running through the varied descriptions of play we have seen is the importance of child choice, that is, a sense of autonomy and control by the child throughout the play. Most theories and definitions of play are articulated from the perspective of the adult and aligned to observations of play behaviours or indicators. The importance of a child perceiving an activity as play or as playful is essential to children being able to gain the benefits of engaging in meaningful play opportunities. Understanding a child's perception of play is therefore important. Studies have indicated that children have higher levels of emotional wellbeing and are more engaged in their learning when they perceive an activity as 'play' versus 'not-play' (Howard & McInnes, 2013). Howard (2002) explored what cues children used to determine whether an activity is 'play' or 'not-play' in order to understand what influenced a child's perception of play in an early years setting. Through an apperception test with children using pictures of environmental and interactional cues, the study identified that the three most significant factors were the child's choice of whether to engage, the location of the activity and the proximity or involvement of the adult. Interestingly, all three of these aspects can be influenced by the adult in setting up opportunities for play. In Howard's (2002) study, in order for an activity to be identified as 'play' the child needed to be able to choose whether to engage or not, the activity needed to take place on the floor or in an open space (not seated at a table) and the adult could be nearby but was not directly engaged in the activity (see Chapter 15).

According to Bilton and Crook (2016), the role of the adult when working with young children is multifaceted and complex. It is important that adults working with young children take every opportunity to engage in and support authentic play and play experiences with children. Authentic and purposeful play experiences have meaning for children and are driven by their interests and choices. Adults need to be able to undertake careful observation and planning in order to scaffold children's learning and development, yet their attitude towards play and their role within it needs to be fully understood and carefully enacted in order to become a partner in the play and not overtake it.

For most classical theorists, the role of the adult is key; Frobelian perspectives on the role of the adult resonate with the understanding that play is in the control of the child, not the adult. The role of the adult should be to facilitate time and opportunities for children to engage in play, not to decide or dictate the content or outcome of it (see Chapter 4). Vygotsky believed that social interactions and relationships are drivers for children's cognitive development. A critical aspect of this is the development of imagination through play. Vygotsky developed the theory of the zone of proximal development which articulates the level at which children require support in order to further their development (see Chapter 6). Nilsson and Ferholt (2014) use Vygotskian ideas to argue that the most effective way to provide this support is through play. How this support can be most effectively implemented in line with understandings of what play 'is' or 'should be' can be difficult to balance. Bruner, Froebel and Piaget all viewed children as active learners who need real-life first-hand experiences through play to facilitate their learning and development. Bruner also believes (like Vygotsky) that the role of the adult is important. This is evident within Bruner's spiral curriculum theory, in which children require time to play, master skills and develop working theories, through autonomous and independent play, before being supported to move on to the next stage of development, when they may be introduced to formal learning.

Supporting and extending children's learning and development needs to be balanced without tipping the scales into adult-led tasks, in order to avoid losing the benefits, for children, of engaging in play. Playwork practice provides examples of the role of the adult during each element of the play cycle. Firstly, the adult acts as an observer: observation allows us to gain an understanding of the child's interests, level of engagement and stage of development. This information is key to supporting the planning of play spaces and opportunities for children, as well as recording or evidencing outcomes of children's development. Observing children during play is the optimal time to see what their capabilities are and what interests them. When observing children in a child-led play-based environment we can be more certain that we are seeing a true reflection of the child (Howard & McInnes, 2013).

Secondly, the adult can respond to play cues given by the child to become involved in the play with the child. The crucial aspect for the adult to understand here is that the content, direction and process of the play must remain with the child. Children may invite adults to engage in their play for a few different reasons, it may be simply to provide something to continue with their play such as a resource or moving a heavy object, or they may be invited to engage in the play at a more complex level where they become part of the play themselves. When adults are engaged in the play care must be taken not to 'adulterate' the play by trying to change the direction, improve or educate within the play.

A further role of the adult is in the facilitation of the environment, including the resources, time and space to enable children's play (see Chapter 11). Often practitioners can fill a child's day with routine, numerous transitions and set times for activities. For example, in sessional care lasting a morning or an afternoon, after greeting time, snack time, focused tasks and large group story or song time, very little of the session is left for children to engage in their choice of play without interruption. The setting up of the environment and resources is an important consideration when supporting children's learning and development. A range of resources to facilitate choice is essential.

Open-ended resources and loose parts provide endless opportunities for inspiration and prompting curiosity and exploration (see Chapters 10, 15, and 20).

This chapter has already outlined the benefits of children engaging in play, including increased well-being, focus, and motivation, in addition to the development of skills and dispositions that support learning and development. The role of the adult in creating spaces and opportunities where children perceive their activity as *play* is critical (McInnes et al., 2013); adults must strike a careful balance so that they support and enhance children's play without taking it over for their own agenda and changing the child's perception to *not*-play.

Case Study 1.1

Rosie, Jack, and Ruby are in the creative area of an early years setting during free play. The area has been set out with large sheets of paper covering the tables and laid out on the floor, a variety of different resources are available for children to use including paint, chalks and pens. A number of practitioners are within the vicinity observing or engaging in other activities with children in the room.

The children begin exploring with mark-making, testing out different resources independently; although sharing the same space and resources very little interaction is happening between the children. Rosie walks over to the resource area and picks up some red paint, she squirts some of the paint onto the paper, Jack notices this and begins to swirl his finger in the paint. Rosie responds with a giggle and starts to create her own swirls and patterns on the paper with the paint. Ruby picks up some blue paint and adds this to the paper. All three children continue to mix the colours and paints on the paper, creating patterns and exploring colour; the children engage with each other laughing, pointing, and smiling.

One of the practitioners nearby notices the children's excitement, goes over to them and asks Rosie – 'What are you drawing?' The children all stop and think, Rosie says 'I don't know' then gets up and wanders off. Jack and Ruby continue to make marks with the paint but explore independently.

Reflection Point 1.3

- What happened, here, to the children's play?
- Why do you think this may have happened?
- What should the practitioner have done?
- Have you experienced this in your own practice?
- What would you do differently next time?

Summary

- Play is difficult to define yet the key to supporting children's learning through play is to understand it.
- Play is central to children's learning and development, evidenced through the ongoing commitment to play within early years curricula and approaches.
- The child's perception of an activity as *play* is fundamental to their level of engagement within the play and the impact on their development and well-being.
- Play needs to be child-led, freely chosen by and in the control of the child. The adult role in play should be as a partner and/or facilitator and not to lead the play.

Further Reading

Bottrill, G. (2018) *Can I Go & Play Now? Rethinking the Early Years*. London: Sage. Bottrill's book explores the issue of children's perceptions of play and how they relate to practice. The book includes useful chapters on child-centred practice and 'what play is and what play isn't'.

McInnes, K., Howard, J., Crowley, K. and Miles, G. (2013) The nature of adult-child interaction in the early years classroom: Implications for children's perceptions of play and subsequent learning behaviour. *European Early Childhood Education Research Journal*, 21(2), 268–282. This paper explores children's use of adult presence as a cue for children's perception of an activity as 'play'. Interesting points related to control and choice are discussed.

Wood, E. (2013) *Play, Learning and the Early Childhood Curriculum* (3rd ed.). London: Sage. The third edition of this book challenges policy on 'educational play' and explores international perspectives on play. Chapters include useful case studies to illustrate practice.

References

Aubrey, K., & Riley, A. (2019). *Understanding and using educational theories* (2nd ed.). London: Sage.

Bilton, H., & Crook, A. (2016). *Exploring outdoors ages 3–11: A guide for schools*. London: Taylor & Francis.

Bottrill, G. (2018). *Can I go & play now? Rethinking the early years*. London: Sage.

Davis, J. A., Davey, B., Segers, E., Talati, Z., Silva, D., Prescott, S. L., & Gibson, L. Y. (2025). The flourishing child: Understanding how adults and children perceive flourishing from the start of life. *International Journal of Applied Positivist Psychology* 10(18). https://doi.org/10.1007/s41042-024-00213-x

Dowling, M. (2013). *Young children's thinking*. London: Sage.

Dumford, N. (2009). *The effects of external rewards on intrinsic motivation*. Available at: www.semanticscholar.org/paper/THE-EFFECTS-OF-EXTERNAL-REWARDS-ON-INTRINSIC-Dumford/38da2034a8ec0d850d1ab11b4331fda283eab7be#related-papers

Eberle, S. G. (2014). The elements of play: Toward a philosophy and a definition of play. *American Journal of Play*, 6(2), 214–233.

Harvard University. (2021). *Resilience.* Centre for the Developing Child. Available at: https://developingchild.harvard.edu/science/key-concepts/resilience/

Howard, J. (2002). Eliciting young children's perceptions of play, work and learning using the activity apperception story procedure. *Early Child Development and Care,* 172, 489–502.

Howard, J., & McInnes, K. (2013). The impact of children's perception of an activity as play rather than not play on emotional well-being. *Child Care, Health and Development,* 39(5), 737–742.

King, P., & Newstead, S. (2020). Re-defining the play cycle: An empirical study of playworkers' understanding of playwork theory. *Journal of Early Childhood Research,* 18(1), 99–111. https://doi.org/10.1177/1476718X19885991

Lepper, M., & Greene, D. (1975) Turning play into work: Effects of adult surveillance and extrinsic rewards on children's intrinsic motivation. *Journal of Personality and Social Psychology,* 31(3), 479–486. https://doi.org/10.1037/h0076484

McInnes, K., Howard, J., Crowley, K., & Miles, G. (2013). The nature of adult-child interaction in the early years classroom: Implications for children's perceptions of play and subsequent learning behaviour. *European Early Childhood Education Research Journal,* 21(2), 268–282.

NHS. (2017). *Play & leisure.* Available at: www.nhsggc.org.uk/kids/life-skills/play-leisure/

Nilsson, M., & Ferholt, B. (2014). Vygotsky's theories of play, imagination and creativity in current practice: Gunilla Lindqvist's 'creative pedagogy of play' in US kindergartens and Swedish Reggio Emilia inspired preschools. *Perspectiva,* 32(3), 919–950.

Play Wales. (2020). *Playing and hanging out.* Available at: https://playwales.org.uk/eng/playinghangingout

Play Wales. (2021). *Playwork.* Available at: https://playwales.org.uk/eng/playworkprinciples

Rutter, M. (1985). Resilience in the face of adversity: Protective factors and resistance to psychiatric disorder. *The British Journal of Psychiatry,* 147, 598–611.

Scottish Government. (2013). *Play strategy for Scotland: Our vision.* Available at: www.gov.scot/publications/play-strategy-scotland-vision/pages/5/

Siraj, I., Sylva, K., Muttock, S., Gilden, R., & Bell, D. (2002). *Researching effective pedagogy in the early Years (REPEY).* London: Department for Education and Skills/Institute of Education, University of London.

Sturrock, G., & Else, P. (1998). 'The Colorado paper' – the playground as therapeutic space: Playwork as healing. In P. Else and G. Sturrock (Eds.), *Therapeutic playwork reader one 1995–2000.* Eastleigh: Common Threads.

Sylva, K., Melhuish, E. C., Sammons, P., Siraj, I., Taggart, B. with Smees, R., Toth, K. and Welcomme, W. (2014). *Effective pre-school, primary and secondary education 3–16 project (EPPSE 3–16): Students' educational and developmental outcomes at age 16.* Research Report RR354. London: Department for Education.

Tovey, H. (2020). *Froebel's principles and practice today.* London: Froebel Trust.

UN Committee on the Rights of the Child. (2013). *General comment No. 17 on the right of the child to rest, leisure, play, recreational activities, cultural life and the arts* (Art. 31). Geneva: United Nations.

UNICEF. (1990). *United Nations Convention on the Rights of the Child.* London: UNICEF.

2
Children's Right to Play

Jane Waters-Davies

Chapter Objectives

This chapter will help you to:

- Position play as a right for all children.
- Consider children's agency and recognise how adults can support or limit children's enactment of their rights.
- Recognise that diverse childhoods mean some children can enact their rights more easily than others.

Play as a Right

In 1989, the Convention on the Rights of the Child (CRC) was ratified by the United Nations (UN) General Assembly. This meant that the rights of children were recognised in international law; the signatory countries agreed to implement the Convention and take part in monitoring systems that evaluate their progress in implementation. Broadly speaking, the UNCRC addresses children's interests across 'the three Ps', covering children's rights to provision, protection, and participation (see Theobald, 2019; Williams, forthcoming). There are 54 articles in total within the UNCRC. This chapter explores Article 31, which is summarised as 'Every child has the right to relax, play, and take part in a wide range of cultural and artistic activities' (UNCRC, 2017). In this chapter, we explore some of the issues and tensions that can arise in ECEC practice and policy around recognition of children's right to play.

In full, Article 31 states the following:

1 States Parties recognise the right of the child to rest and leisure, to engage in play and recreational activities appropriate to the age of the child and to participate freely in cultural life and the arts.

2 States Parties shall respect and promote the right of the child to participate fully in cultural and artistic life and shall encourage the provision of appropriate and equal opportunities for cultural, artistic, recreational and leisure activity (UNCRC, 2010).

This article places a duty on governments to ensure that children have the opportunity to play and take part in a range of cultural, recreational, and artistic activities. The article does not instruct governments about how to do this. David (2006) highlighted concerns that the obligations to uphold Article 31 were not being addressed by governments and this led to the publication of General Comment No. 17 (UNCRC, 2013). This elaborates on the right of every child to play, as well as identifying groups at risk of not achieving this right, including girls, children living in poverty, children with disabilities and children from indigenous or minority communities (UNCRC, 2013, pp. 15-16). The General Comment defines play as behaviour *'initiated, controlled, and structured by children,* as non-compulsory, driven by intrinsic motivation, not a means to an end', and emphasised that it has key characteristics of fun, uncertainty, challenge, flexibility, and non-productivity (UNCRC, 2013, pp. 5-6, my italics).

Governments may respond to this duty differently. For example, traditionally Nordic countries have embraced rights-based perspectives as core to policy, curriculum, and pedagogy. In those countries, young children are increasingly recognised as active participants in their communities, especially in early childhood programmes. Children's play choices in their early years are respected and playful environments are available across ECEC provision for children up to at least the age of six (Einarsdottir et al., 2015).

In New Zealand, one of the five strands of the Te Whāriki curriculum (see chapter 20) is *Exploration*, which includes the domain 'exploration through play'. This strand brings together children's play and children's learning through provision for active playful exploration of the environment. In Wales, children's rights are embedded in policy (Murphy et al., 2024) and young children are recognised as learning best through playful engagement with their surroundings (see Chapter 14). Taking a play-based approach to curriculum design for young children might be understood as these countries enshrining a child's right to play within their early childhood education curricula, however we may find a tension here. Recognition that children learn through play, and making use of this characteristic to enhance children's educational outcomes, is not the same as recognition that children have a right to play – for its own sake, irrespective of specific outcomes (see also Chapters 1 and 15). Remember how General Comment 17 defined play: *initiated, controlled and structured by children,* non-compulsory, driven by intrinsic motivation, *not a means to an end.* Where play-based activities form part of the curriculum, these are often adult-led and outcome-focused, and can be perceived by children as 'work' rather than play (Goodhall & Atkinson, 2017). We might understand this tension as sitting at the nexus between two categories of rights in the 'three Ps': *provision* and *participation,* and the tension centres around the role of the adult in ensuring children's rights can be realised.

Let's think again about the right to play. This might be understood as a *provision* right; that is, adults need to provide for, or facilitate, children's play so that children can enact this right. Alternatively, the right to play might be understood as a *participation* right; that is play can be understood as the way in which children participate in their communities. This tension may not feel important; you might suggest that if children have access to play then that's enough, surely? However, when we consider what aspects of children's play are permitted, and provided for, in different settings then we can realise this tension further. For example, play with loose parts, such as rocks, tree trunks, sticks, and stones, is appealing to most young children (see Chapter 12). Climbing trees is also often appealing and yet such play can be considered as too risky by some adults, and as a result this activity may not be supported. In this situation, the opportunity for children to *initiate, control, and structure* their play, as intended in the UNCRC Article 31, is restricted by adults. Indeed, when we consider the opportunities that young children have to engage in play, we can recognise that in almost all situations, these opportunities are structured by adult choices (see Chapter 15).

Thinking about how children's play is managed, shaped, and controlled by adults allows us to recognise some of the tensions for ECEC providers that sit within children's right to play. In another everyday example, let's think about 'tidy up time'. Clearing up play materials is generally not part of children's natural engagement in play, and some play theorists advocate that children should be able to return to their play spaces over time, in order for their play to develop. It is common practice in many UK-based play spaces associated with ECEC provision that play equipment is set up by adults and needs to be tidied up often, even as regularly as each half-day session. This sits in contrast to ECEC providers who leave some play materials for children to revisit day after day, offering and introducing new items for play in response to children's interests. Settings adopting the latter approach can look messy and disorganised but, arguably, allow for children to *initiate, control, and structure* their play to a much greater extent than settings where play spaces are routinely and regularly 'tidied up'.

Within this book, the child is viewed as a competent and capable individual, and a rights-holder. Children's rights, like human rights, are *inalienable*, this means that they cannot be taken away. Article 31 means that play is not a reward that needs to be earned by children enacting certain behaviours or completing certain tasks; the right to play cannot be removed as a reprimand or punishment. And yet, it is not uncommon in early learning contexts for adults to position play in just that way, often in order to meet the demands of the context or curriculum.

Reflection Point 2.1

Read the following sentences and consider how they frame children's play. Would children learn that play is their right or a reward from such statements?

- When you have finished this (task), you can go and play.
- When we are all sitting nicely then we can go to play.
- You have been so well behaved today that we will have some extra playtime.

In early learning contexts there can be an emphasis on core task completion, development of specific skills, and alignment to certain expectations of behaviour and systems of reward. These are in place for good reason – they support children to align themselves with the expectations for engagement and behaviour that exist within the setting, often established with the intention that such alignment eases transition to more formal school environments. However, the unintended consequences are that children's freely chosen, self-initiated play can be marginalised and time spent on it limited. The British Psychological Society (BPS) became so concerned about this issue that it published a position paper in 2021, defending the right of children to play, reporting the erosion of children's playtime at school in the last 20 years and highlighting the use of playtime as a reward, or loss of playtime as a punishment. The BPS state that children

> are often more capable of playing than adults give them credit for and find time and space for play wherever and whenever conditions allow. However, children will struggle to play when their basic needs are not met or where the environments they live in are so constraining that they are unable to play. Schools can provide children with the access to time, space and permission for playing, which is an essential part of their everyday lives. This is particularly important for children who have their play restricted by factors such as poverty, domestic or environmental circumstances. (2021, p. 3)

The United Nations recognises the early years as a 'critical period for realizing children's rights' (2006, p. 3). Young children are rights holders, and yet their rights are often overlooked due to perceptions of immaturity. That adults are generally expected to act in the best interests of the child means that adult concerns often over-shadow decisions about provision and therefore shape children's enactment of their rights. As Theobald (2019) explains, children's rights are intertwined with adult knowledge and personal position. Pedagogical approaches do not always attend to children's views and opportunities for participation, especially in the case of young children (Rekers & Waters, 2021). ECEC practitioners and teachers may unintentionally reduce children's participation, contribution and agency (Waters-Davies et al., 2024). Yet, early childhood organisations and programmes catering for children, aged birth to eight years, at local, state and global levels can become more active in addressing young children's rights and recognising the important shaping force of how adults engage with young children.

Reflection Point 2.2

How is play managed in an ECEC setting with which you are familiar? What are the choices made by adults about children's play and what choices are in the domain of the child? To what extent do children have the opportunity to *initiate, control, and structure their play*?

   Think about a time when young children were rewarded with play for doing something the adult wishes them to do. Why did this happen? In the example you are thinking about, do you think this was OK? Why/why not? How does this reflect on children's right to play? Are there tensions that you can identify for the adults managing the provision?

Children's Agency

In this section, we explore the notion of agency and specifically address children's agency within the inherent power relationships that exist between children and adults, exploring what it means for children to enact their right to play.

The word 'agency' can be broadly described to mean: *the capacity of an individual to actively and independently choose and to affect change; free will or self-determination*. The extent to which young children are agentic (that is, the extent to which they have and enact agency) has been contested and generally, in the United Kingdom, our view of the child has changed over the last century. We recognise that children are not represented by the Victorian image of blank slates upon which to be written, passive and lacking agency. We now tend to recognise that children have a capacity to act and to make choices and that this capacity is structured by the adults and the environment around the child. Within ECEC contexts, we might think of the growing child as growing in their capacity to enact their rights, as Quennerstedt and Quennerstedt suggest:

> Children as rights subjects are seen as agents in inter-dependent social networks, in which they both act on their rights and grow in capacity to understand and act on rights. The socio-political surrounding of the child and her immaturity and dependence on others together constitute her powers as a growing human rights subject. (2014, p. 129)

When we plan for children's play in care and/or education settings we can support, or limit, children's choices and their enactment of agency. As adults then, we structure children's engagement and opportunities to act, and we have to manage many demands while we do this (Tur Porres, forthcoming). Adults working in ECEC have a duty to ensure the safety of children in their care, and this duty includes attending to the needs, rights and voices of all the children in their care, not just one child or one group of children. Governments and regulatory authorities place restrictions on spending, staffing and space in ECEC provision. Statutory guidance and ECEC curriculum documentation set out expectations for children's outcomes and may include the requirement to engage with specific activities and/or develop certain skills and knowledge. These outcomes are associated with the concern to ensure that young children gain literacy, numeracy, and self-regulation skills in their young lives that will enable them to succeed at school and play a part in society in their futures. All of these factors are important when we consider provision for children's play. As we have seen in the discussion above, these demands upon adults can create tensions that need to be negotiated to ensure children can enact their rights.

Sometimes, adults working in education-based settings, teachers and senior leaders, may feel that there are tensions between the recognition of children's right to play, the place of the school to provide access to play, and the need to ensure that children are provided with learning experiences that support their development in specific 'core' domains, for example literacy and communication or numeracy. Schools are held accountable, through the inspection system, for children's academic outcomes. This means that a school may be judged on whether children reach certain levels of attainment in these 'core' domains. This causes a pressure to 'teach' more formally than an early years play-based curriculum may advocate (see Chapter 14). The term 'schoolification' was adopted by the OECD (2006) to describe this downward pressure on ECEC to mirror primary school practices. The term is generally synonymous with negatively held views relating to peda-gogies that are formalised and seen to be in tension with play-based approaches to children's learning. The arguments around this issue are complex, however there are approaches and choices that adults make in how they organise ECEC settings that can support or limit children's agency and their enactment of their right to play.

Case Study 2.1

- A nursery class for 3- to 4-year olds includes three adults, one lead educator and two learning support staff, and 28 children.

Scenario A

At the start of the nursery session, the children enter and begin to play in an area of the classroom of their choice. This routine occurs every morning and allows the teacher to talk to parents and carers as they drop the children off, and the adults help settle children as needed. Sioned joined the class a month ago and is one of the youngest of the children there; she has begun to settle easily into playing in the sand and water areas as her dad drops her off each day.

The lead educator has planned for a morning literacy-focused session, which engages the children in repeating rhymes that occur in a story. She would like to work with the whole class and read the story at the start. She calls the children to come together and sit on the carpeted area of the room. The learning support staff encourage the children to leave their playful activity and sit on the carpet. Sioned does not want to and begins to get upset when she is told again to leave the sand area. The lead educator and class wait for Sioned who is told again to leave the sand area. A learning support staff member takes Sioned's hand and moves her towards the carpet to join the other children. Sioned complies and sits down; she does not pay attention to the story or join in any of the rhyming or singing that the lead educator encourages during and after the story.

Scenario B

At the start of the session children arrive and they choose where they would like to play. The lead educator in the nursery engages with each child as they come in and the learning support staff join children's play around the room. This is an established routine. Today the lead educator is going to read a story that two of the children chose the day before. She is planning to ask the class to repeat the rhymes that occur in the story and then lead some singing rhymes.

About 20 minutes after the start of the session, the lead educator invites the children to join her for a story on the carpet. Most children join her on the carpet; the learning

(Continued)

support staff are sitting round the edge of the carpet. Aled is playing in the home corner setting out a picnic for his favourite toy. Josh and Alexa are working on a den in the construction corner. The lead educator calls over to Aled, Josh, and Alexa and asks them to join in. None move. The lead educator starts the story. After a few minutes, Josh moves to stand next to a learning support staff member on the edge of the carpet and listens to the story. Aled remains in the home corner and Alexa continues building. When the lead educator invites children to join in with the rhyming and singing associated with the story most children join in, though Josh does not. Alexa joins in from the construction area. Aled is deep in fantasy play and does not join in.

Reflection Point 2.3

Discuss the two scenarios above:

- In which scenario do children have more agency? Why?
- What do you think are the motivations for the lead educator's actions?
- What does this say about choice, rights, and power in the two classrooms?
- What is the position of play in these settings?
- Is *play* in tension with *learning* in these scenarios?

Children's experiences of agency in early education are largely framed by teachers' authority and the social and moral order of the setting/school culture (see also Chapter 18). Pedagogically, the adults who work with children can listen closely to children's voices in order to strengthen opportunities in classrooms and to support children's sense of personal agency. Do read Sirkko et al. (2019) if you are interested in a nuanced exploration of agency in ECEC practice.

Canning's work on *empowerment* in play is useful; she argues that, in an adult-free play environment, children are able to experience autonomy in decision-making and a sense of empowerment in developing their social and emotional relationships.

Empowerment can be understood as an enabling process where experiences are made possible through opportunities and by establishing support networks that nurture self-belief, competence, and confidence. Accordingly children who regularly encounter empowering experiences believe in their own capability and will engage with a positive attitude resulting in positive outcomes. In social play contexts, empowerment may be explained by focusing on ways in which children use their relationships with others through participation, expression of voice and their environment to influence contexts they are involved in. (Canning, 2020, p. 1)

Using Canning's empowerment framework in child observations allows us to consider how to observe and understand children's play from a position of respect for children's right to play, as well as recognising the need for ECEC practitioners and teachers to consider how learning and development are supported through play. This approach also supports practitioners to provide empowering experiences in which children enact their right to play, in the manner intended according to the General Comment 17, *and* practitioners are able to recognise and record social and emotional learning and development (see Canning, 2020).

Play Provision Outside ECEC Settings

Consideration of play provision and the child's right to play sits outside of early learning and care settings as well as within them. There are various bodies that work to support children's right to play across the United Kingdom. See the links provided below to the International Play Association and the four National Play Councils across the United Kingdom. The Play Councils take children's right to play as their foundation stone, and campaign to ensure that this right is realised through effective professional learning for adults who work with children, and effective planning for play at local, regional, and national level.

'Play sufficiency' is the term used to describe an assessment of children's opportunities for play. The United Nations Committee on the Rights of the Child encourages countries to embrace the principle of play sufficiency. In 2012, Wales became the first country in the world to legislate specifically in support of children's play when the Welsh Government introduced the Play Sufficiency Duty. This duty places a responsibility on all local authorities in Wales to carry out an assessment of children's opportunities for play every three years and in between times take action to secure sufficient opportunities based on their findings. It is clear that securing sufficient play opportunities for children is not just about designated provision but is dependent on the ability of local authorities to cultivate the temporal, spatial, and psychological conditions needed for children to play. See Barclay and Tawil (2013) for a great document that explains in detail what can be involved in a Play Sufficiency Assessment, don't be put off by the date – this is a thorough overview of the issues involved. Scotland introduced play sufficiency requirements in 2019 and, as this volume goes to print in 2025, there are campaigns to introduce similar in England, and Northern Ireland.

One of the advantages of having organisations whose mission it is to campaign for children's opportunities for, and access to, play is that children's right to play becomes an agenda item in local and national planning decisions. This means that it may be more difficult for local councils to make funding cuts to services that provide play opportunities for children. However, when funding is restricted, and in times of austerity, children's play can be diminished as less important than other priorities that are funded through the local government.

Reflection Point 2.4

- You are a local authority official and have to decide how to make 5% savings across your budget. There are three suggestions up for discussion; one involves cutting back on the maintenance of all the local playgrounds, despite some being in a poor state of repair; one involves postponing plans to make playgrounds accessible to children who have restricted mobility; and the third involves cutting back on care provision for elderly, vulnerable adults.
- You are aware of children's right to play, and also the right of individuals to access publicly owned sites, and also the rights of the ageing population to high-quality care.
- What factors do you discuss as you debate your decision?

To conclude this chapter, the words of Maryanne Theobald (2019) remind us that the enactment of children's rights is constrained by adult positions, as we have considered above, but also by circumstance and context.

> Very young children, children living in poverty, children in vulnerable circumstances, or in contexts in which children and their families are marginalised, are not well positioned to enact rights. (p. 253)

This statement resonates with that made by Quennerstedt and Quennerstedt: 'the sociopolitical surrounding of the child and her immaturity and dependence on others together constitute her powers as a growing human rights subject' (2014, p. 129).

We are reminded that when working with young children, there are structural and contextual issues (e.g., poverty, conflict, migration, health, and bereavement) that mean children in differing circumstances are more or less able to enact their rights than others. As adults working with children we should be mindful to ensure that all children are supported to enact their right to play under our care, not just those who are already advantaged to do so. We need, therefore, to be aware of structural and contextual inequalities that may be experienced by our children, and work to ensure that these do not constrain their agency and participation.

Summary

- Children's right to play is enshrined in international law; this right, like all other rights, is inalienable, which means it cannot be taken away.
- Play is defined in the UNCRC General Comment 17 as 'behaviour initiated, controlled and structured by children, as non-compulsory, driven by intrinsic motivation, not a

(Continued)

(Continued)

    means to an end, and emphasised that it has key characteristics of fun, uncertainty, challenge, flexibility, and non-productivity'.

- Children are agentic and able to enact their right to play according to structural and contextual circumstance; this means some children have reduced opportunities to enact this right and may need specific support to ensure equitable enactment of this right.
- Adults structure children's enactment of their rights and agency; this means adults working in ECEC and school contexts need to be mindful of tensions that arise in their professional work that may inadvertently limit children's agency, and need to ensure children in their care have equitable access to their right to play. Observation is a powerful tool for the ECEC professional in this regard.
- Play Councils proactively support and defend children's right to play in communities across each of the four nations of the United Kingdom.

Further Reading

Theobald, M. (2019) UN Convention on the Rights of the Child: 'Where are we at in recognising children's rights in early childhood, three decades on...?' *International Journal of Early Childhood*, 51, 251–257. https://doi.org/10.1007/s13158-019-00258-z. This is a summary of the progress of implementation of the UNCRC and highlights tensions within and around this. See this entire special issue for a thorough assessment of the progress in, and tensions inherent in, implementation of the UNCRC.

Canning, N. (2019) Just 5 more minutes! Power dynamics in outdoor play. *International Journal of Play*, 8(1), 11–24. The paper considers some of the dilemmas and intricacies of power dynamics between children, adults and the environment, exploring the way in which children navigate those situations.

Moss, P. (2007) Bringing politics into the nursery: Early childhood education as a democratic practice. *European Early Childhood Education Research Journal*, 15, 5–20. Peter Moss, a powerful thinker about ECEC, provides an impassioned call for re-consideration of ECEC practice and its democratic potential. A great read if you are interested in children's voices and adults' role in hearing them.

Play Matters, Early Years Reviews. This freely available resource edited by Aaron Bradbury is an impassioned plea from researchers and practitioners for the value of children's access to play in ECEC. Available from: https://www.early-years-reviews.com/play-matters

Ludicology (2019). *The Concept of Play Sufficiency* (October 3). Available from: https://ludicology.com/store-room/the-concept-of-play-sufficiency/

International Play Association: https://ipaworld.org. 'IPA's purpose is to protect, preserve and promote the child's right to play as a fundamental human right'.

Play Scotland: www.playscotland.org. 'Play Scotland is the lead organisation for the development and promotion of play in Scotland. We work to make the child's right to play a reality. More play, better play'.

Play Wales:

- English: www.play.wales
- Welsh: www.chwarae.cymru

Play Wales is 'The national charity for children's play in Wales. We champion every child's need and right to play'.

Play England: www.playengland.org.uk. 'Play England's vision is for England to be a country where everybody can fully enjoy their right to play throughout their childhood and teenage years, as set out in the UN Convention on the Rights of the Child Article 31 and the Charter for Children's Play'. Playboard NI: www.playboard.org. 'PlayBoard is the leading charity in Northern Ireland dedicated to the development and promotion of children and young people's play. '.

References

Barclay, M., & Tawil, B. (2013). *Wrexham play sufficiency assessment 2013: Abridged.* Wrexham: Wrexham County Council Wales.

British Psychological Society. (2021). *Division of educational and child psychology (DECP) position paper: Children's right to play.* Available at: https://www.bps.org.uk/guideline/childrens-right-play, https://cms.bps.org.uk/sites/default/files/2022-06/PP17 Children%27s right to play.pdf

Canning, N. (2020). *Children's empowerment in play: Participation, voice and ownership.* Abingdon: Routledge.

David, P. (2006). *A commentary on the United Nations convention on the rights of the child, article 31: The right to leisure, play and culture.* Leiden: Brill.

Einarsdottir, J., Purola, A.-M., Johansson, E., Broström, S., & Emilson, A. (2015). Democracy, caring and competence: Values perspectives in ECEC curricula in the Nordic countries. *International Journal of Early Years Education*, 23(1), 97–114.

Goodhall, N., & Atkinson, C. (2017). How do children distinguish between 'play' and 'work'? Conclusions from the literature. *Early Child Development and Care.* http://doi.org/10.1080/03004430.2017.1406484

Murphy, A., Roberts, L., Williams, J., Clement, J., Chicken, S., Waters-Davies, J., & Tyrie, J. (2024). Participative rights in Welsh primary schools: Unpicking the policy rhetoric. *Policy Futures in Education* 23(2), 295–315.https://doi.org/10.1177/14782103241257281

OECD. (2006). *Starting strong II: Early childhood education and care.* Paris: OECD.

Quennerstedt, A., & Quennerstedt, M. (2014). Researching children's rights in education: Sociology of childhood encountering educational theory. *British Journal of Sociology of Education*, 35(1), 115–132. https://doi.org/10.1080/01425692.2013.783962

Rekers, A., & Waters, J. (2021). "All of the wild": Cultural formation in Wales through outdoor play at forest school. In L. T. Grindheim, H. V. Sørensen & A. Rekers (Eds.), *Outdoor learning and play: Pedagogical practices and children's cultural formation.* New York: Springer. Available at: https://library.oapen.org/bitstream/id/bca22612-0e0d-45e1-b699-9e18ab81e203/978-3-030-72595-2.pdf (Accessed 26 February 2025).

Sirkko, R., Kyrönlampi, T., & Puroila, A.-M. (2019). Children's agency: Opportunities and constraints. *International Journal of Early Childhood*, 51, 283–300. https://doi.org/10.1007/s13158-019-00252-5

Theobald, M. (2019). UN Convention on the Rights of the Child: 'Where are we at in recognising children's rights in early childhood, three decades on …?'. *International Journal of Early Childhood*, 51, 251–257. https://doi.org/10.1007/s13158-019-00258-z

Tur Porres, G. (forthcoming) Embracing children's agency in early childhood education and care. In J. Tyrie & J. Waters-Davies (Eds.), *Young children's participation: Exploring practice in early education and care*. Routledge.

UNCRC. (2010). *The United Nations convention on the rights of the child*. Available at: https://www.unicef.org.uk/wp-content/uploads/2010/05/UNCRC_united_nations_convention_on_the_rights_of_the_child.pdf

UNCRC. (2013). *General comment No. 17 on the right of the child to rest, leisure, play, recreational activities, cultural life and the arts (Art. 31)*. Geneva: United Nations.

UNCRC. (2017). *Accessible summary of the UNCRC*. Available at: www.unicef.org.uk/rights-respecting-schools/wp-content/uploads/sites/4/2017/01/Summary-of-the-UNCRC.pdf

United Nations. (2006). *General comment No. 7: Implementing child rights in early childhood*. CRC/C/GC/7/Rev.1. Geneva: UN Office of High Commissioner for Human Rights (OHCHR). Available at: www2.ohchr.org/english/bodies/crc/docs/AdvanceVersions/GeneralComment7Rev1.pdf

Waters-Davies, J., Murphy, A., Tyrie, J., Chicken, S. & Clement, J. (2024). Constructing child participation in early years classrooms: An exploration from Wales. *Children & Society*, 38(50), 1824–1841. Available at: https://doi.org/10.1111/chso.12848

Williams, J. (forthcoming). Participation and participative rights. In J. Tyrie & J. Waters-Davies (Eds.), *Young children's participation: Exploring practice in early education and care*. Abingdon: Routledge.

3
Types of Play

Alison Rees-Edwards

Chapter Objectives

This chapter will introduce:

- Theory of the stages of play.
- Traditional categories of play.
- Contemporary typologies of play.
- The concept of 'free play' and its benefits.

Introduction

The chapter begins with a brief introduction to traditional understandings of categories of play, supported with the work of Mildred Parten Newhall and Sara Smilansky. Contemporary thinking, where there is more focus on children's holistic development, in relation to play types, is then explored. Several types of play are defined, and a brief description of how each type of play can be beneficial for babies, young children and practitioners included. This is followed with a comparison of free play and structured play, presented as a case study with questions for students. See also Chapter 9 for further consideration of how we might observe and understand play.

Stages of Play

Considered by many as one of the earliest researchers of play in the early years, the American sociologist and researcher Mildred Parten (1902-1970) developed the theory about Stages of Play from her 1929 study of young children at play. She observed and recorded children's behaviours, particularly how children interacted with others when playing, and found that as they mature, children's play and interactions become more complex. Based on her research, Parten divided play into six categories.

Unoccupied Play

At this stage, babies and young children explore their environment by observing their surroundings rather than engaging in play. They perform random movements or explore while standing still. Unoccupied play provides children with opportunities to practise their fine motor skills while manipulating objects and to master self-control and patience. This type of play also enables children to learn about how the world works.

Solitary Play/Independent Play

When children play alone, focusing on their own activities and seeming uninterested in others, they are engaging in solitary or independent play (see Figure 3.1). Seeing young children play alone can cause concern, however they are simply entertaining themselves. Thought to be more common in 2- and 3-year-olds, solitary play enables children to master their motor skills and cognitive skills.

Figure 3.1   A 2-Year-Old Engaging in Solitary Play

Onlooker Play/Spectator Play

Onlooker play describes children who observe other children at play rather than participating with them in their games. As they observe, children are learning to recognise social rules, how different relationships work and that there are different ways of playing. Common in 2 and 3 year olds, this type of play is considered a normal part of play development and does not necessarily mean that children are lonely or wary of joining others at play.

Parallel Play

Participating in parallel play enables children to learn new ways of how to engage with others. Although they may play in close proximity to other children, and may mimic others' actions, they are happy to play independently.

Associative Play

In this type of play, children express interest in other children but have no interest in what they are doing. They will interact with each other and engage in activities, but there is no particular goal to their play.

Cooperative Play

Cooperative play describes a more sophisticated type of play where children are interested in other children as well as the activities they are engaged in. Their play appears to be more organised where each child has assigned roles. However, cooperative play is also usually associated with conflict as children learn social skills, such as having to share and take turns.

Smilansky's Four Types of Play

The developmental psychologist Sara Smilansky (1922-2006) worked with the renowned psychologist Jean Piaget, and later broadened his theories of children's cognitive development based on her own studies of children at play. Although Smilansky agreed with Piaget's theory of play, and later found a correlation between sociodramatic play and children's academic success, she argued that play does not develop in stages. Smilansky believed that children engage in four types of play, which contribute to their learning at all stages of development.

Functional Play/Practice Play

Functional or practice play begins at an early age, and is where children learn about physical attributes of objects in their environment. Children use their senses, taking in how something feels, tastes, smells, sounds and what objects can do. They also use their muscles, strengthening and fine-tuning their motor skills as they repeat actions several times. Some children often talk to themselves, engaging in monologues and describing what they are doing.

Constructive Play

After gaining experiences playing with different objects, young children build on what they have learnt and then engage in constructive play. Children build, shape, and manipulate objects and materials to create something new. Constructive play includes play with sand, water, cardboard boxes, dough, as well as construction blocks, and promotes skills such as collaboration and cooperation, problem-solving and creativity.

Dramatic Play

As young children begin to understand their surroundings, they engage in dramatic play, such as role play. This type of play provides children with valuable opportunities for language learning, especially a second language (or more). Smilansky is credited with the introduction of the term '*sociodramatic play*' (Robertson et al., 2020) where children incorporate what they have learnt from their surroundings in their play. This is demonstrated by children's use of dialogue, characterisation, and imaginative play.

Games with Rules

Thought to be the most highly organised form of cooperative play, children engaging in games with rules, such as board games and playground games, are introduced to the concept of rules, how to accept rules and to play by the rules. Not only do children follow intended rules of games, which provide structure and a sense of fairness, children also make up rules as play develops, demonstrating their imaginative and creative skills.

Contemporary Types of Play

Many organisations and charities, such as Play England and Play Wales, have a common goal to raise awareness of children's right to play, as underpinned by Article 31 of the United Nations Convention on the Rights of the Child (UNCRC, 1989, cited in Play Wales, 2024). Not only do they campaign for, and promote, quality play experiences, they also provide advice and guidance for those responsible for providing play opportunities for children (see Chapter 2). Based on the work of the playworker Bob Hughes, play is often categorised into different play types which are thought to promote different areas of child development.

Communication Play

Communication play is a type of play where children use words, gestures, facial expressions, and posture to express their opinions and feelings. Adults can often determine how children are feeling by observing their body language at play. Observing babies enables practitioners to gauge how they are developing and to see which strategies they are using while playing. This can inform future planning, such as play opportunities or changes to the environment. Observing older children enables adults to identify play cues, such as a look or verbal invitation, letting them know if they are required to intervene in their play or not. Playing with other children promotes oracy skills, including speaking, listening, collaborating, and discussing. There must be plenty of time for children to communicate with each other as well as opportunities for turn-taking. Communicating with others during play introduces children to new vocabulary. Singing, storytelling, telling jokes, and miming provides children with opportunities to experiment with language and to develop their understanding of different ways of communicating.

Creative Play

Creative play is often associated with arts and craft-type activities. However, any activity where children are provided with opportunities to satisfy their curiosity, to explore and to express themselves can promote children's creativity. As children come across challenges while playing, their ability to problem-solve enhances their creativity. Problem-solving enables children to develop ideas and their imagination, and when successful, their self-esteem and self-confidence grows. Allowing children time to find the answers and to try out new ideas supports their cognitive development, such as divergent thinking. To promote creative development, children need to feel confident that they can change the environment, and objects within the environment, without fear of being scolded or judged. This, and allowing children to choose what happens while playing, nurtures their emotional health (see also Chapter 7).

Deep Play

Deep play is also known as risky play. These terms describe types of play that enable children to experience risks, problems, challenges, and dangerous activities, such as climbing trees, balancing, jumping from high surfaces and swinging from ropes. Pretend games that include monsters and 'baddies' and telling scary stories are further examples of deep play. Deep play experiences are beneficial for children as they discover what they are physically and mentally capable of doing. They learn how to manage and overcome risk, which, in turn, can help them conquer their fears. Although usually associated with older children, younger children are also drawn to risky play. However, opportunities for deep play are usually limited as many adults are averse to children taking risks (see Chapter 16). Allowing children to engage in deep play challenges adults' instincts to protect children. Increased regulations and restrictions within settings also limit children's deep play opportunities.

Deep play can also be used to describe children who are deeply involved in their play, concentrating hard and difficult to distract from what they are doing.

Dramatic Play

Dramatic play, or thematic play, describes play where children recreate scenarios they have encountered from listening to stories, from reading books themselves and from other examples of media (television, films, and the internet). Children often assign themselves with roles and 'perform' what they have seen and heard. Although dramatic play is often associated with children playing independently, other children, as well as adults, may be invited to participate as an audience. Dramatic play, where children can repeat their actions, enables children to have a better understanding of characters, of narrative and themes. This type of play also provides opportunities for children to act out their emotions and feelings, and by acting out their experiences, dramatic play increases their understanding of the world and helps them cope with reality.

Exploratory Play

One of the first types of play children experience, exploratory play involves finding out about the properties of toys and objects in their environment, and what happens to these toys and objects when manipulated. Exploratory play promotes children's natural curiosity and encourages them to investigate and explore. It is a type of play that involves all of the senses. For example, when engaging in water play, children will look at the water and will touch the water with their mouths and hands. They will listen to the sounds water makes when moved and children's sense of smell can be stimulated if ingredients are added to the water. Exploratory play involves trial and error, which stimulates children's cognitive development. It is a type of never-ending play, and with no expectations, there is no pressure on children to achieve certain outcomes. When successful, after putting an object back together for example, children's self-confidence, self-esteem, and critical thinking skills grow. Exploratory play in the outdoors, where children have freedom to investigate their environment, is also a positive play experience for children. Exploring leaves, stones, foliage, etc. enables children to connect with the natural world (see Chapter 9). Children become more active and engrossed in their surroundings, which, in turn, improves their fitness, muscle strength, and coordination.

Fantasy Play

Also known as 'pretend play', fantasy play is a term used to describe play where children engage in scenarios which they are unlikely to encounter in real life. For example, pretending to be a superhero with superhuman powers or pretending that a soft toy horse is a unicorn. Fantasy play enables children to improve their understanding of the world, as they take on different roles, exploring the boundaries between what is real and unreal. It is a type of play that promotes children's imagination and creative thinking, as they use unreal characters and events to help them address 'what if' situations. Fantasy play also acts as an outlet for children as they use the unreal scenarios to act out anything that may be making them anxious. As the children themselves determine the result of these situations, they experience a sense of achievement, which promotes their self-esteem and self-worth.

Imaginative Play

Similar to fantasy play, children engaging in imaginative play participate in activities that provide them with opportunities to solve problems, create new possibilities, and to make sense of the world they are living in. However, in contrast to fantasy play where scenarios are based on unreal situations, imaginative play is usually associated with events that have happened, or are likely to happen, to children. For example, children may pretend to be teachers and their toys are their pupils, acting out an event that happened to them at school. By re-enacting the event while playing, children are able to take control of what is happening and act out different outcomes. As a result, they may experience different emotions and feelings, which helps them to develop an understanding of empathy (Hashmi et al., 2020). Children may play alone or with others when engaged in imaginative play. If alone, children are often heard talking to themselves. This is known as private speech. As children develop, and their thoughts and feelings become more internalised, their imaginative play decreases.

Locomotor Play

Young children's first physical skills, such as crawling, walking and running, develop naturally in typically developing children. However, children need opportunities to engage in locomotor play to practise and develop additional physical skills, including jumping, hopping, skipping, cycling, and ball games. Locomotor play is beneficial for children's physical development as these types of activities promote the development of muscles needed for strength, flexibility, and endurance. Engaging in locomotor play also enables children to learn how to control their movements for balance and spatial awareness. Locomotor play is beneficial to children's health and well-being, especially if activities are undertaken in the outdoors, where there is sufficient space to move. At a time where there is an increase in children's physical and mental health problems, including childhood obesity and depression, children need regular opportunities to engage in physical activities. Locomotor play, where children can practise their physical skills, has been found to reduce levels of cortisol – the stress hormone – and helps children develop the connection between nerve cells and the brain, which, in turn, promotes their cognitive skills, such as concentration and memory.

Mastery Play

Mastery play is a term used to describe play experiences where children have opportunities to repeat actions and activities until they have been mastered. To facilitate this, children need to feel safe and comfortable, and provided with plenty of time. Mastery play is often associated with activities that are challenging for children, such as walking along a high surface for the first time. At first, they appear apprehensive and may walk slowly as they work out what they are capable of doing. They may need reassurance and support as they work their way across. By repeating the activity, their confidence and self-belief becomes visible as they approach the high surface in a more confident manner, their pace used to walk across the surface increases and they may decline any offers of support. Mastery play provides children with opportunities to take control over their actions and their learning. By undertaking challenging activities, they learn how to recognise and how to manage risk. They develop trust in themselves, have respect for their environment and recognise which skills they have yet to master.

Object Play

Similar to 'exploratory play', object play includes the examining and manipulating of objects. As children develop, and have further opportunities to practise their fine motor skills, they are able to control objects for longer, turning them around, pushing and pulling, looking inside them, and exploring what can be done with them. Some adults may not understand the benefits of object play nor children's fascination for objects, especially those unfamiliar to them. However, object play provides opportunities for exploration, for discovery and can be used to represent children's feelings and interests. Some objects can have multiple uses, keeping children engrossed in their endless possibilities, such as cardboard boxes and other examples of packaging. For example, children may enjoy placing objects inside a box, opening and closing the box flaps. If large enough, children may also enjoy climbing and hiding inside boxes. The skills acquired by engaging in object play are thought to be a foundation for later learning, such as mathematics, science and engineering.

Recapitulative Play

Recapitulative play is described as a deep and complex type of play, often associated with evolutionary behaviours. It is a type of play where children can be seen building dens, nests and shelters and making use of natural resources as weapons, such as using sticks to represent guns. Recapitulative play also includes play with water and mud, and rubbing sticks together as if to create fire. It is thought that engaging in these activities reflect behaviours and experiences associated with our ancestry and history, and as it is unlikely that children will have first-hand experiences of these, recapitulative play is said to be instinctive. Further examples of this type of play include exploration of our history, relaying stories, myths and legends, and creating languages. Recapitulative play often occurs in outdoor environments where children have access to nature. As a result, children can investigate properties of natural resources and phenomena such as light and darkness. Recapitulative play is thought to be challenging to identify as the types of play children engage in overlap with other types of play.

Role Play

Considered to be an important part of child development, role play describes play where children imitate people who are familiar to them, as well as people in different occupational roles, including builders, teachers, and police officers. As for imaginary play, role play provides children with opportunities to explore different characters, either demonstrating identifiable features of others (tone of voice, body language, and facial expressions) or with more exaggerated features. Roles explored can be both real-life and fictional situations, and children often incorporate situations that different people may experience in their play. Role play is beneficial for children's language and communication skills as they make plans, discuss ideas with others and use different forms of speech as they act out different roles. Although adults may be invited by children to join them in their play, role play that is child-led is more likely to promote children's creativity, imagination, and problem-solving skills.

Rough and Tumble Play

Also known as 'play fighting' or 'pretend fighting', rough and tumble play includes behaviours such as children pushing and tickling each other, wrestling, climbing over, and chasing each other. It is a type of play often misunderstood by adults, who are concerned that children may hurt themselves or each other. It is thought that today's attitudes and expectations, along with having to abide by safety regulations, have contributed to a decline in rough and tumble play. Adults are often concerned that this type of play is a sign of aggressive behaviour and may develop into actual fighting. However, it is possible to distinguish between the two by looking at children's facial expressions. If children are seen smiling and laughing, they are demonstrating that they are happy and content. If children appear unhappy or uncomfortable, adults should investigate and intervene if necessary. When engaging in rough and tumble play, there is no deliberate intention to hurt each other. Observed in children as young as 18 months old, it is a type of play that promotes physical, cognitive and language development, and social-emotional growth. Children can learn about self-control, balance, coordination and body awareness. Rough and tumble play also provides children with opportunities to establish friendships, to work out relationships and boundaries, such as what is, and what is not, acceptable behaviour.

Social Play

Described as one of the most common behaviours observed in children (Play Wales, 2017), social play is any type of play where children interact with others. During infancy, early examples of social play can be seen as babies smile and coo, imitate facial expressions and enjoy peek-a-boo games. These actions, and those reciprocated by others, are thought to be precursors for turn-taking in conversations. As children develop and begin to play with others, they are introduced to social skills, such as learning how to share, how and when to take turns, listening to others, and noticing and understanding social cues. These skills enable children to see that others may have different perspectives to themselves, which is fundamental if they are to develop empathy. As children's play becomes more complex, their social skills grow and they learn how to form and maintain friendships. They share ideas as well as toys, cooperating with each other when building something as they play, or playing games together. They can negotiate and compromise, working together as they follow (and break) established rules of play.

Socio-Dramatic Play

Often associated with 'fantasy play', socio-dramatic play can be a solitary experience or a type of play that involves others. As they play, children may imitate experiences that have actually happened to them, but they often incorporate elements of make-believe in their actions. For example, children pretend to be cooking a 'meal' in the home corner but that meal is for a cartoon character or superhero. Socio-dramatic play is an advanced form of play and is sometimes viewed as a form of therapy, as children use play as an outlet to deal with negative experiences, such as being bullied or witnessing abuse. Children are able to express emotions and feelings that may be causing anxiety, confusion, and fear through play. Similarly to social play, socio-dramatic play provides children with opportunities to explore how others may be feeling; they learn how to interact, how to communicate and how to cooperate.

Symbolic Play

Thought to develop at around 18–24 months of age, symbolic play is a term used to describe play where children use objects, actions, and ideas to represent something else. Examples of symbolic play can include using payment cards as mobile phones, a toy hairdryer used as a firefighter's hose or a twig as a police officer's gun. Prior to this stage, babies engage in functional play, where objects are used according to their intended purpose. During symbolic play, children are often observed interacting with the objects, talking to them and expressing emotions, thoughts and feelings. These emotions can either be their own thoughts and feelings, or children transfer thoughts and feelings onto the objects themselves; this is also known as animism. Symbolic play is beneficial for children's creativity as they do not always need to have actual objects as they play – children can imagine that an object is present. In addition, symbolic play promotes symbolic thought, essential for children's language development, literacy and numeracy skills. Letters, in their written format, are symbols used to represent sounds and words, essential for speaking, reading and writing, and numbers are symbols used to enable us to count and make calculations.

Musical Play

Music play or musical play is an additional type of play, often excluded from taxonomies of play, and thought to be overlooked by some adults, as not all understand the value of children's exposure to music. From an early age, babies and children are often introduced to nursery rhymes and songs, and have opportunities for creative play. In today's thinking, young children's exposure to music and benefits of musical experiences are thought to be an important part of child development, with growing interest and extensive research in the field. Included in Howard Gardner's multiple intelligences theory (Moyles, 2015), children with musical intelligence are those who respond to music by singing and clapping, can remember tunes, move and dance, and can create their own rhythms and music. Experiences with music have been found to promote children's cognitive and language development, especially in their ability to acquire language and to read. Learning to play a musical instrument aids children's mathematical development. Singing with children introduces them to sounds and meanings of words, while dancing to music promotes children's motor skills.

Case Study 3.1

Three Year 1 children are sitting at a table, playing with LEGO® in a classroom. They are content in each other's company, sharing ideas and listening to each other in their attempt to construct a 'house'. One child attaches some LEGO® bricks together and holds up his creation to show the other children. 'Look, I've made a gun!; ' exclaims the child. The child points the 'gun' towards them and makes 'shooting' noises. The other two children smile and seem to be studying the 'gun'. They attach LEGO® bricks together and create their own 'guns'. The children stand from the table and pretend to 'shoot' each other. They are engrossed in their play, laughing and hiding from each other by crouching behind the furniture. One of the adults in the classroom stands up abruptly and walks quickly towards the children. She immediately scolds the children and tells them to dismantle what they have created. She states that 'shooting' each other is 'not nice' and is not allowed in the school. The children look upset, sit back down at the table and take their creations apart.

Reflection Point 3.1

- Consider how you would explain the benefits of gun play/weapon play to the practitioner.
- How could you support your explanation?
- If gun play/weapon play is not permitted at a setting, how would you explain this to children engaging in this type of play?

Free Play vs Structured Play

According to Play England, free play is defined as:

> children choosing what they want to do, how they want to do it and when to stop and try something else. Free play has no external goals set by adults and has no adult imposed curriculum. Although adults usually provide the space and resources for free play and might be involved, the child takes the lead and the adults respond to cues from the child. (National Children's Bureau, 2007, p. xi)

Children who appear to be engrossed in one activity, but then spontaneously begin to play something else, are said to be engaging in free play. They are acting on their natural curiosity, following their own interests and having fun. Free play is beneficial for children as it:

- Encourages children to develop imagination.
- Promotes creativity.
- Involves pretending and role play.
- Provides problem-solving opportunities (see also Chapters 1, 6, and 8).

Besio (2017, p. 9) describes free play as '*play for the sake of play*', where children are completely absorbed in what they are doing. Free play gives children a sense of freedom, as it is the child who is in control, deciding on what and how to play, and where to play. Children can also decide whether to play alone or with others, when to start playing and when the play ends, as there is no time limit. Engaging in free play is a rewarding experience for children as there is no prescribed way to play and no expectations placed on them. Having the freedom to make choices is crucial for children's cognitive development, their mental health and their well-being, as they are more likely to learn how to be autonomous. Children who do not have sufficient opportunities to make independent choices are more likely to be dependent on others for longer and easily influenced by others. They are also more likely to have low self-esteem. Therefore, it is important that adults understand the importance of children's autonomy and facilitate choice wherever possible.

Structured play or play-like activities are terms that describe play which has been initiated by adults. In contrast to free play, where activities are child-led, structured play tends to be adult-led and includes activities that have a particular purpose, often with objectives that can be measured for either educational or clinical reasons. Examples of structured play are games with rules, organised sports, and activities where children have to follow instructions. Although structured activities enable adults to identify children's individual needs, to monitor their progress and to inform future planning, they are not always considered beneficial. An increase in structured play often results in fewer opportunities for free play, and is thought to cause stress and anxiety in children. This could be linked to fewer opportunities where children can express themselves and be creative. Children may lose interest and lack concentration when participating in adult-led activities, and they are less likely to become independent in their thinking and actions.

Reflection Point 3.2

According to O'Connor (2017), there has been a significant decline in opportunities for children to engage in free play and concern that there may be lasting negative consequences for children.

- Discuss possible reasons for the decline in free play.
- Consider what these 'negative consequences' could be.
- How can opportunities for free play be reintroduced?

Summary

In this chapter, we explored:

- Traditional categories of play and how they inform today's practice.
- Contemporary thinking about play with examples of activities undertaken by children.
- The role of the adult when facilitating and supporting play opportunities.
- Why 'free play' is important for children.

Further Reading

Owen, K. (2021) *Play in the Early Years*. London: Sage. This book provides an insight into the importance of play, and provides an overview of key concepts and approaches to children's play. Prominent theorists in the field of child development are included, enabling students to link theory to practice.

Waller, T. and Davis, G. (2014) *An Introduction to Early Childhood* (3rd ed.). London: Sage. Not only does this publication explore contemporary issues related to children and child development, Part 3 looks at how play promotes children's creativity as well as the importance of play in the outdoors.

Wood, E. (2013) *Play, Learning and the Early Childhood Curriculum* (3rd ed.). London: Sage. Another useful resource that looks at the benefits of play, with useful case studies to support students' understanding.

References

Besio, S. (2017). *The need for play for the sake of play*. Available at: www.researchgate.net/publication/316306731_1_The_Need_for_Play_for_the_Sake_of_Play

Hashmi, S., Vanderwert, R. E., Price, H. A., & Gerson, S. A. (2020). Exploring the benefits of doll play through neuroscience. *Frontiers in Human Neuroscience*, 14, 560176. https://doi.org/10.3389/fnhum.2020.560176

Moyles, J. (Ed.). (2015). *The excellence of play* (4th ed.). Maidenhead: Open University Press.

National Children's Bureau. (2007). *Free play in early childhood: A literature review*. Available at: www.playengland.net/wp-content/uploads/2015/09/free-play-in-early-childhood.pdf

O'Connor, S. (2017). *The secret power of play*. Available at: https://time.com/4928925/secret-power-play/

Play Wales. (2017). *Play types*. Available at: https://issuu.com/playwales/docs/play_types

Play Wales. (2024). *Play for Wales: Playing in the early years*. Available at: https://play.wales/wp-content/uploads/2024/10/Play-for-Wales-issue-63-Spring-Summer-2024.pdf

Robertson, N., Morrissey, A. & Moore, D. (2020). From boats to bushes: Environmental elements supportive of children's sociodramatic play outdoors. *Children's Geographies*, 18(2), 234–246.

4
Play Pioneers and their Legacy

Alison Murphy

Chapter Objectives

This chapter will:

- Explore the work of the play pioneers and their theories.
- Reflect on their ideas of how play should be planned and implemented.
- Consider how the pioneers have influenced contemporary policy and practice in early years settings.

Play Pioneers

A play pioneer is a person who has helped to shape and change our ideas about play and how it is integral in supporting children's learning and development.

Jean Jacques Rousseau (1712-1778)

One of the earliest pioneers to recognise the value of play was Jean Jacques Rousseau. He was a philosopher born in Geneva in 1712, who extolled the child's right to play and explore the natural world. He spent much of his adult life in France and in 1762 his novel *Emile* was published. This book told the story of a young boy and his fictitious education journey. Fundamentally this book sets out Rousseau's view on education and emphasises how the innate goodness in humankind can be nurtured with the right educational approaches. This book was seen as revolutionary at the time and was banned in Paris and Geneva as it did not correspond with the views of the church which were then dominant in France.

Rousseau saw childhood as a time of innocence which needed to be respected and revered as a distinct phase of life. During the eighteenth century children were often seen as miniature adults and were dressed and treated accordingly. However, Rousseau recognised the differences between adults and children; he saw childhood as a separate stage of life. Children and childhood should not be governed by the demands of society according to Rousseau's philosophy. He saw that children needed to be nurtured and protected from harm and not subject to punishment and threats, and provided with a secure, loving environment.

Rousseau proposed that educational experiences should be child-centred and individually structured to meet the needs of each child. Play was central to this, fostering the child's natural curiosity to explore the world. This emphasis on nurturing the child's innate desire to explore the natural world was later echoed in the work of Jean Piaget. Rousseau saw the adult as a guide, who would react and respond to the child's instinct to explore, rather than as an instructor. He considered experiential learning rather than didactic instruction as fundamental, with the child leading the learning process.

Rousseau also went on to influence other pioneers such as Pestalozzi (1746-1827). Pestalozzi implemented Rousseau's ideas about education and nature in orphanages and subsequently inspired his student Friedrich Froebel (1782-1852). Froebel was the educator (or 'pedagogue') who went on to formulate the 'kindergarten'.

Rousseau's Key Influences
- Childhood is a distinct stage of life to be respected and revered.
- Children need to be nurtured and protected from harm.
- The child has a right to play and explore the natural world.
- Educational experiences should be child-centred and individually structured to meet the needs of each child and their interests.

Friedrich Froebel (1782-1852)
Friedrich Froebel was a German educator who is credited with pioneering the kindergarten approach for children aged 2-7 years. Froebel's mother died when he was only nine months old and as the fifth child of a clergyman, he was often left to his own devices. He spent much of his young life engaging with the natural world where he acquired knowledge about plants and natural phenomena. After training as a forester, then studying surveying and architecture, Froebel decided to pursue education as his chosen profession. He began teaching at a school in Frankfurt which used the ethos of Pestalozzi, which endorsed a child-centred, holistic approach to education. Here, children's natural curiosity and innate desire to learn were fostered. Froebel then went on to study under Pestalozzi at Yverdon, where he became deeply influenced by Pestalozzi's ideas specifically the notion of nurturing the head, heart and hands, that is, holistic learning which was based around each child's needs in a relaxed permissive environment.

Froebel's own philosophies are underpinned by his strong spiritual and religious beliefs. He believed in the inherent goodness of the child and that children needed to be nourished by the adults around them in an enriched environment. He sought to give children a wide range of meaningful play experiences which allowed them to develop their creativity and self-expression. These activities were child-led and self-chosen, powered by the child's intrinsic motivation to learn through being active. The outdoors was an important aspect of this; allowing children to interact with the natural environment, he saw the natural world as an influential means for learning about the physical, moral, and spiritual world. The word *kindergarten* translates as 'children's garden'.

As part of his curriculum, Froebel designed educational materials which he called the 'Gifts'. These sets of cubes, spheres, and cylinders were presented to the children in a sequential way, moving from the simple to the complex. Children played with the 'Gifts' which allowed experimentation and enabled children to build on their knowledge and skills, making connections in their learning through open-ended play. He also formulated 'Occupations' which included painting, singing and other creative expressions as integral to his curriculum and supported by the adults within the setting. The children were given a mixture of directed and free-flow play which focused around the children's development and interests.

Relationships and interaction with other children were an important aspect of Froebelian principles. The adult's role was central in knowing what a child can do and therefore intervening sensitively. Froebel saw the adults as nurturers of ideas, feelings, and relationships, supporting children to develop their confidence, skills, and independence. He recognised the importance of educators of young children being trained.

Froebel's Key Influences

- Engagement with the natural world.
- Learning through self-directed play and reflection.
- Creative experiential learning.
- Nurturing, well-trained practitioners.

Maria Montessori (1870-1952)

Maria Montessori was a doctor; she was the first woman in Italy to graduate with a medical degree in 1896. During her career she worked with children who lived in squalid impoverished conditions deprived of medical and social interventions; these children were deemed uneducable. Montessori went on to establish a pre-school in the slums of Rome. After observing these children, she created her distinctive approach which combined her knowledge of paediatric medicine and education (she taught medicine and produced many academic papers based on her observations and theories). Montessori was heavily influenced by the work of Froebel and Pestalozzi. Her holistic approach to education was based on nurturing children's inherent desire to learn.

Montessori viewed children and childhood with respect in an era where children were meant to be seen and not heard. She was an advocate for children's rights and social reform. Like Rousseau,

Montessori promoted a child-centred approach which recognised the need for individual teaching and self-directed activity. Play was seen as a purposeful action and was encouraged via particular activities and interaction with objects. This pragmatic approach regarded play approaches such as fantasy play as trivial.

The Montessori method focused on fostering children's independence and motivation and advocating that children had the greatest capacity to learn between the ages of 0-6 years. Montessori identified that physical activity had a primary role in establishing concepts and achieving mastery. She believed that young children learnt best through sensory-motor activities; knowledge and skills were gained through mastery of simple aspects before leading on to proficiency in more complex aspects. Therefore, Montessori considered the learning environment critical and argued that this needed to be matched to the developmental level of the children. Thus, Montessori settings were divided into specific learning areas and included child-sized furniture and equipment to allow for independent learning. Settings were multi-aged so that children can learn from each other and children were free to move around the setting and engage in the planned activities as part of Montessori's self-directed ethos. The planned learning activities were designed to develop the senses and to create opportunities for mastery.

The role of the adult was that of director or enabler, rather than instructor. Assessments were formulated via careful observations of the children. They were carried out to gain an understanding of reactions to the activities and learning; the observations fed into further planning to support and guide the children's next steps. Mutual respect was implicit in the adult–child relationships.

The Montessori method is still very popular and there are many early years settings and schools throughout the world which use her ideas and principles. Maria Montessori's approach to play and learning has influenced early years curricula and learning environments. For example, the Early Years Foundation Stage in England is very much based on active learning and learning through experience. The principles of the EYFS (Department for Education, 2024) are reminiscent of Montessori's ideas, seeing the child as a unique competent learner from birth, the need for the child to be nurtured through positive relationships with parents and key workers and the role of the enabling environment as the key to supporting development and learning. Montessori qualifications have been approved on several national qualification frameworks; the training has been acknowledged as addressing relevant criteria for those wishing to enter the workforce as early years educators.

Montessori's Key Influences

- Promotion of carefully planned environment with child-sized equipment to allow for independent learning.
- Division of nurseries into specific areas – mathematical, language, etc. Purposeful play with sequenced learning activities to develop the senses.
- Adult as an enabler.
- Observations as a tool for assessment.

Reflection Point 4.1

- Rousseau, Froebel, and Montessori all advocated child-centred approaches; these are now integral to early years curricula throughout the United Kingdom. Consider how child-centred notions are enacted in the early years curricula and settings that you are familiar with. How do practitioners support these child-led learning opportunities?
- The role of the adult as a guide and enabler for learning rather than an instructor was fundamental to Rousseau and Montessori's notion of child-initiated learning. From your own observations, are adults working in early years settings 'guiding' or 'instructing' in their delivery of learning experiences? Does the approach differ according to the type of early years setting?

Margaret McMillan (1860-1931)

Margaret McMillan was a pioneer of nursery schools and an advocate for outdoor learning. Margaret McMillan was born and partially educated in the United States. She returned to Scotland where she completed her education and then became a governess. She then relocated to London where she took up a job as a junior superintendent in a home for young girls. Her sister Rachel also worked in a similar role. Both sisters became Christian socialists and were politically active in the Independent Labour Party. They relocated to Bradford where Margaret became a member of the Bradford School Board. While inspecting schools in Bradford, Margaret witnessed children in poor physical health. Margaret McMillan believed that many of the conditions she had seen such as malnutrition and poor physical and dental health could be overcome with fresh air, nutritious meals, and appropriate health care. Like the psychologist Maslow (1987) who developed theoretical ideas around the hierarchy of needs, she considered that once their physical and emotional well-being needs were met, then the children would be able to learn and develop. Therefore, she and Rachel decided that they should focus their attention on improving the lives of children who lived in poverty.

Subsequently, Margaret was responsible for the introduction of a school medical service, school meals and baths in Bradford schools, the first board in the United Kingdom to introduce these measures. She and Rachel went on to work in Deptford, London, where they lobbied parliament for compulsory school medical inspections. This law, enacted in 1907, precluded children under the age of 5. Following this the sisters championed nursery education. In 1911, they set up an open-air school for 6- to 14-year-olds which used a holistic approach to education. This was followed by a camp for younger children in 1914 which emphasised the need for care alongside education.

Margaret McMillan was greatly influenced by the work of Froebel. McMillan advocated active learning through first-hand experiences and felt that physical activity was vital and as such the outdoor environment was critical. She thought that 'the best classroom and the richest cupboard is roofed only by the sky', that is, the outdoors (McMillan, 1919). Play was viewed as a means of self-expression and an application of learning and understanding. The environment was designed to encourage creativity, exploration, and experimentation to stimulate learning. Adults in the setting were trained to understand how to capture the attention of the child and engage them in playful activities. McMillan also recognised the importance of working alongside parents and helping them to learn how to engage positively with their children.

Margaret McMillan acknowledged the requirement for teachers to be properly trained to meet the care and educational needs of young children and that this role should be given professional status. As the development of nursery schools gained pace in England, the Rachel McMillan Teacher Training College was established in 1930 (by this time Rachel had died and the college was named in her honour). The three-year course designed by McMillan taught students to nurture the whole child, work alongside parents and the community.

Undoubtedly Margaret McMillan's philosophy of educating early years teachers is still influential today, with greater moves to raise the status and further professionalise the early years workforce in the United Kingdom and beyond through the introduction of a suite of qualifications aimed at ensuring high quality early education. Her use of the outdoor environment was ground-breaking, and the revival of outdoor provision continues in early years practice; many young children now regularly access stimulating outdoor spaces where they can explore and experiment. Parental partnership and community engagement are a key feature of legislation, policy, and practice not just within the early years but throughout the education sector, this is particularly evident in the Curriculum for Wales (Welsh Government, 2023) where community focused school model is advocated.

McMillan's Key Influences

- Teacher training for early years teachers.
- Holistic approach – promoting the child's physical and emotional well-being as well as encouraging learning.
- Outdoor learning, forerunner to forest schools.
- Parental and community partnerships.

Susan Isaacs (1885-1948)

Susan Isaacs was a psychologist and educationalist; she too promoted child-centred approaches and embedded her knowledge of child psychology into her ideas about how children learn and develop. Isaacs was born in Lancashire in 1885. When she left school, she travelled abroad and became a governess. She returned to the United Kingdom to undertake a teaching course and study further for a degree in philosophy as well as studying psychology at Cambridge. She also trained as a psychoanalyst. In 1924, she set up the Maltings House School which catered for children aged 2 to 7. Much of her subsequent academic theories were generated from the observations and findings established while she was there.

Isaacs saw play as integral to learning and development and a vehicle for self-expression which could support children's emotional well-being. She acknowledged the role of play as the safe way for children to explore the world and experiment and recognised that 'Play is indeed the child's work and the means whereby he grows and develops' (Isaacs, 1929, p. 9). Isaacs also valued cooperative play as a means for developing social interactions. Her school environment was carefully planned to support learning through play. Like Montessori she provided the children with child-sized furniture and resources, areas were set out to encourage role play through dressing up, creativity through experimentation with art and craft materials and there was also a quiet area where children could rest. The garden was also arranged in a specific way to encourage enquiry and natural curiosity via playful experiences and interaction with the resources. Children were given responsibilities such as tidying up and planning.

According to Isaacs, the role of the adult was fundamental to the learning environment in providing a safe, secure place nurturing the child's social and emotional development and fostering a child-centred approach. Observation provided a valuable instrument for the adult to gain detailed knowledge of the individual children in their care and respond accordingly. 'By patient listening to the talk of even little children and watching what they do... we can wish their wishes, see their pictures and think their thoughts' (Isaacs, 1929, p. 15). Isaacs introduced record cards into the classroom so that teachers could build up a picture of the whole child.

Isaacs' influences on current policy and practice are evident in the way in which theoretical ideas about children, their development and learning are considered from a range of perspectives including psychological, philosophical, and historical viewpoints. Also, her analysis and data gathering in the Maltings House School has paved the way for further use of observational findings to support planning and development. Perhaps her most important contribution was the recognition of the social and emotional benefits of play; providing an environment which supports this is implicit in early years contexts.

Isaacs' Key Influences
- Carefully planned enabling environment.
- Social and emotional benefits of play.
- Theories of psychology embedded into ideas about how children learn and develop.
- Observation as a tool for planning.

Elinor Goldschmied (1910-2009)
Elinor Goldschmied was a pioneer of heuristic play (heuristic means enabling someone to discover or learn something for themselves, see Chapter 6) and the use of the treasure basket with babies. Elinor was born in rural Gloucestershire and she felt that her freedom to explore the natural world and everyday objects in the family's large garden had influenced her ideas and thinking around how children learn and develop.

Elinor trained as a teacher at the Froebel Institute alongside Susan Isaacs and was greatly influenced by Froebel's ideas about nature and creativity. Following on from this she also qualified as a psychiatric social worker. In 1946, she moved to Italy where she worked in an institution for single mothers and their babies and began to introduce sensory learning activities to babies via the treasure basket. Goldschmied then began teaching and training in other institutions throughout Italy, transforming childcare practice there in daycare and orphanages. She returned to the United Kingdom in 1955 and began working at the Tavistock Institute with John Bowlby who was developing his attachment theory.

Goldschmied's treasure baskets were introduced in Italy in 1955 and embraced by the Italian childcare systems, however her ideas about heuristic play only came to the forefront of practice in the United Kingdom in the 1980s. The treasure basket is a collection of natural objects such as shells and pebbles and everyday things such as wooden spoons and small pots (around 100 items) which babies explore. The children experience the characteristics of these objects using their senses. Advances in neurological research in the 1990s supported Goldschmied's ideas about the value of sensory learning and therefore treasure baskets gained popularity and were soon part of early years practice in nurseries. She believed that young children could learn scientific and mathematical concepts through their play and interaction with sensory materials and containers. She produced detailed guidance on how these heuristic play sessions could be set up with pre-verbal toddlers, with the adult providing a calming but attentive influence, allowing the children to freely explore the objects in front of them.

The role of the adult was also a theme in Goldschmied's work. She pioneered the Key Person Approach which stemmed from her time in Italian orphanages. This system of personal care is described as 'a way of working in nurseries in which the whole focus and organisation is aimed at enabling and supporting close attachments between individual children and individual nursery staff' (Elfer et al., 2003, p. 18). In the Key Person Approach, a nursery practitioner is allocated a small number of children. He or she is then responsible for the group and forms an attachment with each child through interactions while meeting the child's physical needs and playing with them. The Key Person will also liaise with parents at the start and end of the day, providing a link between the setting and the home.

Goldschmied's Key Influences

- Sensory play.
- The use of treasure baskets.
- Heuristic play as a means of understanding mathematical and scientific concepts.
- Key Person Approach.

Janet Moyles (1942-)

Janet Moyles became interested in play and how it can impact on learning and development while being a parent, playgroup leader, and parent helper. She then trained as a teacher and went on to teach in both nursery and primary schools. After being seconded to work on an early years research project with Cambridge University Institute of Education, she then worked in a variety of roles in higher education.

Janet Moyles produced her seminal text *The Excellence of Play* in 1989 where she outlined the key features and importance of play. Moyles (1989) identified that play opportunities should support experimentation and exploration and allow children to make choices and decisions and organise their own time. She noted that when children have confidence in play activities, this impacts positively on motivation, concentration, and self-image. Other features described by Moyles include play as a vehicle for children to use their imagination and creativity, and she also noted that when applying this approach there is often little need for expensive materials. According to Moyles, play contributes to the overall development of the child, aiding motor and perceptual development alongside social development as children collaborate with peers in activities.

Moyles stated that mastery of skills and concepts is intrinsic in play and suggested that the learning process is like a spiral. It begins with free play, continues with structured or directed play and then returns to enriched free play as knowledge and abilities are acquired and consolidated. The first session of free play allows exploration, whereas the second brings a degree of mastery, and this is followed up by the adult who offers more structured play opportunities leading to a new cycle of play and exploration. This spiral goes on and on as children go through these cycles.

Reflection Point 4.2

Here is an example of Moyles' play spiral.

Free Play

- Lexie is sitting at the modelling table for the first time. She has just been watching some children playing with dough and clay for a couple of days but hasn't sat down and tried it herself. Today she experiments with the dough by pushing and squeezing it and making holes with her finger.

Mastery

- As Lexie plays freely with the dough over the next few days she becomes more and more skilful in the way she manipulates the dough.

Adult-Led Structured Play

- The early years worker sets up a dough baking activity to make fruit shapes for the shop and Lexie joins in. Over the next few weeks, she develops further skills in modelling dough.

Free Play

- Lexie starts to investigate clay in the same way.

Identify how Lexie could be encouraged to develop her skills further. Use Moyles' play spiral to reflect on what further opportunities could be provided to develop mastery both in terms of enriched free play opportunities and adult-led structured play.

In 2002, Janet Moyles coordinated the SPEEL (Study of Pedagogical Effectiveness in Early Learning) project. The main outcome of this project was the development of the 'Framework for Effective Pedagogy' that provided a set of competencies which identified the role of the effective practitioner in supporting children's learning in the early years. Moyles advocated that reflective and responsive adult-child interaction is the foundation to children's wellbeing, requiring practitioners to engage in debates around pedagogy. She championed the notion of playful pedagogies whereby practitioners have a clear understanding that 'play is the essential pedagogical strategy to enhance children's deeper learning' (Moyles, 2010, p. 8).

Moyles' Key Influences

- The play spiral.
- Playful pedagogies.
- Play as a tool for holistic development.
- Reflective practitioner.

Tina Bruce (1947–)

Tina Bruce trained as a primary school teacher at the Froebel Educational Institute. She went on to become an educator who was guided by Froebel's principles including developing a holistic approach to teaching young children. Bruce worked for many years at the Froebel Institute and has made a distinguished contribution to the field of early years through writing and editing education books and co-founding the Centre for Early Childhood Studies at Roehampton University. She has worked with numerous advisory groups playing an instrumental role in laying the foundations of today's approach to the early education experienced by children aged 0–5 years in England.

Bruce (2001) is an advocate for free-flow play where the children themselves govern what to do, how to do it, and what to use. She argues that when children are playing freely, play is coordinated, moves fluidly from one phase or scenario to the next and makes young children feel powerful and contented. Free-flow play according to Bruce equals wallowing in ideas, feelings, and relationships and application of developed competence, mastery and control.

She emphasises that:

> Children at play are able to stay flexible, respond to events and changing situations, be sensitive to people, to adapt, think on their feet, and keep altering what they do in a fast-moving scene. When the process of play is rich, it can lead children into creating rich products in their stories, paintings, dances, music making, drawings, sculptures, and constructions, or in the solving of scientific and mathematical problems. (Bruce, 2001, p. 46)

Tina Bruce (1991) identified features of free-flow play in her second book, *Play in Early Childhood Education*; these are summarised below:

1 It is an active process without a product.
2 It is intrinsically motivated.

3 It exerts no external pressure to conform to rules, pressures, goals, tasks, or definite direction.

4 It is about possible alternative worlds, which involve 'supposing' and 'as if', which lift players to their highest levels of functioning. This involves being imaginative, creative, original, and innovative.

5 It is about participants wallowing in ideas, feelings, and relationships. It involves reflecting on and becoming aware of what we know or 'metacognition'.

6 It actively uses first-hand experiences which drive the child to manipulate materials, explore and discover.

7 During free-flow play, we use the technical prowess, mastery, and competence we have previously developed and so can be in control.

8 It can be initiated by a child or an adult but if by an adult he/she must pay particular attention to features 3, 5, 11.

9 It can be solitary.

10 It can be in partnerships or groups of adults and /or children who will be sensitive to each other.

11 It is an integrating mechanism, which brings together everything we learn, know, feel, and understand.

Bruce supports the need to promote creativity, with adults providing a supportive role rather than an obtrusive one. This exploration of creativity should be based on the child's interests and motivations. The role of the adult is to value and respect these while encouraging but not taking over. This view of the adult in the supportive role while the child initiates play is a key feature of Bruce's work.

Bruce's Key Influences

- Free-flow play.
- Promoting creativity.
- The role of the adult in supporting play.

Case Study 4.1

Green Lane Primary is a village school in central Wales. Matthew (3 years and 7 months) attends nursery class five mornings a week. The nursery follows a planning scheme that changes the topic on a weekly basis. Matthew is fascinated with the water area and in week one of the project the water area has jugs and pipes with connectors in. Matthew enjoys filling and pouring using jugs and watching the water flow down the pipes. Every morning on entry to the setting, he is engrossed in experimenting with the resources provided.

After the week ended, the focus of the planning changes and the resources in the water area were taken and replaced with different materials. When Matthew comes into nursery that week, he is disheartened to find all the resources have been changed. He explores the area for a short time but then loses interest and moves away.

Reflection Point 4.3

Consider the scenario above and reflect on the philosophies expressed by the play theorists we have explored in this chapter.

Identify how staff at Green Lane could use play to support Matthew's learning and development. Think about the following questions:

- How could the staff initiate a child-centred approach which supports Matthew's holistic development?
- What methods of assessment could they use to assess his skills and knowledge to plan and support Matthew's learning and development?

Summary

We have looked at some of the play pioneers spanning a journey of over 200 years from Rousseau in the eighteenth century to Moyles and Bruce in the twenty-first century. In summary, although their approaches may differ, they all agree fundamentally on the following:

- The value of play as necessary to support learning and development.
- Children have a natural curiosity which needs to be nurtured through playful experiences.
- These experiences need to be child-centred.
- The role of the adult is important in planning and supporting play both indoors and outdoors.

Further Reading

The references below provide you with further reading about the pioneers discussed here and also other influential theorists who have shaped current practice in the early years.

Bradbury, A. and Swailes, R. (2022) (Eds.) *Early Childhood Theories Today*, London: Sage https://early-education.org.uk

Osgood, J., Archer, N. J., Albin-Clark, J. and Mohandas, S. (2024) Bewildering early childhood 'pioneers'. *Pedagogy, Culture & Society*, 32(4), 875–883. https://doi.org/10.1080/14681366.2024.2355096

References

Bruce, T. (1991). *Time to play: Play in early childhood education.* London: Hodder and Stoughton.

Bruce, T. (2001). *Learning through play – babies, toddlers and the foundation years.* London: Hodder Education.

Department for Education. (2024). *Early years foundation stage statutory framework.* Available at: https://assets.publishing.service.gov.uk/media/670fa42a30536cb92748328f/EYFS_statutory_framework_for_group_and_school_-_based_providers.pdf. (Accessed 12 February 2025)

Elfer, P., Goldschmied, E., & Selleck, D. (2003). *Key persons in the nursery: Building relationships for quality provision.* London: David Fulton.

Isaacs, S. (1929). *The nursery years: The mind of the child from birth to six years.* London: Routledge.

Maslow, A. H. (1987). *Motivation and personality* (3rd ed.) New York: Harper and Row.

McMillan, M. (1919). *The nursery school.* London: J.M. Dent and Sons.

Moyles, J. (1989). *Excellence of play.* Maidenhead: Open University Press.

Moyles, J. (2010). *Thinking about play: A reflective approach.* Maidenhead: Open University Press.

Welsh Government. (2023). *Annex 4: Developing community engagement in community focused schools.* Available at: https://www.gov.wales/sites/default/files/pdf-versions/2023/9/3/1695804238/annex-4-developing-community-engagement-community-focused-schools.pdf (Accessed 12 February 2025).

5
Contemporary Playful Pedagogies

Lauren Whale and Louise Atkins

Chapter Objectives

This chapter will help you to:

- Explore provocations for play based on ideas of both contemporary and established pioneers.
- Consider how STEAM can be implemented within a play-based curriculum.
- Reflect on your own understanding and confidence in planning playful experiences for children.

Introduction

Chapter 4 has already introduced the established pioneers of play based practice, but what are our most contemporary thinkers considering that can further shape how we understand play practice in our everyday routines?

We are going to delve into current ideas based around empathy and advocacy, professional love, neuroscience, sustainability, STEAM, and finally asking you to reflect on your own practice and confidence to lead play while considering these contemporary ideas.

Empathy, Advocacy, and Empowerment

Exploring empathy and advocacy in early years through the lens of the protected characteristics as outlined in the Equality Act (2010) is an essential and impactful focus. In early childhood education, these concepts can help shape inclusive, and equitable environments where children develop an understanding of diversity, social justice and fairness. Daniel's (2023, p. 87) considerable work in the anti-racist sphere acknowledges that racism is 'heavy', 'unpacking racism is a process that will take us out of our comfort zones if we are truly trying to learn and make a difference'. She comments that the pedagogy and practices related to early years have potential for strategies for real-world change. Daniel (2023) considers the concept of 'in-the-moment planning' (Ephgrave, 2018) and what it requires early years practitioners to know, understand and apply to practice. For example, considering statutory duties, understanding what children need to know, and shaping the curriculum for children to learn. Daniel acknowledges that although practitioners may plan to address racism in settings, they often have no idea of the various ways in which racism will be manifested, so practitioners need to be skilled and 'informed enough' to respond, 'in the moment', in what is referred to as 'the teachable moment' in in-the-moment planning. Education settings play a key role in empowering children as responsible and informed members of society. Preparing children effectively for the future can solidify their roles and self-efficacy as agents of change, capable of positively impacting their surroundings, understanding and anticipating how their actions affect themselves and those around them (OECD, 2024).

Let's break down the ideas around empathy and advocacy for equality, diversity and inclusion (EDI) in early childhood settings:

Fostering Empathy through Representation and Diversity

Diverse Materials and Resources: Providing books, dolls, and toys representing various racial and ethnic backgrounds helps children see diversity as a norm. Early exposure to a variety of cultures, languages and histories promotes empathy by showing children the value of diversity.

Inclusive Storytelling and Real-Life Examples: Stories and resources that feature characters from everyday life that portray the protected characteristics allow children to connect emotionally with experiences that can be different from their own or validate their own family and community experiences. Grimmer's (2022) work around 'theory of mind' considers its impact on empathy, how it is a skill that takes time to develop and can be fostered through role-playing, storytelling, and dialogue around thoughts and feelings. For example, creating situations where children can role-play problem-solving when they see exclusion or unfair treatment will nurture empathy and advocacy. The goal is to let children practice inclusive behaviour in a controlled, positive way.

Creating Safe Play Spaces for Conversations about EDI

Guiding Children in Conversations: Creating safe spaces for discussing the protected characteristics in age-appropriate ways can foster understanding. Educators can gently introduce conversations about EDI, naming the experiences that might arise from bias or prejudice in everyday life. Children can be empowered to understand what advocacy looks like in everyday life. Empowered children have the opportunity and ability to act on issues important and relevant to them, can learn by making mistakes, and are key contributors to democracy (OECD, 2024).

Normalise Conversations: Discussing inequality openly can prevent discomfort around these topics. Normalising these discussions in early childhood encourages children to understand that it is okay to ask questions and talk about differences without fear of judgement. Henry-Allain and Lloyd-Rose (2021, pp.18–21) have developed a set of practice principles for talking to very young children about issues such as inclusion, empathy and racism, giving ideas for developing quality play opportunities.

Modelling Inclusive Language and Cultivating Allyship: Adults can model respectful and inclusive language. This can include using correct terminology and show how to be a thoughtful and active ally. Louis and Betteridge (2024) present an inspirational dialogue that can support educators to self-reflect and consider how to facilitate these open and honest conversations. Teaching young children to be allies for those who may be marginalised helps them develop a sense of responsibility for creating a more inclusive environment. Allies speak out against bias, bullying, and racism. Having the privilege of working with a diverse range of young children and their families enables early years educators to be instrumental in advocating for others. A fantastic example of starting the conversations around allyship with young children is present in the children's book 'My skin, your skin' by Henry-Allain (2021).

Challenging Stereotypes: Activities that challenge gender, racial, and cultural stereotypes are crucial. The 'redraw the balance' campaign (2016) asked 66 children aged 5–6 to draw a picture of a firefighter, a surgeon and a fighter pilot. 61 children drew men, five children drew women. The women in these roles then joined the children in the class. Watch the video and begin to reflect on ways you can challenge stereotypes in a playful, inspiring, and age-appropriate way. (See: https://www.inspiringthefuture.org/campaigns/inspiring-women/redraw-the-balance/).

Conflict Resolution: By focusing on teaching empathy during play, such as how to resolve conflicts in non-violent ways, children can learn to advocate for themselves and others, standing up against unfair treatment and promoting kindness and fairness. Grimmer (2022) advocates for the High/Scope approach and its six steps to conflict resolution, a problem-solving method that can be used during those everyday squabbles observed during play.

Parent and Community Involvement

Engaging Families and the Community: Working with families and caregivers is essential in promoting an inclusive play environment. Inviting guest speakers, such as community leaders, artists or family members from diverse backgrounds, can provide children with models of empathy and advocacy from real-life experiences.

Hunt (2022) concludes that the more engaged parents are in their child's learning, the more likely it is for their children to succeed.

Reflection Point 5.1

Before you begin to think about your own teaching practices you need to be able to self-reflect on any unconscious biases. Use this online resource to support you in navigating your own unconscious bias. https://www.changingfaces.org.uk/for-professionals/employers/training-guidance/unconscious-bias-training/

Now think about your own teaching practice. How do you:

- Develop your own understanding of EDI?
- Build cultural competence (cultural competence refers to the ability to understand, communicate with, and effectively interact with people across cultures).

(Continued)

(Continued)

- Ensure you have an inclusive play environment?
- Lead inclusive play practices?

Professional Love and Play

Professional Love builds on Noddings' (2003) 'ethic of care' where there is a *compulsion* on behalf of one person to care for the other. Dr Jools Page coins the term *Professional Love* (Page, 2018) to describe the situation where reciprocity and a deepening relationship exist between practitioner and children in ECEC. Professional love in the context of play refers to the deep commitment educators show to the children's well-being, growth, and success. It involves nurturing relationships, being empathetic and providing support, all while maintaining professionalism. When combined with play, this creates a dynamic approach where children learn through exploration, imagination and interaction, supported by practitioners who are genuinely invested in their development. According to the Love and Nurture Rating Scale (Grimmer & Bradbury, 2024), love and nurture are the foundation of early childhood education. This idea stresses the importance of fostering an environment where practitioners bring passion, care and enthusiasm (professional love) to their work while also embracing the value of play as a crucial learning tool. Parents and early years educators can work in partnership to share information about what the child is interested in playing with both in the setting and at home and children can remind the adults in their lives how to play and to be playful, a reciprocal playful model for all (see Figure 5.1).

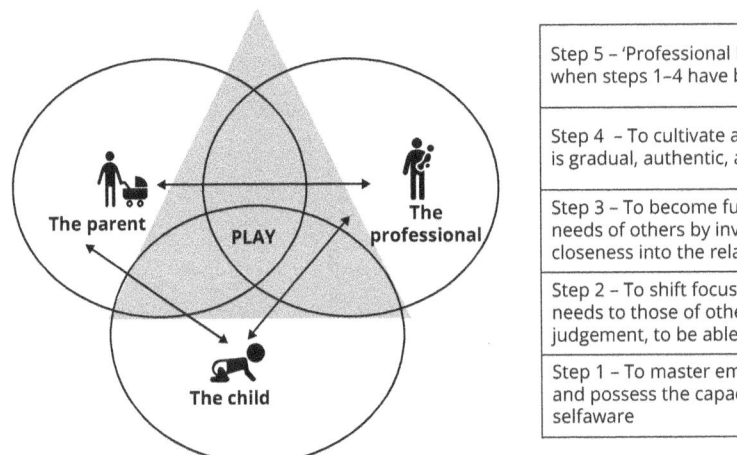

Figure 5.1 Thinking about How Professional Love can Be Supported through Play
Adapted from Page, 2018.

How can Professional Love Support Play?

Professional love in education supports play by creating a nurturing, safe, enriching, and supportive environment where children feel valued, respected, and free to explore. When educators show professional love - through empathy, encouragement, and care it helps foster positive relationships with children, allowing them to fully engage in play without fear of judgement or failure. In turn, this emotional security empowers children to take risks, explore new ideas, and express themselves creatively during play. By showing a deep commitment to each child and their well-being, practitioners can create rich, playful experiences that challenge children's thinking, foster social interactions and promote collaboration. Practitioners who demonstrate professional love, understand the importance of play in supporting child development and learning. Through professional love, educators also model patience, kindness, and resilience - qualities that children can mirror during their own play and further enriching the learning experience. Neuroscience also confirms that love and nurture shapes children's brains, helping them develop resilience, emotional intelligence and a strong sense of self (Bradbury & Grimmer, 2024).

Professional love helps children feel safe and supported during play, allowing them to explore, learn and grow in meaningful ways becoming a medium for both discovery and emotional growth. This balance helps children develop holistically, fostering both cognitive and emotional skills that are essential for lifelong learning.

Reflection Point 5.2

- Reflect on and list the ways in which your practice promotes professional love.
- Do you see professional love being practiced by others in your setting?
- How can you lead others to encompass professional love in their play practices?

Brain Development and Play

Advances in neuroscience support the idea that play has a vital role in brain development. Harding (2024) agrees, commenting that research tells us that the best way for children to learn is through play and therefore play is integral to nurturing brain development.

During the first few years of life, a child's brain is highly malleable, and the experiences they have, particularly through play, help form and strengthen neural connections that are vital for learning and growth. Play-based learning actively promotes what is known as *neuroplasticity*. Neuroplasticity is the brain's ability to reorganise and form new neural connections in response to experiences. When children engage in varied types of play, they create a rich network of experiences that help the brain grow and adapt (Harding, 2024). Below are some examples of how play supports the different types of brain development:

Cognitive Development: Play stimulates brain activity by encouraging children to explore, solve problems, and engage with their environment. For example, building blocks can improve spatial awareness and problem-solving skills, while pretend play fosters creativity and language development. As children engage in different types of play, they develop critical thinking, memory, and attention skills.

Emotional Development: Play helps children process emotions. Through imaginative play, children may act out different scenarios that help them understand and manage their feelings. This supports the development of emotional regulation, empathy and resilience and are skills that the OECD (2019, p. 11) highlight as trends shaping the future of education. Conkbayir (2023) has been instrumental in supporting early years educators and parents to understand early brain development, particularly around the importance of self-regulation as a critical skill that can be nurtured and developed through play. Conkbayir (2023, p. 2) defines 'Self-regulation is our ability to regulate (or manage) our thoughts, feelings, and behaviour'.

Social Development: When children play together, they practice social skills such as sharing, cooperation, reasoning, and negotiation. Social play helps them learn to understand and respect other people's perspectives, building their ability to collaborate and communicate effectively. This interaction strengthens brain areas involved in social cognition, such as recognising facial expressions or interpreting body language.

Motor Development: Physical play, whether it's running, jumping or playing with tactile materials like sand or clay, supports the development of both fine and gross motor skills. These activities help form connections between the brain and muscles, improving coordination and physical awareness.

To further support children's skills in self-regulation through play, it is useful for early years educators to begin to understand the concept of the 'upstairs brain' and 'downstairs brain' (Siegel & Bryson, 2011). These terms are often used to explain the brain's functioning in simple terms, particularly in relation to child development to illustrate how different parts of the brain influence behaviour and emotional regulation.

Imagine your brain is a two-storey house. The 'upstairs brain' is the part of the brain responsible for our executive function, that is higher-order functions like decision-making, problem-solving, planning, impulse control, self-regulation, and empathy. It's the 'thinking brain' that helps us pause before acting, reflect on consequences, and make thoughtful choices. It helps us to become self-aware. It develops very slowly. Between the upstairs and downstairs brain is a 'staircase' – this is the network of neurons and synapses, that carries information up and down, to and from different parts of the brain. The 'downstairs brain' is responsible for basic survival functions, emotions and instincts. This part of the brain controls automatic reactions like fight-or-flight responses, basic emotions (anger, fear, joy), and regulation of heart rate and breathing. It tends to dominate when a person is stressed or overwhelmed, which can lead to impulsive or emotional responses. Conkbayir (2023) advocates that when a child can self-regulate, they remain calm when responding to such emotions and can think before they act.

In young children, the 'downstairs brain' is often more developed than the 'upstairs brain', meaning they may react more emotionally or impulsively to situations. As children grow, the upstairs brain becomes more developed, enabling them to regulate their emotions and make more thoughtful decisions. Educators, parents and caregivers can help children develop their upstairs brain by offering play-based strategies for emotional regulation, mindfulness and problem-solving, helping them shift from reacting impulsively (downstairs brain) to thinking through situations calmly and thoughtfully (upstairs brain). This practice can be developed through play by incorporating what we have already discussed above in terms of professional love and empathy and advocacy.

Sustainability

The UN's seventeen Sustainable Development Goals are:

- No poverty (SDG 1)
- Zero hunger (SDG 2)
- Good health and well-being (SDG 3)
- Quality education (SDG 4)
- Gender equality (SDG 5)
- Clean water and sanitation (SDG 6)
- Affordable and clean energy (SDG 7)
- Decent work and economic growth (SDG 8)
- Industry, innovation, and infrastructure (SDG 9)
- Reduced inequalities (SDG 10)
- Sustainable cities and communities (SDG 11)
- Responsible consumption and production (SDG 12)
- Climate action (SDG 13)
- Life below water (SDG 14)
- Life on land (SDG 15)
- Peace, justice, and strong institutions (SDG 16)
- Partnerships for the goals (SDG 17)

O'Sullivan and Corlett (2021, p. 4) describe education as ;a very powerful pathway to sustainability. . . that is central to the whole learning experience and needs to be part of a broad and inclusive quality education'. By fostering an awareness of nature and the world around them, children learn the importance of taking care of the planet from a young age. This can be done through play-based activities that involve experiences like gardening, recycling, nature walks and discussing topics like water conservation or energy use (see also chapter 12). In early childhood settings, sustainability education can also involve exploring themes like respect for all living things, reducing waste and creating a sense of responsibility for the environment.

The impact of sustainability education in the early years is far-reaching, as it not only instils eco-conscious behaviours in children but also helps to cultivate critical thinking and problem-solving skills. Furthermore, incorporating sustainability into early childhood education supports the development of values such as empathy, cooperation and respect, which can lead to more socially responsible and environmentally aware adults in the future.

Reflection Point 5.3

Drawing on O'Sullivan and Corlett's (2021) 8 R's on sustainable options below, reflect on how you would plan play based activities that encourage children to engage in sustainable experiences in a playful, positive and fun way.

- **Respect** nature, foster an understanding of natural processes, minimise harm to the natural world. Act with kindness and empathy towards humans and animals.
- Be **reflective** and cultivate the habit of asking questions and being thoughtful.
- **Reduce** the consumption and waste of food, materials, and resources.
- Be **responsible** in your actions, be economically sustainable and support ethical causes.
- **Recycle** items and material, understand options beyond throwing away rubbish and teach children on the significance and impact they can have by recycling in their own lives.
- **Repair** things instead of throwing them away.
- **Reuse** items multiple times for various purposes.
- Allow things to **rot,** return to the earth to sustain future plant life and supporting habitats for small rodents and insects.

(based on concepts from O'Sullivan & Corlett, 2021)

Provocations for Play

Stripping back the labels put upon play and theories of play pioneers, we want to address provocations for play in their most basic sense. 'Put simply, provocations provoke. This includes all aspects of learning and development, provoking interest, curiosity, discussion, and discovery. They also provoke children's questions, queries, thoughts, and ideas' (Longstaffe, 2020, p. 15), encouraging them to explore, inquire and discover through play (see also chapter 10). These provocations help set the stage for playful learning and can take many different forms, depending on the context and the goals of the activity. The idea is to inspire children to think, experiment and deepen their understanding by engaging with the environment, materials or ideas which offer openings and pathways where children may enter the world of knowledge.

There has been some concern that setting up provocations for children are, in fact, an extension of adult-led activities; however, the role of the adult in a provocation is to 'recognise the interests of the children, plan and set up a particular provocation and then to observe as the children explore, discover and interact with the resources' (Longstaffe, 2020, p. 17). In an adult-led activity, it is the adult who leads and directs the children to a particular outcome, something which is not the case for provocational and child-led learning and opportunities.

Here are some examples of provocations for play.

Sensory Play Provocations

- **Textures**: Providing a variety of materials with different textures (e.g., sand, water, fabric, clay)
- **Light and Shadow**: Setting up a space with objects and a light source, inviting children to explore how shadows change and what patterns they can create.
- **Sound Exploration**: Offering objects that make different sounds (e.g., drums, bells, spoons, plastic bottles) and encourage children to explore how they can create sound, rhythms or melodies.

Loose Parts Play Provocations

- **Open-Ended Materials**: Providing a collection of loose parts (e.g., wooden blocks, buttons, fabric scraps, bottle caps)
- **Building**: Setting up an area with various building materials.
- **Nature Items**: Gathering items from nature (e.g., sticks, leaves, rocks, pinecones)

Imaginative and Creative Play Provocations

- **Role-Playing**: Setting up a pretend play area (e.g., a kitchen, a shop, or a doctor's office) and offer costumes or props
- **Story Sacks**: Providing story sacks with props related to familiar stories
- **Found Objects**: Place a random collection of items in a space (e.g., a cardboard box, hats, scarves) and see what happens
- **Open Art Stations**: Setting up art materials (e.g., paint, crayons, paper, clay) for children to access freely
- **Collaborative Art**: Setting up a large canvas or a mural space where everyone can contribute

Mathematical and Inquiry-Based Play Provocations

- **Sorting and Categorising**: Presenting a collection of objects (e.g., coloured blocks, buttons, shells)
- **Measuring Play**: Offering rulers, measuring tapes, or different containers and invite children to compare sizes or volumes.
- **Hypothesis Building**: Set up a simple science experiment (e.g., baking soda and vinegar reaction, magnets and metal)

Exploration of New Tools or Technologies

- **Digital Play**: Introduce simple coding games or apps, such as beebots, light boxes.
- **Interactive Displays**: Set up a touchscreen display, smart board, sound buttons, or other interactive technologies.

These provocations are meant to stir curiosity, inspire action and encourage children to explore, experiment and expand their thinking in playful, hands-on ways. They work by providing just enough structure to guide exploration while leaving plenty of room for imagination, creativity, and personal interpretation.

> ## Reflection Point 5.4
>
> Who are the pioneers of play and contemporary pedagogical thinkers that you resonate with?
>
> What can you draw out and combine from these key thinkers to develop your own pedagogy of play?
>
> Based on your pedagogy of play, how do you/can you encourage children's curiosity through play in your setting?

STEAM

With the large-scale rise of STEM (science, technology, engineering and maths) within education all over the world educators are now choosing to add an 'A' into their underpinning philosophies. The settings that choose to embed STEAM (science, technology, engineering, art, and maths) into their practice as their learning approach will interweave these to create a strategy for children to gain twenty-first century knowledge and skills in communication creativity, collaboration, and technology mastery through play (Leung, 2023).

Fostering STEAM in Early Years

Practitioners need to be able to develop skills in critical thinking and open-ended questioning alongside ensuring that the play-based learning process is fully child centred. This enables children to talk about their creations based on their design and creation (Amri et al., 2024). When planning for a STEAM rich environment practitioners need to provide children with a multitude of materials. This enables them to create, explore and wonder, foster curiosity and critical thinking through hands-on, interactive experiences. Activities that integrate STEAM concepts encourage exploration, experimentation and collaboration, while also promoting an understanding of how different areas of learning are interconnected. By engaging in age-appropriate projects, children not only grasp appropriate knowledge but also build the confidence to ask questions, make decisions and approach challenges with a creative mindset.

STEAM and Practitioners

Effective practitioners in STEAM education use inquiry-based approaches. They must be flexible, adapting their strategies to meet the diverse needs and interests of the children. Practitioners should create a safe and supportive atmosphere where failure is viewed as a learning opportunity. This helps to build resilience and confidence as children develop their skills in the cross curricula areas of learning and development.

Case Study 5.1

STEAM: Contemporary Playful Pedagogies at More2Nurseries (Greenwich)

STEAM allows us to equip children with 'twenty-first-century skills' necessary for our rapidly changing world. Many of our nursery parents work in financial services, law, media or office roles, limiting children's early access to scientific and engineering concepts. STEAM helps broaden their horizons and introduces them to diverse subjects. Additionally, the rise in local construction, traffic-free zones, and environmental issues in Greenwich are meaningful to the children. We could have chosen the more familiar 'STEM' approach, but the inclusion of art reflects our love for messy play, big art projects, and creativity. STEAM in our setting is a playful, inquiry-based approach that encourages children to observe, question and explore their environment. It is not about rigid lessons or fixed outcomes but fosters curiosity, critical thinking and problem-solving. From exploring light and shadows to constructing bridges from crates, STEAM is integrated into everyday play.

Staff buy-in to the philosophy is important so we engaged staff through training sessions, staff meetings, and discussions that showed how STEAM is much more than complex science experiments. We explained that we were already doing many of the STEAM activities, such as exploring shadows or building with bricks. Staff were encouraged to think how they could integrate STEAM concepts into everyday play. The team were excited and very receptive. Ongoing support for staff is important so each nursery has STEAM leads who have attended external training. Our pre-school leaders have also completed maths champion courses. An external trainer demonstrated practical STEAM activities, and we've built a library of photos and online training resources. Every year, we celebrate National Science Week, using their early years resources on their website. New staff members cover STEAM principles as part of their induction.

Observation of a 2.5-Year-Old Child Doing a STEAM Activity (Milk and Food Colouring)

Activity: Creating patterns with milk and food colouring. Setting: The activity took place in the maths area with a plastic tray, a shallow dish of milk, food colouring, and cotton swabs.

Observation: The child curiously observed the milk and asked, 'What's that?' while pointing at the food colouring. The adult explained, 'These are colours that we can make dance in the milk!' The child tested the milk's temperature, noting, 'It's cold'. When a drop of red food colouring was added, the child named the colour, 'Red!' They used a cotton swab to swirl the colours, blending red and blue to create purple. The child used swirling motions, pressing the swab gently and hard to see the colours spread and mix.

Engaged by the sensory experience, they dipped their fingers into the milk, saying, 'It's so soft!' and asking, 'Why did it do that?' as colours blended. The adult showed them how mixing two colours could create a new one.

(Continued)

(Continued)

Skills Demonstrated:

- Fine Motor Skills: Manipulating the cotton swab improved hand-eye coordination.
- Cognitive Development: The child explored cause and effect by mixing colours.
- Language Development: They described their observations and asked questions, expanding vocabulary.

This activity combined science (colour mixing), art (patterns) and sensory exploration, nurturing curiosity and basic scientific understanding.

Final Thought

For any setting thinking about adopting this approach we would urge you to consider how STEAM will benefit your children and reflect their interests and surroundings. For instance, if your setting is rural, adapt STEAM to focus on farm machinery or food production. Help staff understand that STEAM is about exploration and curiosity, not rigid 'science experiments'. Soon, STEAM will become a part of your every day!

Source: More2Nurseries – More2Childcare and More2Riverside, Greenwich, South East London https://more2nurseries.com

Impact of STEAM

Research in the implementation of STEAM has shown the increase in children's creativity (Wahyuningsih, 2020), and independence (Septiani & Kasih, 2021) preparing children for future careers in fields that require interdisciplinary knowledge. It helps to bridge gaps in gender and socioeconomic disparities by providing equal access to engaging, hands-on learning experiences, and builds the necessary skills to thrive in a dynamic world.

Having Confidence in Your Own Pedagogy of Play

Having confidence in your own *pedagogy of play* is crucial as it directly influences how effectively you can engage, teach and support the children, and lead the colleagues that you work with. Harrison et al. (2022, p. 36) supports this stating that the process of leading others is a 'process of influence which is enacted by individuals and teams as they connect with each other to make changes that reflect a shared vision'. The pedagogy of play refers to the approach or philosophy you use to incorporate play into learning. Being confident in it can lead to positive outcomes for both you and the children. Here's why it's important:

- **Trust and Engagement**: When you're confident in your approach, children are more likely to trust and engage with the activities you're providing. Play is only effective when it's enjoyable and feels natural, and if you show confidence, children are more likely to follow your lead and embrace the experience.

- **Creating a Safe Space**: Confidence helps you maintain a safe, supportive atmosphere where children feel comfortable experimenting, making mistakes and expressing themselves. Play often requires vulnerability, so being confident reassures children that the environment is one where they can take risks.
- **Embracing Play's Flexibility**: Confidence helps you adapt to the needs of the children and be flexible with how play unfolds. Play-based learning is often spontaneous and being comfortable with this allows you to shift and tailor experiences to the children's interests and developmental needs.
- **Inspiring Others**: Confidence in your own pedagogy conveys passion for the value of play. When children, parents and colleagues see that you genuinely believe in the power of play for learning, they are more likely to see it as a valuable tool themselves.
- **Stronger Rapport with Children**: When you are confident in your pedagogy, you are more likely to build strong relationships based on trust and respect. Children are more likely to engage with you in a playful, positive way, as they see you as a secure figure (Page, 2018).
- **Understanding Individual Needs**: Confidence allows you to be observant and responsive to individual needs, whether it's adjusting play-based strategies to accommodate different developmental levels or offering different play options that cater to diverse needs.
- **Embracing Mistakes**: Confidence helps you embrace mistakes as part of the learning process. Play is often trial and error, and when you're confident in the process, you're more likely to model a growth mindset (Dweck, 2017).
- **Creative Problem Solving**: Confidence in your pedagogy helps you respond creatively to challenges that arise during play. Whether it's an unexpected behaviour, an environmental challenge, or a need to modify an activity in the moment, being confident in your approach allows you to adjust without losing sight of the learning goals.
- **Advocating for Play-Based Learning**: Developing and understanding your own pedagogy will enable you to advocate for play-based learning (see pause for thought).

Having confidence in your pedagogy of play is essential because it allows you to create a positive, adaptable, and effective learning environment where children can thrive. It encourages engagement, supports risk-taking and exploration and helps you lead and advocate for the value of play in learning. This is supported by Harrison et al. (2022) who argue that each of us has the ability to lead within our diverse workforce.

Reflection Point 5.5

How can you use your own play pedagogy to advocate for play-based learning in an environment that does not understand the benefits of learning through play?

How will your own play-based pedagogy support you to shape policy and practice in play-based learning?

Summary

- Whether it's being invited into a child's play or developing a provocation to spark children's curiosity, play taps into the natural way we learn to make sense of the world around us.
- Early years educators are required to make intentional actions for developing language and dialogue through play. They should foster environments by creating safe spaces for discussion, understanding, inclusivity, justice, equality, and fairness to empower children to grow into compassionate individuals who advocate for themselves and others.
- To support children to feel safe during play the notion of professional love is fundamental. Building these trusting, meaningful relationships provides children with the confidence to explore, learn and grow holistically.
- Widening our knowledge and understanding of early brain development can help us to rationalise the behaviours and emotions we might observe during children's play. Supporting children to self-regulate will equip them with the tools they need to face challenges, build positive relationships and thrive academically and socially.
- If we are to instil a love of life-long learning in children, we need to ensure we are preparing them for what the future may hold. STEAM and sustainable play are fundamental in supporting children to develop critical thinking skills, be eco-conscious, empathetic and respectful, which are the qualities of being socially responsible and environmentally aware.
- To conclude, play should be a wonderous, joyful experience for all who participate in it. Early educators are privileged to be able to observe or participate in play with young children and although play is a powerful tool for learning, we must not forget that play is there to be enjoyed by all. Having confidence in your pedagogy of play will serve as a reminder of the joy because you will be offering opportunities to play in positive, adaptable and effective learning environments where children are encouraged to thrive.

Further Reading

Conkbayir, M. (2023) *The neuroscience of the developing child self-regulation for wellbeing and a sustainable future*. London: Routledge. This book draws upon a wide range of resources to show readers how they can nurture self-regulation through their daily interactions with children and the environment and experiences they offer them.

Grimmer, T. (2022) *Supporting behaviour and emotions in the early years*. London: Routledge. This book focuses on the idea that all behaviour is a form of communication and explores central areas such as self-regulation and attachment, offering strategies that can be used to support challenging behaviour.

Louis, S. and Betteridge, H. (2024) *Lets talk about race in the early years*. London: Routledge. This resource offers practical and accessible guidance alongside the tools and techniques you need to identify and confront discriminatory practices, with strategies to break down barriers and tackle these complicated issues sensitively and constructively.

Page, J. (2018) Characterising the principles of Professional Love in early childhood care and education. *International Journal of Early Years Education*, 26(2), 125–141. https://doi.org/10.1080/09669760.2018.1459508. To develop a deeper understanding of 'Professional Love' as a term to comprehend the reciprocal pedagogic relationship which develops in positive interactions between primary caregiver, child and parent, this paper is an essential read.

OECD (2019) *Trends shaping education 2019*. Paris: OECD Publishing. https://doi.org/10.1787/trends_edu-2019-en. This publication provides guidance for educators who are asking 'What does this trend mean for the future of my education system? And what can I do'?

Reedsy (n.d.) *60 Children's books about diversity to read with little ones*. Available at: https://reedsy.com/discovery/blog/childrens-books-about-diversity

This is a well-crafted list of 60 books to introduce to young minds about range of subjects: from cultural differences to gender fluidity, from social expectations to identity construction. The list features a diverse cast of writers and artists, these stories offer different lenses through which children can see the world.

PEDAL is the centre for research on play in education, development, and learning at the University of Cambridge. PEDAL conducts academic research into the role of play in children's lives in order to inform wider practice and policy. Available at: https://www.educ.cam.ac.uk/centres/pedal/

References

Amri, K., Syarfina, S., & Veryawan, V. (2024). Enhancing early childhood educator proficiency in implementing STEAM-loose parts using a project-based learning model. *JPUD · Journal Pendidikan Usia Dini*, 18(2), 350–357. https://doi.org/10.21009/jpud.v18i2.48987

Bradbury, T., & Grimmer, T. (2024). *Love and nurture in the early years*. London: Learning Matters.

Conkbayir, M. (2023). *The neuroscience of the developing child: Self-regulation for wellbeing and a sustainable future*, London: Routledge.

Daniel, V. (2023). *Anti-Racist Practice in the early years*, London: Routledge.

Dweck, C. (2017). *Mindset · updated edition: Changing the way you think to fulfil your potential* (6th ed.) London: Robinson.

Ephgrave, A. (2018). *Planning in the moment with young children: A practical guide for early years practitioners and parents*. London: Routledge.

Equality Act. (2010). Available at: https://www.gov.uk/guidance/equality-act-2010-guidance.

Grimmer, T. (2022). *Supporting behaviour and emotions in the early years*. London: Routledge.

Grimmer, T., & Bradbury, A. (2024). *Early years love and nurture rating scale*. LuLu.

Harding, J. (2024). *The brain that loves to play: A visual guide to child development, play and brain growth*. London: Routledge.

Harrison, J., Munn, H., Thistle, R., Atkins, L., & Whale, L. (2022). *Leadership in early childhood. Challenges and complexities*. London: Sage.

Henry-Allain, L. (2021). *My skin, your skin*, London: Ladybird.

Henry-Allain, L., & Lloyd-Rose, M. (2021). *The tiney guide to becoming an inclusive, anti-racist early educator.* Tiney. Available at: https://assets.ctfassets.net/jnn9p19md0ig/4ntGEh21KNXyB9aLxq9gCY/61847fa97f563ba4d9b281cf89d8a8ef/Guide_Inclusive_Education.pdf (Accessed 1 December 2024).

Hunt, M. (2022). *Helping every child to thrive in the early years How to overcome the effect of disadvantage.* Abingdon: Routledge.

Leung, W. M. V. (2023). STEM education in early years: Challenges and opportunities in changing teachers' pedagogical strategies. *Education Sciences*, 13(5). http://doi.org/10.3390/educsci13050490

Longstaffe, M. (2020). *Provocations for learning in early years settings. A practical guide.* London: Jessica Kingsley Publishers.

Louis, S., & Betteridge, H. (2024). *Let's talk about race in the early years.* London: Routledge.

Noddings, N. (2003). *Caring: A feminine approach to ethics and moral education* (2nd ed.) Berkeley, CA: University of California Press.

O'Sullivan, J., & Corlett, N. (2021). *50 fantastic ideas for sustainability.* London: Bloomsbury.

OECD. (2019). *Trends shaping education 2019.* Paris: OECD Publishing. https://doi.org/10.1787/trends_edu-2019-en

OECD. (2024). *What does child empowerment mean today?: Implications for education and well-being, Educational Research and Innovation.* Paris: OECD Publishing. https://doi.org/10.1787/8f80ce38-en

Page, J. (2018). Characterising the principles of Professional Love in early childhood care and education. *International Journal of Early Years Education*, 26(2), 125–141.

Redraw the Balance (2016). Available at: https://www.inspiringthefuture.org/campaigns/inspiring-women/redraw-the-balance/ (Accessed 28 March 2024).

Septiani, I., & Kasih, D. (2021). Implementasi Metode STEAM Terhadap Kemandirian Anak Usia 5-6 Tahun di Paud Alpha Omega School. *Jurnal Jendela Pendidikan*, 01(November), 192–199.

Siegel, D., & Bryson, T. (2011). *No drama discipline: The whole brain way to calm the chaos and nurture your child's developing mind.* London: Scribe.

Wahyuningsih, S., Pudyaningtyas, A., Nurjanah, N. E., Dewi, N. K., Hafidah, R., Syamsuddin, M. M., & Sholeha, V. (2020). The utilization of loose arts media in STEAM learning for early childhood. *Early Childhood Education and Development Journal.* Department of Teacher Training of Early Education and Faculty of Teacher Training and Education Universitas Maret. https://doi.org/10.20961/ecedj.v2i2.46326

Part II
Why is Play
Important?

Part II

6
Play, Learning, and Development

Natalie Canning and Angela Rekers

Chapter Objectives

This chapter will help you to:

- Understand the holistic role of play for development and how physical and social-emotional development are interlinked with cognitive development.
- Consider how play can support brain development leading to enhanced skills in the areas of self-regulation, communication, and social-emotional skills.
- Understand the role of play in concept development.

Introduction

This chapter establishes that children's play is at the heart of their learning and development. Play provides children with opportunities to explore, make meaning, test, and problem-solve. It enables them to process their thoughts and emotions through making choices and decisions. All these attributes are linked to cognitive development; all are significant for learning and growing up in a complicated world. In this chapter we examine the impact of play from a socio-constructivist position where young children's knowledge and understanding is shaped through engagement with their social and material environment.

From the neonatal period to pre-school and beyond, children are exposed to new experiences and different encounters, which contribute to their holistic development across social, emotional, cognitive and physical domains. In this chapter, we discuss how play experiences, such as schematic behaviours can be observed when children interact with objects and heuristic play. We also consider how engagement with open-ended resources can shape children's interests and curiosity, and how concept development supports holistic development. Adults can facilitate children's engagement by providing resources, observing and supporting and we draw upon Vygotsky's concept, The Zone of Proximal Development. The role of adults in play is explored more fully in Chapter 15.

Understanding the basic principles of neuroscience helps us to consider how play supports brain development and skills related to executive functioning, such as self-regulation, as well as communication, and social-emotional wellbeing. Early concept development is explored as a cognitive benefit of play. Children are never 'just playing'. Their development, cognitive, and social learning are all entwined with the opportunities they have for play, the adults and children with whom they play and the materials and environments they explore. Consequently, as early childhood professionals, the skill is to acknowledge the significance of play for children's development, allow time and space for play to happen and be prepared to stand up and make a case for why play should be at the heart of practice.

Holistic Development

Play is important for children because it is where they explore, try out new things and build relationships with other children. It acts as a vehicle for nurturing their interest and provides a platform for exploring curiosity and creativity (Canning, 2025). Active engagement in play supports whole child development as children bring what they already know to the situation and build on this knowledge through their play. Children come with their experiences from home, their family and other interactions that have impacted their thinking (Donner et al., 2024). They use this knowledge in how they approach play situations, how they act within them and how they respond to and negotiate with other children. Play is an opportunity for children to mirror real-life events; within a play space they are able to experiment with different scenarios, see the reactions of their peers and learn from those encounters. Social play also enables children to experience power relationships and negotiate different agendas. This happens through verbal and nonverbal communication and action.

Children are influenced by their formal and informal education at nursery and school and home, in relation to socially acceptable behaviour. Yet, in play, children can explore a sense of freedom. The game does not always have to conform to the rules, and children can test the boundaries of what they are doing. That might mean testing their physical ability – climbing higher than they have done before, their creative ability to come up with something new for them and their friends to explore, their cognitive ability to work out a new problem like how to divert water using the materials they have to hand (Canning, 2020). In acknowledging play as a foundation for learning and learning as a pathway to development, the importance of play is significant in the success and positive impact of the other two.

The holistic role of play means embracing everything that a context has to offer, including all the stimulating factors that surround the situation. These include the environment, the materials within that environment, the other people that are there, what they are doing and saying and how they are acting. The dynamics between people is also important – how many children and how many adults, the age range of the children and whether they are already friends or coming together for the first time. Thinking about what children and adults bring to the situation helps to understand the way in which they interact. In the following case study taken from Rekers-Power (2020), a group of children are involved initially in an adult-led, experiential activity that is focused upon concept development. As you read, consider how children develop the activity in response to the environment, and what that might tell us about how play supports holistic development.

Case Study 6.1

Painting in the Woods

In a reception year class, there are 36 children aged between 4 and 5 years old, six of whom are learning English as an Additional Language. During an outdoor play session with half of the class, the teacher presents a large roll of newsprint paper placed on the ground and some different shaped pieces of wood. The teacher explains how the logs of wood are *cylinder* shapes, with ends that are both *oval* and *circular*, as some logs have been cut straight across and others at a slant. These terms are vocabulary words the children have been learning in class to support their cognitive development of mathematical concepts.

The children use different colours of paint that the teacher has brought to the space to make shapes on the paper with the wood acting as stencils. However, some of the children begin to use their hands to paint or begin to draw different shapes with the logs and nearby twigs. They are engaged in reproducing the shapes as well as exploring the affordances of the paint, paper and their own hands. A small group of children quietly engage and watch what others are reproducing, working side by side. Some children then begin to use sticks that they have picked up from the woodland floor to paint other designs and some start to use their hands, making circles with their fingers and palms, exploring how their fingerprints make oval shapes and their palms circles. The teacher tells them they are doing it 'wrong' and to stop using their hands and painting other shapes. Finally, after a few minutes and once the children have produced some recognisable shapes with the wood that may be displayed later in the classroom, the teacher says, 'OK, you can go and play now!' Most of the children jump up to play in nearby puddles or on swings that have been attached to tree branches while others continue to paint using the logs and their hands. The teacher then gathers up the paper and puts away the paint, urging them to 'just go play'.

Throughout the activity described in the case study the children who spoke English as an Additional Language were carefully observing how, initially, the other children were using their bits of wood, to ensure that they understood and followed the teacher's directions. The inviting nature and affordances of the paint enabled children to explore with their hands; so, although the aim from the teacher's point of view was to use the logs as stencils, dipping them into the paint and then onto the paper, children saw the opportunity to put their hands in the paint, using their hands as tools rather than the logs. Once one child had experimented in this way, others followed, and the teacher found this challenging to address as it deviated from her instructions. Additionally, the calm setting and soothing nature of painting in the outdoors seemed to offer therapeutic and creative benefits; while some children ran off to play with different features of the woodland, many stayed on, engaged in the task and enjoying the peacefulness of the painting activity without directives.

This example can be understood as one with specific intention from the teacher to support the children's *conceptual* learning in relation to shapes, using a playful activity. Although the activity supported the intention, the materials and the environment influenced the way in which the children responded to the task. Cognitive development was supported by using three-dimensional shapes found in the woodland; executive function, including focus and self-regulation supported by the children's engagement; and, physical development of fine motor skills by the hands-on nature of manipulating intended and found objects. Opportunities for creative, social, and emotional development were also visible.

Within every play experience there is a learning opportunity (Aslanian et al., 2024). However, it is the role of the teacher to understand that learning opportunity and consider its relationship to an individual child's progress in any given situation. Often an adult's intention for play opportunities has an objective or outcome in mind; yet, if we consider the holistic nature of play, we can often 'find' multiple outcomes that may be unexpected. Therefore, understanding both the play opportunities available and the individual learning possibilities is significant for the teacher. Consequently, providing open-ended play opportunities can be an effective and dominant strategy to encourage positive attitudes towards developing cognitive, socio-emotional skills, and physical development (Canning, 2020).

Reflection Point 6.1

Think again about the case study:

- Why do you think the teacher told the children to 'go play' rather than supporting the children's playful approach to the task?
- How does play support more than one developmental aim?
- What do you think are the most important elements for effective play-based learning in this scenario?

We have considered some of the elements associated with holistic play, and now we ask whether what we know about brain development supports the argument that play is significant. In this next section we consider neuroscience research and its contribution to our understanding of play, learning and development.

Brain Development

Play is most often valued in an educational context for its contributions to learning and development (Aslanian et al., 2024). Play's contribution to brain development, or neurological development, is important because children's cognitive, language and communication, physical, socio-emotional and self-regulatory skills start within the brain (Vygotsky, 1967; Yogman et al., 2018). Quality play is 'exercise' for the brain, impacting brain structure and helping with skill development as well as social relationships and well-being (Ham et al., 2024).

From an evolutionary perspective, playfulness is a characteristic of mammalian species (Hughes, 2012). Playfulness is essential from a developmental perspective, because in its absence, humans and non-human species risk social, emotional, and cognitive impairment (Siviy, 2016). The neural structures of the brain are programed through the wiring of neural circuits, in which the pruning of synapses contribute to healthy human brain development and executive neocortex functioning, such as decision-making, planning and regulating stress responses (Yogman et al., 2018). Play seems to build resilience, as it supports the developing brain's flexibility in navigating and responding to unexpected or challenging situations (Siviy, 2016).

Importantly, theorists argue that the ways in which adults and peers impact children's inter- and intra-personal relationships are critical to developing complex, self-regulatory play behaviours from a neurological standpoint (Martin-Garcia & Rico-Gonzalez, 2024, p. 429). Forming secure attachments with caregivers in playful interactions contributes to the secretion of neurotransmitters and increases levels of oxytocin, the hormone responsible for creating a sense of well-being (Stewart et al., 2016). Even rough and tumble play, in nurturing contexts, supports complex organisational responses from the brain and reduces stress levels (Yogman et al., 2018). Also, by engaging in play, children develop skills in observation and restraint that support development of understanding of rules of a game and intentional play behaviour (Vygotsky, 1967). Such skills may be supported by more capable others such as adults, peers or older siblings when children are engaged in mixed-aged play. Vygotsky (1967, p. 16) argues that play 'is the source of development and creates the zone of proximal development', within which the child and adults and/or more capable peers can co-construct healthy and complex play behaviour and other valued skills.

Reflection Point 6.2

- Can you think of examples in play that illustrate what processes take place in the brain when children navigate and respond adaptively to unexpected encounters?
- How could play increase children's resilience?

Concept Development

In the case study, painting in the woods, we can see that the children were able to put the concept of 2D and 3D shapes, namely *cylinder*, *oval* and circle, into 'real-life' contexts by exploring the different shapes of the wood and using them as stencils to mark-make on paper. Another concept that children might have explored is the mixing of natural materials to mark-make such as using earth and puddled water to make mud. This might have been an appropriate activity sup-porting concept development, by utilising the affordances explored in the natural environment of the woodland. When play is viewed as a motivating activity for children, adults can use the foundation of play to develop children's conceptual thinking by linking the abstract with the concrete (Fleer, 2011). For example, in the classroom, the vocabulary of cylinders, ovals and circular shapes is abstract, especially if only seen in a book, or on a worksheet or screen. When the children are able to explore the possibilities of 2D and 3D shapes, the concept of shape can become real, or 'concrete'. Of course, such learning can take place in the classroom with everyday objects; indeed, providing young children with manipulatives is a teaching strategy to support concept learning. Yet, the flexible nature of the outdoor environment also afforded children the opportunity to further explore and follow their interests in mark-making with twigs and sticks. Such playful exploration creates opportunities for the teacher to use children's own interests and discoveries to support further conceptual development. For example, one of the authors observed that during outdoor play, when a child found an insect crawling along one of the sticks he was about to pick up, he and the teacher began to wonder about where the insect lived. The teacher facilitated scientific concept development by having a conservation with the child about *habitats*.

This strategy of supporting children's concept development in play is called *sustained shared thinking*. This involves adults using conversations to extend children's thinking, creating a mutually inquisitive relationship in which the adult and child collaborate to explore materials, concepts and together begin to problem-solve. In the example above, the teacher recognised the child's interest in the insect crawling on the stick and used her own knowledge about habitats to provide a rich opportunity for a conversation about insects. The teacher was able to build on the child's interest and current knowledge by engaging in a meaningful and relevant conversation with him. The critical factor in concept development and sustained shared thinking is the engagement and interest of those involved in the learning opportunity. Collaborative interactions support children's social, emotional and cognitive outcomes and such interactions are especially effective when children's existing knowledge and experience from home or other environments is recognised and considered (Chesworth, 2016). Children's interests are made visible to adults through their play and playful exploration of their environments.

Schematic Play

As you have learnt so far, there are many ways in which teachers and practitioners can observe and make sense of children's play, in order to support their holistic development. Another way is through identifying children's schematic behaviour. This means looking for repeatable patterns of actions or behaviours called schemas (Athey, 2007). Athey (1990) defined a schema as:

> a pattern of repeatable behaviour into which experiences are assimilated and ... gradually coordinated. Coordinations lead to higher-level and more powerful schemas (Athey, 1990, p. 37).

Athey was strongly influenced by Piaget (1952) and built on his concept of schemas, which he explained as mental structures or representations into which we organise our knowledge about the world. Athey observed children at play and identified a number of observable schemas that can be used to support adults observing children's interactions with their environment. Table 6.1 describes some of the most common observable schemas.

Table 6.1 Summary of Schematic Behaviour Definitions

Schema	Definition
Trajectory	Interest in up-and-down and along-and-back movements
Rotation	Interest in things that go around and around
Enclosure	Interest in boundaries
Enveloping and containing	Interest in covering objects and putting them into containers
Connecting	Interest in joining things together in various ways and forms
Transporting	Interest in moving things about in different ways
Sensorimotor	Interest in objects and contexts dominated by the senses (taste, smell, sight, touch, and sound), particularly when these are also triggered by movement, such as a child taking delight in pushing a toy along the floor and it making a sound as they do so
Symbolic	Interest in turning one object into a pretend object to support imaginative play, such as a stick becoming a sword

Schematic behaviour is important for children's development because it is a way in which we can make sense of what children are doing, what and how they are exploring, and how they transfer practice of their cognitive and physical skills to different objects and contexts. Schemas can often be observed within children's play and can also operate on different levels. For example, sensorimotor schemas are dominated by the senses and movement, whereas symbolic representation schemas focus on pretend and imaginative play. Schemas also relate to functional dependency, i.e. cause and effect. Children's interactions with objects around them help us understand how they are testing out or exploring the limits of what they can do with something; for example, trying to fit square objects into a round hole. Schematic behaviour may not be the focus of the play, but it is noticeable because it is a repeated behaviour the child becomes deeply immersed in. The following case study highlights the way in which children use schemas in their imaginative play.

Case Study 6.2

A Giant's House

Katcha, a practitioner at a mobile, 'pack-away' playgroup, decided to fill the community hall space with lots of different sized cardboard boxes she had been collecting over the previous weeks. When the children came into the hall, they were initially shocked not to

(Continued)

(Continued)

see their usual resources and toys. However, they soon started to explore, with some children stacking the boxes and some getting inside the larger ones. The group had been reading *Jack and the Beanstalk* and one child took on the role of being 'Jack', pretending to enter the giant's house and finding all the boxes. Katcha observed Mohammad carrying around one of the smallest boxes. He was looking for something, she thought. She focused on him and noticed that he was picking up different boxes, similar in size and shape, and trying to put his first box inside another. He discarded a few options and settled on one that was just a bit bigger and had flaps which could be turned in to create a covered lid. He kept exploring the boxes, choosing another that was bigger so that he could put his new box inside another box. By the end of the play, he had enveloped five boxes around the original small one. As he was absorbed in his play, Katcha heard Mohammed talking to himself, making up the story as he went along. From what he was saying, Katcha surmised that Mohammad was 'Jack'. He had a secret in his box and needed to protect it. The other boxes were magic and putting the secret in lots of boxes made it harder for the giant to find.

Mohammed's play was all about his quest to hide his secret in magic boxes; however, as well as this imaginative play, he was also engaged in an *enveloping* schema (see Table 6.1). Children often demonstrate deep concentration and seek out ways to continue their schematic behaviour by finding materials in their environment which will support their actions, such as gathering all available boxes and containers and items to put in the boxes to continue an enveloping schema. Schematic behaviour is a good starting point to think about children's development and learning. When a child is involved in an enveloping schema, it is important to consider all the different elements that they are learning from their activity. In gathering boxes of different sizes and shapes Mohammed was identifying what was a good container for his purpose and thinking about how it could be used. More generally, in looking for items to put into boxes or containers children are demonstrating creativity and curiosity in the items chosen and experimenting with size and shape. They are working out if more than one thing can be put in a box and if the lid will still be able to close. Through experimenting with different items being put in different sizes and shaped boxes children are beginning to understand the idea of volume, i.e. many smaller items will fit, but only one larger item.

An important aspect of Athey's work involved showing how schemas are fed by experiences provided in the home and in an educational context. In the following case study of Omar, who is four years old, practitioners in the nursery where he attended talked to his parents about his play at home and, as a result, practitioners provided *transporting* activities. Observing children in this way provides adults with a framework for developing an understanding of children's interests and patterns of play, and an opportunity to share these observations with parents.

Case Study 6.3

Omar's Play

In a brief conversation with Omar's mother as she was picking up her son, Greta, the nursery manager, began to wonder what other opportunities the nursery could provide for him. His mother mentioned that he was an active child at home, and a favourite game was taking items from the rooms in the house and putting them under his bed. He would take one item at a time, put it under the bed, then retrieve a different item from under the bed and take it back to its original place. Each time he moved an item he would do it in a different way: hopping to and from one location to another, putting the item in his sister's doll buggy, carrying it in a fishing net. He often repeated the game to the annoyance of his older sister whose dolls and teddies often went missing only to suddenly reappear. Greta had noticed something similar in the nursery. Omar liked to be mobile, often carrying an item from one place to another in the push along trolley or balancing something on a toy car to transport it. She had heard other practitioners asking him to return toy dinosaurs to their box rather than leaving it in the sandpit across the other side of the room. She noticed that he seemed to choose the furthest point from one place to another to move his items but would, at some time in the day, retrieve the item and move it back. It occurred to Greta that Omar was fascinated by the act of *transporting* the items rather than the actual item itself; this insight helped Greta and the other practitioners under-stand Omar's play more fully. Previously they had focused upon the items themselves, rather than thinking about the connection between them, Omar, and movement. Talking to his mother, Greta realised that the different forms of transport were the linking factor.

Reflection Point 6.3

- What could Greta do to support Omar's fascination with a transporting schema?
- How could understanding the transporting play schema help Greta support Omar in meeting classroom expectations, for example putting toys away?
- How might a transporting schema support Omar's learning and development?

The role of the adult as an observer, curious about every aspect of children's interactions with other children, adults and the environment, is important in order to understand the child's perspective. In acknowledging children's interests and considering alternative opportunities for learning, richer and more creative ways of seeing the child can be created (Corsaro, 2017). Utilising schemas can be a starting point for understanding children's play and learning from a different perspective. Some children will want to keep revisiting their schematic behaviour while others will quickly move on. It can be fascinating as a practitioner to get to know the children you work with and notice the ways in which they are playing.

The final section of this chapter relates to heuristic play. Like schematic play, understanding the processes children engage with through heuristic play can help us to identify different ways in which play and learning are intertwined.

Heuristic Play

Heuristic play is an approach to helping babies and young children learn (see Chapter 4: treasure baskets). The word *heuristic* originates from the Greek word *eurisko* which means, 'I discover' or 'I find', so it is about a personal action which holds significance for the individual. The process of heuristic play enables children to be in control and lead their own play by presenting natural and everyday household objects to children allowing them to experiment and discover independently (Hughes, 2016). For example, a baby might be presented with a saucepan, wooden spoon, beads on a string, large pinecones, a plastic container with a lid and a plastic cup. This collection of random objects does not have to be used in any particular way – or at all, if the baby is uninterested – thus, providing endless possibilities to explore as there are no agendas attached to the items. They are regarded as *open-ended resources* that enable open-ended play because no one is showing the baby what to do, there is no expectation of an outcome, and the baby has autonomy over what to do with them and how to use them. The everyday objects provide opportunity for the baby to explore, investigate and discover on their own. Heuristic play helps children to develop their preferences, curiosity, and imagination because of the numerous ways with which the objects can be played. Heuristic play supports abstract thinking, which in developmental terms begins before the development of expressive language (Atherton & Nutbrown, 2016). It also links to functions of the brain as the deep concentration used to explore different objects requires all of the senses. This leads to intense neural activity as explored previously in this chapter.

Summary

As stated at the beginning of this chapter, children are never 'just playing'. Awareness of the different components of play, the theories and research that provide a rich and deep knowledge base about play, provides the basis for understanding the significance of play in child development. This chapter has given a brief insight into how play supports holistic development across developmental domains and the significance of play to brain development. From the neonatal period to pre-school and beyond, the child is shaped by their social and material environment, learning through exploration with objects and materials and through interactions with their peers, siblings, and significant adults. Having an awareness of concept development, schematic and heuristic play can support how you, as practitioners and teachers, guide children through the process of formal learning, while recognising the immense importance of informal learning.

Play gives children the opportunity to mirror real-life events, and within that space they are able to experiment with different scenarios, see the reactions of their peers and learn from those encounters (see also Chapter 7). As practitioners, the knowledge that you have about child development can translate into meaningful and positive learning encounters. Understanding the processes that happen when children engage in play helps you to focus your attention and observe approaches to learning, so that you can document a holistic picture of children's current engagement, interests, knowledge, and understanding. This enables you, as educators, to plan for their future learning trajectory, and to feel confident in practice that prioritises play.

Key Messages

- Play should be at the heart of all early childhood practice.
- Active engagement in play supports whole child development as it brings what they already know to the situation and builds on this knowledge through play.
- Play is a foundation for learning and learning is a pathway to development.
- Play is exercise for the brain and helps with skills development as well as social relationships and well-being.
- Schematic behaviour is important for child development because it is a way in which we can make sense of what children are doing, what and how they are exploring and how they transfer practice of their cognitive and physical skills to different objects and contexts.
- Heuristic play includes everyday objects that are regarded as open-ended resources with multiple possibilities for play. It helps children to develop their preferences and be curious and imaginative because of the numerous ways in which the objects can be played with.

Further Reading

Bruce, T., Hakkarainen, P. and Bredikyte, M. (2017) *The Routledge international handbook of early childhood play.* Abingdon: Routledge. This book contains chapters from highly respected researchers whose work has been critical to building knowledge and expertise in the field of play and early childhood. It focuses on examining historical, current and future research issues in play and learning scholarship and offers diverse perspectives to help see play in new ways.

Harding, J. (2023) *The brain that loves to play: A visual guide to child development play and brain growth.* London: David Fulton. This visual book provides an accessible introduction to how play affects the holistic development and brain growth of children from birth to five years. It brings current theory to life by celebrating the developing brain that loves to play and is hungry for sensitive human interaction and rich play opportunities. Chapters focus on different areas of development, providing snapshots of play exploring children's play preferences and the theory that underpins play behaviour.

Goodliff, G., Canning, N., Parry, J. and Miller, L. (Eds.) (2018). *Young children's play and creativity: Multiple voices.* Abingdon: Routledge. This book draws on the voices of practitioners, academics and researchers to examine young children's play, creativity and the participatory nature of their learning. Bringing together a wide range of perspectives from the UK and internationally, it focuses on the level of engagement and exploration involved in children's play and how it can be facilitated in different contexts and cultures.

References

Aslanian, K., Bjerknes, A. L., & Andresen, A. K. (2024). Children's holistic learning during self-initiated outdoor play in a Norwegian kindergarten. *European Early Childhood Education Research Journal, 32*(3), 371–382.

Atherton, F., & Nutbrown, C. (2016). Schematic pedagogy: Supporting one child's learning at home and in a group. *International Journal of Early Years Education, 24*(1), 63–79.

Athey, C. (1990). *Extending thought in young children.* London: Paul Chapman.

Athey, C. (2007). *Extending thought in young children* (2nd ed.). London: Paul Chapman.

Canning, N. (2020). *Children's empowerment in play.* Abingdon: Routledge.

Canning, N. (2025). 'Outdoor play opportunities in UK contexts and the impact of pedagogic action: Using the empowerment framework to re-orientate outdoor play and learning provision towards children's empowerment'. In M.Mart, G.Gessiou & J.Waters-Davies (Eds.), *Exploring the pedagogy of learning and playing outdoors: Questions of purpose and intention.* Oxon: Routledge and EECERA.

Chesworth, L. (2016). A funds of knowledge approach to examining play interests: Listening to children's and parents' perspectives. *International Journal of Early Years Education, 24*(3), 294–308.

Corsaro, W. A. (2017). *The sociology of childhood* (5th ed.). Thousand Oaks, CA: Sage.

Donner, P., Lundström, S., & Heikkilä, M. (2024). A case study of young children's play negotiations in free play. *Early Years, 44*, 3–4, 889–902. https://doi.org/10.1080/09575146.2023.2266590

Fleer, M. (2011). Conceptual play: Foregrounding imagination and cognition during concept formation in Early Years education. *Contemporary Issues in Early Childhood, 12*(3), 224–240.

Ham, J. R., Szabo, M., Annor-Bediako, J., Stark, R. A., Iwaniuk, A. N., & Pellis, S. M. (2024). Quality not quantity: Deficient juvenile play experiences lead to altered medial prefrontal cortex neurons and sociocognitive skill deficits. *Developmental Psychobiology, 66*(2), e22456. https://doi.org/10.1002/dev.22456

Hughes, B. (2012). *Evolutionary playwork: Reflective analytic practice* (2nd ed.). London: Routledge.

Hughes, A. (2016). *Developing play for the under 3s: The treasure basket and heuristic play* (3rd ed.). London: David Fulton Books.

Martin-Garcia, A., & Rico-Gonzalez, M. (2024). The effect of free play on preschoolers' physical activity level and motor, cognitive, and socioemotional competences: A systematic review of randomized controlled trials. *European Early Childhood Education Research Journal, 32*(3), 429–447.

Piaget, J. (1952). *The origins of intelligence in children.* (M. Cook, Trans.). W W Norton & Co. (Original work published 1936).

Rekers-Power, A. (2020). *Exploring young children's participation and motive orientation in the classroom and at forest school* (Doctoral thesis, University of Wales Trinity Saint David).

Siviy, S. (2016) A brain motivated to play: Insights into the neurobiology of playfulness. *Behaviour*, 153(6-7), 819-844.

Stewart, A. L., Field, T. A., & Echterling, L. G. (2016). Neuroscience and the magic of play therapy. *International Journal of Play Therapy*, 25(1), 4-13.

Vygotsky, L. (1967) Play and its role in the mental development of the child. *Journal of Russian and East European Psychology*, 5, 6-18.

Yogman, M., Garner, A., Hutchinson, J., Hirsh-Pasek, R., & Michnick Golinkoff, R. (2018). The power of play: A pediatric role in enhancing development in young children. *Pediatrics*, 142(3), 1-16. https://pediatrics.aappublications.org/content/pediatrics/142/3/e20182058.full.pdf

7
Play, Early Language, and Communication

Amanda Bateman

Chapter Objectives

This chapter will:

- Explain in detail the connection between play and communication.
- Explore children's peer-peer social organisation practices and rule-making during play.
- Demonstrate how impromptu play activity is co-produced by children through talk.
- Consider how adults can use verbal and non-verbal resources to extend children's learning through play.

Co-Constructing Play Activities

Children's play can be observed as both a social and a solitary activity (see Chapter 3). Piaget's research using a developmental psychology approach considers stages of play, beginning with children's solitary engagement in play and developing in social complexity the older the child becomes. This suggests that children become increasingly intelligent in interacting with others as they become older – the more social the child is, the more cognitively advanced they are. Research subsequent to the work of Piaget has also suggested that children's social interactions in play require very complex thought and intelligence, but that even very young children are able to competently manage their social worlds independent of adult intervention (Corsaro & Everitt, 2024). There is increasing understanding that toddlers and young children intelligently co-produce play activity in their everyday lives with peers, but what is less understood is *how* they do this. The following transcripts and discussion aim to shed light on the process of children's early play through investigating how they use their verbal language and non-verbal gesture in social play with peers and adults.

A Note on Transcription

The transcripts provided in this chapter use conversation analysis transcription conventions to show as clearly as possible how and when the talk was spoken, and gestures performed. For example, arrows pointing up or down show that the word is spoken in a high or low pitch; words in double brackets show the action that is performed; and the time of pauses is recorded in single brackets (see appendix to this chapter for a list of symbols used). Importance is placed on the sequence of interaction, so writing the turn-taking of the participants on each line of transcription is quite significant. As we first look at children's peer-peer play, the symbols will help to show how it is that the children are using their talk, including pitch and tone, to co-produce their social networks in competent and intelligent ways.

Children's Peer-Peer Play

The first section of this chapter looks at children's play together as peers. The following transcripts explore children's peer-peer play to reveal how together, children demonstrate intelligent social competencies in negotiating their social play situations. The importance of providing time and space for children to play together away from adults is discussed, as this supports the practising of social rules through verbal and non-verbal participation.

Transcript 1 (Bateman, 2011)

This first excerpt demonstrates how, in just a few seconds, children can use their environment in intelligent ways to manage the inclusion and exclusion of their peers in their play. The scene is located in one of the playground huts in a primary school playground in Mid-Wales. Although the playground huts were built to facilitate and encourage children to play together, the ways in which children actually use these structures is much more complex.

Here we see Tina and Jess (both aged four years) entering one of the playground huts that is currently occupied by Emma, and Emma orienting to their entrance as problematic. Emma uses gesture to indicate who her talk is aimed at through eye gaze and pointing, and verbally produces a rule that Tina and Jess have broken (shown with the → arrows). Emma's orientation to a rule being broken here gives a strong rationale for the exclusion of Jess and Tina from the hut and so the play activity. The transcript begins when Jess and Tina have run into the hut.

01 Emma: ↑those ju:st went in without a:sking. ((*gaze toward Keira*))

02 Keira: ((*looks at Tina and Jess and continues eating her snack*

03   *without speaking*))

04   Emma: you're not allowed in to play ((*looks directly at Jess and*

05   *Tina*))

06 Kim: who ((*looks at Emma*))

07 Emma:→   you ((*points at Tina and Jess*)) (0.1) get out

08 →   you're supposed to ask one of these ( ) (0.1) before

09   you come in ↑aren't you.

10 Tina: what?

11 Emma:→   you're supposed to say the magic word (0.2) ple::ase (0.2)

12   when you come in this hut.

13 Jess: °let's go in another part.° ((*Jess and Tina run to another hut*))

Source: Reprinted from Bateman, A. (2011) Huts and heartache: The affordance of playground huts for legal debate. *Journal of Pragmatics*, *43*(13), 3111-3121. Copyright (2011), with permission from Elsevier.

Running into a playground hut to initiate play with its occupants might seem like an easy thing to do, but here we see there are specific social rules around play entry for children. As soon as Jess and Tina enter the hut, their entrance is made visible through Emma's announcement 'those just went in', which is then oriented to as problematic at the end of the utterance 'without asking' (line 01). As she speaks, Emma places emphasis on the word 'asking' (the elongation of the word 'asking' is indicated by the : symbol), drawing attention to that specific part and directing her gaze towards Keira to demonstrate that she is speaking to her. This utterance immediately marks Jess and Tina as rule-breakers.

Emma then moves on to direct her speech to Jess and Tina through her gaze shift so that she is looking at them, and by clearly articulating the exclusion – that they are 'not allowed in to play' (line 04). By using the words 'in' and 'play' Emma makes the specific exclusions clear – access 'in' the hut is prohibited as is the activity of 'play'. This is followed by an extension on the exclusion as Emma verbally instructs them to 'get out', using her gaze and a pointing gesture towards Jess and Tina (line 07). Further identification of the rule that was broken is then given 'you're supposed to ask one of these' (line 08) and 'say the magic word "please"' (line 11) to give a clear rationale for the exclusion. Jess and Tina demonstrate their understanding that this social situation cannot be rectified and that they will not be granted permission into the play as they run off into another playground hut. This small sequence of talk lasting just a few seconds demonstrates how complex entering play activities can be for children, and also highlights the social competencies of children in co-producing their own social order through talk and gesture.

Transcript 2 (Bateman, 2016)

In this second transcript we once again look at children's play with each other in their everyday peer-peer interactions, this time across the globe in New Zealand. Here, two 4-year-old children are engaging in pretend play using puppets to stage a puppet show. This transcript demonstrates how the children negotiate turn-taking to show an awareness of inclusion in play where each person has a turn to participate. The transcription symbols here also illustrate how the children use voice pitch and tone (prosody) to apply a 'creaky voice' (identified with *) and quieter tone (identified with °) when the puppet speaks to differentiate this talk from their own talk.

01 Sienna: *no:w* do it (2.2) >your turn< (0.8) >now

02   you=*no:w*< *yo:::u* (.hh) go °for shower° (0.6)

03   ((*imitates shower noise*)) sh::[:::

04 Matai   [go for shower e:ither

05   >here< ER:::::=ah ((*sings*)) de boo bah:: de boh

06   do be:: bo bi de=bo bi de[e:: dee dee dee dee]

07 Sienna: [SH:::::] (0.7)

08   °it's camera (>looking=at<) us° ((*singing*))

Lines omitted

09 Matai: oh wa ca di ca do:: ((*holds his turtle puppet up to*

10   *centre-stage and uses a character voice, singing.*

11   *He moves the puppet as he talks*)) *ah hello:: (0.5)

12   I can go jump un:der:: >in the< (*juggling*)

13   jelly=argh*::

Source: Bateman, A. (2016) Ventriloquism as early literacy practice: Making meaning in pretend play. *Early Years: An International Research Journal*, 38(1), 68-85. Copyright © TACTYC, reprinted by permission of the publisher (Taylor & Francis Ltd, www.tandfonline.com) and Informa UK Limited, trading as Taylor & Francis Group, www.tandfonline.com on behalf of TACTYC.

This puppet play can be seen as a cooperative play where each turn at talk works to build the play episode. It begins with Sienna indicating to Matai that it is his turn to perform and giving him instructions on the type of performance he can give – going for a shower (line 02). As directed, Matai takes his turn in the next space (lines 04-06), making his puppet go for an imaginary shower as he sings a song. Sienna then uses a very quiet 'different' type of voice to her usual one to ventriloquise her puppet noticing the researcher's video camera (line 08). After he has finished showering, Matai's puppet makes the final utterance in this performance (lines 09-13) as the puppet is placed centre-stage and uses a 'different' creaky type of voice to speak to announce his actions to the audience. These initial turns of talk and puppet action build the scene of a puppet show performance, where each child takes a turn to collaborate in their improvised play activity.

Adult-Child Interactions in Play

Transcripts 1 and 2 demonstrate how children competently manage the inclusion and exclusion of peers in play episodes through the use of talk and gesture, without the assistance of adults. We now turn to explore the role of the adult in children's play by considering adult verbal and non-verbal contributions that might help and/or hinder play activities. To explore this, we consider the difference between adult involvement in children's play through commenting on and asking questions *about* children's pretend play (transcript 3), compared with adults fully engaging *in* children's play as co-players (transcript 4).

Transcript 3 (Bateman, 2015)

In this play episode, we see the toddler teacher (JAM) approach two 2½-year-old toddler girls, Juda and Tia, who are sitting in a very large sand area in an early childhood centre garden. The children are engaged in play involving spooning sand into bowls and then pretending to eat the bowls of sand. The teacher sits down in the sandpit with them and asks them questions about their play.

01 JAM: what are we gonna put in here ((*looks at Tia's*

02   *bowl and then looks away from the children*))

03 Tia: ((*looks at JAM and puts handfuls of sand*

04   *into her bowl*))

05 JAM: what we gonna put in here Juda (0.3) what are we

06   cooking ((*looks at Juda*))

07 Juda: ↑We:lla:↓ ((*Juda makes eye contact with JAM*

08   *then looks away*))

09   (1.2)

10 JAM: what is ↓wella↓

11 Juda: in the ↓wella↑ ((*looks at JAM and points to the*

12   *bowl in front of her*))

13 JAM: ↓ok what are we going to put in there

14 Juda: ↓wella↓ ((*looks away and starts digging the sand*

15   *and giggles quietly*))

Here we see that even at the age of two years, the toddlers are capable and competent in co-producing an interaction with their teacher through turn-taking sequences. The teacher begins the conversation, making the play the topic to be talked about, as she asks one of the toddlers what she is going to put in her bowl. The toddler replies with gesture as she spoons sand into her bowl, so answering the teacher's question. Satisfied with this answer, JAM then moves to the second toddler, Juda and asks the same question to her. Juda replies verbally with 'wella', which is treated by the teacher as problematic in the next turns of talk – first marked by the long silence (line 09), then the teacher's request for clarification (line 10). Juda shows her understanding of the need to repair her delivery of her answer as per the teacher's request and so elaborates further 'in the wella' with added gesture, as she points to her bowl. However, the shared understanding is still not apparent here in this slightly awkward interaction as the teacher repeats her question and Juda gives the same answer.

When talking *about* the play here, there develops a breakdown in understanding. This failure to reach a shared understanding is not productive in the extension of children's learning. If we consider the role of the adult in children's play, we are expected to extend or stretch children's learning through playful activities that children are interested in; guidance on how to extend children's thinking in everyday play activities is offered by Houen et al. (2020) (see Further Reading link below). In this transcript we see that, through asking questions *about* the play, the interaction became more about practical matters of what was going into the bowl, which led to a breakdown in understanding. In the next transcription, we see how adult engagement *in* the child's play can work more productively to co-produce a collaborative play activity.

Transcript 4 (Bateman, 2015)

The same teacher from transcript 3 (JAM) has returned to the sandpit and is now sitting just with Tia, as Juda has left. Tia now has a different container in front of her that she is adding sand to. This time, rather than asking questions *about* what is being put inside the container as with transcript 3, the teacher begins engaging *in* the play activity, as she fills her own bowl with sand and offers a monologue of her play activity – cooking a delicious meal.

```
01 JAM:   got some ↑celery to put it in there and I'll put
02        some spi:ce sprinkle some spice in there and do you
03        like ↑curry powder↓ ((sprinkles sand into bowl))
04 Tia:   °↓yeah↓°
05 JAM:   put some curry powder in here and then I'm gonna
05        tip some stock from here ((adds more sand to bowl))
Lines omitted
06 JAM:   put some ↑stock in here ((holds small saucepan and
07        pretends to transfer liquid into her bowl))
08        ok↑ and then I'm gonna put my- (1.3) ↑chicken to
09        cook on the::- (1.2) ↓oh=pretend this is our stove
10        and I'll cook it on there (1.3) and then we gotta-
11        ((rests the bowl on top of a saucepan))
12 Tia:   → ((lifts up the bowl that she has been adding the
13        sand to and places it on top of JAM's bowl))
14 JAM:   you wanna add some of your food in there too↑
15 Tia:   → ((nods her head))
16 JAM:   °↓ok↓° (0.8) we gotta make sure it's mixed all nicely
17        in there. ((stirs the bowl of sand with her spoon))
18 Tia:   → ((joins in the stirring))
19 JAM:   ↓stir ↑it nice:ly: (1.0) give it a big stir (1.2)
20        tha::t's it.
```

The collaborative action of cooking a pretend meal is observable here through the turn-taking sequences of talk and gesture, where Tia's gestures are accepted and responded to as just as important as her verbal contributions by the teacher. In this instance, the teacher has noticed the child's interest in pretend cooking, recognised her play as providing an opportunity for shared learning, and responded in a way that supports and extends Tia's play. Through engaging in the play *with* Tia, the teacher supports her love of learning about how the world works, supporting a strong disposition to engage in playful learning activities (Sands & McChesney, 2022).

This sequence of notice, recognise, and respond as a systematic approach to pedagogical practice in early childhood education is recommended in the New Zealand early childhood 'exemplars' *Kei Tua o te Pae* (Carr et al., 2004-2009). The 'exemplars' are a set of books that provide support for early childhood teachers' pedagogy through offering examples of practice. Although written for New Zealand practice, there are valuable examples of good-quality teaching practices that are salient across countries, and which are particularly helpful in bilingual contexts where early childhood practice is also guided by a *curriculum framework*. Book 1 makes specific reference to noticing, recognising and responding where 'Teachers notice a great deal as they work with children, and they recognise some of what they notice as "learning". They will respond to a selection of what they recognise' (Carr et al., 2004, p. 6); see Further Reading for links to the *Kei Tua o te Pae* 'exemplars'.

Pretend play offers many opportunities for extending learning, including early socialisation and cultural practices where the real-life activity of cooking a meal is practised and early storytelling where the participants act out impromptu roles and storylines. In transcripts 2-4 we see how both of these learning activities are managed in a collaborative way through talk and gesture.

Questions in Play

Within many early childhood curricula across the globe, teachers are set the task of supporting children's disposition to learn with an aim to encourage lifelong learning. From transcript 4 above we can see how children and teachers might engage in playful and enjoyable activities together that encourage a love of learning. Learning dispositions are an attitude to learning where strong dispositions to learn can be encouraged by supporting and extending children's learning through their interests and encouraging them to make sense of their world through working theories. Working theories are linked to learning dispositions as they are both learning outcomes of *Te Whāriki*, the New Zealand early childhood curriculum, where working theories are 'the evolving ideas and understandings that children develop as they use their existing knowledge to try to make sense of new experiences' (Ministry of Education, 2017, p. 23). As infants, toddlers and young children explore their worlds in everyday interactions with people, places and things, they develop their working theories about how their world works and their place in it. Opportunities to engage in interactions that are enjoyable and interesting help support a strong disposition to learn:

> as learners intentionally engage in learning contexts, a developing combination of dispositions and working theories lead to transformational learning (Sands & McChesney, 2022, p. 3)

Children can be encouraged to make sense of and understand their world through playful activity and through the use of questions in their everyday interactions with others. Children's use of questions is promoted in early childhood education as it supports their knowledge seeking and their right to express their interests and views (Murray, 2022); adults' use of open-ended questions is also recommended to support and extend children's thinking – further advice about how to use questions effectively is available in Houen et al. (2020) in the Further Reading section below.

In the following transcript, we see how children's disposition to learn and working theories are supported by the teacher who offers encouragement with their line of enquiry and problem-solving during sand play. Here we will see the teacher asking questions that prompt the children to work out how to solve the problem of the water sinking into the sand as they try to make a well. Through the collaborative co-construction of this interaction, children build working theories about the scientific properties of sand and water.

Transcript 5 (Bateman, 2013)

In this interaction, the early childhood teacher (Shar) is sitting at the edge of a large sandpit in the garden area of an early childhood centre. With her are two 4-year-old children, Levi and Frank. The ongoing activity involves the children digging a hole next to where the teacher is sitting and then pouring water into it with the aim of making a well, but when the water is poured into the hole it is soaked up by the sand. Rather than immediately explaining why the sand soaks up the water, the teacher prompts the children to work the problem out for themselves. She manages to encourage the children's working theories about the situation through asking open-ended questions, leaving time for replies and offering some solutions.

01 Shar: ↓The:re we go:↑=look how its ↓flowing down=but
02   ↑what's happened↑(0.6) ↑where's the water gone↓
03 Frank: ↓gone↓ ((holds palms of hands out to sides))
04   (2.9)
05 Levi: it' s not working↓ ((runs to get more
06   water))
07 Shar: $it's not working ↑anymore↓why do you think
08   it's not working anymore↓$((continues digging))
09   (3.2)
10 Frank: coz it's ↑not↓ ((digs with Shar))
11 Shar: coz it's ↑no::t↓
12 Frank: [no]
13 Shar: [but] why isn't it working anymore ↓do you
14   know why↑
15   (6.5)
16 Frank: ((runs to get more water))
17 Levi: ((runs up to the trench and pours another bowl
18   of water into it))
19 Shar: now ↑watch what happens when you pour the water↓
20   ↑what happens↓ ((holds palm of hand out))
21   (1.7)
22 Levi: $it's it's ↓go::ne↓$

23 Shar: it's gone but where's it ↑gone↓

24 Levi: I (think) it's gone ↑un:der↓

25 Shar: it's gone under (0.6) under where↓

26 Levi: under the ↑ho:le↓

27 Shar: under the ↑ho:le↓

28 Levi: the:re (*points to the hole*)

Source: Bateman, A. (2013). Responding to children's answers: questions embedded in the social context of early childhood education. *Early Years: An International Research Journal, 33*(2), 275-289. Copyright © TACTYC, reprinted by permission of the publisher (Taylor & Francis Ltd, www.tandfonline.com) and Informa UK Limited, trading as Taylor & Francis Group, www.tandfonline.com on behalf of TACTYC.

In transcript 4, the example demonstrated how teachers might take on a role in children's pretend play to extend and support their engagement with the play. Here in transcript 5 we see a much more explicit scaffolding of children's learning through a cognitively challenging problem-solving activity afforded by sand and water play.

At the beginning of the transcript, the teacher identifies the problem of the sand soaking up the water with her open-ended question 'what happened' (lines 02). There has been research on the effectiveness of the use of the open-ended question 'what happened' which recognises it as a verbal teaching strategy for prompting children's working theories around specific topics (Houen et al., 2020). In this sequence of talk 'what happened' works to prompt each child to respond with an articulation of the specific problem at hand – identifying what the problem is can be seen as the first step to solving it.

The teacher continues to collaborate on solving the problem with the children, where we see how this question-answer sequence is co-constructed through turns at talk between the child and teacher in ways that secure an interaction around knowledge sharing of a specific problem. This helps the children develop working theories about how to solve problems in context, helping them to see themselves as competent learners and so developing a strong positive learner identity and strong learning dispositions to become lifelong learners (Sands & McChesney, 2022).

It is also possible that there may be some questions that teachers might ask which inhibit children's contribution though. For example, if we look at the teachers' talk on lines 07 and 13, we see the use of the question 'why' followed by a significant pause on the subsequent lines 09 and 15. Rather than responding to the teacher's question in the usual turn by turn process of conversation, the children do not answer straight away – this can indicate a problem. In this instance we might see that 'why' type questions could be problematic for children to answer, perhaps for the following reason:

Why-formatted interrogatives ['why' questions] display a challenging stance toward the accountable event and responsible agent(s) and are, thus, frequently co-implicated in complaining, criticising, and blaming (Bolden & Robinson, 2011, p. 94)

Through examining the sand and water play interaction in great detail we can see how the turns of talk and gesture work to mobilise working theories around scientific enquiry, which could be extended to exploring the properties of sand and water in more detail if the child shows interest in such an activity.

Reflection Point 7.1

- Consider your own personal observations of children's play. In what ways do the children in your observations demonstrate social competencies through their playful actions?
- Think about how you have used questions when you are interacting with children in their play, what types of responses these questions prompted from the children and how you might use questions in future playful interactions with children.
- When and how might you intervene in various types of children's play going forward? What strategies might you use, for example, to engage with children as co-player in their pretend play?

Summary

- Collaborative play activity is co-produced by verbal and non-verbal turns of talk and action between the players in systematic ways.
- This close investigation into children's peer-peer play reveals how together, children demonstrate intelligent social competencies in negotiating their social situations and make sense of their worlds through their verbal and gestural communication. It is important we do not underestimate their social competencies.
- This chapter highlights the importance of providing time and space for children to play together to practise social rules independent of adult intervention so that they can explore and negotiate their own social worlds.
- When considering the role of the adult when engaging in children's play, we see that children's holistic learning can be supported and stretched if the adult uses their talk and gesture in ways which position themselves as a co-player so that they are in a position to extend working theories and learning dispositions.

Further Reading

For very useful strategies to use in everyday play with children see: Houen, S., Staton, S., Thorpe, K. and Toon, D. (2020) Building your evidence engine: Five evidence-informed strategies for promoting rich conversations with young children. *Early Learning.* Available at: www.educationtoday.com.au/news-detail/Building-your-evidence-engine-4776.

For the latest edition of Corsaro's work on children's social competence through play see: Corsaro, W. and Everitt, J. (2024) *The Sociology of Childhood* (6th ed.). London: Sage.

To explore and consider the use of questions in play interactions: Bateman, A. (2013) Responding to children's answers: Questions embedded in the social context of early childhood education. *Early Years: An International Research Journal, 33*(2), 275-289.

Links to the Kei Tua o te Pae 'exemplars' books are available online and are very helpful in considering children as competent and capable learners as well as offering guidance for effective practice for early childhood teachers: www.education.govt.nz/early-childhood/teaching-and-learning/assessment-for-learning/kei-tua-o-te-pae-2/.

References

Bateman, A. (2011). Huts and heartache: The affordance of playground huts for legal debate. *Journal of Pragmatics*, 43, 3111-3121.

Bateman, A. (2013). Responding to children's answers: Questions embedded in the social context of early childhood education. *Early Years: An International Research Journal, 33*(2), 275-289.

Bateman, A. (2015). *Conversation analysis and early childhood education: The co-production of knowledge and Relationships*. Farnham: Ashgate/Routledge.

Bateman, A. (2016). Ventriloquism as early literacy practice: Making meaning in pretend play. *Early Years: An International Research Journal*, 38(1), 68-85.

Bolden, G. B., & Robinson, J. D. (2011). Soliciting accounts with why-interrogatives in conversation. *Journal of Communication*, 61, 94-119.

Carr, M., Lee, W., & Jones, C. (2004). *An Introduction to Kei Tua o te Pae: He Whakamōhiotanga ki Kei Tua o te Pae (Book 1)*. Learning Media. Book 1 available at: www.education.govt.nz/assets/Documents/Early-Childhood/Kei-Tua-o-te-Pae/ECEBooklet1Full.pdf

Carr, M., Lee, W., & Jones, C. (2004-2009). *Kei Tua o Te Pae: Assessment for learning: early childhood exemplars*. Learning Media. All books available at: www.education.govt.nz/early-childhood/teaching-and-learning/assessment-for-learning/kei-tua-o-te-pae-2/

Corsaro, W., & Everitt, J. (2024). *The sociology of childhood* (6th ed.). London: Sage.

Houen, S., Staton, S., Thorpe, K., & Toon, D. (2020). Building your evidence engine: Five evidence-informed strategies for promoting rich conversations with young children. *Early Learning*. Available at: www.educationtoday.com.au/news-detail/Building-your-evidence-engine-4776

Jefferson, G. (2004). Glossary of transcript symbols with an introduction. In G. H. Lerner (Ed.), *Conversation analysis: Studies from the first generation*. Amsterdam: John Benjamins.

Ministry of Education. (2017). *Te Whāriki. He Whāriki mātauranga mō ngā mokopuna o Aotearoa: Early childhood curriculum*. Wellington: Ministry of Education.

Murray, J. (2022). Any questions? Young children questioning in their early childhood education settings, *EECERJ*, 30(1), 108-130.

Sacks, H., Schegloff, E. A., & Jefferson, G. (1974). A simplest systematics for the organisation of turn-taking for conversation. *Language*, 50, 696-735.

Sands, L., & McChesney, K. (2022). How learning stories influence children's learning identities, *New Zealand Journal of Education Studies*. https://doi.org/10.1007/s40841-022-00273-0

Appendix: Conversation Analysis Transcription Conventions for Chapter 7

The conversation analysis symbols used to transcribe the data are adapted from Jefferson's conventions described in Sacks et al. (1974) and Jefferson (2004).

. falling intonation

? rising intonation

↑ sharp rising intonation

↓ sharp falling intonation

:: lengthening of the prior sound

[the beginning of an overlap of talk

] the end of an overlap of talk

= latching of speech between the speakers

(0.4) time of a pause in seconds

Underscore emphasis placed on the underscored sound

°degree° spoken in a quiet tone

(brackets) utterance could not be deciphered

((*brackets*)) unspoken actions

$ smiling while talking

> arrows< utterance spoken quickly

→ Points to a phenomenon of interest, to be discussed by the author

– Utterance stops abruptly

8

Play, Creativity, and Well-Being

Charlotte Greenway and Laura Hutchings

Chapter Objectives

This chapter will help you:

- Understand the importance of well-being in childhood.
- Identify how play can promote well-being in children.
- Be aware of how well-being can be supported in the early primary school setting.
- Understand the concept of creativity.
- Identify how creativity develops through play.
- Be aware of the importance of creativity and play in the development of coping and resilience.

Introduction

In recent years, well-being has become a key concern for those who work with children. Its complex nature coupled with multi-faceted definitions makes understanding its development challenging. The term 'well-being' has been used interchangeably with concepts such as happiness and quality of life and measured objectively and subjectively. Definitions also reflect theoretical, disciplinary, and political viewpoints. In policy contexts, well-being may be associated with mental state and emotional health, or it may relate to physical health and developmental milestones. The focus, in policy, is on objective indicators that monitor whether a nation is leading or lagging in well-being. Such indicators aim to facilitate the government's promotion of well-being across the lifespan to ensure a healthy nation. From a psychological perspective, well-being is conceptualised as some combination of positive affective states such as happiness and life satisfaction (the hedonic perspective) and functioning with optimal effectiveness in daily life (the eudaimonic perspective).

Based on hedonism, Diener (2000) proposed subjective well-being, which refers to an individual's affective state and cognitive evaluations of life. In contrast, eudaimonic theorist Ryff (2014) argued for the importance of a sense of meaning, purpose and fulfilment in life.

Despite these conceptualisations, there is no single, universally accepted definition of wellbeing in early childhood. Generally, well-being refers to children feeling loved, secure and supported. Research shows that secure relationships and the role of others significantly have an impact on a child's positive state of mind (see Clark, 2017). In the United Kingdom, there has been increasing awareness around emotional well-being and mental health concerns for children, highlighting the importance of supporting children's emotional development from a young age. This is particularly crucial given the reported rise in emotional disorders among children aged 5-15. This highlights the importance of focusing on well-being from an early age and understanding its influence on children's social, cognitive and psychological development to ensure that children and young people develop the knowledge, understanding and skills needed for a healthy childhood and future.

The Importance of Well-Being in Children

Numerous policies in the United Kingdom emphasise the importance of well-being in childhood. In Wales, the Well-Being of Future Generations Act (Welsh Government, 2015) promotes individuals' well-being in schools. Furthermore, health and well-being is at the core of the new Curriculum for Wales as it is an Area of Learning and Experience. The Scottish Curriculum for Excellence 3-18 (CfE, 2013) contains health and well-being experiences and outcomes that focus on mental, emotional, social and physical well-being. In addition to this, the Scottish Mental Health Strategy (Scottish Government, 2017) states that schools should provide access to mental health and well-being support for all children and young people. In England, the Foundation Stage statutory framework (DfES, 2017) links wellbeing to the theme of 'a unique child', highlighting physical and emotional well-being through the promotion of resilient, self-assured children (see also Chapter 12).

Typically, statistics on children's well-being in the United Kingdom focus on the perceptions and lives of older children. However, the National Children's Bureau Young Children's Well-Being project (National Children's Bureau, 2009) concentrates explicitly on the well-being and mental health of children aged 0-8. The project found that within an education setting, relationships and practitioner characteristics impact well-being in children. For practitioners, it is essential to reflect on one's own qualities such as self-awareness, empathy, patience and respect to promote positive well-being among children within the setting. The project also highlighted that the setting/classroom organisation and space affected children's well-being. In particular, play positively influenced well-being and the play spaces that encouraged risk-taking positively impacted several characteristics such as self-efficacy, self-esteem and self-concept.

Play and Well-Being

Play provides children with a valuable platform to learn about themselves and the world around them. Through play, children can symbolically re-enact recent life events in a safe environment and learn to problem-solve, which can reduce tension. Play allows children to learn about their feelings through expressing emotions such as fear, anger, love and happiness. In addition to this, play enables children to experiment with different behaviours and learn social skills (see Chapter 6 and 7). They learn to navigate the responses of others to their actions and regulate their emotions accordingly, helping to build self-discipline and self-regulation. Play, therefore, provides children with social and behavioural tools that have a positive impact on well-being immediately and later in life.

Play activities also support physical health, which in turn boosts confidence and self-esteem, both which are important to a child's well-being. Furthermore, the physical exertion often involved in play releases endorphins and has a 'feel-good factor' that promotes joy in children, increasing dopamine levels in the brain. Dopamine, a neurochemical associated with motivation and reward, contributes to the sense of joy and pleasure that children experience during play. This positive reinforcement helps to develop a 'can do' attitude, motivating children to pursue the rewards offered by play thus increasing their self-esteem and self-efficacy.

Promoting Well-Being Through Risky Play

Risky play lets children experience a range of emotions in a controlled and safe environment. It encourages children to take risks, overcome challenges and seek out potentially frightening situations, whether these are real or imagined. According to Sandseter (2007), there are six characteristics of risky play:

- Playing with harmful tools.
- Playing at height.
- Playing at speed.
- Rough and tumble play.
- Playing near dangerous elements.
- Play where children can disappear/get lost.

While risky play is most commonly associated with outdoor contexts, it can also occur indoors. For example, activities such as beam walking, climbing, sliding and using tools all involve elements of risk. Risky play in the outdoors is not a new concept in the early years setting. McMillan (1930) considered that the ideal outdoor environment would allow children to 'play bravely and adventurously' (see Chapter 4). Inside setting activities, such as stacking large objects or using a safety knife to allow children to cut fruit and vegetables, can also be seen as risky play examples. Many early years practitioners may be concerned about the health and safety aspects surrounding a risk (see Chapters 12 and 18); however, we must consider whether the skills children gain from such activities outweigh the risks involved.

Children are naturally curious, and risky play gives them the opportunity to experience excitement. In one study (Coster & Gleeve, 2008), children engaged in risky play for fun, excitement, and enjoyment however, the authors also reported that risky play increased self-esteem and independence because children could push boundaries and respond to challenges. Dweck (2000) coined the term 'mastery approach', which explains how children rise to challenges and develop a 'can do' attitude. As risky play allows children to test their capabilities and push limits, it becomes a crucial tool for developing self-belief. Kernis (1995) argued that a sense of well-being is linked to past experiences and success. Thus, if a child injures themselves through risky play, they may develop a sense of failure due to the negative experience. However, Hendry and Kloep (2002) suggest that providing that the outcome is not too severe, the experience can foster resilience and positively prepare children for future challenges.

Supporting Children to Develop Self-Efficacy and Self-Regulation Through Play

Self-efficacy relates to the belief in oneself to succeed and overcome challenges. The leading proponent of self-efficacy, Bandura (1997), argued that it refers to the belief of an individual in their own abilities, influenced by past performance, social models, social persuasion and emotional states. Evidence supports the idea that self-efficacy and well-being are closely related, as the more capable a child feels, the better they feel about themselves.

Similarly, self-regulation is essential for well-being. It involves how children respond to challenges and the strategies they use to cope with difficult situations. While self-efficacy focuses on a child's beliefs about their own abilities, self-regulation relates to the thoughts and actions generated in response to a given situation. Self-esteem is also intertwined with these concepts but relates to feelings of self-worth rather than actions or beliefs. Both self-regulation and self-esteem can be developed through play. Here we explore how the early years setting and practitioners assist with the enhancement of these in relation to play.

From Bandura's theory, self-efficacy is greatly influenced by others' support, role models in the environment and past experiences. Therefore, if a child in the setting is encouraged sensitively and unobtrusively throughout the play activity by the practitioner and the practitioner presents themselves as a positive role model, this will help build on the foundations of self-efficacy within a child. The practitioner who is responsive to a child's needs and adjusts the play activity accordingly supports the development of self-efficacy (see also Chapter 15).

Play presents children with the opportunity to practise self-control, manage emotions, and behaviours and develop self-regulation. By examining how others react to their actions, children become more independent and more able to regulate their own emotions. Well-being is positively affected when children effectively use self-regulatory skills to adjust emotions in challenging situations. It is believed that child-initiated play promotes self-regulation more than structured play. During child-initiated play or free-play (see Chapters 1 and 3), children can experiment with boundaries, be creative, become independent thinkers and devise their own strategies to regulate emotions. To support self-regulation within the early years, we need to organise space to facilitate child-initiated activities. Such activities enable children to set goals and evaluate their performance, failures and successes. Bandura's self-efficacy theory suggests, therefore, that child-initiated play is likely to have a positive effect on self-efficacy as the child is more likely to meet their goals and will consequently be competent in similar activities in the future.

Measuring Well-Being in the Setting

There are several benefits of measuring well-being in childhood, including the early identification of individual issues and provision of appropriate support. Data gathered on children's well-being could also influence policy and practice in education settings. However, measuring well-being is not a simple task, particularly among younger children. Well-being relates to an individual's internal state, making it somewhat subjective. Since well-being relates to psychological and emotional aspects, its nature is difficult to assess. In addition, young children may not yet have the language skills to fully express their feelings. Instead of focusing directly on well-being we might focus on indicators relating to well-being and involvement in young children rather than measuring well-being per se (Laevers, 2000).

Within the early years environment, observations are commonly used to gather data on children's behaviour. This is a data collection method that you are likely to be familiar with (see Chapters 9 and 14). As you have seen in this chapter, play is beneficial to well-being. Therefore, an observational tool that allows the indicators of well-being to be measured while play takes place is valuable for practitioners. The Leuven Scale of Well-Being and Involvement (Laevers, 1994) is an observational tool that allows practitioners to measure children's emotional well-being and involvement, two vital components of learning, development and progress in children. Laevers defines the term 'involvement' as the individual's engagement in learning activity and indicates that children who are 'involved' in activity are demonstrating high levels of well-being, which is linked to self-esteem, self-confidence, resilience, spontaneity and freedom. For Laevers, children with high well-being will fully engage in setting/classroom experiences, whereas children with low well-being may withdraw from learning activities. Scores for involvement and wellbeing on the Leuven Scale range from one to five, with one being the lowest and five being the highest. It is thought that unless children are functioning between levels 4 and 5 and therefore demonstrating high involvement, they will not fully benefit from the learning experience, which in turn affects their overall well-being.

Reflection Point 8.1

Think back to when you were in early primary school. Do you think your well-being was directly supported by the approach taken to play and to learning? If so, in what ways? Maybe the approaches you recall detracted from your well-being. If so, in what ways? What activities supported, or detracted from, your well-being? What actions by teachers supported, or detracted from, your well-being? How would you ensure early primary school experiences promoted well-being?

There are many ways in which children's sense of well-being can be increased. One example is through creativity. Research demonstrates that creativity promotes happiness, mood and mental health and reduces stress and anxiety. It also fosters resilience and coping by allowing children the freedom to explore their emotions and to develop and test strategies for future use.

Creativity

There are many definitions of creativity (see Sternberg, 1999). Most include two distinctive features: the creative product and the creative process. The creative product is the output, which must be both original and appropriate, and the creative process facilitates the creative act. For something to be original, it must be new and be something that has never been seen or heard of before. However, originality alone is not sufficient; something that is original may be useless. That is why any new creation must also be appropriate for the task at hand in a way that is useful in order to be creative.

An important consideration when exploring creativity in children is whether children can create something original and appropriate. The answer lies in whether the product of creation is age-appropriate and whether the product 'makes sense' for children within that age group. To ensure these qualities and understand children's creativity, we must focus on children's creative process and development. Wallas' (1926) four-stage model of creativity remains a foundational framework for researchers and educators. The four processes outlined in Figure 8.1 provide a lens to understand creativity. The four-stage model helps us see where we are in our creative process, where we need to go and how to navigate through the mental processes to reach our goal. The stages are non-linear; individuals may revisit them multiple times, and the benefits of following a framework allow us to re-centre our thoughts if we veer off course and provide structure in educational contexts, allowing practitioners to guide children's creative exploration.

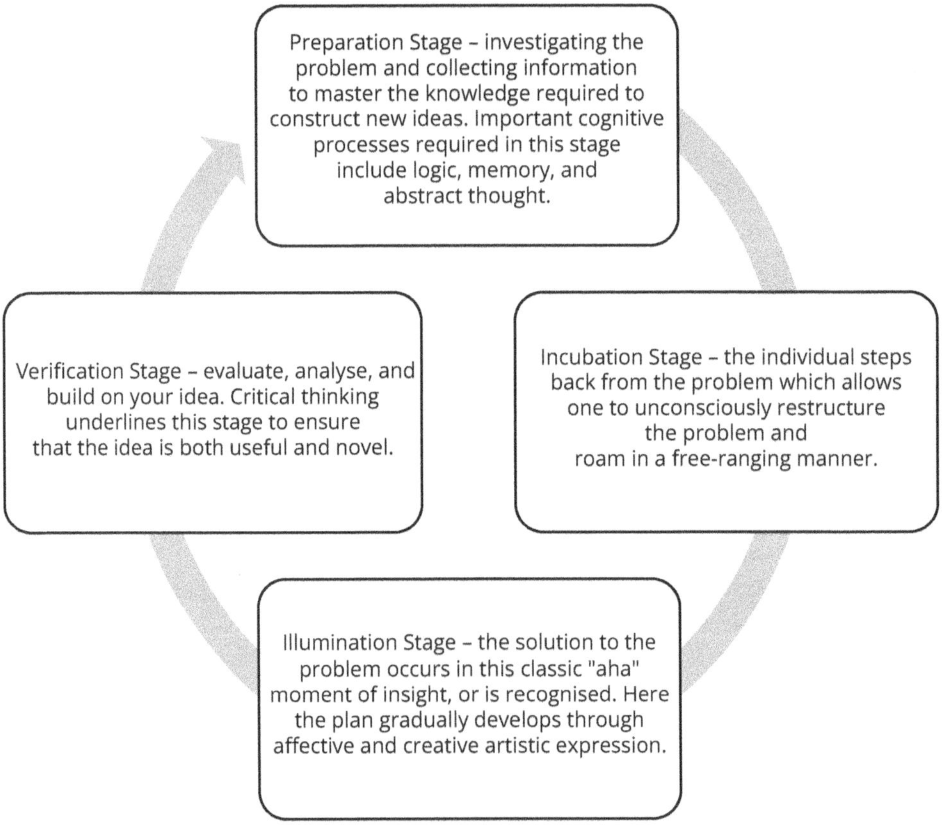

Preparation Stage – investigating the problem and collecting information to master the knowledge required to construct new ideas. Important cognitive processes required in this stage include logic, memory, and abstract thought.

Incubation Stage – the individual steps back from the problem which allows one to unconsciously restructure the problem and roam in a free-ranging manner.

Illumination Stage – the solution to the problem occurs in this classic "aha" moment of insight, or is recognised. Here the plan gradually develops through affective and creative artistic expression.

Verification Stage – evaluate, analyse, and build on your idea. Critical thinking underlines this stage to ensure that the idea is both useful and novel.

Figure 8.1 Four-Stage Processes of Creativity
Source: Adapted from Wallas (1926).

Why Is Creativity Important?

The cognitive components of creativity equip children with critical life skills, including communication, problem-solving, and emotional expression. Encouraging creativity from an early age helps children develop resilience, adaptability, and the ability to navigate the complexities of modern life. Particularly, creativity supports the development of:

- Verbal and non-verbal communication skills.
- Coordination and motor skills (e.g., music and dance).
- Self-expression and identity formation (e.g., arts and crafts).
- Imaginative play as a means of understanding the world.
- Problem-solving, decision-making, and innovative thinking.

The essential link between creativity and learning is reflected in curriculum developments across the United Kingdom. All four nations have acknowledged the significance of creativity in their Early Childhood Education and Care (ECEC) and primary education frameworks. For instance:

- England: The Early Years Foundation Stage (EYFS) emphasises 'expressive arts and design' as a critical area of development, encouraging children to explore and use their imagination.
- Scotland: The Curriculum for Excellence (CfE) integrates creativity into 'experiences and outcomes' across subject areas, aiming to nurture skills for life, learning and work.
- Wales: The Curriculum for Wales (CfW) prioritises creativity under its 'Four Purposes', particularly as part of the 'Expressive Arts' Area of Learning and Experience.
- Northern Ireland: The Foundation Stage curriculum promotes creativity as a key component of play-based learning.

How Wallas' (1926) four-stage model of creativity fits today's UK educational landscape can be seen below:

1 Preparation – gathering information, developing skills and exploring problems.
   - England: Encourages exploration and active learning through play, promoting inquiry-based approaches to problem-solving.
   - Scotland: Focuses on developing skills for learning, life, and work through interdisciplinary activities and experiential learning.
   - Wales: Promotes curiosity and inquiry as part of the 'Four Purposes' to create ambitious, capable learners.
   - Northern Ireland: Emphasises problem-solving and thinking skills within child-initiated learning.

Fit with Wallas: Preparation aligns with fostering curiosity, research skills, and foundational knowledge across all UK frameworks.

2 Incubation: Unconscious processing happens, and ideas are allowed to develop naturally.
   - Play-Based Learning: Through periods of free play and unstructured activities give children the mental space to reflect and process ideas subconsciously.
   - Connection with Nature and the Outdoors: Outdoor play and exploration allow children to step away from structured activities, giving their minds space to rest and process information.

○ Art and Creative Activities: Activities like drawing, painting or sculpting allow children to work without explicit goals, promoting a free flow of ideas that supports unconscious thought.

Fit with Wallas: UK curricula increasingly value non-linear learning processes, where children take breaks and revisit tasks later, mirroring this stage.

3 Illumination: The 'aha' moment when solutions or creative ideas emerge.
   ○ Collaborative Learning: Classroom strategies that promote group discussions and brainstorming facilitate moments of insight.
   ○ Teacher Facilitation: Educators play a critical role in guiding children to connect ideas, often through questioning and scaffolding.
   ○ Creative Subjects: Art, music, and drama lessons across the United Kingdom encourage students to experiment and arrive at creative breakthroughs.

Fit with Wallas: The structured spontaneity supported in UK classrooms allows children to experience moments of illumination through guided exploration and collaboration.

4 Verification: Evaluating and refining ideas to ensure they are viable and effective.
   ○ Formative Assessment: Encourages self-reflection and peer evaluation, helping students refine their ideas.
   ○ Iterative Design in STEM (Science, Technology, Engineering, and Maths): Projects often involve cycles of prototyping, testing and improvement, echoing this stage of the model.
   ○ Cross-Curricular Projects: These projects allow students to apply creative solutions to real-world problems, ensuring their ideas are original, appropriate and useful.

Fit with Wallas: UK curricula increasingly emphasise the iterative process of creativity, where students assess and improve their outputs.

Wallas' model thus provides a timeless framework that resonates with the UK's evolving educational priorities. It fosters creativity as an essential skill for personal growth and societal advancement.

Creativity and Play

Vygotsky (2004) emphasised the role of imagination in fostering creativity, which he viewed as a foundation for art, science, and technology. He suggested that creativity is shaped by the amount and variety of an individual's knowledge and life experiences, the heart of which is imagination. He sees imagination as intentional, and with development, it can work alongside daydreaming, inventing and planning to create something new. Vygotsky's ideas are evident in all four nations. Each system reflects its cultural and educational priorities while promoting creativity and imagination as essential aspects of early learning by integrating pretend play into structured and free-choice activities and fostering skills like collaboration, problem-solving and emotional expression through imaginative activities.

The development of creativity through play encourages children to depart from reality and explore and comprehend the world around them by creating enjoyable and meaningful situations. Through their imagination, children move between the past, present and future to communicate their thoughts and feelings and think about and create representations and new meanings to construct a reality that fulfils their wishes and needs. Despite the departure from reality observed in a child who imagines the stick they are holding is a sword, for Vygotsky, imagination remains deeply connected to social reality. He speaks about play as imagination in action: a creative process that develops in play because a real situation takes up a new and unfamiliar meaning. From his description, imagination is both emotional and intellectual, and therefore it develops creativity.

Creativity and Pretend Play

The relationship between creativity and play has been examined more recently by Russ (2004, 2014), who suggests that many similarities exist between the processes that occur in creativity and pretend play. Pretend play, a hallmark of early childhood, uses fantasy and make-believe to represent one object or scenario for another. It allows the child to manipulate objects; hold mental images; make up stories; to imagine a waterfall and how that may feel on their skin; to express positive or negative feelings. It is most prominent within the 3- to 5-year age range of a typically developing child but continues into middle childhood and beyond. Through pretend play, children structure and restructure their experiences in unique ways that facilitate the development of divergent thinking. Studies that demonstrate a relationship between pretend play and divergent thinking abilities show that children who participate in more frequent pretend play and display a variety of emotions offer more responses on divergent thinking tasks. As seen in Vygotsky's account of creativity, Russ discusses the importance of emotions. She uses the term 'affect' rather than 'emotion' and describes two affective processes that occur during pretend play: access to affect-laden thoughts and openness to affect states. For Russ, the two processes mean that children access, explore and experience emotional thoughts and feelings (e.g., aggression, anxiety), and learn to express and regulate their emotions during pretend play. If children express both processes, they could develop a wide variety of affect-laden associations that ought to facilitate divergent thinking. Additionally, the fact that pretend play can promote both cognitive (divergent thinking) and affective (express emotions) abilities suggests that children who frequently engage in pretend play should generate many solutions for and respond better to everyday problems, thus suggesting a link between pretend play, coping, and even resilience.

Reflection Point 8.2

- As creativity is increasingly embedded in ECEC guidance and primary education across all four UK nations, how can ECEC practitioners and teachers promote creativity amidst busy curriculum schedules?
- As children enter the school system, what are the tensions teachers may have to face in making curriculum space for the development of creativity?

Play, Coping, and Resilience

Coping involves any cognitive or behavioural effort made to manage internal or external demands and conflicts with its purpose to control or alter the source of the stress and to regulate stressful emotions (Folkman & Lazarus, 1980). Effective coping strategies provide resilience (the ability to bounce back) to lessen the likelihood of adverse outcomes, help the adjustment to stressful life events and improve well-being later in life. Studies have found that children with good pretend-play skills demonstrate effective coping skills that endure over time. Using the Affect in Play Scale (APS; Russ, 2004) – a five-minute play task designed to assess affect and imagination in play using puppets – Christiano and Russ (1996) examined the effect of pretend play on children undergoing an invasive dental procedure. The authors found that children who expressed affect and fantasy in their play demonstrated better coping strategies and less distress during the dental procedure.

More recently, in their study of 61 children, Hoffmann and Russ (2012) used the APS, a divergent thinking task and a storytelling task to assess creativity, and the Emotion Regulation Checklist (ERC). They reported a relationship between pretend play and creativity and emotion regulation, and a relationship between divergent thinking and creativity in storytelling. Their findings have important implications not only because they suggest play, creativity, and emotion regulation are linked but also for children's future coping and resilience. Emotion regulation is the ability to manage one's emotional experiences and is essential for children's psychological and social well-being (Shipman et al., 2003). The ability to engage adaptively with daily challenges afforded by emotion regulation coupled with divergent thinking abilities makes it crucial to the child's ability to manage and alter strategies so they can overcome adversity and rise above disadvantage.

It appears that the creativeness and imagination abundant in pretend play allow children to explore and test the consequences of many alternative situations. Through shared experiences, cooperation, and negotiation, children can overcome challenges in a safe environment. Such activities help to develop a range of behavioural, social and emotional skills that can facilitate coping and resilience. Therefore, creativity and pretend play should be encouraged so children can live fulfilling and healthy lives.

Case Study 8.1

George (aged five) and his 7-year-old brother, Reuben, are sitting on the kitchen floor. They have gathered a bundle of kitchen paraphernalia to build a fortress so that Kevin and Fudge, the hamsters, can have a day of adventure out of the cage. George begins by rolling up two tea towels to act as walls for the fortress and places them adjacent to one another. Reuben finishes the square enclosure by doing the same with two cereal boxes. Reuben places an empty kitchen roll tube in the middle of the fortress and says, 'a tunnel to run through'. George adds a mixing bowl saying, 'they can climb up and over that'. Reuben says, 'no silly, how can they? It's too slippery'. They both look at the items they have left. George motions to the colander, saying, 'foot holes for grip?' Reuben looks horrified and says, 'no, their feet will fall straight through the holes, and that will hurt them'. George gets up and stomps off, shouting to his mum that 'Reuben won't let me

(Continued)

choose'. Reuben calls back at George, 'look, George, a ramp'. George turns to watch as Reuben places a wooden chopping board on the side of the mixing bowl and says, 'good idea George, they will love running up that hill'. Reuben picks up a wooden spoon and puts it to his mouth, and yells, 'let the games begin'. George smiles and returns to the floor with his older brother.

Reflection Point 8.3

The case study shows George and Reuben building a fortress for hamsters Kevin and Fudge.

- How might Wallas' Four-Stage Model of Creativity be applied to George and Reuben's process of building a fortress for their hamsters? How might George and Reuben use the skills they have learnt in the future to cope with an everyday problem?
- How did Reuben support George in being resilient?

Summary

- Play activities, especially risky play, can enhance skills such as problem-solving, confidence and independence, which can positively impact self-esteem, self-efficacy, and self-belief.
- The practitioner plays an important role in supporting children to develop skills associated with well-being.
- Creativity allows children to try out new ideas and new ways of thinking and problem-solving.
- Creative experiences can help children to express and cope with their feelings.
- Pretend play is a child's natural vehicle for creative experiences that can help foster resilience and develop a wide range of coping skills for the future.

Further Reading

Clark, C. (2017) *Play and well-being.* London: Routledge. This book examines the role of play in health and well-being across a variety of contexts. Through its exploration of research evidence, it challenges the assumptions that play is insufficient and unproductive.

Goodliff, G., Canning, N., Parry, J. and Miller, L. (Eds) (2017) *Young children's play and creativity: Multiple voices.* Abingdon: Taylor and Francis. This book examines children's play, creativity and the participatory nature of learning. Through the voices of practitioners, academics and researchers, it explores the benefits of play and creativity for children's well-being and development.

Laevers, F. (2000) Forward to basics! Deep-level learning and the experiential approach. *Early Years*, 20(2), 20-29. This article offers an insight into the Leuven Scale of well-being and involvement. It examines experiential education, deep-level learning and well-being within the early years environment.

Sternberg, R. J. and Kaufman, J. C. (Eds) (2018) *The nature of human creativity.* Cambridge: Cambridge University Press. Sternberg and Kaufman provide an overview of the approaches of leading scholars to understanding the nature of creativity, its measurement, its investigation, its development and its importance to society.

References

Bandura, A. (1997). *Self-efficacy: The exercise of control.* New York: W. H. Freeman.

Christiano, B. A., & Russ, S. W. (1996). Play as a predictor of coping and distress in children during invasive dental procedure. *Journal of Clinical Child Psychology*, 25(2), 130-138.

Clark, C. (2017). *Play and well-being.* London: Routledge.

Coster, D., & Gleeve, J. (2008). *Playday! give us a go: children and young people's views on risk-taking.* Available at: www.playday.org.uk/wp-content/uploads/2015/11/give_us_a_go___children_and_young_peoples_views_on_play_and_risk_taking.pdf

Curriculum for Excellence (CfE). (2013). *Health and well-being: experiences and outcomes.* Available at: www.educationscotland.gov.uk/Images/health_well-being_experiences_outcomes_tcm4-540031.pdf

Department for Education and Skills (DfES). (2017). *Statutory framework for the early years foundation stage.* Available at: www.gov.uk/government/publications/early-years-foundation-stage-framework-2

Diener, E. (2000). Subjective well-being: The science of happiness and a proposal for a national index. *American Psychologist*, 55(1), 34.

Dweck, C. S. (2000). *Self-theories: Their role in motivation, personality, and development.* Hove: Psychology Press.

Folkman, S., & Lazarus, R. S. (1980). An analysis of coping in a middle-aged community sample. *Journal of Health and Social Behavior*, 21, 219-239.

Hendry, L., & Kloep, M. (2002). *Lifespan development – Resources, challenges and risks.* Washington, DC: Thompson Publishing.

Hoffmann, J., & Russ, S. (2012). Pretend play, creativity, and emotion regulation in children. *Psychology of Aesthetics, Creativity, and the Arts*, 6(2), 175-184.

Kernis, M. (1995). *Plenum series in social/clinical psychology: Efficacy, agency, and self-esteem.* New York: Plenum Press.

Laevers, F. (Ed.) (1994). *The Leuven involvement Scale for young children: Manual and video.* Experiential education series, No. 1. Leuven: Centre for Experiential Education.

Laevers, F. (2000). Forward to basics! Deep-level learning and the experiential approach. *Early Years*, 20(2), 20-29.

McMillan, M. (1930). *The Nursery School.* London: J. M. Dent and Sons.

National Children's Bureau. (2009). *Young children's well-being: Domains and contexts of development from birth to age eight*. Available at: www.ncb.org.uk/sites/default/files/field/attachment/NO97%20-%20young_childrens_well_being_final.pdf

Russ, S. W. (2004). *Play in child development and psychotherapy: Toward empirically supported practice*. Mahway, NJ: Erlbaum.

Russ, S. W. (2014). *Pretend play in childhood: Foundation of adult creativity*. Washington, DC: American Psychological Association.

Ryff, C. D. (2014). Psychological well-being revisited: Advances in the science and practice of eudaimonia. *Psychotherapy and Psychosomatics*, 83(1), 10–28.

Sandseter, E. (2007). Categorising risky play: How can we identify risk-taking in children's play? *European Early Childhood Research Journal*, 15(2), 237–252.

Scottish Government. (2017). *Mental health strategy 2017–2027*. Available at: www.gov.scot/publications/mental-health-strategy-2017-2027/

Shipman, K., Zeman, J., Fitzgerald, M., & Swisher, L. M. (2003). Regulating emotion in parentchild and peer relationships: A comparison of sexually maltreated and non-maltreated girls. *Child Maltreatment*, 8(3), 163–172.

Sternberg, R. J. (Ed.) (1999). *Handbook of creativity*. Cambridge: Cambridge University Press.

Vygotsky, L. S. (2004). Imagination and creativity in childhood. *Journal of Russian and East European Psychology*, 42(1), 7–97.

Wallas, G. (1926). *The art of thought*. London: Jonathan Cape.

Welsh Government. (2015). *Well-being of future generations (Wales) Act*. Available at: www.futuregenerations.wales/wp-content/uploads/2017/02/150623-guide-to-the-fg-act-en.pdf

9
Observation and Assessment of Play

Tereza Aidonopoulou-Read

> ### Chapter Objectives
>
> This chapter aims to:
>
> - Challenge traditional perceptions of play.
> - Explore neuroatypical engagement with play.
> - Reflect on how we, education practitioners, choose what we assess in play and how we assess it.
> - Explore alternative play assessment frameworks that can promote inclusive assessment.

Definitions

Neurodiversity: a term for diverse neurological differences in the human brain, which can impact thinking and learning, and is viewed as a range of natural variations rather than a deficit in individuals (Kircher-Morris, 2022).

Neuronormative: a term used to signify that there is one main way of thinking which is valued in society, and it often is the type of thinking that the hypothetical 'majority' of neurotypical individuals follow.

Neurotypical: a term used to describe individuals whose neurological development and functioning align with what is considered typical or expected by societal standards.

Introduction

Autistic children often demonstrate different patterns of visual attention when compared with neurotypical children. For example, they may show a higher visual preference towards trains over faces.

Even though initially it was assumed that this preference related to a lack of interest in faces, it is now understood that it is linked with personal interests (Alcañiz et al., 2021). There are studies that suggest that both neurodivergent and neurotypical children show a visual preference for trains over faces, driven by personal interests as opposed to avoidance of faces (Scheerer et al., 2021), opposing the traditional view that babies and young children are naturally drawn to faces. Eye-tracking devices also revealed different patterns of eye gaze in autistic children, such as looking at bodies more than faces. Similarly, instead of interpreting this as a lack of interest in social interactions, it is understood that autistic individuals process social information differently (Alcañiz et al., 2021). This reveals that autistic children engage differently with the world. Our assumptions about typical developmental patterns led to pathologising deviations from the 'norm' due to the overwhelming dominance of the medical perspective in education (see also Chapter 16).

This suggests that the lens through which we observe and assess children's play and social interactions during play may be unhelpful and damaging to their progress. This chapter focuses on play assessment through various lenses and approaches. The aim of this chapter is to challenge assumptions about the hierarchy of play types through the exploration of processing styles that deviate from the assumed 'mainstream norm'. This can inform the start of a much-needed discussion around what we value as educators and how we can aspire to learn from children and help them grow both in confidence and in academic achievement.

The Issue of Play Assessment

Play is crucial for young children's development in several key areas, including thinking skills, social interactions, emotions, physical abilities and language. Although there are various tools to evaluate how young children play, agreeing on a definition of play can be challenging (see Chapter 1). This lack of consensus makes it difficult to determine what specific aspects to assess. Most assessments focus primarily on the social and cognitive aspects of play, neglecting the emotional side, such as the positive feelings associated with oxytocin, a hormone that promotes bonding and happiness (Rebelo et al., 2024). This trend reflects the types of evaluation tools commonly used, which look at how children play together and their involvement in pretend or imaginative play. Examples of this type of assessments include Child-Initiated Pretend Play Assessment (ChiPPA); Structured Play Assessment (SPA); Test of Pretend Play (ToPP).

Non-statutory guidance for early years provision in England, Birth to 5 Matters (Early Education, 2021) explicitly references theorists like Vygotsky, Piaget, Bruner, and Bronfenbrenner. Their work helps us understand child development better, yet there is still a gap in how these theories address the unique developmental pathways of children with special needs. Governmental guidance in England, Development Matters (Department of Education, DfE, 2023), recognises that development can vary significantly for children with special needs. It suggests that educators may need to conduct in-depth observations to understand these children's individual needs. However, it remains somewhat vague about what 'detailed observations' entail.

This chapter explores how neurodivergent children play differently compared to their neurotypical peers. We will look at how understanding these differences can improve how we, their educators, observe and support children in Early Years settings, helping create inclusive environments.

This discussion challenges research that often remarks how autistic children may seem less engaged in play but doesn't always recognise the unique and meaningful ways they interact with their surroundings.

Observational Assessment of Play: A Step Towards Inclusive Practice

Assessment frameworks highlight the skills we deem important enough to merit our attention and investment in development. This chapter uses England as a key example, where the Early Years Foundation Stage (EYFS, DfE, 2024) framework provides practitioners with a set of predefined principles and objectives that children are expected to achieve. Development Matters (DfE, 2023) complements this by outlining how assessment should be carried out. According to Development Matters, practitioners must have a solid understanding of child development to accurately assess what children have learnt.

A significant issue that neither the EYFS nor the Development Matters documents address is that perceptions and understanding of child development are based on traditional theoretical models. For instance, Piaget established age-specific expectations for child development that remain widely accepted. While the contributions of such theories are invaluable, the fact that they unchallenged in educational practice poses problems. These theoretical benchmarks establish a standard against which education professionals and parents measure a child's success, which may not reflect individual circumstances.

Developmental theories related to autism suggest that early and subtle variations in a child's interactions with their environment can lead to atypical developmental trajectories, resulting in features commonly associated with autism (Happé, 2015). The Neurodiversity Paradigm suggests that there is a natural diversity among humans, which means that different processing and thinking styles naturally exist. It is now known that neurodevelopmental conditions such as autism are lifelong and neither can be nor should be treated. Yet, despite this natural variation, the aim of interventions, including those focused on play skills, often is to acquire neuronormative standards of play, failing to consider whether different developmental pathways and expressions of play might be valuable. This raises a question: How can we support children as unique individuals rather than classify them simply as 'successful' or 'failing' based on standardised norms, which expect every child's journey to be identical?

To genuinely assess individuals with a deep understanding of who they are, we must consider how to achieve this while they are required to meet specific targets. Additionally, we need to ensure that we fulfil our statutory obligations, set appropriate targets and avoid disadvantaging any child when determining our priorities and assessment methods.

Is the Development of All Children's Play Identical?

Early theorists such as Piaget (1951) and Parten (1932) viewed play as a means of developing cognitive and social skills. The former identified types of play linked with cognitive growth, such as sensory play, symbolic play and games with rules. The latter suggested there was an 'evolution' of play, and children progressed from solitary to parallel and then cooperative play (see Chapter 3). Due to the dominance of such theories, it is easy to forget that their development was based on a neurotypical lens. Suppose we were to assess an autistic child's play using these theories as our baseline. They would very likely be found to be 'lacking' as they follow a different neuro-developmental pathway.

Some attempts to shift this type of perception of play have been made, in which the activity itself and its level of 'sophistication' play little role, and the child's approach to a task is focused on instead (Sheridan et al., 2010). Howard (2010) observed that a playful attitude towards activities is more beneficial than trying to enforce different 'types' of play; being free to explore behaviours and feeling free from the potential to fail can benefit children's mental health and confidence.

Playfulness reflects an internal attitude towards an activity, showcasing the essence of play: even though those processes are internal, attempts have been made to assess the level of play-fulness each child displays. According to Westby (2022), evaluating playfulness is possible and the four elements used to evaluate playfulness include: 1. intrinsic motivation: enjoying the process of play and engaging with play because they want to; 2. internal control: being in charge when it comes to choosing when to play, who to play with and how to play; 3. The ability to suspend reality: children can pretend that they are someone else or that the object is something else or that they pretend to be doing something they are not actually doing; and 4. Framing: children recognising the activity as play, therefore communicating and interpreting social cues during play. Based on the author's observations, autistic children are less likely to be perceived as experiencing pleasure from play: the 'evidence' related to this is that they show repetitive behaviour with objects and restricted play interests. They may also focus on obscure topics. This type of interpretation, however, is flawed. Who is to decide what feels pleasurable to another person? And why is intense focus on one aspect or object of play rated as restricted? External observations are unlikely to produce accurate results when one attempts to rate playfulness from a professional or personal perspective. Therefore, rating an experience can be seen as flawed as attempting to measure a person's feelings externally.

Reflection Point 9.1

Can we assume that experiencing emotions such as pleasure can be observable from the outside?

What would your own criteria for observing playfulness include?

External play focuses on what is done with the objects of play and with the play partners. External play has a hierarchical classification: exploratory, relational, functional, pretend, symbolic (Westby, 2022; see also Chapter 3). This type of hierarchy, and age-related expectations of play go against the neurodiversity paradigm. This is because the scientific basis for this classification is based on expectations of neurotypical development.

What we consider play will inevitably affect the frameworks we use to assess children's play. There is little nuance regarding play assessment frameworks and ensuring they are used authentically. For example, most studies define functional play as *using one object as its function denotes*; however, Hancock's (2020) free play observation research findings revealed that it is a much more complex process. Developing a framework based on the observations of autistic children with Severe Learning Difficulties (SLD), Hancock captured the detail and development of their research participants' play, enabling them to establish what progress in functional play could look like to help inform the assessment of children with autism and SLD.

In relation to functional play skills, studies tell us that ideational praxis can be an area of difficulty in neurodivergent children: ideational praxis encompasses the process of recognising object affordances (what actions objects allow) and forming a mental plan for how to use them in a meaningful way (Moon & Dezember, 2023). Since ideational praxis is a significant predictor of playfulness in autistic children, explicitly teaching those skills can support play development (Serrada-Tejeda et al., 2024).

To successfully create enabling environments in which adults respond to individual interests, several prerequisites need to be met: adults supporting play need to have a clear understanding of the child's current abilities and interests, know what steps need to be taken to enhance learning, and hold a firm understanding of the curriculum and child development (Kilburn & Mills, 2019). This, however, can be partially effective. Knowing an individual and understanding their perspective should also be developed through understanding each child's thinking, which can be far removed from mainstream perceptions of child development. Without, for example, a firm grasp and understanding of the neurodiversity paradigm, it is difficult for practitioners to consider that there is an alternative perspective or different developmental pathways that neurodivergent children or children from different cultural backgrounds might follow when developing their play skills or learning through play.

Locus of control can be a further challenge for practitioners. For example, child-initiated play can be seen as repetitive and meaningless in autistic children, resulting in the child having limited freedom with their choices. The specific skills outlined in each child's education plan (Maynard, 2016) might dictate different priorities to those preferred by the child, limiting their sense of agency. Another study that highlights the importance of environmental control of the classroom environment (Unwin et al., 2021) found that when autistic children had control over the sensory equipment, they paid more attention and exhibited fewer repetitive and sensory behaviours. They also engaged in less stereotyped speech, produced fewer vocalisations, and demonstrated lower levels of activity. This highlights the importance of locus of control and the fact that what is seen as non-engagement maybe withdrawal due to lack of control or need for sensory regulation.

For years, the focus has been on developing autistic children's social skills by focusing on social play and ensuring children are taught how to act like their neurotypical classmates. Studies have found that combining lateral tutorship – defined as the parallel and unsynchronised exposure to information – with the principle of synchrony, which emphasises early dyadic communication and engagement, can lead to a new generation of strengths-based interventions that will support neurodivergent children develop their skills (Mottron & Gagnon, 2023). Lateral tutorship refers to a type of learning or teaching where individuals are exposed to information or experiences in a parallel and unsynchronised manner. It often involves exploring multiple pieces of information or tasks independently and without strict alignment in time or order. Parallel play, often identified as a 'preferred' type of play among autistic children is based on this principle. Synchrony, on the other hand, highlights the importance of reciprocal interactions, such as turn-taking in communication, joint attention, and shared timing in activities, which promote social skills. Combining lateral tutorship and synchrony may align well with neurodivergent learners, who can benefit from self-paced, exploratory, and flexible learning environments that don't rely on rigid, top-down instruction.

It is evident in the various examples given in this book that adult intervention limits children's imaginative play, while studies confirm that adults may also influence physical activity, negatively (Woodfield et al., 2021). In the case of neurodivergent children, however, adult support has been found to enable children to immerse themselves in their environment, which is crucial for the development of social skills (Syrjämäki et al., 2023). It is generally accepted that autistic children favour processing non-social information, while neurotypical children favour social information. For this reason, combining approaches can create more inclusive environments that focus on developing strengths as opposed to compensating for deficits. Since adult support is key for the engagement of autistic children, a balanced approach to ensure all children feel supported but also not obscured can transform neurodivergent children's relationship with play, their classmates and education environments.

Types and Stages of Play

In Chapter 3 of this book, types and stages of play have been discussed. Most research studies use concepts that agree with traditional theorists' models of play. Parten's Stages of Play, in which solitary, onlooker, parallel, associative and cooperative play are distinguished, remain dominant in ECEC, with cooperative play being the ultimate/most sophisticated stage and one to be pursued for all children. Smilansky's types of play include Functional, Constructive, Dramatic play, and games with rules.

Free play was also discussed in the chapter, discussing this type of play's high value and importance. What is rather problematic, however, is that play is defined through a neurotypical lens; here, we emphasise that play might look different for children with different neuro-developmental conditions. Play is also influenced by culture: even though the act of play is universal, cultural influences shape how play is perceived, structured and valued across different cultures. Cultural elements influence how children engage in and interpret play, leading to variations in how play is manifested (Gaskins et al., 2007; Norbeck, 1974; Oers, 2012). While this has been established through research, the Western normative paradigm of 'play' is rarely questioned. In the English context, for example, Development Matters (DfE, 2023), dictates that when observing a child and focusing on their personal, social and emotional development around the age of four, practitioners ought to be observing whether the child plays alongside others or alone; or if they take part in pretend play; if they take different roles when role-playing; and whether they can negotiate solutions to conflict. Considering that these are areas of difficulty for autistic children, using these criteria to assess their play may be problematic as it will focus on what they cannot do instead of valuing what they can do. Further to this, and again in the English context, the way early learning goals have been detailed in the EYFS handbook (2024) heavily rely on cooperative play to achieve the 'expected' level of development.

The goals also suggest that the neurotypical lens has been applied to come up with the assessment descriptors. If, for example, under 'Building Relationships', a neurodivergent child is being assessed against working cooperatively and taking turns, forming 'friendships' and 'showing sensitivity to others' they will not meet those targets, purely due to being expected to adapt to the way neurotypical children play. Even if there were to 'succeed' in this, they would achieve 'fitting in' rather than 'building relationships'. Since relationships are two-way and depend on the effort at least two different individuals put into that relationship, it would be appropriate to consider how neurodivergent children play and form relationships through play and teach neurotypical children how to be attuned to different types of play. The guidance and aims, therefore, should reflect this development of sensitivity to others, something that will benefit the broader children's population.

Assessment Frameworks

How do we assess progress related to play using frameworks, and how do we know that those frameworks represent the authentic experience of our Early Years learners? In this section, we explore some frameworks that can support observation-based play assessments.

One such example is Sproule's (2019) framework, in which the three assessment foci include the degree of playfulness, the locus of control and the type of learning taking place. These three areas are flexible as they do not dictate a hierarchy of types of play; on the contrary, 'playfulness' is described as an inner state of affairs rather than solely externalised behaviours. In the case of autistic children, this paradigm would be more inclusive since externalised social behaviours are less likely to occur. The success of such a framework also depends on the skilfulness of the observer and their subjective interpretation of the observed individuals and activities. To eliminate such a risk, using Hancock's (2012) method of breaking down functional play into multiple skills and levels within those skills can help practitioners record progress accurately. Functional play, seen through the eyes of autistic participants, is a complex and detailed task with multiple steps that can be achieved, and reveals the complexity of that task and teaches children how to problem-solve.

Hancock et al. (2012) identified different areas of functional play, such as 'one play object', 'two or more play objects', 'with self' and 'with environment' (p. 7) to capture the nuance of the children's play. She also suggested other areas to be considered such as 'facial expression', 'problem solving' and 'vocalisations' (p. 7). Those were broken down into smaller steps, such as 'accidentally touching an object, attempting action with the object, touching and manoeuvring the object with interest, using part of the object' (p. 6). Observing how autistic children learn and identifying the smaller steps they take enabled Hancock to capture progress and understand the unique characteristics of play in children with autism and SLD. This type of nuance ought to form part of any observation framework to enable teachers to monitor progress and ensure all children are supported in developing their strengths. Without detailed guidance and understanding of individual play, it is unlikely for neurodivergent children to excel in Early Years settings, where standard expectations are far removed from their style of play and forming relationships and relating to the environment. Other schemes that can be used to monitor progress of play are the *Show Progress assessment scheme* (n.d.), developed by the Autism Education Trust and the *Early Years Standards Framework* (Department for Education, 2024), also developed by the Autism Education Trust. Using such schemes can help evidence overall progression and ensure staff can support autistic children in Early Years settings through forming a deep understanding of the individual and assessing them based on smaller, discrete and externally observable aspects of play.

Case Study 9.1

Muriel is forming shapes with playdough in the sensory corner of her Reception class. Jacob approaches the table and takes one of the playdough tubs to take the blue playdough out. Without making eye contact, Muriel snatches the pot out of Jacob's hands and pushes him away. Jacob starts crying and protesting. The teaching assistant approaches Muriel and sternly states: 'You need to share and use kind hands. Jacob can use the blue playdough – you have the red tub'. The teaching assistant takes the blue tub from Muriel and hands it to Jacob. Muriel starts screaming and throwing things. She is moved to the 'calming corner' until she is able to calm down and rejoin the group. The class teacher explains to the other children that Muriel is autistic, and they need to be careful when they approach her because she finds interacting with other children difficult. As part of her formative assessment practice, the class teacher notes that Muriel does not yet show sensitivity to her own and to other's needs.

Reflection Point 9.2

1 If Muriel is assessed as 'not yet showing sensitivity to her own and other's needs', how should Jacob be assessed?
2 Would you, as a teacher, be able to state with confidence that Muriel did not show sensitivity to her own needs and to other children's needs?
3 What are your thoughts in relation to how the teaching assistant handled the situation?
4 Do you feel that the teacher's approach of advising children to be careful around Muriel can help Muriel and the other children achieve the goal of showing sensitivity to their own and to other's needs? How would you have handled the situation?

Play and the Autistic Child

Several studies have examined play as an intervention to support learning. Still, few consider play as the dependent variable (Kuhaneck et al., 2020): for example, changing the classroom setup, adults and children in a space, and using outdoor environments (independent variables) can induce changes in the nature of play (for example, solitary versus cooperative play) or level of engagement with play. For example, an autistic child may play with others when the classroom is set up with familiar board games they enjoy. However, they might only engage in solitary play when transferred to an outdoor environment that is devoid of familiar play equipment. If one were to observe this child in the earlier environment, they would conclude that the child enjoys playing with others, while if they observed the child in the latter environment, they could conclude that they only enjoy playing on their own. Additionally, there is a lack of a universally accepted intervention to enhance play outcomes in autistic children. Play ability is often perceived as fixed, with a child's tendency to engage with others seen as unchangeable. Unlike reading, where there are well-established, evidence-based interventions and a widespread belief that improvement is both possible and expected, play lacks equivalent structured approaches. As a result, little is known about how to systematically support the development of play. Evident from various studies has been the focus on play 'deficits' or 'differences' in relation to autistic children, using neurotypical frameworks when assessing play. Four of such 'deficits' are challenged in this section.

1   Autistic children play less frequently and show less flexibility and creativity, using play items in unusual or repetitive ways (Bodison, 2015; Kasari & Chang, 2014). For example, an autistic child might pick up a toy car and spin its wheel repetitively as a form of play. This can be judged as non-functional use of the object, and the type of play rated as 'less imaginative'. How confident do you feel as a practitioner that this is the correct observational judgement of this type of play? In a world that encourages us to specialise, could this not be rated as advanced play due to noticing the qualities of parts instead of the whole? Why is this of less value than playing with a car by pushing it against the floor and making 'vroom, vroom' sounds?

2   Autistic children lack symbolic play. This can lead to being socially rejected, having limited friendships and being victimised, which leads to more significant anxiety in relation to peer interaction over time (Mazurek & Kanne, 2010; Rowley et al., 2012; Schupp et al., 2013). This, however, often promotes a common misconception that autistic children cannot play imaginatively. However, autistic children can play imaginatively: what they may have difficulties with is social imagination. This involves understanding what it is like to be another person. For example, pretending to be a parent could be challenging for an autistic child to imitate or relate to. However, they might be excellent at pretending to be a superhero they are familiar with through watching TV, performing the role with great accuracy. The difference potentially lies in situations related to being a parent (such as putting a doll to bed or pretending to feed a teddy) being too close to reality; while being a pirate and finding a treasure is removed from day-to-day life and the surrounding narrative is intangible. Would we, therefore, say with conviction that, when observing play, a child is not good at symbolic play because they don't act out day-to-day interactions?

3   A further assumption in literature is that autistic children seem *unmotivated* to engage with their peers (Carré et al., 2015; Chevallier et al., 2012). The use of the term 'unmotivated' is problematic at many levels. It appears that when adults observe children play, their assessment of the situation often lies with the autistic child not wanting to engage with others. It also assumes that autistic children can join in but are not motivated to do so. Perhaps, there is an element of truth in the second statement: if the types of games neurotypical children play do not interest autistic children, is the problem that the autistic child does not find those games interesting or is the problem with the education professional that has not taken into account what the autistic child values so as to incorporate it into play provision?

4   Play has been cited as the goal of interventions (Warreyn et al., 2014), implying that autistic children do not know how to play. Is it, however, likely that the way autistic children play is not valued, and the way we assess their play is focused on what they lack as opposed to what they can bring to the table? The Neurodiversity Paradigm encourages us to value different types of thinking. How about valuing different expressions of play and judging them on their own merit? And how about teaching neurotypical children how to play with autistic children? If 'teaching' neurotypical play skills is of value to autistic children as it helps with socialisation, what could 'teaching' autistic play achieve for neurotypical and neurodivergent children alike?

The question is not whether play is of value or whether it helps children feel included. It is whether how we assess play tells us a lot more about our limited preconceptions of play and less about children's 'ability' to play. As established in an earlier chapter (See Chapter 1), the definition of play can change depending on whose perspective it is being defined. If we accept that '...play is any behaviour, activity or process initiated, controlled and structured by children themselves...' (UNCRC), how is it acceptable that play-focused research for autistic children insists on 'teaching' play skills to them? Could it be that we value certain play behaviours and not others? And could it be that our play frameworks lead us to a narrow-minded assessment of play?

Restricted and Repetitive Behaviours

'Restrictive and Repetitive Behaviours' (RRBs) in autism are often characterised as meaningless and interfering with the acquisition of life skills, negatively affecting the quality of life of individuals and their families (Leekam et al., 2011; Wolff et al., 2014). The term RRBs is used to describe behaviours and interests perceived as inflexible, restricted, and highly fixated, different from those of their peers (Evans, 2017; Oakes et al., 2016). Repetitive behaviours have received less attention than social communication difficulties in autism research, and often, when focused on, they have been approached as a trait to eliminate as they 'interfere' with learning skills. RRBs, based on the RBS-R questionnaire (Repetitive Behaviour Scale – Revised), 2024), a tool used by psychologists, teachers, or researchers, assess repetitive behaviours in autistic individuals include the following: stereotyped behaviour, compulsive behaviour, ritualistic behaviour, sameness behaviour, restricted behaviour and self-injurious behaviour (Esbensen et al., 2009). Repetitive behaviours can be observed in neurotypical and neurodivergent children in their toddler years (Kim & Lord, 2010). They tend to weaken as neurotypical children grow older (Larkin et al., 2017), but they persist or aggravate with age in neurodivergent children (Joseph et al., 2013).

Howard's (2012) study confirmed that repetitive behaviours include characteristics related to playfulness. It is further recognised that refusing to acknowledge repetitive activities as play disempowers autistic children and identifies them as 'unable' to play, dehumanising them and negating the originality of their play experience (Eisele & Howard, 2012). Ferguson et al. (2024) remark that RRBs are a tool to express or cope with anxiety, a form of emotional expression and regulation and a communicative tool, especially for those with limited verbal abilities. This negates the idea that RRBs are 'meaningless', and reinforces the idea that this type of nonverbal expression is a communicative tool and a form of personal expression. A positive correlation between repetitive sensory-motor behaviours and the development of social skills during toddlerhood has been identified (Chaxiong et al., 2021), suggesting that repetitive sensory-motor behaviours are an essential part of socialisation in autistic children's early years.

Case Study 9.2

Oliver is five years old and is starting in the Reception class at his new school. The staff are aware of his difficulties when exploring unfamiliar environments and meeting new people, so they want to make his transition as smooth as possible. After meeting with his mother in advance, they learnt that Oliver enjoys playing with Lego figures, particularly Ninjago. They proactively gathered resources related to this interest, including books, minifigures, Lego bricks, and colouring pages, and created a Ninjago corner.

A key staff member made a video to introduce herself and share her own special interest in needle felting. On the first day, it was agreed that Oliver would arrive 15 minutes earlier than his peers, so he could be taken through a quieter route to his classroom. The keyworker collected both Oliver and his mother and led them straight to the Ninjago corner. She sat down with her felting kit and began explaining her actions. Initially hesitant, Oliver looked at the minifigures and asked the keyworker where Lloyd the Green Ninja was. She identified Lloyd and placed him in front of Oliver while continuing her felting.

Oliver looked to his mother for encouragement, and she assured him that he could play with the toys. Once Oliver appeared comfortable playing with the resources, his mother mentioned she would leave and return to collect him at 3 o'clock when school finished. The keyworker confirmed that they would call her during the day if Oliver needed to speak to her or was uncomfortable in the setting.

When the other children arrived, they interacted with each other and the teacher in a separate area. Oliver asked the keyworker a question about Ninjago, which she couldn't answer, but she offered to bring in another expert to discuss Ninjago with him if he wanted. He agreed to this. Knowing that Ahmed, one of his new classmates, also liked Ninjago, the keyworker brought him over and asked if he would like to play. Ahmed began playing his game, and Oliver asked him his question, which Ahmed was able to answer. They continued playing alongside each other.

The keyworker's assessment reported that Oliver was building relationships with his peers and showed sensitivity to the needs of others.

Reflection Point 9.3

1 What areas of good practice can you identify in the practitioners' approach?
2 To what extent do you agree with the keyworker's assessment around Oliver 'building relationships' and 'showing sensitivity' and why?
3 How do you think Oliver's style of play can be extended to different areas of learning?

The Early Years Environment and Choices

Early Years environments in the United Kingdom are known for being 'rich' and offering 'choices' (see Chapter 14). They include diverse learning contexts such as role play, physical activities, and construction. Children are given the freedom to gravitate towards what they wish to play with and engage with their choices in their own way. In such an environment comes the assumption that neurodivergent children may engage with what is judged as a 'limited' range of materials, and in a 'restricted or repetitive' manner (typically the case for autistic children). Other neurodivergent children may briefly touch up all resources, without focusing on any of them in what would be classed as 'meaningful engagement' (this is typical engagement for children with Attention Deficit Hyperactivity Disorder). The main limitation of such observations is the failure to understand why neurodivergent children interact superficially with their environment and how they can be enabled to interact with it meaningfully. Questions we may ask include: Have children been gradually introduced to each of the resources? Without knowing what the resources are, how to interact with them, whether they are safe and whether they are available to them, autistic children are likely to choose to play with familiar toys in familiar environments. The lack of interaction in certain areas and with certain items, therefore, may have nothing to do with a child's capacity to play in that area and with that item but a lot to do with familiarity. Keeping this in mind, the way an area is set up can influence a child's behaviour and the results of observation/assessment of their play.

Summary

- Traditional theories of child development, promoting a mainstream 'norm' need to be challenged.
- Using alternative lenses when assessing neuroatypical children can enhance play opportunities for neurodivergent children and their neurotypical peers.
- Questioning the deficit approach to play assessment can transform the way we evaluate skills and support children develop their strengths. Focusing on what the child can do and does achieve gives practitioners more of an insight as to how the child develops.

- More nuance is needed in breaking down different types of skills demonstrated during play to ensure we observe all aspects of play and recognise their value while explicitly teaching skills that can enhance our children's play experiences.
- Identifying and explicitly teaching skills that enable more nuanced play such as ideational praxis skills as opposed to 'showing' children how to play can be a more productive and beneficial approach for all children.

Further Reading

Kuhaneck, H., Spitzer, S. L. and Bodison, S. C. (2020) A systematic review of interventions to improve the occupation of play in children with autism. *OTJR: Occupation, Participation and Health*, 40(2), 83–98. https://doi.org/10.1177/1539449219880531

This paper provides a helpful review of interventions targeting play that have been seen to be effective. It is written from an Occupational Therapy perspective, however the methods are highly relevant in education.

Westby C. (2022). Playing to pretend or "pretending" to play: Play in children with autism spectrum disorder. *Seminars in Speech and Language*, 43(4), 331–346. https://doi.org/10.1055/s-0042-1750348. Epub 2022 Jul 27. PMID: 35896409.

This article explains what different types of play entail and examines the different elements of each type of play that can be considered by practitioners when assessing a child. It also examines the relationship between learning new skills and play and how the one influences the other.

Conn, C. (2015). 'Sensory highs', 'vivid rememberings' and 'interactive stimming': Children's play cultures and experiences of friendship in autistic autobiographies. *Disability & Society*, 30(8), 1192–1206. https://doi-org.northampton.idm.oclc.org/10.1080/09687599.2015.1081094

This article contains autistic children's perceptions of play based on autobiographies. It offers some everyday examples of play experiences.

References

Alcañiz, M., Chicchi-Giglioli, I., Carrasco-Ribelles, L., Marín-Morales, J., Minissi, M., Teruel-García, G., Sirera, M., & Abad, L. (2021). Eye gaze as a biomarker in the recognition of autism spectrum disorder using virtual reality and machine learning: A proof of concept for diagnosis. *Autism Research*, 15, 131–145. https://doi.org/10.1002/aur.2636

Bodison, S. C. (2015). Developmental dyspraxia and the play skills of children with autism. *American Journal of Occupational Therapy*, 69(4), 1–6. https://doi.org/10.5014/ajot.2015.015909

Carré, J. M., Geniole, S. N., Ortiz, T. L., Bird, B. M., Videto, A., & Bonin, P. L. (2015). Digit ratio (2D:4D) and psychopathic traits moderate the effect of exogenous testosterone on socio-cognitive processes in men. *Psychoneuroendocrinology*, 62, 319–326. https://doi.org/10.1016/j.psyneuen.2015.08.022

Chaxiong, P., Burrows, C., Botteron, K., Dager, S., Estes, A., Hazlett, H., Schultz, R., Zwaigenbaum, L., Piven, J., & Wolff, J. (2021). Relations of restricted and repetitive behaviors to social skills in toddlers with autism. *Journal of Autism and Developmental Disorders*, 52, 1423-1434. https://doi.org/10.1007/s10803-021-05014-8

Chevallier, C., Kohls, G., Troiani, V., Brodkin, E. S., & Schultz, R. T. (2012). The social motivation theory of autism. *Trends in Cognitive Sciences*, 16(4), 231-239. https://doi.org/10.1016/j.tics.2012.02.007

Department for Education. (2023). *Development matters: Non-statutory curriculum guidance for the early years foundation stage*. London: Department for Education. Available at: https://www.gov.uk/government/publications/development-matters-2

Department for Education. (2024). *Statutory framework for the early years foundation stage: Setting the standards for learning, development and care for children from birth to five*. London: Department for Education. Available at: https://www.gov.uk/government/publications/early-years-foundation-stage-framework-2

Early Education. (2021). *Birth to 5 matters: Non-statutory guidance for the early years foundation stage*. Available at: www.birthto5matters.org.uk

Eisele, G., & Howard, J. (2012). Exploring the presence of characteristics associated with play within the ritual repetitive behaviour of autistic children. *International Journal of Play*, 1(2), 139-155. https://doi.org/10.1080/21594937.2012.692202

Esbensen, A. J., Schwichtenberg, A. J., & Shattuck, P. T. (2009). Sleep problems in children with autism spectrum disorders: A review. *Research in Autism Spectrum Disorders*, 3(1), 151-161. https://doi.org/10.1016/j.rasd.2008.04.001

Evans, B. (2017). *The metamorphosis of autism: A history of child development in Britain*. Manchester: Manchester University Press.

Ferguson, E., Spackman, E., Cai, R., Hardan, A., & Uljarević, M. (2024). Characterizing associations between emotion dysregulation, anxiety, and repetitive behaviors in autistic youth with intellectual disability. *Autism Research: Official Journal of the International Society for Autism Research*. https://doi.org/10.1002/aur.3207

Gaskins, S., Haight, W., & Lancy, D. (2007). *The cultural construction of play* (pp. 179-202). Taylor & Francis. https://doi.org/10.4324/9780203936511

Hancock, C. (2020). We don't play that way, we play this way: Functional play behaviours of children with autism and severe learning difficulties. *Research in Developmental Disabilities*, 103, 103688. https://doi.org/10.1016/j.ridd.2020.103688

Hancock, K. J., Lawrence, D., Mitrou, F., & Zubrick, S. R. (2012). The association between playgroup participation, learning competence and social-emotional wellbeing for children aged 4-5 years in Australia. *Australasian Journal of Early Childhood*, 37(2), 72-81.

Happé, F. (2015). Autism as a neurodevelopmental disorder of mind-reading. *Journal of the British Academy*, 3, 197-209. https://doi.org/10.5871/jba/003.197

Howard, J. (2010). In P. Broadhead, J. Howard, & E. Wood (Eds.), *Play and learning in the early years: From research to practice*. London: SAGE Publications.

Howard, J. (2012). The impact of children's perception of an activity as play rather than not-play on emotional well-being. *Child: Care, Health and Development*, 39(5), 737-742. https://doi.org/10.1111/j.1365-2214.2012.01405.x

Joseph, L., Thurm, A., Farmer, C., & Shumway, S. (2013). Repetitive behavior and restricted interests in young children with autism: Comparisons with controls and stability over 2 years. *Autism Research*, 6(6), 584-595. https://doi.org/10.1002/aur.1316

Kasari, C., & Chang, Y. -C. (2014). Play development in children with autism spectrum disorders: Skills, object play, and interventions. In F. Volkmar, S. Rogers, R. Paul, & K. A. Pelphrey (Eds.), *Handbook of autism and pervasive developmental disorders* (4th ed., pp. 207-229). Hoboken, NJ: Wiley.

Kilburn, V., & Mills, K. (2019). Play for children with special educational needs. In T. Bruce, L. Brooker, & C. Nutbrown (Eds.), *The Routledge international handbook of early childhood education*. London: Routledge.

Kim, S. H., & Lord, C. (2010). Restricted and repetitive behaviors in toddlers and preschoolers with autism spectrum disorders based on the Autism Diagnostic Observation Schedule (ADOS). *Journal of Child Psychology and Psychiatry*, 51(8), 911-920. https://doi.org/10.1111/j.1469-7610.2010.02251.x

Kircher-Morris, E. (2022). What is neurodiversity?. *Raising twice-exceptional children*. https://doi.org/10.4135/9781529767438

Kuhaneck, H., Spitzer, S. L., & Bodison, S. C. (2020). A systematic review of interventions to improve the occupation of play in children with autism. *OTJR: Occupation, Participation and Health*, 40(2), 83-98. https://doi.org/10.1177/1539449219880531

Larkin, F., Hobin, E., & van Kessel, S. (2017). *Play in autism: Evidence-based approaches to promoting social communication*. York: York St John University.

Leekam, S. R., Prior, M. R., & Uljarević, M. (2011). Restricted and repetitive behaviours in autism spectrum disorders: A review. *European Child & Adolescent Psychiatry*, 20(4), 221-232. https://doi.org/10.1007/s00787-011-0166-8

Maynard, T. (2016). *Exploring outdoor play in the early years*. Maidenhead: Open University Press.

Mazurek, M. O., & Kanne, S. M. (2010). Friendship and internalizing symptoms among children and adolescents with autism spectrum disorders. *Journal of Autism and Developmental Disorders*, 40(12), 1512-1520. https://doi.org/10.1007/s10803-010-1014-y

Moon, M., & Dezember, M. (2023). Learning connections: From practice to praxis. *Journal of Museum Education*, 48, 89-91. https://doi.org/10.1080/10598650.2023.2215961

Mottron, L., & Gagnon, D. (2023). Debate: How far can we modify the expression of autism by modifying the environment?. *Child and Adolescent Mental Health*. https://doi.org/10.1111/camh.12686

Norbeck, E. (1974). Anthropological views of play. *Integrative and Comparative Biology*, 14, 267-273. https://doi.org/10.1093/ICB/14.1.267

Oakes, A., Thurman, A. J., McDuffie, A., & Abbeduto, L. (2016). Repetitive behavior in fragile X syndrome: Profiles and predictors in adolescence and adulthood. *Journal of Intellectual Disability Research*, 60(8), 777-787. https://doi.org/10.1111/jir.12307

Oers, B. (2012). *Culture in play* (pp. 957-988). https://doi.org/10.1093/OXFORDHB/9780195396430.013.0046

Parten, M. B. (1932). Social participation among pre-school children. *Journal of Abnormal and Social Psychology*, 27(3), 243-269.

Piaget, J. (1951). *Play, dreams and imitation in childhood*. London: Routledge & Kegan Paul.

Rebelo, J. A., Diniz, A., & Esgalhado, G. (2024). Assessment of play in preschool-age: A systematic review. *European Journal of Psychological Assessment*. Advance Online Publication. https://doi.org/10.1027/1016-9040/a000520

Repetitive Behavior Scale-Revised. (2024). *A comprehensive tool for assessing autism spectrum disorders*. Available at: https://neurolaunch.com/repetitive-behavior-scale-revised/#google_vignette

Rowley, E., Chandler, S., Baird, G., Simonoff, E., Pickles, A., Loucas, T., & Charman, T. (2012). The experience of friendship, victimization and bullying in children with an autism spectrum disorder: Associations with child characteristics and school placement. *Research in Autism Spectrum Disorders*, 6(3), 1126–1134. https://doi.org/10.1016/j.rasd.2012.03.004

Scheerer, N., Birmingham, E., Boucher, T., & Iarocci, G. (2021). Attention capture by trains and faces in children with and without autism spectrum disorder. *PLoS One*, 16. https://doi.org/10.1371/journal.pone.0250763

Schupp, C. W., Simon, D., Corbett, B. A., Ryan, N., & Mendoza, S. (2013). Cortisol responsivity differences in children with autism spectrum disorders during free and cooperative play. *Journal of Autism and Developmental Disorders*, 43, 2405–2417. https://doi.org/10.1007/s10803-013-1796-9

Serrada-Tejeda, S., May-Benson, T., Bundy, A., Santos-Del-Riego, S., Rodríguez-Pérez, M., & Pérez-De-Heredia-Torres, M. (2024). Ideational praxis, play, and playfulness: A cross-sectional study of autistic children. *American Journal of Occupational Therapy: Official Publication of the American Occupational Therapy Association*, 78(4). https://doi.org/10.5014/ajot.2024.050397

Sheridan, M., Howard, J., & Alderson, D. (2010). *Play in early childhood: From birth to six years* (3rd edn.). London: Routledge.

Show Progress. (n.d.). *AET autism progression framework 2.0 powered by show progress*. Available at: https://www.showprogress.co.uk/aet-progression-framework.html

Sproule, L., Walsh, G., & McGuinness, C. (2019). More than 'just play': Picking out three dimensions of a balanced early years pedagogy. *International Journal of Early Years Education*, 27, 409–422. https://doi.org/10.1080/09669760.2019.1628011

Syrjämäki, M., Reunamo, J., Pesonen, H., Pirttimaa, R., & Kontu, E. (2023). The involvement of autistic children in early childhood education. *European Journal of Special Needs Education*, 38, 879–893. https://doi.org/10.1080/08856257.2023.2179310

Unwin, K., Powell, G., & Jones, C. (2021). The use of Multi-Sensory Environments with autistic children: Exploring the effect of having control of sensory changes. *Autism*, 26, 1379–1394. https://doi.org/10.1177/13623613211050176

Warreyn, P., Roeyers, H., & de Groote, I. (2014). Social-communicative abilities as treatment goals for preschool children with ASD: The importance of imitation, joint attention, and play. *Developmental Medicine & Child Neurology*, 56(8), 712–716. https://doi.org/10.1111/dmcn.12455

Westby C. (2022). Playing to pretend or "pretending" to play: Play in children with autism spectrum disorder. *Seminars in Speech and Language*, 43(4), 331–346. https://doi.org/10.1055/s-0042-1750348. PMID: 35896409.pmid:35896409

Wolff, J. J., Boyd, B. A., Elison, J. T.,et al (2014). Longitudinal patterns of repetitive behaviour in toddlers with autism. *Journal of Child Psychology and Psychiatry*, 55(8), 945–953. https://doi.org/10.1111/jcpp.12207

Woodfield, L., Tatton, A., Myers, T., & Powell, E. (2021). Predictors of children's physical activity in the early years foundation stage. *Journal of Early Childhood Research*, 20, 199–213. https://doi.org/10.1177/1476718X211052797

10
Planning for Play

Karen Boardman and Jennie Swift

Chapter Objectives

This chapter will support you to:

- Understand some of the underpinning principles of planning spaces for playful learning indoors and outdoors, with the child as the focus.
- Explore the key features of an effective enabling environment to support children in following their own play interests as active learners.
- Reflect on the role of the adult and the use of resources in the learning environment to support active play and exploration, so that children can explore their own ideas and interests in depth.

Introduction

The definition of 'play', its relationship with the curriculum and the role of adults in children's learning through play are explored in previous chapters of this book. This chapter is focused on planning experiences and environments for play. We invite you to reflect and delve deep into your pedagogical approach – your philosophy of play and how you purposefully plan for play that is meaningful for young children.

The field of Early Childhood Education and Care (ECEC) is universally contentious in the United Kingdom and often internationally, particularly relating to debates about quality and playful pedagogies (McDowall Clark, 2017; Moyles et al. 2002; Wood, 2013). When you include planning for play, the debate becomes utterly confusing based on how adults plan for play within busy curriculum and setting timetables. Murray (2018) highlights that there appears to be no unanimously agreed definition of play to support planning for play. However, substantial research evidence (Campbell-Barr et al. 2023; Evangelou et al. 2009; Goouch, 2008; Siraj-Blachford et al. 2002; Sylva et al. 2010) tells us that learning is very much dependent on social interactions and contexts - cultural, relational and environmental. Spaces, places, adults, other children and resources all influence learning and development (Fairchild, 2021). The quality of these early relationships and social interactions within play ensures that there are then opportunities for further learning (Meltzoft, 1995; Whitebread, 2012).

In this chapter, we draw upon the seminal research of the Researching Effective Pedagogy in the Early Years (REPEY) study (Siraj-Blatchford et al. 2002) and the Effective Provision of Pre-school Education (EPPE) Project (Sylva et al. 2004), focusing on the collaborative process between practitioner/teacher, the learner and the learning environment where children develop natural learning strategies by learning though active play, investigation and social contexts – it is about the children and their play. We will also explore the contemporary research from Suzanne Axelsson's 'Original Learning Approach' (OLA) theory and 'Playarista' concepts in planning for play. Axelsson (2023) refers to play responsive adults with 'deep pockets filled with play' to nurture a pedagogy of hope, which is a good starting point to think about planning spaces for play.

Planning Spaces for Play: An Enabling Environment

McDowall Clark (2017) and Sharp et al. (2002) highlight that formal learning (academic skills-based) is just too abstract for many children's development. Therefore, young children need to have plenty of active, hands-on learning experiences to fully embed their own learning. For example, children may know that a paintbrush can make marks on paper, yet to hold the paint-brush in order to make these marks requires the physical skills to do this in a certain way. Next, to paint a picture that has meaning for the child – to consider the texture of paint, how it drips, blobs, shapes and is sized on the paper, needs to be continuously explored and experimented with in a variety of ways led by the child, which can only be developed through independent hands-on experiences learnt over time. In essence, an enabling environment is an environment that priori-tises interactive hands-on learning over structured learning, alongside the opportunity to build and sustain reciprocal social and emotional relationships. Let's unpick the concept of planning spaces for play within an enabling environment further, given that many voices (policymakers, regulatory bodies, and families) often sit in this vague place where only formal learning through structured tasks is valued.

Birth to Five Matters (Early Education, 2021, p. 35) outlines the key points of an effective learning environment having a focus on:

- individual and diverse development needs of all children;
- safety security, comfort, choice, access, and opportunity;
- opportunities to be physically active – movement, interaction, creativity, and imagination;
- experiences that nurture independent exploration and collaborative exploration;
- inclusive access to open-ended resources indoors and outdoors.

Clement explores enabling environments indoors and outdoors in Chapter 11, with a focus on where play happens. Here, we build on this and encourage you to reflect on the key features of an effective enabling environment in supporting children to follow their own play interests as active learners – not structured adult-led activities.

Reflection Point 10.1

Think about planning spaces for play. Consider the following points:

- Mental well-being, physical, and socio-emotional enjoyment (Andreopoulou & Moustakas, 2019) – where is the fun?
- Open-ended spaces and resources versus closed spaces and movement – can children move resources and their play around in the spaces you have planned?
- Collaborations – between the child, adult, the family, and community?
- Permissions for play – do children feel like they have permission to play in the way that they wish to?
- 'Enabling' refers to making something possible or easier for the child.
- The child's voice in play spaces.

Axelsson's (2023) OLA explores how play evolves when the children take the lead. This OLA is holistic and is sensitively connected to culture, context and building relationships, especially outdoors in nature (see also Chapter 12). When we are planning play spaces, it is vital that we listen to the children and go even further to ensure that their voices, choices, and interests are positioned within the play spaces to enable the children to take the lead in their own playful learning – having ownership and agency. For example, most settings have a writing area or a mathematics exploration area. What if the children decide to take the resources from these areas to the sand tray to try to work out a concept for themselves? Consider firstly if the children have permission to do this and secondly, if the spaces allow these connections to be developed.

Axelsson (2023) advocates for ten essential threads to embed within playful learning:

1 wonder;
2 curiosity;
3 joy;
4 knowledge;
5 imagination;
6 interaction;
7 risk;
8 time;
9 reflection;
10 listening.

> ## Reflection Point 10.2
>
> Think about the ten essential threads from Axelsson's OLA.
>
> Reflect on how you could build these threads as opportunities for all children within your planning for play spaces - where might the joy and wonder come from in your planning for play?
>
> Consider the time afforded to play - the time to *wallow and belong* within these play spaces to create meaningful experiences for the children.

Does All Play Need to Be Planned for?

Let's extend our discussion on planning for play with a critical provocation – can play be planned? Should we be planning for play at all?

Initially, the Early Years Foundation Stage (EYFS) documentation (DfES, 2007) in England clearly emphasised active learning and child-initiated learning through play. Although the message about play was clear – unhelpfully, how the adult sets about planning for play was not so plainly defined. The later version of the EYFS in 2008 offered specific definitions about child-initiated learning versus adult-led learning, still leaving the debate about planning for play open to inter-pretation. The current version of the EYFS (DfE, 2024) is still highly ambiguous about planning for play. Yet, we can hold on to the strength of the Characteristics of Effective Teaching and Learning (CoEL) which underpin the EYFS curriculum in England:

- playing and exploring – children investigate and experience things, and 'have a go';
- active learning – children concentrate and keep on trying if they encounter difficulties, and enjoy achievements;
- creating and thinking critically – children have and develop their own ideas, make links between ideas and develop strategies for doing things.

(DfE, 2017, p. 10)

The CoEL are very clear about the position of the child within playful learning and the position of play for learning. However, the CoEL are not always embedded within our pedagogies in our settings in England in the same way that play permeates Reggio Emilia practices (Rinaldi, 2005) or other international approaches (see also Chapter 20). For some strange reason, we seem to separate play from 'work' in our settings and schools in England – children can go and play after the work is done (Moyles, 2010), which suggests that we are not listening to the plethora of evidence-based research or the children. Because of this pressure to foreground 'work' or more formalised learning over child-led play agendas, many educators are resisting and subverting their practice to enable children to play (Albin-Clark & Archer, 2023).

Reflection Point 10.3

If you are working in early years settings or schools in Wales, Scotland or Northern Ireland, to what extent do you think there are similar issues to those we have outlined in England?
   Reflect on the formal learning versus play agenda.

Children's cultural experiences and connections in every aspect of their lives (families and communities) influence their play choices – how they play, who they choose to engage with and the resources they play with. Vivian Gussin Paley (1993) championed the power of play and community in fostering empathy, social justice and a sense of belonging alongside imaginative playful learning. Her seminal work on storytelling, fantasy, fairness and friendship has influenced educators worldwide in shaping our understanding of children's learning and development. The Learning Stories approach, based in New Zealand, also aligns with Paley's emphasis on valuing children's individual narratives through play (Carr & Lee, 2012). However, we should not assume that children naturally engage in storytelling or friendships within their playful learning, given that Chesworth (2016) reminds us about the importance of the many cross-cultural contexts within play – the funds of knowledge that children bring into their play.

It is highly problematic to define the concept of play or to capture the essence of play because play is a process (Moyles, 2005). Moyles (2015: p. 16) highlights that the many attempts to define play are consistent with the concept of 'catching bubbles' (see also Chapter 1). Consequently, Bruce (1991, 2011) argues that play is a demonstration of the way that young children apply, use, test and combine the responses of their own first-hand experiences, which makes perfect sense viewed from the perspective of the child. Remember that play can and does happen anywhere and does not necessarily need to have resources, given that children's play preferences are noticeable whatever the location. For example, children will still play football without having a ball. Bringing us back to planning for play and if play does indeed need to be planned for, let's explore what play as a process can accomplish which is observable and measurable by adults and able to be documented, given successful achievement of outcomes is required within our settings and schools. During play, children can with opportunity and permission:

- develop their confidence and competence;
- experiment with people and things;
- make choices, test out choices and make significant decisions;
- organise their own time and activities;
- build up their memory stores for transferable learning;
- think, know and remember more;
- investigate cause and effect, and solve problems;
- build language, talk, and vocabulary;

- develop interpersonal interactive and negotiation strategies;
- develop imagination and creativity;
- learn about self-regulation and co-regulation;
- adapt behaviours and attitudes to fit in with the cultural habits and practices of social communities;
- master a wide range of skills and concepts;
- interpret new events and interpret trauma affects;
- make meaning through new and established experiences and build connections;
- become emotionally engaged and highly motivated in their own learning;
- develop self-concepts and the concept of social self in relation to others;
- build fine and gross motor physical skills.

(Bradbury et al., 2025)

When children are responsible for organising their own learning, they will investigate and engage with things that interest them. How we set up our environments, the resources we provide and the interactions versus interference as adults (Fisher, 2016) will either offer the children valuable experiences to take the lead on their learning or limit their learning (Taggart et al., 2015). Remembering that valuing the qualities, uniqueness and potential of all children is at the core of the EYFS (DfE, 2024) principles and practice in England (Siraj-Blatchford, 2010b) as well as those across other UK nations (see Chapter 14), and within international frameworks of learning (Leggett, 2020).

Reflection Point 10.4

Using the list above, consider your role in planning for play:

1 How will you organise your environment to enable playful learning?
2 What do you need to plan?

Reflect on how the indoor environment will be different to the outdoor environment and offer further opportunities for open-ended play.

Remember that all the seminal and contemporary research evidence advocates learning environments that prioritise interactive hands-on learning over structured adult-led learning, with embedded opportunities for developing, building and sustaining reciprocal social and emotional relationships to offer the highest quality outcomes (Broadhead, 2006; Evangelou et al., 2009; Siraj-Blachford et al., 2002; Siraj-Blachford & Sylva, 2004). Positioning children at the centre of the process, as experts in their own playful learning, shifts the focus from adults measuring specific outcomes to children having choices to follow their own interests and lead their own learning.

Organising Resources in the Learning Environment to Support Active Learning, Play, and Exploration

There are many approaches to designing a learning environment to meet the needs of all children. Often these are designed to initially consider the space available, the vision and values of the setting (philosophy) and how the environment can support children to learn and develop holistically and across all areas of learning of the curriculum. Previously in this chapter and within many other chapters of this book, we have considered the learning environments that effectively meet all children's needs and their interests. This section will now consider some key considerations for organising the learning environment to support active learning, play and exploration. The focus is on open-ended resources to enable the children to creatively make connections within their play and within the spaces for play. While embracing open-ended materials encourages active learning, creativity and flexibility, we also need to ensure that we are offering children the freedom of agency and autonomy – it is about their choices. Once again, we need to ask ourselves about the permissions we give for children to play. Here are some key considerations for creating and maintaining an effective learning environment to support active play for you to consider:

- Evaluate your thinking about your environment – how is it reflective of your philosophy (vision, values, and beliefs). Consider the key messages you wish to convey about the voice of the child and the learning opportunities.
- Think carefully about the layout of your environment and how this will affect the way in which children play, connect and explore. Are you making the best use of your available space and resources?
- Reflect on how you choose and display the resources in your environment – this will define how the children use them – or not. Choose resources that are flexible and allow open-ended experiences for children.
- Evaluate how you afford permission to play and connect – can children move the resources freely between spaces? For example, wild weaving outdoors, loose parts play, sound and music resources, easily transportable?
- Think about how your environment actively engages and welcomes families and communities – can children see themselves reflecting within their realities respectfully?
- Reflect on the spaces you are providing for quality interactions with peers and adults indoors and outdoors.
- Consider how your environment enables learning across all the areas of learning, including children's well-being.
- Think about defining flexible spaces for creativity, quiet relaxation, hiding, pretend play, noisy play, spaces for sleep, food and rest, social spaces;
- Extend how you choose 'loose' rather than fixed materials and resources.
- Carefully consider the outdoor environment and resources – open-ended, natural, in and within nature (Boardman, 2024).

- Challenge the need for fixed zoned areas – mark-making area, writing tables, etc. – if children are free to lead their own learning, then they really do not need to be in a zoned space to carry out this learning – writing can be done anywhere and should be done everywhere.
- Conduct learning walks to see, feel and hear how children engage with the environment and the resources.
- Consider how the child is at the centre of the planning for play.
- Create provocation spaces.

Learning Provocation Spaces

Learning provocation spaces are open-ended spaces for children to explore a variety of different objects or experiences – creating awe and wonder and nurturing creativity. Longstaffe (2020) explains that a provocation is something that provokes action and/or stimulates thinking (see also Chapter 5). The beauty of provocations is that there is no right or wrong way and no imposed outcome, as they are completely open-ended explorations. Learning provocations are very different to scenario-based learning experiences, where the scenario might be that the children receive a letter from the Wolf inviting Red Riding Hood to visit him. Here the children are exploring many scenarios and possibilities for learning, guided by the adults, with an outcome in mind. For example, the children might be encouraged to design a poster to warn Red Riding Hood about the dangers of the woods and wolves. With learning provocations, there are infinite possibilities to spark the children's interests and develop their critical thinking skills. Adults may be invited into these play spaces by the children but are not necessary and are not there to lead any outcomes. The play is led by the children.

Here are a few examples to consider:

- maps, magnifying glasses, and magnets;
- picture frames, framed outlines;
- suitcase, treasure chests, and interesting shaped boxes;
- sculptures, artefacts, natural art;
- conceptual – seasons, weather, light, and shade;
- loose parts from nature, buttons, ribbon, and fabric selections.

A word of warning – try not to put all your learning provocations in a tuff tray. The children will soon see this as a defined, structured space and may not choose to engage.

Case Study 10.1: Voice of the Practitioner in Planning for Provocations

Rebecca planned and set up a learning provocation outdoors for the children in Reception with ice 'baubles' in early Spring. Rebecca checked allergies and risk-assessed the provocation. She placed a selection of everyday objects (metal spoon, plastic figure, toothbrush,

(Continued)

beaded bracelet, and wooden fork) and some unusual objects (unusual pebble, colourful stones, crystals, tiny clockface, fabric, etc) into an ice mould, filled these with water and froze the bauble-shaped moulds. Just before they froze solid, Rebecca placed pieces of string in each bauble so that she could hang these from the branches outdoors. Rebecca also placed some (the ones that didn't quite work out) on the outdoor wooden table.

The awe, wonder, curiosity, and joy were truly fabulous when the children first noticed the ice baubles hanging from the tree. The children took great delight in investigating the ice baubles hanging from the tree branches and picking up or trying to pick up the ice baubles from the outdoor table – obviously they are frozen and are cold to touch. The provocation maintained the children's interest for a long period of time – some children returning to this provocation to check-in on the objects, the ice structure and state of solidity. Rebecca observed that some of the children independently came inside to get their gloves to continue to explore, other children sought out objects to try to crack the baubles, some children watched, touched, used magnifying glasses, while other children brought timers to their play – sand and counting timers. Rebecca had not planned an outcome – she didn't really know if or when the ice baubles might or would melt, given the temperature in Spring. The possibilities for learning were endless – the range of materials offered greater scope for discussion about how they got there, will they melt, when they might melt, the position of the sun and many more critical thinking skills at play. More importantly, this provocation included children that sometimes did not engage with other provocations, perhaps because it was outdoors or perhaps because it was an abstract concept not previously experienced or explored.

Rebecca reflects on this provocation and notes that although this is still a planned activity, led by the adult, it was difficult to predict and set the learning outcomes for this prior to the provocation taking place, as expected by her planning format and the links to the areas of learning required for all planned activities in Reception. In addition, Rebecca appreciates that the learning from the ice baubles will continue to develop further than 'in the moment'. Rebecca reflects on her planning documentation and realises that capturing the learning beforehand is very much adult-driven in her planning approach. Rebecca decides to utilise a more child-led focus for documenting children's playful learning. Rebecca now uses Floorbooks with the children so that the children can document their own learning collaboratively and independently. She also shares the Floorbooks with parents and families.

Challenges of Planning to Support Playful Learning

The challenges of planning to enable playful learning will always be an enigma, particularly while situated within a narrow outcomes-driven standardised agenda (Boardman, 2024; Moss, 2016;

Roberts-Holmes, 2015; Roberts-Holmes & Moss, 2021; Wood, 2019). The outcome appears to be more important than the process – the process being play here. Fairchild (2021) considers the inter-related place-space environments within ECEC and how as professionals, we negotiate the mapping of policy environments (curriculum documentation, regulatory bodies), professional (networking, professional development) and practice (play spaces, adult-child interactions, documenting learning). This is a challenge for us all in ECEC, given that planning for play is a complex mix of all these issues. It is important to remember that curriculum frameworks are a guide for interpretation. The statutory guidelines are non-negotiable, but the 'how' in the planning for your own learning environment is to be negotiated and matched to the needs of the children in the setting (see also Chapter 16). Nonetheless, this is much easier said than done. The following case study highlights the complexity of provision for open-ended playful learning.

Case study 10.2: 'Getting Rid of the Bikes and Trikes'

The practitioners in a busy 60-place nursery setting always raise the bikes and trikes outdoors as a challenge for planning outdoor activities, staffing, health and safety. For example, a team member needs to be carefully observing the bikes and trikes as the children go too fast, bump into objects and other children, fall off, argue with each other and it always feels like a chore. Plus, the team feel like they are using negative language with the children outdoors, which is not part of the ethos of the setting, and it is making them feel uncomfortable.

The new setting Manager suggests that they might need to reflect on these resources and asks the team to carefully consider the value of bikes and trikes as an open-ended resource for outdoors. At first, this causes uproar from the team, given that the setting is situated within a disadvantaged area of the Local Authority identified as an Education Investment Area (EIA) by the Department of Education (DfE). The team feel that the children need to continue to develop their physical development skills, especially their fine and gross motor skills, given they may not necessarily have these opportunities at home. The team feel that the wheeled toys meet the development needs of the children in their setting. The setting Manager disagrees and asks the team to consider other open-ended resources for outdoor play. She suggests that bikes and trikes only really do one thing, particularly as the setting does not encourage the children to use them for any other reason other than riding on.

The Manager tasks the team with rethinking their outdoor resources with a focus on only having open-ended materials to support the children in the setting. She removes the wheeled toys from the provision for the time-being.

Bilton and Crook (2016) advise that setting up an environment to support playful learning outdoors should not include bikes, plastic wheeled toys or any fixed climbing equipment (plastic or otherwise). Instead, Bilton (2017) advocates for a wider range of materials to encourage building, designing, movement, space and, most importantly, to enable the children to express agency and to be empowered to play in the way they want to play. However, bikes, trikes and wheeled toys do offer many other possibilities for young children – there is space to support all play, planned and unplanned in our settings. Canning's (2020) research explores children's empowerment in play – participant, voice and ownership (see also Chapter 6). Canning highlights that all discussions about play are challenging without adding the further complexity of empowerment in the play debate. Yet, this is a significant feature for us all to consider. Offering children choices in their play, enabling children to be confident in making these choices and placing the child at the centre of all planning for play is the challenge facing us all.

Summary

- Young children need to have plenty of active, hands-on experiences to fully embed and direct their own learning.
- When planning play spaces, consider the voice and participation of the child first and foremost.
- Embed the CoEL within provision and pedagogy.
- Plan spaces with open-ended resources, lots of opportunities and afford children permission to play.
- Challenge your thinking about defined fixed spaces and zoned areas.
- Consider learning provocation spaces.

Further Reading

STATE OF PLAY. An interim report from the Raising the Nation Play Commission. Centre for Young Lives (2025) 67b5f05190b914fe09e20a6f_462085d4548883cf952c57eb8118aec7_[FINAL - Digital] State of Play - Raising the Nation Play Commission.pdf

This report highlights the importance of play for all children and makes a series of recommendations for policymakers, schools and communities and regulatory bodies. It is a useful read alongside the debates for play in settings and schools.

Bradbury, A., Wright, D., Boardman, K., Thompson, P., Jarvis, P., Cowley, S., Veale, V., Wayne, D., Swailes, R., Scollan, A., Grimmer, T., & Renshaw, K. (2025). Play matters. Available at: https://www.early-years-reviews.com/play-matters

This essential guide, created by leading early childhood professionals, is packed with research, insights and practical strategies on the power of play in early childhood. With contributions from top experts and a foreword by Michael Rosen, this guide is a must read for educators, parents, families and anyone passionate about children's playful learning.

Olsen, A., Tangen, S., Sando, O. J., and Hansen Sandseter, E. B. (2025). Toddlers' actualisation of affordances during free exploration in a varied natural environment. *International Journal of Play*, 1–15. https://doi.org/10.1080/21594937.2025.2464349

This study investigates how toddlers use a varied natural environment when allowed to explore freely. The findings advocate that toddlers should be given ample time and space to explore nature freely, in areas with varied and challenging surfaces and a rich diversity of natural elements and materials to explore.

Canning, N. (2020) Children's Empowerment in play. Participation, voice and ownership. London: Routledge.

Read more about Natalie's research on empowerment in children's play. This TACTYC research-informed edition of the TACTYC book series includes lots of examples and Natalies' Empowerment Framework to support planning for play.

References

Albin-Clark, J., & Archer, N. (2023). Playing social justice: How do early childhood teachers enact the right to play through resistance and subversion? *Prism*, 5(2), 1-22.

Andreopoulou, P., & Moustakas, L. (2019). Playful learning and skills improvement. *Open Journal for Educational Research*, 3(1), 25-38. Centre for Open Access in Science. http://doi.org/10.32591/coas.ojer.0301.03025a

Axelsson, S. (2023). The original learning approach: Weaving together playing, learning, and teaching. In *Early childhood*. St Paul, MN: Redleaf Press.

Bilton, H. (2017). *Taking the first steps outside; under threes learning and developing in the natural environment*. Abingdon: Routledge.

Bilton, H., & Crook, A. (2016). *Exploring outdoors. Ages 3–11 a guide for schools*. Abingdon: Routledge.

Boardman, K. (2024). *Early literacy for under-fives*. London: Sage.

Bradbury, A., Wright, D., Boardman, K., Thompson, P., Jarvis, P., Cowley, S., Veale, V., Wayne, D., Swailes, R., Scollan, A., Grimmer, T., & Renshaw, K. (2025). *Play matters*. Available at: https://www.early-years-reviews.com/play-matters

Broadhead, P. (2006). Developing an understanding of young children's learning through play: The place of observation, interaction and reflection. *British Educational Research Journal*, 32(2), 191-207. https://doi.org/10.1080/01411920600568976

Bruce, T. (1991). *Time to play in early childhood education*. London: Hodder and Stoughton.

Bruce, T. (2011). *Learning through play: For babies, toddlers and young children* (2nd ed.). London: Hodder Education.

Campbell-Barr, V., Evans, K., Georgeson, J., & Tregenza, S. (2023). *Insights into a high-quality early years curriculum*. University of Plymouth and Montessori Global Education.

Canning, N. (2020). *Children's empowerment in play. Participation, voice and ownership*. London: Routledge.

Carr, M., & Lee, W. (2012). *Learning stories: Constructing learner identities in early education*. London: Sage.

Chesworth, L. (2016). A funds of knowledge approach to examining play interests: Listening to children's and parents' perspectives. *International Journal of Early Years Education*, 24(3), 294-308.

Department for Education. (2017). *Statutory framework for the early years foundation stage.* London: Department for Education. Available at: https://www.foundationyears.org.uk/files/2017/03/EYFS_STATUTORY_FRAMEWORK_2017.pdf

Department for Education and Skills. (2007). *The early years foundation stage. Setting the standards for learning, development and care for children from birth to five.* London: DfES.

Department for Education (DfE). (2024). *Early years foundation stage statutory framework. For group and school-based providers. Setting the standards for learning, development and care for children from birth to five.* London: Department for Education (DfE).

Early Education. (2021). Birth to five matters. Early Education. Early Years Coalition. Available at: https://birthto5matters.org.uk/wp-content/uploads/2021/03/Birthto5Matters-download.pdf

Evangelou, M., Sylva, K., Kyriacou, M., Wild, M., & Glenny, G. (2009). *Early years learning and development literature review. Research report DCSF-RR176.* London: DSCF. Available at: http://dera.ioe.ac.uk/11382/2/DCSF-RR176.pdf

Fairchild, N. (2021). Pedagogies of place-spaces: Walking-with the post-professional, practice. https://doi.org/10.1080/25783858.2021.1968279

Fisher, J. (2016). *Interacting or interfering? Improving interactions in the early years.* Maidenhead: Open University Press.

Goouch, K. (2008). Understanding playful pedagogies, play narratives and play spaces. *Early Years*, 28(1), 93–102. https://doi.org/10.1080/09575140701815136

Leggett, N. (2020). Play and early childhood pedagogies. In A. Kilderry & B. Raban (Eds.), *Strong foundations: Evidence informing practice in early childhood education and care* (pp. 138–155). ACER Press. Available at: https://doi.org/10.37517/978-1-74286-555-3_10

Longstaffe, M. (2020). *Provocations for learning in early years settings: A practical guide.* Jessica Kingsley Publishers.

McDowall Clark, R. (2017). *Exploring the contexts for early learning. Challenging the school readiness agenda.* London: Routledge.

Meltzoft, A. N. (1995). Understanding the intentions of others: Re-enactment of intended acts by 18-month-old children. *Developmental Psychology*, 31, 838–850.

Moss P. (2016). Why can't we get beyond quality? *Contemporary Issues in Early Childhood*, 17(1), 8–15.

Moyles, J. (2005). *The excellence of play.* Maidenhead: Open Press University.

Moyles, J. (2010). Empowering children and adults: Play and child-initiated learning. In S.Featherstone & P.Featherstone (Eds.), *Like bees, not butterflies* (pp. 29–44).

Moyles, J. (2015). Starting with play: Taking play seriously. In J. Moyles (Ed.), *The excellence of play* (pp. 1–15, 14–24). Maidenhead: Open University Press and McGraw-Hill Education.

Moyles, J., Adams, S., & Musgrove, A., Department for Education and Skills (2002). *SPEEL : Study of pedagogical effectiveness in early learning.* Research report. Available at: https://dera.ioe.ac.uk/id/eprint/4591

Murray, J. (2018). The play's the thing. *International Journal of Early Years Education*, 26(4), 335–339. https://doi.org/10.1080/09669760.2018.1527278

Paley, V. G. (1993). *You can't say you can't play.* Cambridge, MA: Harvard University Press.

Rinaldi, C. (2005). *In dialogues with Reggio Emilia: Contextualising, interpreting and evaluation early childhood education.* London: Routledge Falmer.

Roberts-Holmes, G. (2015). The 'datafication' of early years pedagogy: 'if the teaching is good, the data should be good and if there's bad teaching, there is bad data'. *Journal of Education Policy*, 30(3), 302-315.

Roberts-Holmes, G., & Moss, P. (2021). *Neoliberalism and early childhood education: Markets, imaginaries and governance*. Abingdon: Routledge.

Sharp, C., Hutchison, D., & Keys, W. (2002). Comparing school systems to explain enduring birth date effects: A response to McDonald (2001). *Compare: A Journal of Comparative and International Education*, 32(2), 239-241.

Siraj-Blatchford, I., Sylva, K., Muttock, S., Gilden, R., & Bell, D. (2002). *Researching effective pedagogy in the early years*. London: Department for Education and Skills, Research Report 356.

Siraj-Blatchford, I., & Sylva, K. (2004). Researching pedagogy in English pre-schools. *British Educational Research Journal*, 30(5), 713-730. https://doi.org/10.1080/0141192042000234665

Siraj-Blatchford, I. (2010b). Learning in the home and at school: How working class children 'succeed against the odds'. *British Educational Research Journal*, 36(3), 463-482. http://dx.doi.org/10.1080/01411920902989201

Sylva K., Melhuish E., Sammons P., Siraj-Blatchford I., & Taggart B. (2004) *The effective provision of pre-school education (EPPE) project: Final report*. London: DfES/Institute of Education, University of London.

Sylva, K., Melhuish, E., Sammons, P., Siraj-Blatchford, I., & Taggart, B. (Eds) (2010). *Early childhood matters: Evidence from the effective pre-school and primary education project*. Abingdon: Routledge.

Taggart, B., Sylva, K., Melhuish, E., Sammons, P., & Siraj, I. (2015). *Effective pre-school, primary and secondary education project (EPPSE 3-16+). How pre-school influences children and young people's attainment and developmental outcomes over time*. Research Brief. Department for Education (DfE).

Whitebread, D. (2012). *Developmental psychology and early childhood education*. London: Sage.

Wood, E. A. (2013). Free choice and free play in early childhood education: Troubling the discourse. *International Journal of Early Years Education*, 22(1), 4-18. https://doi.org/10.1080/09669760.2013.830562

Wood E. (2019). Unbalanced and unbalancing acts in the early years foundation stage: A critical discourse analysis of policy-led evidence on teaching and play from the office for standards in education in England (Ofsted).*Education 3-13*, 47(7), 784-795.

Part III
Where Does Play Happen?

PROCESS

11

Enabling Environments: Indoors and Out

Jennie Clement

Chapter Objectives

This chapter will help you:

- Understand the importance of the environment in young children's play in early childhood.
- Recognise the role of the environment in shaping individual roles and relationships.
- Question different playful learning spaces (indoors and out).
- Consider environments for child-initiated play (from children's interests).

Introduction

The chapter focuses upon the physical environments we create and provide for young children, how they are constructed and how this construction can shape children's play and learning experiences. There is a plethora of terms used to describe the physical environments we create and provide for young children's play – classroom, play room, continuous provision, outdoor classroom, play area, outdoor area. This chapter considers an 'enabling environment' to be all physical spaces that have been purposefully created or provided for children's play and learning. These spaces could be in a school setting, private nursery or community group and they could be both indoors or outdoors; their unifying quality is that they have been created or provided for young children's play and learning. The chapter initially explores the significance of the physical environments we create for ourselves and considers the powerful role of the architect in the design and creation of physical space. When considering play spaces for children, the practitioner is positioned as the architect, designing and creating the physical spaces. The term *practitioner* is used to include any adult with responsibility for designing, creating, and developing spaces for young children's play.

The chapter then explores different approaches to the construction of play spaces and finally considers how spaces can be created, used and manipulated by young children themselves to support their interests and ideas.

The Importance of the Environment in Shaping and Supporting Children's Day-to-Day Experiences

Before we start to consider the importance of the environments we create for young children, let us consider the importance of the environment in our day-to-day lives. Picture this – it is your first day in a new city. In the morning, you visit the library to look for information on the local area, you then have lunch at a café close by and buy a few items for your new house in a craft shop on the way home. Later, you go to a yoga centre to take a class and then end the day at a street market choosing some snacks for later that evening. Even though you've never been to these places before, you know what to do, how to act and interact with the space and the other people within it. And while your 'spatial history' (your experiences of other similar spaces) will provide you with a 'spatial map' that might allow you to understand these new spaces, you also have the ability to read these spaces as you would any written text. Consequently, the physical and material nature of these spaces shapes your actions and interactions, your roles, responsibilities, and identities within the physical space.

The Role of the Environment in Shaping Individual Roles and Relationships

Recognising the influence of physical space and the powerful role of architecture in our day-to-day lives, Blundell Jones (2016) explains how architecture is capable of shaping human experience, structuring our way of being in the world. Considering our physical environments through this architectural lens, different buildings and different physical spaces are created for particular purposes, for particular actions to take place (e.g., a hospital, a gym, a cafe). These physical spaces are designed, by an architect, to support an end 'user' of the space. The 'user' will be guided by the physical spaces to do, to be and to interact with the space and with other people within the space in different, but specific ways. Architect Hill (2003) reflects on three types of user created within space: the passive, the reactive and the creative. A passive user of space transforms neither its use nor its meaning. The reactive user is able to modify space but only has a limited number of possibilities defined by the space. Both passive and reactive users become dependent upon their existing spaces. The creative user is able to create a new space or adapt an original use or meaning. At this point, it is important to recognise the practitioner as an architect and the powerful role they have in supporting a particular 'type of user' within their setting. Using this architectural frame, the spaces we create for children modify pedagogical actions, roles, and relationships. Physical space regulates the course of the day-to-day lives of both practitioners and children.

While equal importance must be given to how practitioners and their interactions support play and learning (McNally & Slutsky, 2018; see Chapters 6 and 15), design and creation precede use and it is the powerful role these play in the physical make-up of space which is foregrounded here.

Placing the spatial nature of children's lives as important draws on Massey's (2005) understanding of day-to-day experiences as a series of material practices, which happen with and through materials and spaces. Fenwick (2015) describes this relationship as a 'sociomaterial' one. A sociomaterial understanding reinforces the importance of the nonhuman elements of our experiences and focuses our attention on materials and spaces. Similarly, Lenz-Taguchi (2014, p. 80) positions the material aspects of practice as having agency of their own. She presents objects and materials as being able to shape and transform a child's 'notions, conceptions and emotions' as much as a child can transform the objects and materials they use. In one example, Lenz-Taguchi (2010) uses the dots on a pre-school floor, the ones assigned for young children to sit on at circle time. She remembers from her own childhood that her dot 'was burning under [her] buttocks, screaming out to me "Sit still!" "Don't move!" "Be quiet!"' (2010, p. 2). Pacini-Ketchabaw et al. (2016) also discuss the relationality between humans and non-humans in early childhood, noticing the entangled lives of young children and classroom materials. These examples serve to exemplify a sociomaterial understanding and how physical spaces and materials are shaping our pedagogical practices and the roles and relationships which form within them (see also Chapter 10). This serves to remind us that space is not neutral and play within space is not only supported by the relationships between the people within space but by the spaces in which these happen.

Creating Different Playful Learning Spaces (Indoors and Out)

Having accepted that the physical environments we provide for young children perform an important role in shaping their day-to-day experiences, it then follows that the environment should be fervently discussed. However, this is often not the case! The environments we create and provide for young children's play and learning and their theoretical constructions are often overlooked, neglected or not considered. In practice, physical spaces are often inherited, and as you start work in a new setting, you will often work within existing physical spaces, with existing spatial practices that have often become so naturalised within the setting they have become accepted as 'just the ways things are'. Emphasis is often placed on the activities you will provide within these spaces, rather than how you might re-design, re-create, re-conceive, or re-imagine the spaces themselves. This construction of space is problematic as it creates a blindness towards how we think about the spatial factors of practice and reinforces an inappropriate assumption that the physical environments we create for young children are neutral and disconnected from their play and learning (Lenz-Taguchi, 2014). This blindness towards the environment appears to neutralise physical space, making it an almost invisible part of provision. It is often rendered unchallengeable and creates pedagogical practice that does not adequately explore, question or consider the spatial nature of play and learning.

While we can recognise the physical environments we create for young children are not always foregrounded when discussing playful practice, there are a number of noteworthy examples of approaches to young children's play and learning which explicitly consider the environment. I will discuss two here – Froebel's (1899, 1838/1912) approach to the construction of children's gardens (see also Chapter 4) and the recognition in the pre-schools of Reggio Emilia of the physical environment as the 'third teacher' (see also Chapter 20). These two interesting examples explicitly weave spatial constructions through their theoretical considerations and practical applications of play and playful learning.

Froebel's Communal Gardens

Fredrick Froebel, often considered the most influential pioneer of early childhood education (Bruce, 2016; see Chapter 4), carefully considered the role of the environment in young children's play and specifically discussed the construction of these spaces. Here we consider the gardens he provided for children. Froebel (1899) created both individual and communal garden spaces for children. Froebel's gardens were seen as 'no mere arrangement; rather, [they] illustrated in a tangible form of Froebel's philosophy of unity between the parts and the whole, individual and community, freedom and responsibility' (Liebschner, 1992 in Tovey, 2014, p. 17). Froebel's spaces recognise these powerful material relationships and the interconnected nature of learning through children's and teachers' construction of their surrounding physical spaces. Within Froebel's communal garden spaces, children were positioned as participants in the construction of the gardens themselves. Their involvement in the construction of these spaces was seen to reflect the idealised notion of what a democratic society could be (Froebel, 1899). The gardens were divided into individual and communal plots with 'the little garden-beds of the children… surrounded by the common garden… showing [the] relation of the particular to the general, of the part to the whole, and so symbolising the child in the family, the citizen in the community' (Froebel, 1838/ 1912, p. 238). Developing practice in this way, where everyone is involved in the construction of their spaces for living and learning, values children equally as citizens and supports a democratic and collaborative approach to play and playful learning. The explicit recognition of the power of space to influence and support the roles and relationships within it is also recognised in the pre-schools of Reggio Emilia.

The Pre-Schools of Reggio Emilia

Within the pre-schools of Reggio Emilia (see Chapter 20), the environment is often called the 'third teacher' in recognition of the physical nature of teaching and learning. Spaces within the pre-schools are explicitly considered within the pedagogical enactments and relationships of the pre-schools, for example, 'the piazza', a space within the pre-schools that represents the main square in Italian cities. These spaces, within the community and within the schools, are seen as spaces where people can meet and talk to one another. These physical layouts and considerations are seen to have a 'pedagogical connotation [and] the piazza supports the formation of relationships, symbolising the "pedagogy of relationships" in the sense it fosters encounters, group interaction, stories, social relations, and the children's assumption of a public identity' (Ceppi & Zini, 1998, p. 37). The construction of the physical space itself is important; it becomes a 'key source of educational provocation and insight' enabling a view of classroom and school spaces which 'can take on a life of their own that con- tributes to children's learning' (Strong-Wilson & Ellis, 2007, p. 40).

The Practitioner as Architect

Reflecting on these two different constructions of space for children's learning, we can see within both practices, the construction of the space is important as it can value and support a particular type of play and playful learning and a particular view of children as learners. The teacher within these spaces can be considered the architect, carefully planning and designing these pedagogical spaces to support specific interactions and pedagogic practices. In Froebel's gardens, the teacher provides spaces for individual and communal growing. These spaces support children's relationships, and their roles and responsibilities can change through the different constructions of physical space. This individual and communal approach to the construction of physical space supports children's identity as individuals but also as members of the whole classroom community with responsibilities to their community. Similarly, within the piazza, the teacher explicitly creates a space to support the relationships of the individual children as part of the wider school community.

Positioning the practitioner as an architect allows us to draw on architectural theory to understand the powerful role the designer and creator of space holds. As we can see from the examples above, the pedagogical spaces created are not autonomous physical structures but become the mediator between children and the wider pedagogical values, demonstrating how children, play and playful learning are conceptualised and valued.

Reflection Point 11.1

Creating an 'Environments' Map

Before we start to consider any specific physical spaces within early years settings, please draw a rectangle (A4 portrait) about 4 cm in from the edge of the paper. Within the rectangle, draw a map of an early years setting you have spent time in (this could be a baby room in a private nursery, a classroom in a school or an outdoor play space). Maybe you have worked there, been a volunteer or been a pupil, but it doesn't matter, what matters is your ability to reflect on some of the spaces you have spent time in that have been specifically created to support children's play and playful learning. On your map, draw all the spaces created and provided for children. In the border, annotate the map - include the names of the spaces, expectations of the spaces, what the children did/do in the spaces.

Once you have completed your map, discuss with colleagues, or the people around you - what are the children doing in each space? What are the expectations of the space itself? Who created the space? What play and playful learning is valued? Do the spaces create different types of play and playful learning? Do the spaces create different roles and relationships for the teacher and the children?

The different spaces we create for children tell us a lot about how we view and value play within our setting. Spaces can either support or curtail play; they can be open or directive.

Please consider the case studies below.

Case Study 11.1

Setting One

- A reception class for 4-to 5-year-olds includes two adults, one lead practitioner and one learning support staff, and 18 children.

Seb is playing in the block corner. It is one of the largest spaces in the room and has enough wooden blocks and floor space for ten children. Additional resources, in the form of loose parts, both natural (small slices of wood, pebbles, and sticks) and man-made (fabric, mini figures, animals, and vehicles), are housed in baskets and boxes and placed on shelves that run the length of the space. George and Betsy come to join Seb, and they quickly start working together, excitedly planning, designing and building. The lead practitioner watches for a little while and then chats to the group about their design. She offers a book from the reading nook so the group can develop their ideas using the images. Betsy then uses paper, pens and a clipboard from the writing station to draw pictures of their plan and Seb adds some magnets from the science table to their design. The group are developing a complex construction, and they chat and build excitedly. After some time, the lead practitioner signals to the class it's time for lunch. Seb and George tidy away some of the unused bricks, pebbles, and slices of wood. Betsy makes a sign to show their creation is a work in progress and that they will return to it later.

Setting Two

- A reception class for 4-to 5-year-olds includes two adults, one lead practitioner and one learning support staff, and 18 children.

Frances is playing in the block corner. It is a small space with enough wooden blocks and floor space for three children; there are other larger plastic blocks and a large box of Lego available for the children to build with. There are a number of 'challenge cards', linked to the class theme, posted on the back wall. One says 'Can you make a new train for Thomas the Tank Engine to play with?' Frances initially starts to build a train, but when James joins her, they decide to reassemble the blocks to make a castle. James loves castles and has visited four out of the six castles near his home. The lead practitioner asks what they are building and reminds them they are building trains this week. Frances tries to bring a long cardboard tube, scissors, and cellotape from the craft corner to make a sword for the castle but is asked to take them back to the area where they belong. After some time, the lead practitioner signals to the class it's time to tidy up because it's lunchtime. They play the tidy up song, and Frances and James are encouraged by both adults to tidy the space and put all of the blocks back on the shelves.

Reflection Point 11.2

Think about and discuss the different spaces and materials above. What implications do the different spaces pose for young children's play and learning? What roles and relationships are fostered in the different spaces? How do the spaces offer (or not offer) opportunities for young children's creativity, independence, exploration, and agency?

So far, this chapter has considered how play and learning can be shaped by the spaces in which it happens. As such, when thinking about creating an 'enabling environment' for children, we must first think about what experiences we want to enable. Using different approaches to support children's learning and development, and different methods depending on what you are intending children to learn, is common practice. Similarly, we need to use different spaces and different approaches to the construction and use of these different spaces. There are a number of excellent sources which have previously considered resources and materials that can be provided for different types of play and learning; see the list provided in Further Reading.

As you develop your reading, research and practice, you might consider the following questions on your own, with the colleagues you work with and with the children who will use your spaces. Make these questions part of your regular discussions about children's play, learning and development with the whole community, reflecting on your existing spaces and re-imagining possible future spaces together.

Ten Questions about Space

1 In which spaces do children feel welcome, secure and safe within the environment?
2 Do children have a range of spaces that will support them to take on different roles and responsibilities – developing their identity as an individual and as part of a group?
3 What are the perceived expectations and values within the environment?
4 Is the outdoor space readily accessible for play? If not, are children supported to access outdoor spaces on a regular basis?
5 How are spaces flexible, supporting play choice and independence?
6 How do spaces support children to be physically and cognitively active during their play – to experiment, to problem solve?
7 Are there spaces that support children to be passive, reactive and creative?
8 Which are considered favourite spaces? Why?
9 Are there spaces for quiet contemplation?
10 How can children's ideas and interests be reflected in physical spaces?

Environments for Child-Initiated Play: From Children's Interests and Needs

This final question needs a different approach. Up until this point, we have positioned the teacher as the architect, creating and providing the physical environments for children. Architecturally, the spaces communicate what is expected to happen in the space, directing the learner and their learning. Architect Jilk (2005) notes these outcome-driven environments can become barriers to any actions which have not been permitted. Within this architectural construct, pedagogical space becomes static and restrictive as each space already has a pre-determined use. In practice, this may mean children's play choices become repetitive and lose spontaneity, authenticity and creativity.

Question 10 asks us to consider children's interests and ideas. We will continue to use the architectural lens and explore what happens if we allow children, based on their ideas and interests, to take on the role of the architect. We will consider, through different examples, how we can support children to design, create, and manipulate playful spaces in line with their interests and ideas - fostering a sense of autonomy, choice and control over their physical spaces and the play that is enabled - and further their roles and relationships within the play spaces.

Spaces which explicitly build on children's ideas and interests are positioned to **need** children's involvement in the design, creation or manipulation of the spaces themselves. There is an existing argument which acknowledges children can subvert the intended use of any space as 'children are not simply influenced by their environments but act in ways that change them' (Wood, 2014, p. 14). However, this spatial practice does not value or enact their ideas and interests; it only 'turns a blind eye' if they are not using the space in the way it is intended. Children's ideas or voices are not valued or represented in these spaces, since they are only able to subvert space, not create it. Architecturally, children's participation in the design and creation of their space is positioned as a reconsideration of the spatial values and meanings of the physical spaces created. Arguably, this also encourages a repositioning of children as architects within their play and learning.

Pedagogical research undertaken by Broadhead and Burt (2012) considered collaborative constructions of space within their 'whatever you want it to be place' (p. 142). Their research, in an early years unit, focused on children's cooperative play in an open-ended role play space. The space itself lacked traditional play equipment and did not have any pre-determined outcomes or ways of using the space. Practitioners provided milk crates, tarpaulin, ropes, barrels, and cable reels, and the children were then free to use the materials provided, or bring materials from other areas, to create their play space. Staff were encouraged, through observation, to develop the children's experiences based on the children's play. The study concluded that this type of space, and allowing children opportunities to manipulate and create space, could support children's voice alongside the planned curriculum.

Positioning children as architects, Clement (2019) develops spatially democratic pedagogy (SDP) as a way of supporting children as designers and co-creators of space. Underpinned by democratic and participatory values which seek to support children's ideas and interests, Clement (2019) documented notable differences in the roles and relationships formed between the children, the practitioner and the space when children's designs were used to create a playful space within the classroom. The democratic and sociomaterial principles that underpin the children's role as architect were seen to be reflected in the roles and relationships which formed during the design and creation process. SDP became the mediator for the way in which the children's ideas and interests were supported and developed through their construction of space.

Summary

Moving forward, one of the most important things to do as a practitioner is to make visible your environments and, most importantly, the construction of these environments. Ask yourself who has made these spaces and what roles and relationships they are trying to support. Try to develop an explicit approach to the design and creation of the spaces you provide for young children, especially when you intend for children to take control and direct their play. Develop professional dialogues with your colleagues about the existing environments and possible alternative spaces you could create for and with the children in your care. Developing a shared understanding about the importance of space through personal and collaborative research, through observation and reflection about how the children use the existing spaces, is a fundamental aspect for supporting and developing your professional understanding of space. Talk to the children about their views, support their creation of new spaces, visit different settings and explore different theoretical constructions and uses of space. It is through these professional practices we can demonstrate the importance of the physical nature of provision. It can give the material and spatial nature of the environments you create for children equal importance to the activities you place within the spaces and the way in which you use the space. Include the spaces and how they will be constructed in your planning. Have discussions about them – about play, about learning, about mess, about risk, about participation and about how your spaces support or constrain these aspects of practice. Developing a shared understanding of the spatial aspects of children's play and learning will allow you to form a collective language with your colleagues and with the children in your care about the physical nature of play and learning. This is important because the physical spaces you provide are important.

Key Points

- **Make the physical environment important:** Talk to the people around you, colleagues, children and parents, about the physical spaces and materials you create and provide. Research the physical environment through different disciplines. Make discussions about physical space a common practice in your setting and with your colleagues.
- **Be an architect:** Purposefully design and create physical space to support the opportunities you want to offer the children. Do not accept existing or external constructions of space or activities unless they relate to you and the children with whom you are working with.
- **Be brave:** If you inherit a physical setting with lots of existing materials, spaces and activities with specific ways of being, doing and acting don't feel you have to 'fit in'. Re-design the physical spaces around you. Build physical environments based on you, your children and your pedagogical approach to play and learning.

(Continued)

(Continued)

- **Support children to be architects:** Allow children to purposefully design and create spaces for play and learning. What are they interested in? Where, how, what, and with whom do they want to play?
- **Observe, reflect and discuss:** Observe how children use the spaces available. Make observation an essential aspect of your reflective practice when creating an enabling environment and observe and reflect before, during and after you make changes to the spaces in your setting. Always discuss the spaces with the children; include their perspectives on the spaces that you are creating for them.

Further Reading

Cardellino, P. and Woolner, P. (2020) Designing for transformation – a case study of open learning spaces and educational change. *Pedagogy, Culture & Society*, 28(3), 383–402. This article considers the dynamics between teaching and learning and the space in which it happens. It argues for balance between the design of learning environments and the educational agenda.

Merewether, J. (2015) Young children's perspectives of outdoor learning spaces: What matters? *Australasian Journal of Early Childhood*, 40(1), 99–108. This article looks at 3- and 4-year old children's perspectives of the outdoor environment in their early years setting. Findings consider the need for children to be able to pretend, move, observe and be social. These discussions could have implications for all practitioners who design both the curriculum and physical outdoor spaces for young children.

White, J. (2020) *Playing and learning outdoors: The practical guide and sourcebook for excellence in outdoor provision and practice with young children.* London: Routledge. This book gives practical guidance on developing outdoor play and learning provision for young children. It offers materials, books, resources and lots of practical examples to support outdoor provision.

References

Blundell Jones, P. (2016). *Architecture and ritual: How buildings shape society.* London: Bloomsbury.

Broadhead, P., & Burt, A. (2012). *Understanding young children's learning through play: Building playful pedagogies.* London: Routledge.

Bruce, T. (2016). Fredrich Froebel. In T. David, K. Goouch, & S. Powell (Eds.), *The Routledge international handbook of philosophies and theories of early childhood education and care.* London: Routledge.

Ceppi, G., & Zini, M. (Eds.) (1998) *Children, spaces, relations: Metaproject for an Environment for young children.* Milan: Domus Academy Researcher Center.

Clement, J. (2019). Spatially Democratic Pedagogy: Children's design and co-creation of classroom space. *International Journal of Early Childhood*, 51(3), 373–387. https://doi.org/10.1007/s13158-019-00253-4

Fenwick, T. (2015). Sociomateriality and learning: A critical approach. In D. Scott, & E. Hargreaves (Eds.), *Sage handbook of learning*. London: Sage.

Froebel, F. (1838/1912). *Froebel's chief writings on education: Part two, the kindergarten* (trans. S. S. F. Fletcher and J. Welton). London: Edward Arnold, University of Roehampton.

Froebel, F. (1899). *Friedrich Froebel's education by development: The second part of the pedagogics of the kindergarten* (trans. J. Jarvis). London: Edward Arnold.

Hill, J. (2003). *Actions of architecture: Architects and creative users*. Abingdon: Routledge.

Jilk, B. (2005). Place making and change in learning environments. In M. Dudek (Ed.), *Children's spaces*. Amsterdam: Architectural Press.

Lenz-Taguchi, H. (2010). *Going beyond the theory/practice divide in early childhood education*. Abingdon: Routledge.

Lenz-Taguchi, H. (2014). New materialisms and play. In L. Brooker, M. Blaise, & S. Edwards (Eds.), *The SAGE handbook of play and learning in early childhood*. London: Sage.

Massey, D. (2005). *For space*. London: Sage.

McNally, S., & Slutsky, R. (2018). Teacher–child relationships make all the difference: Constructing quality interactions in early childhood settings. *Early Child Development and Care*, 188(5), 508-523. http://doi.org/10.1080/03004430.2017.1417854

Pacini-Ketchabaw, V., Kind, S., & Kocher, L. (2016). *Encounters with materials in early childhood education*. London: Routledge.

Strong-Wilson, T., & Ellis, J. (2007). Children and place: Reggio Emilia's environment as third teacher. *Theory Into Practice*, 46(1), 40-47.

Tovey, H. (2014). Outdoor play and the early years tradition. In T. Maynard, & J. Waters (Eds.), *Exploring outdoor play in the early years*. Maidenhead: Open University Press, McGraw-Hill Education.

Wood, E. A. (2014). Free choice and free play in early education: Troubling the discourse. *International Journal of Early Years Education*, 22(1), 4-18.

12
Outdoor Play

Glenda Tinney

Chapter Objectives

This chapter will help you to:

- Explore the significance of outdoor play for young children's development and well-being.
- Debate the implications of challenge and risk, affordance and loose parts in the context of outdoor play.
- Understand the socio-cultural, historic and theoretical context relating to outdoor play.
- Re-evaluate outdoor play in relation to sustainability and engaging with the natural world.
- Consider the opportunities and barriers outdoor play provides in the context of early years settings.

Case Study 12.1

A nursery provides daily opportunities for the children in their care to play outdoors for extended periods in a small woodland area on the nursery grounds. Alongside the natural features of trees, hedges, stones, soil, fallen tree trunks, rocks, and fallen leaves, the nursery practitioners have also included a range of other resources, such as old saucepans, recycled plastic containers, wooden spoons, tyres, pallets, baskets, paint brushes, paint rollers, sheets, tarpaulin, string, rope, troughs, magnifiers, and nature ID books. There is also access to an outdoor tap linked to a water butt. There are 16 children (3- to 4-year-old) and four practitioners in the woodland setting. Four children can be observed in imaginary play, pretending to be superheroes and magic characters. Two children are building a den with a practitioner's support using string, fallen wood, and tarpaulin. Another

(Continued)

(Continued)

three children are painting on a sheet hung up between two trees, using mud they have mixed in a saucepan. Four children are playing a balancing game on a fallen tree trunk and then jumping on pallets and tyres on the floor, observed by a practitioner. Two children are lifting leaves and logs from the floor, using magnifiers to take a closer look at woodlice and worms. One child has a basket and is collecting leaves, twigs, stones, and other materials to add to the 'magic potion' she has been mixing in a saucepan. The children are wearing layers of clothes including waterproofs and wellington boots as it is raining and it is a cold winter's day.

Reflection Point 12.1

Consider the previous case study.

- Why might the nursery have invested time and resources in developing this woodland area for children's play?
- What does this opportunity for outdoor play offer in terms of children's development and learning?
- Can you see any links between the case study and the ideas of the play pioneers set out in Chapter 4 and contemporary pedagogies described in Chapter 5?

Defining Outdoor Play – Theory and Practice

Outdoor play can include any play that takes place outdoors, be that on a playground, park, beach, street, and so on. However, the properties and features of the specific outdoor environment define opportunities for play, understood here to be 'spontaneous, enjoyable, and self-directed activity with no external goal' (Smith, 2010 cited in Carson, 2019, p. 1). For example, in the case study described above, the environment provided for the children includes natural features such as soil, trees and stones, as well as resources provided by the adults, including tyres, sheets, and rope. All these natural and man-made resources are open-ended in that they have no fixed use, and the children can therefore use them in a variety of different ways. This is a contrast to the type of play that might be possible when children only have a bare concrete yard or specific toys and play equipment available in a playground. Play in the outdoors therefore depends on the unique qualities of a well-considered and planned outdoor environment, if it is to offer play opportunities which are significantly different to those available indoors. This chapter explores some key factors to consider, namely: space and movement, time, holistic development and cross-curricular learning, the adult role, the unique opportunities of the outdoors and risk and challenge. The chapter then goes on to consider the socio-historic context of outdoor play and learning and issues relating to sustainability.

Space and Movement

In the case study, children have space to explore and be curious, allowing them to discover and experiment with their environment. Piaget (cited in Frey, 2018) suggested children are 'little scientists' who develop an understanding of their physical world through exploring and experimenting in their environment. Therefore, space is an essential advantage of outdoor learning, allowing children the room to explore new places and ideas. The space also allows for movement. Gross motor skills are developed when children can control large or whole-body movements involving the muscle groups involved in core stability and posture, and the large muscles of the arms and legs. Movements such as stretching, jumping, bending, pushing, pulling, rolling, crawling, running, hopping, skipping, and hanging off things involve gross motor skills. The woodland in the case study offers space and features including fallen tree trunks, standing trees, logs, soil, rocks and stones to encourage children to climb, stretch, crawl, and lift things, thus supporting them to develop their gross motor skills. Fine motor skills involve the use of the smaller muscles of the hands, commonly in activities like building with bricks and blocks, using scissors and tools, drawing, writing, doing up buttons and zips, using cutlery, pouring drinks, and peeling fruits. Fine motor skills are improved where gross motor skills have been developed well, and gross motor skills develop in children before fine motor skills. Therefore, opportunities to practise gross motor skills are essential to supporting later fine motor skills. Children in the case study stirring mud, collecting leaves and painting are also developing their fine motor skills such as hand-eye coordination, essential in the later development of pencil grip and handwriting.

Time

In the case study, the nursery provides children with regular and extended time to be outdoors. Children therefore have plenty of time to explore and be curious, as well as time to revisit ideas regularly and consolidate what they have learnt from one day to the next. For example, when creating the mud painting or building a den, the design can become more complex and elaborate if children can add to it and develop it daily, without worrying about the resources having to be tidied away immediately. Children will be able to benefit from physical exercise (see next section) by having regular daily access to outdoor play for extended periods. Significantly, even a restricted size of outdoor space can provide time to develop multisensory experiences, support a range of physical movements and allow for the curiosity, exploration, and discovery of child-led play. Clark (2022) has referred to 'slow pedagogy', suggesting the benefits for children of slowing down and allowing children time to revisit ideas and develop deeper understanding. In the case study, the time provided to explore the outdoors may be an example of this since the children are able to take time to follow their own ideas and interests.

Holistic Development and Cross-Curricular Learning

The outdoor play within the case study supports all areas of a child's holistic development simultaneously.

Cognitive

The children are using mathematics and science concepts as they consider how to build a functional den. They can estimate or measure what length of branches they need. They can consider the angles and shapes of the den frame and consider forces when balancing the tarpaulin as a roof.

Language

They are speaking to each other and using vocabulary which may include specialised language linked to building a den such as 'we need to stretch the string', 'we need to unravel the tarpaulin', 'we need to use the oak tree to tie our string'. The objects and experiences outdoors are very different to the indoors, and with the support of engaged adults, children will be encouraged to use words which are new and more likely to occur outdoors. Consider words such as dandelion, daisy, conker, oak, willow, woodlouse, blackbird, and snail. These are words that are inherently related to the outdoors. Significantly, some of these words were removed from children's dictionaries in the early twenty-first century, suggesting they were words which were no longer in common usage by children (see Macfarland & Morris, 2017).

Social

While building the den, the children cooperate, negotiate and support each other, which provides significant social skills. One child can also scaffold another child's learning of a new skill such as tying blankets together or sawing a piece of wood. They can do this either by providing instruction, modelling what to do or providing a helping hand to steady the saw or demonstrating how to tie a knot. The space outdoors allows room for both independent solitary play as well as group play (see Chapter 3). Much of the play highlighted in the case study at the beginning of the chapter encourages cooperation where children benefit from interacting with each other. Superhero play stories, for example, involve agreeing the roles and powers each superhero has, debating how the story unfolds and deciding the rules of their battles.

Physical

Building the den requires children to lift heavy objects and to stretch to tie the different branches in place. They will need to crawl to secure the branches into the ground, and duck to climb into the finished den. They will also have carried different materials into the den, involving dragging, pushing, pulling, and lifting materials and developing gross motor skills. In doing so, their heart rate and breathing rate will be increased as they exert themselves, which provides the benefits of physical exercise. If the children are enjoying the play, their brains may be releasing neurotransmitters such as endorphins that can support relaxation and longer-term emotional health (see Chapter 8), which reinforces the positive association of being outdoors and being active.

Emotional

Emotional development is supported in the case study with children having fun and enjoying creating and playing in the den. They may gain self-confidence and self-esteem from the achievement of creating the den. However, the trial and error of making the den and the fact that there is not one correct den design supports children to make mistakes and learn from these mistakes in a safe environment. They learn that mistakes are opportunities to learn rather than 'being wrong', which also supports longer-term resilience (see Chapter 8).

Cross-Curricular Learning

Such opportunities for choosing and self-directing their play outdoors also support cross-curricular learning, which is the focus of many early years approaches such as Te Whāriki in New Zealand, Reggio Emilia in Italy (see Chapter 20) and the forest school approach (see Waller et al., 2017) where children engage in many subjects or areas of learning at the same time rather than exploring one subject at a time. In the UK context, you may have noticed a similar focus in the early years curricula of England, Northern Ireland, Scotland, and Wales. In the case study, the child making a magic potion will be using her mathematical skills when measuring and counting what ingredients to add. She will develop working theories related to early science concepts when she observes how mud and water, when mixed, change in terms of consistency and viscosity, key concepts in chemistry. She may become aware of different types of leaves as she adds these to the magic potion, a key area in biology. By carrying the saucepan and bending and stretching to collect resources, she will be supporting her physical development. She may try to explain her potion recipe to others or record the recipe in writing or orally, supporting her literacy and communication skills. She may be playing the role of a witch or wizard which could lead to reading stories about similar characters or creating her own stories, supporting her communication and literacy skills. The case study provides many examples of play that you may want to consider further in terms of holistic development and cross-curricular learning.

Adult Role

The case study noted previously, where children can choose what to explore and can direct their own play, may appear to require very little adult involvement. However, this is not an accurate reflection. The adult practitioners have key roles in supporting the children's play cycle (see Chapters 1, 11, and 15) outdoors.

Creating and/or Allowing Access to the Outdoor Environment

The adults in the case study have taken the time to develop the outdoor environment as an integral part of the child's experiences. They have considered the value of children engaging with the non-human world (such as rocks, trees, soil, and water) as well as adding other materials to support children's learning and creativity (see later section on loose parts). In doing so, the adults have created an environment where children want to play (see also Chapter 11). They have also provided the correct personal protective equipment such as waterproofs, wellington boots and coats that ensure the children can fully engage with the experience (see Risk/Challenge section) and have understood the significance of their role as observers who can allow the play cycle to develop uninterrupted. The children painting the sheet with mud have been allowed to do this, without adults suggesting they should stop as they may get messy. The children balancing on the fallen tree trunk have been allowed to do this without an adult telling them to be careful or not to climb. However, the adults would discuss with the children any risk they foresee, for example, if the tree trunk feels wet or slippery. This type of support promotes children as 'competent' (see also Chapters 2 and 18). The children have agency because they can make choices that influence and impact on their experiences, in line with Article 12 of the UNCRC, in terms of children having a right to make decisions about issues that affect them. The adults support children to assess their own risk and to consider their own skills, and therefore construct the young child as agentic and competent.

Observing

The case study includes adults who observe the children's play; in doing so, they can consider what might also support the children's curiosity further. The children imagining they are superheroes spend much of their time jumping and pretending to fly, having developed an elaborate story about using their superpowers to save the universe. The adult observing this play may therefore consider adding more resources to the woodland. Tying ropes to a tree may help the children pretend they are flying when they hold onto the rope and dangle, thus also supporting gross motor skills development. Creating a more diverse environment with more raised areas to jump from may support their imaginary play further, and also the development of leg muscles and coordination. Further open-ended materials such as sheets may support the children to dress up as their superheroes, allowing for creative thinking and problem-solving as well as storytelling skills. By observing, the adults develop the environment as well as record and document the children's learning and interests. By doing this, they may notice specific benefits of the outdoors for specific children. Questions these adults may ask are, for example: Do some children take more of a lead when they play outdoors, which is not the case in their indoor play? Are some children less confident outdoors? Do children, who may have additional learning needs, find outdoor play particularly rewarding or challenging and can practitioners support this appropriately?

Unique Opportunities in the Outdoors

The previous sections of this chapter make a case that the outdoors can be most effective in providing unstructured, open-ended play using open-ended materials to support children's holistic development. The case study refers to open-ended materials both natural and man-made. Another term, often used interchangeably, to mean open-ended materials is 'loose parts', referring to materials that have no fixed use and can be moved, transported and combined. Nicholson (1971) originally developed the theory of loose parts, highlighting that loose parts support curiosity, discovery, creative thinking and trial and error, providing children with stimulating and problem-solving situations. For example, experimenting and trial and error are required when building the den or setting up the mud painting. These play activities require far more planning and trying out ideas than would making a den out of bricks or blocks that slot into each other easily or putting paper on a conventional easel. Children are challenged to make their own decisions on what resources will work most effectively and will have to choose from a range of materials. They will have to move resources around and change their shape and size to fit what they want to do. The children in the case study who are playing superheroes may also use the loose parts available to add to their story, such as small twigs or leaves to denote magic dust.

Affordance theory (see Gibson, 1977; 1979 cited in Waller et al., 2017, p. 41) allows us to understand how objects are perceived in terms of their possibilities for action. In recent years, early years researchers have been considering the implications of affordance theory for children's play and learning and how the resources they encounter can support a variety of affordances. For example, in the case study, the fallen trunk has been perceived by the child as a climbing opportunity and the sheet as a painting opportunity. On other days, the fallen trunk may be a table or an imaginary rocket ship, the sheet a resource for a play den. The outdoors provides the space and opportunity to encounter a variety of loose parts, both natural and man-made, that increase the affordance of an area for children's play. In doing so, the interaction with the area becomes a multisensory experience. For example, the potion-maker has chosen resources which she has perceived as potion-making equipment and resources. In doing so, she is also using a range of senses, feeling and smelling the leaves and mud, gauging the weight of the saucepan, seeing the colours and shapes of her ingredients. The different weather conditions, temperatures and other environmental conditions also make the outdoors a less static environment than the indoors, so that every day there are different possibilities and affordances for the same objects. On a wet day, stones may shine and be afforded the role of diamonds or money in a child's imaginary play. On a warmer day, they may be ideal for painting with water and become art resources.

You may want to consider what loose part resources have a high affordance and would support children's play in an outdoor space that you are familiar with.

Reflection Point 12.2

Consider the case study at the beginning of the chapter.

- What would the adults have had to do before providing the opportunity to play outdoors?
- How are boundaries set so children are not exposed to very dangerous situations?
- How could the adults support children to be challenged and take risks without exposing them to major hazards?
- As a practitioner, how might you feel with some of the play the children are involved in? Might you feel nervous for exposing them to risk? Might you worry that they could get hurt, and be concerned about what parents, the local community and other practitioners might think about allowing children to climb, balance, and get messy? How might you mitigate these worries?

Risk/Challenge

According to the Health and Safety Executive (2012, p. 1), 'When planning and providing play opportunities, the goal is not to eliminate risk, but to weigh up the risks and benefits. No child will learn about risk if they are wrapped in cotton wool'.

In the case study, you may have considered that some of the play experiences might be dangerous. However, you could also argue that the woodland area is offering valuable challenges and that when children learn any new skill there is an element of risk. Children would not be able to build a den or play superheroes if they were not exposed to the risk of a small trip or fall. Significantly, the adults have risk-assessed the environment and resources carefully prior to the case study, in line with legislation linked to health and safety. In doing so, the adults ensure that the children will not be faced with hazards that they cannot foresee, for example, hidden potholes, hidden low lying branches, deep pools of water, or broken glass in the ground. The adults will make sure such hazards are controlled. Boundaries will have been set in terms of areas where the children cannot go without the support of an adult. Certain issues will have been discussed beforehand and reinforced regularly so that children can assess their own risks in terms of surfaces being slippery or low-lying branches. For example, balancing on the fallen trunk and jumping from the palettes and tyres may involve children deciding on what they feel capable of doing and developing their confidence from day to day. Adults will also be observing and nearby to provide support when climbing and balancing. Furthermore, children can be part of the risk assessment process themselves, identifying and considering appropriate behaviour in response to risks, such as spotting rubbish or avoiding stinging nettles or thorny plants and poisonous berries.

Learning a new skill or facing a new challenge is inherently risky, wherever that takes place, and involves trial and error. The children climbing on the fallen tree trunks are taking a risk in trying to climb and balance; they may fall or stumble, but the outcome in a risk-assessed environment is likely to be minor cuts or grazes. By wearing appropriate clothing, children will also feel comfortable and will be wearing clothes and boots that lessen their risks as well. The benefits of the play in terms of supporting the development of gross motors skills, balance (vestibular sense), proprioception (sense of body) and self-confidence will outweigh the risks. In terms of outdoor play, risk–benefit assessments have become more popular, where the benefits of an activity as well as the risks are considered at the same time. This can make it easier to understand why the possible risks in an outdoor play environment are worth retaining as they offer children valuable learning opportunities. It can also help highlight risks that should be removed as they have no perceivable benefits (see Waller et al., 2017, p. 127).

Socio-Cultural and Historic Context

The case study outlined in this chapter takes place in an early years nursery setting. However, the wider context for outdoor play is influenced by society's socio-cultural and historic context. In industrialised Western countries, there have been concerns from the end of the twentieth century onwards that children do not have opportunities to go outside and to engage in challenging outdoor play as part of their everyday life (see Waller et al., 2017). Possible suggestions for this might be that industrialised modern life involves more indoor activities linked to digital technology, which means children may be playing indoors at the expense of outdoor experiences. Others suggest that media reporting has led to the perception of the outdoors as being dangerous, including fears over children having accidents and stranger-danger. During the latter half of the twentieth century the amount of traffic increased, making playing in the road and street more hazardous. However, perceptions of increased stranger-danger may not necessarily reflect reality, but instead reflect society's increased awareness, through social media, of tragedies involving children. There is also an argument that different cultures value the outdoors in different ways, and therefore their children's engagement with the outdoors reflects, for example, the status given to outdoor pursuits, or the status given to nature or the non-human in the religious context of a country or culture. Rogoff (2003) highlights how the social-cultural backdrop of children influences their play. Therefore, it may not be surprising that children in Scandinavian countries have had opportunities for outdoor play as part of initiatives such as forest school for generations, since these initiatives reflect the values of the people in these countries, in terms of pastimes and traditions linked to being outdoors (see also Chapter 18). In the United Kingdom, forest school is a more recent approach adapted from Scandinavian forest schools (see Waller et al., 2017), and the case study earlier in the chapter is in line with a drive to introduce outdoor experiences as part of education and care, to compensate for the general reduction in outdoor play in the United Kingdom, observed during the twentieth century. Some cultural contexts, such as First Nations people, have values which are based on respecting nature and humans seeing themselves as part of the web of life, and thus in such contexts, outdoor play and learning will be an intrinsic part of everyday life.

Beyond the Child – Outdoor Play and Wider Sustainability

The chapter to this point has discussed the benefits of playing outdoors for the child with an emphasis on the opportunities for holistic development and well-being. However, in the twenty-first century, concerns are increasing for the well-being of the whole planet in response to climate change, loss of biodiversity and plastic pollution, highlighting the interconnectedness of the well-being of the human and the wider non human world. Therefore, several authors suggest that opportunities to engage with the non human world are a significant benefit of outdoor play. For example, Louv (2005) suggests that children need to be outdoors and that a lack of these opportunities can lead to 'nature deficit disorder'. Wilson (1984) discusses 'biophilia' and the ideas that humans have an inherent love of nature and that our increasingly urban lives stop children engaging with this natural world. Authors such as Chawla (1998) discuss 'significant life experiences', suggesting that many adults who have gone on to work in organisations that help conserve and look after the environment, when interviewed, recognised their childhood in the outdoor environment as significant to their roles caring for the non human world. There is therefore a growing debate about the responsibility of adults to provide children with play opportunities outdoors, which also allow them to build an understanding and relationship with the non human world.

However, playing outside could have a negative impact on the non human world and not develop sustainable practice.

Reflection Point 12.3

In the case study provided above, one group of children are actively looking for woodlice and worms. Consider:

- Should the children in the case study be allowed to play with these animals in any way they wish?
- Do adults have a responsibility to help them not to harm the creatures they find?
- Are there boundaries in terms of how they treat these animals?
- Should they place them back carefully where they found them so they can rejoin their habitat? Why/why not?
- Are there boundaries in place to support children from leaving rubbish or resources that may become litter at the site?
- Is there consideration given to the impact of play activities on the non human world?
- When playing with water from the water butt, are children encouraged to use water as a precious resource?
- How might these discussions take place at the appropriate level for young children?

Froebel (see Chapter 4, and 11) was a proponent of outdoor play and considered that 'children don't just learn about nature, they learn through engagement with nature' (Louis & Powell, 2020). The children in the case study are provided with time and space to engage with the non-human (natural) world in their play and will be becoming aware of other animals and plants in their world. Some authors suggest that allowing children to engage with the non human world may help industrialised societies to support future generations to be less human-centred (anthropocentric) and to understand the value of the non human world. Such arguments suggest that an ecocentric viewpoint is necessary where the non human world is viewed as intrinsically important and not simply a resource for human use. However, to respect and look after the world around them may entail adults intervening in children's outdoor play (see previous reflection box). For example, being kind to the woodlice may be a discussion that disrupts children's natural exploration and is at odds with the ideals of play as self-directed by the child. It also highlights a possible tension between free self-directed play and wider ethical and environmental considerations.

There is also a growing interest in post-humanist approaches such as new materialism (see Lenz-Taguchi, 2014) which again decentres the child and highlights that the children are in a constant interaction with other materials and that these materials are not passive but have a significant role in the outcomes of a child's play. In the case study at the beginning of the chapter, the play observed would not have been possible without the specific qualities of the outdoor woodland area. Children were interacting with water, soil, air, stone and woodlice. They could only balance, jump, build dens or make potions due to the properties of the materials in the woodland. Therefore, from a new materialist perspective on outdoor play, the uniqueness of the environment is as important to the play observed as the children themselves. These may be ideas you want to consider further in your future practice (see Goodenough et al., 2020; also see Chapter 11).

Making the Most of Outdoor Play

This chapter has outlined how outdoor play provides numerous benefits for children. You may now want to consider the opportunities and barriers you may experience in supporting children to have outdoor play experiences.

Reflection Point 12.4

- Is there training or guidance you might require to support outdoor play? What might help you increase your confidence?
- What are the barriers? Could parents, carers or other adults have concerns about children playing outdoors? How might you work in partnership to support these concerns and help people understand the benefits of outdoor play?
- Would you invest in specific resources such as waterproofs and wellington boots or loose parts resources to support outdoor play? How would you fund these? Could you consider fundraising events, getting donations from local businesses and families? Could parents share their skills with you in terms of helping create interesting outdoor features?
- The nursery in the case study was lucky to have a woodland area. What if you did not have access to significant space outdoors? What could you do? Could gardening initiatives help green what space you do have? Could you use local parks or other areas to provide outdoor play?

Summary

- The outdoors offers significant opportunities for play.
- The outdoors provides unique features to support play including time, space, open-ended 'loose parts' materials and interaction with the non human world.
- Adults have a key role to develop interesting outdoor environments to support play affordance and to develop risk-benefit processes.
- Engagement with outdoor play reflects the historic and social-cultural context and will continue to change in line with recent environmental and sustainability concerns.

Further Reading

Waller, T., Arlemalm-Hagsér E., Sandsester, E. B. H., Lee-Hammond, L., Lekies, K. and Wyver, S. (eds), *The Sage handbook of outdoor play and learning*. London: Sage. This book provides a detailed exploration of many of the key points explored in this chapter.

Nicholson, S. (1971) How NOT to cheat children: The theory of loose parts. *Landscape Architecture*, 62, 30–34. https://media.kaboom.org/docs/documents/pdf/ip/Imagination-Playground-Theory-of-Loose-Parts-Simon-Nicholson.pdf. This is the original article outlining Nicholson's theory of loose parts.

These two texts provide further insights into post-humanist and new materialism approaches:

Lenz-Taguch, H. (2014) New materialisms and play. In E. Brooker, M. Blaise and S. Edwards (Eds.) *The Sage handbook of play and learning in early childhood*, London: Sage, pp. 79–90.

Goodenough, A., Waite, S. and Wright, N. (2020) Place as partner: Material and affective intraplay between young people and trees. *Children's Geographies*, 19(2), 225–240. https://doi.org/10.1080/14733285.2020.1783435

References

Carson, V. (2019). Active outdoor play. In *Encyclopaedia on early childhood development*. Available at: www.child-encyclopedia.com/sites/default/files/textes-experts/en/5223/activeoutdoor-play.pdf

Chawla, L. (1998). Significant life experiences revisited: A review of research on sources of environmental sensitivity. *Environmental Education Research*, 4(4), 369–382.

Clark, A. (2022). *Slow knowledge and the unhurried child*. London: Routledge.

Frey, B. (2018). *The Sage encyclopaedia of educational research, measurement, and evaluation*. London: Sage.

Goodenough, A., Waite, S., & Wright, N. (2020). Place as partner: Material and affective intra-play between young people and trees. *Children's Geographies*, 19(2), 225–240. https://doi.org/10.1080/14733285.2020.1783435

Health and Safety Executive. (2012). *Children's play and leisure – promoting a balanced approach*. Available at: www.hse.gov.uk/entertainment/childrens-play-july-2012.pdf

Lenz-Taguchi, H. (2014). New materialisms and play. In E. Brooker, M. Blaise and S. Edwards (Eds.), *The Sage handbook of play and learning in early childhood* (pp. 79–90). London: Sage.

Louis, L., & Powell, S. (2020). *About Friedrich Froebel, who Invented 'Kindergarten'*. Available at: www.froebel.org.uk/about-friedrich-froebel

Louv, R. (2005). *Last child in the woods: Saving our children from nature-deficit Disorder*. Chapel Hill, NC: Algonquin Books.

Macfarland, R., & Morris J. (2017). *The lost words: A spell book*. UK: Hamish and Hamilton at Penguin.

Nicholson, S. (1971). How NOT to cheat children. *Landscape Architecture*, 62, 33–34.

Rogoff, B. (2003). *The cultural nature of human development*. Oxford: Oxford University Press.

Waller, T., Arlemalm-Hagser, E., Sandseter, E. B. H., Lee-Hammond, L., Lekies, K., & Wyver, S. (2017). *The SAGE handbook of outdoor play and learning*. London: Sage.

Wilson, E. O. (1984). *Biophilia: The human bond with other species*. Cambridge, MA: Harvard University Press.

13

Beyond the Binary Logic: Approaching Play in the Digital Sphere Through Media Cultural Lenses

Pekka Mertala and Saara Salomaa

Chapter Objectives

This chapter helps you to:

- Understand the various affordances the digital media culture offers for children's playful practices.
- Critically reflect conceptions and discussions about children and digital media.
- Understand the concept of media educational consciousness in early childhood education and care (ECEC).

Introduction

Digital, as defined in Cambridge Dictionary (n.d.), refers to recording or storing information as a series of numbers 1 and 0 to indicate whether signal is present or absent. With tongue partially in cheek, we would state that the same logic is present in the vivid scholarly and public discussions around the role and effect of digitalisation to children's play - some consider digitalisation to destroy and diminish play (0) while for others, the new technological innovations appear as novel playful affordances (1). In this chapter, we challenge this binary reasoning by analysing young children's play in the digital sphere through media cultural lenses. Instead of approaching digitalisation only as the use of devices and software, we examine and articulate how children approach, make sense of, and give meanings to the digital in their everyday play-practices.

The chapter is organised as follows: In the first half, we illustrate and illuminate the multimodal and assemblage-like characteristics of digital media culture in young children's play-practices. Various examples drawn from video and observation data are used to present the theoretically and conceptually challenging phenomenon in an accessible manner. The second half of the chapter discusses what these observations and interpretations mean for the pedagogy of early childhood education. Theoretically, we foreground the concept of media educational consciousness (Salomaa, 2023) which refers to educators' awareness of acting in the role of an educator and the rights and responsibilities bound to that role in the context of media culture and institutional education. Before moving further, it should be noted that in the original definition of media educational consciousness, the concept of media included print media as well as the traditional (e.g., TV, radio, desktop computers), new (e.g., smartphones, tablet computers), and emerging (e.g., the Internet of Things [IoT]) forms of digital media. However, our focus in this chapter is mainly on digital media to avoid the risk of incoherence and superficial accounts.

Case Study 13.1: Iitu's First Phone: The Multifaceted Nature of Digital Media Culture

In July 2017, Pekka's then five-year-old daughter Iitu went to an overnight stay with her grandfather. When Iitu came home the next day, she was head over heels: Grandfather had bought her a smartphone. Even though Iitu's parents had quite mixed feelings about the situation, they decided to let Iitu keep the phone. In the end, the decision appeared to be the right one as the phone came out as a handy and multifunctional device. During the remaining summer, Iitu took hundreds of video clips and photos of things she liked. Iitu also used it while she played detective, making sure to take photos of clues and evidence such as footprints in the yard. Additionally, they walked dozens of kilometres while playing Pokémon Go in nearby streets. The supply of e-books, children's programmes, and music streaming services also offered entertainment when needed. Not bad for a cheap plastic Monster High toy phone with no real smartphone functionalities (see Figure 13.1).

So what were the driving forces behind the various ways Iitu used her phone during the summer? The answer, we argue, is the multifaceted nature of the media cultural sphere she lives in: Some of Iitu's smartphone practices drew from first-hand experiences whereas others were influenced by observations, second-hand information, and fantasies. Let us begin with her enthusiasm for taking photos and videos. As the pictures used in this chapter suggest, Iitu's parents tend to take photos and videos regularly – a habit which can be understood to signal the major role of visual mediation and communication in the contemporary media culture. When it comes to listening to music, while Pekka considers himself a vinyl enthusiast, he most often plays music via

(Continued)

streaming services for the sake of convenience. Audiobooks were – and still are – the family's main solution for killing time during long drives on holidays. The detective-themed roleplay was most likely influenced by a children's TV show that Iitu watches regularly, The Mysteries of Alfred Hedgehog, in which Alfred and his friends solve mysteries in their home forest by using modern technologies, including smartphones.

Figure 13.1 Iitu's Monster High Toy Phone

Pokemon Go, in turn, was still in its peak of popularity in 2017. At the time she got the phone, Iitu had not played the actual game but was familiar with the basic logic, narrative, and functions as Pokemon Go was a media phenomenon that was almost impossible to ignore. During one stroll around the neighbourhood, Iitu noticed beautiful flowers and interesting stones on the side of the pavement and wanted to pick them. However, this caused a problem: holding the phone in her hand prevented her

(Continued)

(Continued)

from picking up and carrying the flowers and the stones, and she also didn't want to stop playing Pokemon Go. After a moment of hard thinking, she came up with a solution. Her watch – a basic analogue children's watch illustrated with Moomin characters – turned into a smartwatch with integrated Pokemon Go. This innovation allowed her to get rid of the phone and collect the treasures, while continuing to play Pokemon Go. In other words, the immediate interests of flowers and stones acted as the driving forces for creative playful technological invention. The roots of the invention can at least be partially traced beyond the immediate situation. As a devoted runner, Pekka wears a GPS-enabled sport watch which, when paired with a smartphone app, draws a map of the running route. As one way to motivate Iitu to practice cycling without training wheels, Pekka put the GPS on to see the shape of the route they took while cycling.

One major question remains unanswered: why did Iitu relate to her toy phone as a real one? For example, she corrected everyone who referred to her phone as a toy by stating that it was the real thing. It was not that she couldn't tell the difference between a real and toy phone. Instead, in our interpretation, it was important for her that others contribute to building, sharing, and maintaining the fantasy and the "magic circle" of play (see Huizinga, 1949). For Iitu, a smartphone was not only a technological gadget, but owning a phone can be understood as a symbol of being a "big kid" - a school-aged child. In Finland, children typically get their first phone when they enter primary school at the age of seven (Merikivi et al., 2016), and indeed, some of Iitu's friends had older siblings who had gotten their first phones during the summer holiday.

Pedagogical Implications: Media Educational Consciousness as a Prerequisite for Understanding Children and Their Playful Digital Practices

As the case presented in the previous section illustrates, children's media cultural play draws from various sources and does not necessarily reflect their first-hand experience, as children can be cognisant about the media culture in which they have no first-hand experience (see also Lehtikangas & Mulari, 2016; Mertala & Meriläinen, 2019). Nevertheless, children's media cultural roleplay and other forms of meaning-making are often considered as direct information of children's media use by ECEC practitioners (Lehtikangas & Mulari, 2016; Salomaa & Mertala, 2019). Oftentimes, the content of these beliefs can be best described as negative and anxious because media use is believed to hinder social interactions, deprive imagination, cause health issues, and destroy play (Mertala, 2019a, 2019b). Some kindergartens may even have a total ban on roleplay inspired by a specific children's programme, which can be perceived as a very problematic way to engage children and their interests (Lehtikangas & Mulari, 2016). These beliefs contain notable resemblance with the ways in which children and media are represented in public discussion – headlines suggesting children as vulnerable and victimised media users have been common since the 1980s (Selwyn, 2003) and there are no signs that the discourse would be changing anytime soon (Laidlaw et al., 2021).

It is evident that sensitive and high-quality ECEC cannot be based on false beliefs and inflated concerns. Instead, they produce what Buber (1937) referred to as an "I-It-relationship" where the other – the child – is objectified as a mental representation. To put it another way, in the I-It relationship, the teacher does not recognise the child as a unique subject but rather as a reflection of her/his own fears and desires. To overcome the threat of the I-It -relationship requires constant critical reflection of the interpretations that educators make from children's play themes, drawings, and discussion topics. However, critical reflection of one's observations and beliefs is not an easy task. Instead, rather than questioning their beliefs, people are keen on assimilating new information to support their existing beliefs (Nespor, 1987). To provide tools for this challenging process, we next introduce the concept of media educational consciousness (Salomaa, 2023). The concept draws from Hirsjärvi's (1980) ideas on educational consciousness. In the context of media education, its core tenets include four main themes: (1) Conceptions about media; (2) Conceptions about ECEC goals and values in relation to media literacy; (3) Conceptions about children's growth and development; and (4) Conceptions about oneself as a media educator and the importance of ECEC for human growth in media culture. Each of the themes will be discussed in their own sub-sections.

Conceptions About Digital Media

One prerequisite for conducting media education is to have a conception of what media is. From the outset, we want to emphasise that digital media and its affordances in children's everyday life are not bound to any device. For example, children's drawings and crafts, singing, and role-plays are often inspired by digital media, thus expanding the sphere of media to non digital practices as showcased in the beginning of this chapter. According to a survey answered by 1056 Finnish parents of a minor, 59 % of 4- to 6-year-olds engaged in role-play that included media characters on a weekly or more basis (Kanerva et al., 2020, p. 52). Hence, in the educational context, media should also be seen as an important and broad learning environment that socialises children and adults to culture as well as shapes the image of the world.

While this article argues for a media cultural approach, much of the scholarly and pedagogical discussion is device-centred. A good example of this trend is that much of the debate around children and digital media is built on one blunt measure: screen time (Daugherty et al., 2014). In the context of ECEC, this discussion is present in the form of concerns related to children's eyesight and lack of physical exercise, which are all believed to be the effects of excess screen time (Mertala, 2019b). Screen time is a problematic concept to begin with, due to the lack of conceptual precision as there is no difference between watching TV while lying on the sofa and walking five kilometres while playing a location-based game such as Pokémon Go. The concept of screen time also does not distinguish itself between screen-based consumption (i.e. watching a digital animation via smartphone) from screen-based composition (i.e. creating a digital animation with a smartphone).

Furthermore, the case of Iitu's smartwatch serves as an important example that even digital media devices can no longer be regarded only as screen-based digital technologies. In fact, smartwatches with call function are gaining popularity among parents of young children (Business Research Insight, 2025). Additionally, the proliferation of Internet-connected household devices and toys are increasing rapidly (Allied Market Research, 2024), bringing ubiquitous computing and Internet of Things (IoT) as a part of children's everyday lives. However, for children, it is far from clear whether artefacts, such as toys, can be connected to the Internet (Mertala, 2020a). This uncertainty applies to the Internet in general – instead of a network of connected devices, children tend to conceptualise the Internet as a feature of the device they use (Mertala, 2019a; 2020a).

Some of the contemporary speech-controlled connected toys record and analyse what children say to them while other toys collect location data. Indeed, the ubiquity of Internet and datafication has inspired some scholars to highlight the need for including cyber safety education in ECEC (Edwards et al., 2018). Taking care of children's well-being by protecting them from potentially harmful media practices, content, or conduct is undoubtedly important. With that being said, media education cannot be reduced to mere safeguarding as there is little long-term benefit in forms of digital education that frames children as passive victims (Hope, 2013). Instead, as Pangrazio and Selwyn (2021) argue, cyber safety needs to be re-oriented to complement more critical and agentic forms of pedagogy. Such re-orientation, however, requires educators to reflect on their conceptions about the objectives of education as well as the traits and characteristics they perceive children to possess. This notion serves as a bridge to the next two themes: Conceptions about the objectives and values of ECEC in relation to digital media literacy, and conceptions about the children and their growth and development.

Reflection Point 13.1

- First, observe children's daily routines. How and when is media, in all its forms, intertwined in a child's day? How about your own day? What are the differences and similarities?
- Then, focus your observation on children's media-inspired play. What are the underlying themes the children might be processing through play practices and roleplay?

Conceptions About the Objectives and Values of ECEC in Relation to Digital Media Literacy

As mentioned in the beginning of this chapter, one of our aims is to unpack the binary logic that is often prevalent in discussions around children and digital media. In that respect, we wish to emphasise that such distinction does not exist between media education and the rest of ECEC. Instead, the aim of early years' media education is to promote ECEC's general educational goals by enhancing media literacy (Salomaa & Mertala, 2019). In many cases, making distinctions between media education and "other" education would be artificial and counterproductive. For example, let's take a look at social skills. Respectful behaviour towards others is a valuable educational goal, whether it be the interaction is digitally mediated or taking place face to face. Teaching children about one most likely contributes positively to the other as well.

When talking about educational goals, it is worth acknowledging that not all ECEC are alike in a global sense. In some countries, there is a rather strict division between care and education, which are often provided by different stakeholders, whereas others have opted for a more holistic approach. In Finland, ECEC has three intertwining dimensions: education, socialisation, and care (FNAfE, 2018). Since much of the scholarly discussion around children and digital media is concentrated on education (e.g., how digital media can support children's learning) and care (e.g., concerns about media use to children's eyesight and physical posture), our focus in this discussion is placed on socialisation.

With socialisation, we mean a process through which an individual becomes both a functional member of society "as is" and a unique subject who is able to criticise the prevalent societal structures and act as an agent of change in their own turn as they contribute to the development of a society that "might be" (Biesta et al., 2015). The latter form, the so-called individualistic social-isation process, is seldom addressed in early years' media education (Mertala, 2019b). This is problematic because media culture, like any other culture, is not a static monolith but it is shaped by different agents. In other words, the problematic features of contemporary media culture, such as grooming, online bullying, and dataveillance-based behavioural engineering are not products of deterministic causal processes but are intentional choices. While statements like, "the world is what we make of it," are simplistic and diminish the structural imbalances of power between people with different backgrounds and resources, it is important that children experience that they can affect things in their lifeworld.

Reflection Point 13.2

- Children's participation requires that children can practice skills that will enable them to be actors in media culture. These skills include, but are not limited to, knowledge about media, operational skills, safety skills, evolving critical thinking, and skills of self-expression through media. Name a practical example for each of the media competence areas that are currently relevant for children in ECEC.
- Plan adequate play activities to support the skills mentioned above.

In educational literature, the aforementioned principles of individualistic socialisation are often conceptualised through the concept of participation. Instead of strict hierarchy, participation refers to an idea that children and educators should form a collective where important decisions are made together in a democratic manner (Shier, 2001). In other words, participatory pedagogies are about creating a culture where the children want to participate as they feel welcomed, accepted, and respected, and can contribute to shaping and developing the culture to a great extent (see also Chapter 11 and Chapter 18). We argue that in ECEC, this is best done through playful pedagogies that combine both digital and non-digital practices.

It is vital to remember that education always operates on two different time-levels. Each pedagogical decision must contribute to children's well-being here and now as well as in the future. In other words, by practicing participatory pedagogies, we also aim to contribute to promoting participatory future society and media culture. This philosophy is beautifully and implicitly captured in the article A pedagogy of multiliteracies by the New London Group (1996). According to the article, education can "instantiate a vision through pedagogy that creates in microcosm a transformed set of relationships and possibilities for social futures, a vision that is lived in schools" (New London Group, 1996, p. 72). In our interpretation, the New London Group is suggesting that the everyday praxis and interactions in ECEC should be a micro-version of the kind of future we – children and adults – wish to achieve through education. The term "vision" does not refer to a predetermined and fixed idea of a good citizen/subject, as such a view would be just another form of I-It-relationship (Buber, 1937). This topic will be discussed in more detail in the next section.

Conceptions About the Children and Their Growth and Development

Earlier in the chapter, we warned about the dangers of I-It-relationship (Buber, 1937) in which the child is not recognised as a unique subject but as a representation of educators' fears and hopes. The threat is not only a hypothetical one, as in the context of digital media education, educators' conceptions are often polarised and children are viewed to be either too cognisant or not cognisant enough to be taught about digital media.

One prevalent conception is that digital media education is not needed because children already master the use of digital technologies and understand how these technologies work. Acceptance of this so-called digital native myth is identified among both in-service and preservice ECEC educators and is found to be rather persistent (Mertala & Salomaa, 2020). One explanation behind the popularity of the myth relates to overemphasising children's operational media literacy. What we mean by this is that children's handiness in using the often extremely intuitive and easy touchscreen devices is falsely considered to be an indicator of a holistic media literacy (Mertala, 2020b). However, tapping on an icon on a screen does not mean that the child is aware of the technology behind enabling such functionality or understands the messages received through media.

This notion serves as a bridge to the other common notion that children are too young to understand abstract phenomena, such as the Internet, and thus teaching these concepts should be postponed for later years – a statement we find rather problematic. Even though children may not be able to understand an abstract concept and/or phenomena in a comprehensive manner, this does not mean that they are not able to understand it at all. Nor does it mean that abstract and difficult concepts should be abandoned. For example, instead of merely using the functions, learning about the Internet can begin with the educator being conscious and clear when talking to children about using the Internet for digital practices and focusing on the connection that makes the functions possible. Thus, the concept of news might be best learnt by doing (e.g., by creating the group's own newspaper or 'news broadcast' by the means of playfully practiced journalism focusing on issues of children's interests).

To conclude, we argue that teaching children about digital media is not an either-or question. Media literacy, like all competences, is evolving. If you go back to the case description of Iitu's smartphone and smartwatch, and compare them to the two conceptions of children and media discussed in this section, you will most likely conclude that neither of them manages to capture her relationship with digital media. While she definitely possessed knowledge about the different functions of smartphones and smartwatches, she was far from all-knowing. In other words, teaching children about digital media is about finding the right balance of concrete and abstract explanations, and developing appropriate methods and materials. This topic will be addressed in the following section.

Conceptions of Oneself as a Media Educator and the Importance of ECEC for Human Growth in Media Culture

Based on our extensive research with in-service and preservice educators (e.g., Mertala, 2020b; Salomaa & Mertala, 2019), we argue that much of the hesitation in media education is due to educators' doubts regarding their own competencies as digital media educators. As stated by one preservice teacher: "I think that already small children are much more competent than adults are. Today, children are born around media, especially social media, so they get used to it better, compared to an adult who has lived a different life long before social media" (Mertala, 2020b, p. 33). Such a belief is without research-based support – children attending ECEC are so young that their use of digital media is dependent on adults' assistance and willingness to provide the children with devices and connections as well as socialising them to be digital media users.

Children are not "born around social media" – social media is used by adults. For example, in Finland, it is more common among 35- to 44-year-olds to report that they follow social media "constantly" (i.e. more than few times a day) than it is among 10- to 14-year-olds (Statistics Finland, 2017). The exaggerated uncertainty about practitioners' own competencies is also rather understandable as media culture has gone – and is going – through fundamental changes. This continuous evolution can cause professional uncertainty, especially as the contrast to the static nature of many fundamental ECEC contents is rather notable. For example, today, 1 plus 1 is 2 and so it was 20 years ago as well. Likewise, children in the 2020s need support in learning how to eat and get dressed independently in a similar manner as the preceding generations. This can lead to the misconception that media pedagogies would somehow be particularly difficult.

However, even though media education should embrace the complexity of media culture, the media educational practices do not have to be complex. As stated by one in-service teacher, media education is about "simple everyday things, things we learn in the day care centre and pre-school anyway" (Salomaa & Mertala, 2019, p. 156) but contextualised in a media culture. For example, let's examine the previously discussed IoT. There is empirical evidence indicating that young children can become aware of the existence of the IoT by reading purposefully selected non fictional books and via simple electronic crafting (Mertala, 2020a). Additionally, research suggests that open-ended and game-themed drawing tasks can be utilised in engaging children in pedagogical discussions about the basic mechanics of digital game design (Mertala & Meriläinen, 2019). Both of these examples imply that children can be taught about digital media by using traditional methods and materials, such as books and play-dough. This notion is not surprising, given that children often express their knowledge about digital media through non-digital artefacts, as exemplified in the case study about Iitu's smartphone and smartwatch. Furthermore, as play can be seen as one of the fundamental elements of ECEC and children's learning (Pramling Samulelsson & Johansson, 2006), children's interests in media-driven roleplay should be seen as pedagogically valuable potentials for exploring the media culture we all live in.

The previous section is a long-winded way to say that while the ever-changing media culture can justifiably be seen as a challenge for ECEC, media education provides inspirational possibilities for early years' practitioners. Media education pedagogies that combine children's media cultural interests, their playful expressions of meaning-making, and educators' professional competencies can lead to deeply meaningful learning experiences. The fact that children in ECEC are very young creates a challenge for educators' consciousness: A sensitive approach is needed in order to provide young children with safe and inspiring media education experiences, to recognise and respectfully support the media driven roleplay, and to identify the sparks for evolving media literacy skills that could be further developed alongside the playful everyday activities. However, the same fact can also be seen as comforting. Nothing overly complicated is required to be taught to young children about the media that it would be overwhelmingly difficult for a professional practitioner with a conscious mind to carry out.

Reflection Point 13.3

- Name 1-3 educational principles that are important to you in general. How do these principles become apparent in your educational actions related to children and digital media?

Summary

- Children's digital media-themed forms of play reflect the media culture they live in as well as their first-hand experiences with digital media.
- Even though media education should embrace the complexity of media culture, the media educational practices don't have to be complex.
- Media educational consciousness is a prerequisite for sensitive, safe, and inspiring media education in ECEC.

Further Reading

Mertala, P. (2021) Using playful methods to understand children's digital literacies. In L. Arnott & K. Wall (Eds.), *Research through play: Participatory methods in early childhood* (pp. 179-191). London: Sage. This chapter offers the reader a detailed walk-through of a playful digital literacy project, which combines traditional methods and materials with electronic crafting.

References

Allied Marker Research. (January, 2024). *Smart toys market size, share, competitive landscape and trend analysis report, by type, by technology, by distribution channel: Global opportunity analysis and industry forecast, 2024-2033.* https://www.alliedmarketresearch.com/smart-toys-market

Biesta, G., Priestley, M., & Robinson, S. (2015). The role of beliefs in teacher agency. *Teachers and Teaching*, 21(6), 624-640.

Buber, M. (1937). *I and thou.* Edinburgh: T. & T. Clark.

Business Research Insights. (March, 2025). *Children smartwatch market overview.* http://pxnet2.stat.fi/PXWeb/pxweb/en/StatFin/StatFin__eli__vpa__Tieto_ja_viestintatekniikk a/statfin_vpa_pxt_196.px/

Cambridge dictionary. (n.d.) *Digital.* https://dictionary.cambridge.org/dictionary/english/digital

Daugherty, L., Dossani, R., Johnson, E., & Wright, C. (2014), *Moving beyond screen time: Redefining developmentally appropriate technology use in early childhood education.* Washington, DC: RAND Corporation.

Edwards, S., Mantilla, A., Henderson, M., Nolan, A., Skouteris, H., & Plowman, L. (2018). Teacher practices for building young children's concepts of the internet through play-based learning. *Educational Practice and Theory*, 40(1), 29-50.

Finnish National Agency for Education. (2018). *National core curriculum guidelines for early childhood education.* Finnish National Agency for Education. https://www.oph.fi/en

Hirsjärvi, S. (1980). *Kasvatustietoisuus ja kasvatuskäsitykset. Teoreettinen tarkastelu (Educational consciousness. Theoretical perspectives).* University of Jyväskylä Department of Education. Research reports 88/1980.

Hope, A. (2013). The politics of online risk and the discursive construction of e-safety. In K. Facer & N. Selwyn (Eds.), *The politics of education and technology: Conflicts, controversies and connections* (pp. 83-98). London: Palgrave/Macmillan.

Huizinga, J. (1949). *Homo Ludens: A study of the play-element in culture.* London: Routledge.

Kanerva, A., Niiniaho, A., & Pirilä, L. (2020). Selvitys kuvaohjelmien ikärajatuntemuksesta (Report on age-rating awareness). *Cuporen verkkojulkaisuja*, 64. https://kavi.fi/wp-content/uploads/2020/09/Cupore_ik%C3%A4rajat_saavutettava.pdf

Laidlaw, L., O'Mara, J., & Wong, S. (2021). 'This is your brain on devices': Media accounts of young children's use of digital technologies and implications for parents and teachers. *Contemporary Issues in Early Childhood*, 22(3), 268-281.

Lehtikangas, A., & Mulari, H. (2016). 'Mä en oo kattonu mut mä vaan tiiän ne': Havainnointi, medialeikit ja eronteot päiväkodissa. ('I haven't seen them, I just know them': observation, mediaplay and distinctions in kindergarten). In H. Mulari (Ed.) *Solmukohtia: Näkökulmia lasten mediakulttuurien tutkimusmenetelmiin ja mediakasvatukseen (Viewpoints to research on children's media cultures and media education).* (pp. 55-78). Nuorisotutkimusverkosto/Nuorisotutkimusseura.

Merikivi, J., Myllyniemi, S., & Salasuo, M. (2016). *Media hanskassa. Lasten ja nuorten vapaaaikatutkimus* [Media under control. Leisure Survey of Children and Young People 2016 on Media and Physical Activity]. Helsinki, Finland: Nuorisotutkimusseira.

Mertala, P. (2019a). Young children's conceptions of computers, code, and the Internet. *International Journal of Child-Computer Interaction*, 19, 56-66.

Mertala, P. (2019b). Teachers' beliefs about technology integration in early childhood education: A meta-ethnographical synthesis of qualitative research. *Computers in Human Behavior*, 101, 334-349.

Mertala, P. (2020a). Young children's perceptions of ubiquitous computing and the Internet of Things. *British Journal of Educational Technology*, 51(1), 84-102.

Mertala, P. (2020b). Misunderstanding child-centeredness: The case of "child 2.0" and media education. *Journal of Media Literacy Education*, 12(1), 26-41.

Mertala, P., & Meriläinen, M. (2019). The best game in the world: Exploring young children's digital game-related meaning-making via design activity. *Global Studies of Childhood*, 9(4), 275-289.

Mertala, P., & Salomaa, S. (2020). Looking for digital (alter)natives: Why teachers' beliefs about children matter in media education. In D. Frau-Meigs, S. Kotilainen, M. Pathak-Shelat, M. Hoechsmann, & S. Pyntz (Eds.), *The handbook of media education research*. Hoboken, NJ: John Wiley and Sons.

The New London Group. (1996). A pedagogy of multiliteracies: Designing social futures. *Harvard Educational Review*, 66(1), 60-93.

Nespor, J. (1987). The role of beliefs in the practice of teaching. *Journal of Curriculum Studies*, 19(4), 317-328.

Pangrazio, L., & Selwyn, N. (2021). Towards a school-based 'critical data education'. *Pedagogy, Culture & Society*, 29(3), 431-448.

Pramling Samuelsson, I. & Johansson, E. (2006). Play and learning—inseparable dimensions in preschool practice. *Early Child Development and Care*, 176(1), 47-65.

Salomaa, S. (2023). *Mediakasvatus osana varhaiskasvatuksen opettajien työtä ja koulutusta: Tulkintakehyksenä mediakasvatustietoisuus (Media education as part of early childhood education teachers' work and training: Media educational consciousness as an interpretative framework)*. Tampere, Finland: Tampere Univeristy.

Salomaa, S., & Mertala, P. (2019). An education-centred approach to digital media education. In C. Gray & I. Palaiologou (Eds.), *Early learning in the digital age* (pp. 151-164). London: Sage.

Selwyn, N. (2003). 'Doing IT for the kids': Re-examining children, computers and the 'information society'. *Media, Culture & Society*, 25(3), 351-378.

Shier, H. (2001). Pathways to participation: Openings, opportunities and obligations. *Children and Society* 15920, 107-117.

Statistics Finland. (2017). *How often follows social media, those aged 10 or over %*. Available at: http://pxnet2.stat.fi/PXWeb/pxweb/en/StatFin/StatFin__eli__vpa__Tieto_ja_viestintatekniikk a/statfin_vpa_pxt_196.px/

14

The Place of Play in the Early Years Curricula of the United Kingdom

Carys Jennings

Chapter Objectives

This chapter will help you to:

- Understand how play is conceptualised within the curricula of the home nations.
- Consider how play and learning is planned within the various curricula.
- Understand how children's voice can be embedded into the planning process.
- Think about play and pedagogy.

How Is Play Conceptualised Across the United Kingdom?

The education systems of England, Scotland, Northern Ireland and Wales have each embraced the ideals of play as being a central feature of early childhood and developmental growth. The fundamental role of play within the curricula of the UK nations legitimises a conceptualisation of play as a purposeful means of learning for children in the early years. Since the beginning of the twenty-first century each of the four home nations has undergone an educational reform that includes highlighting the importance of play provision within the curriculum for their youngest citizens. Play is therefore recognised as having positive cognitive, physical, social and emotional 'consequences' on paper. However, there is often a tension between policy and what happens in practice. The last two decades provides much-needed evidence to support those long-held views by early years educators that play is, and can equate to, purposeful learning when in the hands of those who understand child development and how children learn (Walsh et al., 2017). This chapter aims to explore the intention for play within the curricula of the four nations and to consider the challenges and tensions often associated with the implementation of a play pedagogy.

Each nation has a play strategy (see also Chapter 2) as well as an education strategy. Play in England (2025) is England's 'new 10-year Play strategy' (which is currently being 're-imagineered') (https://www.playengland.org.uk/strategy) promotes play for children between 3 and 5 years and during break times in school, whereas Scotland's most recent 'Play strategy' (2024) (https://www.playscotland.org/policy/play-strategy/), Wales' 'Play policy' (2019) (https://play.wales/play-policy-legislation/current-policies/) and Northern Ireland's 'Play and leisure policy' (2016) (https://www.education-ni.gov.uk/articles/play-matters#toc-0) include strategic guidance that outlines and underpins the importance of play within an educational context during traditional contact teaching time in addition to during out of school leisure activities.

Provision varies across each country as regards curricular content; however, each nation highlights the importance of experiential learning and play within their documentation. Table 14.1 provides the links to curriculum content for each of the four nations for the early years sector and beyond.

Table 14.1 Overview of the Documentation Relating to Curriculum Provision for Children 0-8 Years Across the United Kingdom

Nation	Documentation and Age Range	URL Links	Comments RE Relevant Dates
England	Early Years Foundation Stage (EYFS): 0–5 years:	https://www.gov.uk/government/publications/early-years-foundation-stage-framework–2	Revised November 2024
England	Key Stage 1: 5–7+ years	www.gov.uk/national-curriculum/key-stage-1-and-2	Current documentation
Scotland		Curriculum for Excellence 3–18 years: https://education.gov.scot/curriculum-for-excellence/	Current documentation
		Pre-birth to 8 years:	
		https://www.gov.scot/publications/supporting-young-peoples-health-wellbeing-summary-scottish-government-policy/pages/4/	
Northern Ireland		Pre-school 2–4 years:	Current documentation
		https://www.education-ni.gov.uk/topics/early-years-education-and-learning	
		Foundation Stage:	
		www.nicurriculum.org.uk/docs/foundation_stage/UF_web.pdf	
		Key Stages 1 and 2:	
		https://ccea.org.uk/key-stages-1-2/curriculum	

Table 14.1 Overview of the Documentation Relating to Curriculum Provision for Children 0-8 Years Across the United Kingdom *(Continued)*

Nation	Documentation and Age Range	URL Links	Comments RE Relevant Dates
Wales		Early childhood, play, learning and care in Wales https:// hwb.gov.wales/curriculum-for-wales/early-childhood-play-learning-and-care-in-wales	Current documentation
		Curriculum for Wales 3–16: https:// hwb.gov.wales/curriculum-for-wales/	

Each nation organises curriculum content in domains of knowledge and development, for example in Wales these are: expressive arts; humanities; health and well-being; science and technology; mathematics and numeracy; languages, literacy, and communication. Each nation also includes cross-curricular themes, for example relationship education, education for sustainable development and global citizenship, and children's rights.

The following section provides an overview of the place of play within the curriculum documentation described above. In addition, where national play policy provides guidance that relates to the sphere of early years education and care this is also noted.

Play in the English Early Years Curriculum

The curriculum in England supports the notion that children's play reflects their interests and that they should have opportunities to play alone or alongside others in different situations. The Early Years Foundation Stage (EYFS) is a play-based framework that sets out the expected standards for the learning, care and development of children from birth to 5 years across England. It upholds the overarching principles that every child is unique, that they learn to develop strong relationships, that the prepared environments must enable play and development, and that every child learns at different rates and in varying ways. The EYFS outlines three key features of effective learning through play, those being playing and exploring, active learning and creating and thinking critically.

Play in the Scottish Early Years Curriculum

The vision within the education strategy in Scotland outlines that children's play is crucial to Scotland's well-being: socially, economically and environmentally. Scotland's Realising the ambition: Being me (2020) acknowledges play as a key component of good practice in the early years and highlights the importance of planning and supporting play both within and outside school settings.

Challenge and enjoyment are highlighted as important features of the activities undertaken. Additionally, Scottish policy documentation supports the availability and exposure to play challenges that will develop healthy outdoor habits amongst children and young people (Play scotland, 2025).

Play in the Northern Irish Early Years Curriculum

Play as a primary means of learning in the early years, the importance of outdoor provision and engaging families are all aspects that define the curriculum for the early years in Northern Ireland (NI). 'The pedagogy of play provides a holistic learning vehicle for the early years' (Walsh G., 2020, Personal Communication: Interview with the author 05-01-20). Playboard Northern Ireland states that play is the means by which children make sense of the world. 'Both natural and instinctive, play enables children to test their own abilities and learn and to develop new skills and knowledge' (PlayboardNI, 2020). For further information regarding play in Northern Ireland see Doherty and Walsh in Boyd and Hirst (2016).

Play in the Welsh Early Years Curriculum

The Welsh Government or Senedd were the first country in the world to legislate for children's play. Curriculum for Wales (CfW) is the current legislation for the education of 3- to 16-year-old learners in Wales, it builds on the previous play-based Foundation Phase that set a precedent that has remained for play and experiential learning as central to children's learning (see Chapter 2).

The Curriculum for Wales (Welsh Government, 2021) is underpinned by 12 pedagogical principles and four purposes which are aspirations for each child to develop as ambitious, capable learners; enterprising creative contributors; healthy, confident individuals; and ethically informed citizens. Experiential holistic learning is championed as the pedagogy of choice for the Curriculum for Wales with play having a central role within the early years and experiential learning extending across all statutory schooling.

Reflection Point 14.1

Use the links provided above and explore the curriculum guidance for children aged 3- to 5-year-old across the four nations. Try to identify the following.

- What is the expected curriculum content across the four nations for this age group?
- What is the place of play in curricular provision across the four nations for this age group?
  - Is this similar or different across the four nations? In what ways?
  - How might any differences be visible in a nursery class for 3- to-4-year-old children in each country?
  - Now explore differences for children aged 5-6 years.

Planning for Play

Planning in the early years usually takes place in the long, medium and short term, see also chapter 10 for more detail about planning for play.

Short term planning may be for a session, a day or a week, whereas mid-term planning may be for a half term, term or number of months. Long-term planning may provide an overview of learning across a full year, an entire phase or stage. Schools and settings decide upon 'umbrella themes' and overarching goals or objectives to be explored during each of the three time frames. These themes and goals are guided by curriculum frameworks for the children they are planning for. Good practice examples of planning from approaches such as the Reggio Emilia approach in northern Italy (see Chapter 20) and plan-do-review from HighScope (https://highscope.org/) encourage children to be active participants in the planning process, especially in the mid and short term. All four UK nations stipulate that planning should be based on the reflective process of observation of children's activity and interests during teaching and learning events in order to inform and improve provision and practice. Socio-cultural perspectives are employed whereby children learn through shared co-constructed experiences with other children and adults, and integrated models of planning are encouraged as opposed to one particular framework being championed. Learning areas or domains can be combined and placed within a specific context that will make sense to the child, such as when learning about money, a role play area may be set up so that the children can actively engage in activities directly related to the concepts of shopping, buying, and paying using money.

Observing children at play, considering the resources that are available and the scope of the environment both indoors and outdoors (see Chapter 11) are all considerations that contribute to the careful planning of engaging activities. Planning is by no means a simple task, it is challenging; practitioners are required to have a clear understanding of child development, to know about the specific interests of the children in their care and to know the requirements of the relevant curriculum framework (see chapter 10). Ensuring appropriate spaces, engaging themes and providing a variety of resources are some of the initial considerations when planning. Organisation and progression are part of the planning process, however there is a need for flexibility as children will be drawn to some activities more than others; much of what was intended at the planning stage may change according to children's interests and engagement. Often practitioners will then write retrospective accounts of the play and learning activities undertaken.

Documenting planning is an essential and required means of recording proposed activities and information. These planning documents can then be shared with colleagues, parents, or other interested parties for reference. Planning documents map out intended experiences and tasks and can be a record of children's interests, tasks and the progress they have made.

Long-term planning ensures that all the areas and aspects of learning are covered. This coverage can be for a year or for a two-year cycle in some cases. Schools will highlight targets for each term within a cycle to ensure specific skills are developed within that time. Generally, in all four nations practitioners plan the activities to be undertaken in the early years using a thematic or topic-based approach (Boyd & Hirst, 2016), choosing themes that will be of interest to the children. These themes can, and often are, a combination of adult and child chosen themes; umbrella themes tend to be adult chosen and are frequently repeated at later stages in the educational journey of a child but at a deeper level. For example, take a look at Table 14.2–a child may engage in playful learning including recognising and naming body parts by singing 'Heads, shoulders knees & toes' in the *Me, myself & I*, 'Getting to know me' theme during the Autumn term. They will revisit this aspect during movement sessions, moving arms, legs, and head whilst dancing during the *People & the natural world* theme in the Spring term and again revisit and consolidate their understanding through play when comparing and contrasting sizes of people, body parts or role playing a hospital during the *Our community* theme in the Summer term.

Mid-term planning draws on the proposed skills and activities outlined in the long-term planning and focuses on the weekly or fortnightly activity to be undertaken covered within a mini theme or topic. Mid- and short-term themes tend to stem from children's interests within the umbrella theme as they articulate what they already know and what they would like to find out about an idea proposed. For example, if we take the *Our community* theme from Table 14.2, during discussions and in their play the children may indicate they want to investigate recycling and rubbish which could lead to a mini theme of 'Bags and boxes'. Ideas would then be considered that relate to the theme 'Bags and boxes', and that reflect aspects of the curriculum and known areas of playful interest for the children. These are then incorporated into activities for investigation, construction, creating, and discovery play.

Table 14.2 Example of Long-Term Planning by Umbrella Themes

	Autumn Term		Spring Term		Summer Term	
Examples of Focus Areas	**Me, Myself, and I**	**My Friends and Family**	**All Around Us**	**People and The Natural World**	**Making Connections**	**Our Community**
Languages, Literacy and Communication	Sharing, speaking and listening	Vocabulary Songs and rhymes	Early reading skills	Handling texts and books	Emergent writing	Mark-making
Mathematics and Numeracy	Numbers & counting	Number recognition and counting	Counting and sorting	Sorting and comparing Chronology	Measuring (non-standard)	Comparing and contrasting measures
Personal and Social Development	Getting to know me	I like I can	Getting to know you	You are You know	How are we connected?	We are We can
Expressive Arts	Who am I? Portraits focus	Making choices	Music and movement focus	Handling equipment	Drama and role play focus	Experimenting with media
Health and Well-being	Regulating my body	Stances & movements	Balance & co-ordination	Dance & apparatus	Object control	Ball skills
Humanities	Being kind	Christmas Hannukah Diwali	New life	Easter	Special places and spaces	Looking after each other Respecting

Short-term planning will include children's ideas and curiosities regarding the theme; for example in Table 14.3 we see how 'People who help us' has been planned as a cycle (carousel) of activities for a day, with free choice play spaces available.

Table 14.3 Example of Short-Term Planning of Activities for a Day

Introduction to the session

Feely bag with hats and jackets and objects belonging to people who help us – children to choose one item and place on the floor. Discuss what it is and who uses it.

Each child in turn will choose an object and place it in a new pile or with another related to the person who helps us – four people who help us will be portrayed through the objects (doctor/police person/delivery driver/optician). *Carousel activities*

Construction Play	*Role Play*	*Creative Digital Play*	*Sensory Play*
Skills:	Skills:	Skills:	Skills:
Handling objects	Exploration	Hand-eye co-ordination	Fine motor skills
Cooperative play	Language use	Problem-solving	Thinking
Activity:	Activity:	Activity:	Activity:
Build an ambulance/lifeboat from recycled materials.	Recreate roles in the Magic Mirror – children to decide who they will be today.	Move the Bee-bot® ambulance or police car to the destination in order to help the patient get to the hospital.	Create stamps of people who help us (like the Queen's head) to put on a border around the display board.

Free choice activity areas available

Painting area

Outdoors – garden area/den making

Small world – town mat and resources

Interactive whiteboard – matching

Case Study 14.1

Planning

A reception class in School A work on a fluid fortnightly cycle of themes that stem from children's ideas relating to the whole school theme, *Here, there and everywhere*. At the beginning of the term the adults introduce the theme and ask the children to propose some ideas; these stem from their experiences and knowledge, and include rooms, places, villages, towns, and countries. A spider diagram is drawn up with the theme in the centre and the new sub-themes, arising from children's ideas surrounding it. The children decide which theme to choose each fortnight. The planning and discussion about the spider diagram reoccurs fortnightly on a Friday in preparation for the coming weeks. The sub-theme is chosen, and the children share their ideas and what they wanted to find out. For example, Gweno asked 'is Abergwili a village or a town? And Ioan asked 'Can you walk to France?' Next to each idea the child's name is written, this makes pupil voice visible and can also be a source of pride for the individual when the activities and subsequent documentation and display of playful learning comes to fruition.

> ## Reflection Point 14.2
>
> - What playful provision might you provide to enable children to respond to Gweno and Ioan's interests?
> - What tensions might arise for the practitioner who must ensure coverage of a statutory curriculum when she plans playful provision based around children's interests?
> - How might the practitioner ensure at least some provision allows children to have control over the play?

Planning in the Early Years – The Early Excellence Model of Provision

Planning varies across the UK nations and between types of early years setting depending on the size, type of provision (maintained or non-maintained), and whether the provision is within a school or an independent setting. However, there are similarities whereby staff plan as teams and collaboratively with the children, giving children a voice and ensuring playful pedagogies. Various models of planning are created and utilised in order to account for the environments, resources, and priority needs of the children who attend the settings.

One such example that has been used by many settings and schools is the Early Excellence Model of provision found in Figure 14.1 (Early Excellence Ltd – www.earlyexcellence.com).

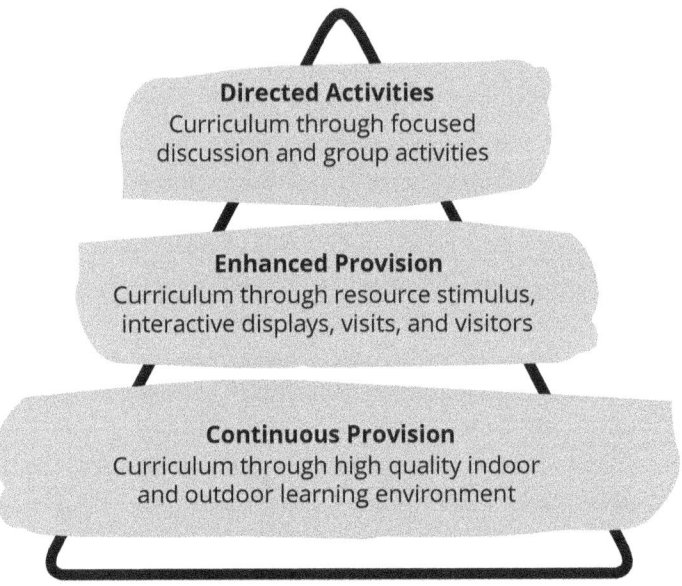

Directed Activities
Curriculum through focused discussion and group activities

Enhanced Provision
Curriculum through resource stimulus, interactive displays, visits, and visitors

Continuous Provision
Curriculum through high quality indoor and outdoor learning environment

Figure 14.1 Early Excellence Planning Model

Source: Guide to Continuous Provision, Early Excellence (2020). Reprinted with permission.

The Early Excellence Model is a bottom-up model that takes account of three interrelated stages of planning and delivery. The model has been developed by Liz Marsden, Founder and CEO of Early Excellence and has been recognised as good practice by inspection bodies across the four nations where schools and settings have used it effectively for planning for play and development of skills.

The bottom or base level of the model is the *continuous provision* – this would include the permanent areas that are available to the children for playful activity indoors and outdoors, e.g. sand area, painting area, role play area, garden, mud kitchen, and the like.

The middle tier is the *enhanced provision* – these are additional resources and new activities that have been chosen carefully for the different areas to enable the children to engage and develop their skills further, e.g., open-ended resources for imaginative play, brushes, paints, sponges, different sizes and textures of paper etc. These enhancements should be based on close observation of the children's play interests, and will seek to extend the playful engagement of the children.

The top tier represents the *directed activities* – these are generally adult led, usually small-group but maybe whole-class activities where new ideas, skills or concepts are introduced to the children that are unfamiliar and require a more able other to demonstrate or lead the learning by modelling. These could be activities, such as letter or number recognition, counting, sorting, and matching activities, handling new equipment, learning songs or rhymes, that could include playful approaches but would not necessarily be considered play provision.

Even though these are three distinct layers each one works with the others to ensure a holistic purposeful provision is being implemented. Resources used within a directed activity to introduce a new skill would then transfer as enhancements (to a continuous provision) so that the children could encounter, explore, practise, and consolidate their understanding.

The provisions we create, and the resources children encounter, should allow for the learning that has been planned to take place, as well as for children to play and engage in further imaginative learning. The Early Excellence philosophy offers children opportunities to interact with their environment to make choices, and to become independent confident participants.

Practitioners in all four nations adopt an integrated approach to planning using aspects from various planning models in order to provide a bespoke provision for the children in their care.

Reflection Point 14.3

- How important do you think it is for adults to include children in planning? Why?
- In the Early Excellence Model, how are children's play interests planned for?
- What are the tensions between enacting a play-based pedagogy and providing directed learning activities? How might these be overcome?

Adults, Play, and Pedagogy

It is clear in all four nations that within structured play, the adults' role is imperative in order to progress the learning. Here, structured play is where the outcome or perceived skills to be developed have been planned beforehand to meet the intentions of curriculum guidelines but include children's interests. Teachers, support assistants or leaders undertake a variety of roles within the pedagogy of play and are encouraged to adopt a 'playful persona' (Walsh G., 2020, Personal Communication: Interview with the author 05-01-20). At times, when children are encountering new learning in knowledge, concepts or skills, the adult will lead the learning by modelling and introducing new vocabulary as in the case of 'directed activities' within the Early Excellence model. Other times, the adults will be supporting or facilitating the play by joining in, when invited, or introducing new ways of handling resources, or by engaging in conversation (see Chapter 12). Sometimes there will be no formal interactions, the adults will observe and reflect on the play as it happens as a means of informing future planning to move the play along. Knowing when to join in with children's activity and when to step back is a skill. Walsh emphasises that children and adults should be partners in play and the child should certainly not be the follower (Walsh et al., 2017); whilst Siraj (2021) underlines the importance of intentional and relational pedagogy to ensure provision is a blend of adult-led and child-initiated opportunities as play will have different purposes for adults and children. We are aware from the work of Montessori that 'play is a child's work' (see Chapter 4) for example. Early years education documents in all four nations describe the features of children's play to include dispositions such as perseverance, object handling, concentration, dealing with challenge and uncertainty, being imaginative, working alone or in cooperation with others. Guided play where adults lead, or support, could be seen as hindering free-flow self-directed play (see Chapter 1). Adults may have specific objectives in mind when planning for play with a time frame and a set of skills that children should encounter along the way. Having adults on hand who sensitively develop children's vocabulary and use of objects can support and extend learning and skill development. However, children may have no particular aim or outcome at the outset of their playful activities; learning occurs, and skills will develop, but these will not have been decided upon beforehand.

Case Study 14.2

A Case Study From Wales

A group of 5-year-old boys were playing in the 'snowy white world' trough (imitation snow, snowflakes, penguins and polar bears along with pompoms and small fir trees were the scene).

The children had chosen the imaginative world and had previous knowledge of life at the north and south poles, and therefore know that penguins and polar bears did not actually live together, but they were happy to continue their play. However, one Monday morning the adults observed two of the boys rummaging in the small world play box for additional resources. The boys proceeded back to the snowy trough with lions and continued with their play. The adults considered joining in and challenging the addition of the lion to the winter scene, but instead decided to observe as the boys engaged in 15 minutes of imaginative and dramatic play with the lions in the snow. When an opportunity

(Continued)

arose later the adults asked the boys about their play. The boys had been to the cinema to see a film over the weekend and they were re-enacting what they had seen. The film was the *Lion, the Witch and the Wardrobe*.

Reflection Point 14.4

- What would have happened if the adults intervened when the boys fetched the lions?
- What was the value of re-enacting parts of the film for the boys?
- What learning might the adults record against the curriculum guidelines for Wales for 5-year-olds?
- How might the adults build on the children's learning and interest in future provision?

There are many tensions and a variety of perspectives regarding play as a means of learning despite the consensus that it is the most appropriate means to develop young children's understanding. 'There is a constant pressure to ensure children are 'school-ready' (Cremin & Burnett, 2018, p. 110). Government requirements are often based on the accountability of settings and schools to show statistics that reflect levels of attainment which can push young children into a formal education before they are developmentally ready to engage (see Chapters 1 and 6). Early years practitioners are profoundly aware that young children are able to play, think and learn in a sophisticated manner that can be observed in ways that formal testing cannot show. The Effective Provision of Pre-School Education project (EPPE) revealed that when well-trained knowing adults engage in play alongside children, they can become involved in episodes of sustained shared thinking (Sylva et al., 2004) with children, in which the adult and the child engage deeply in conversation to solve a problem, or clarify or extend a narrative (Sylva et al., 2004). The skill of the adult in sustained shared thinking is to engage deeply in those conversations that children are interested in, those that are led by the children themselves (Brodie, 2014). Play-based pedagogies reject the false divide between children's 'play' and 'work' (see Chapters 1 and 15) to ensure all playful activities are given equal status and viewed as learning opportunities.

Play and Technology

The ECEC curriculums of each of the four nations include elements of digital technologies as part of the provision. The use of computers, interactive whiteboards, iPads, and digital mobile devices is highly contested within early education circles, with opposing views often unable to agree or strike a balance as to how much, or how often, digital devices should be incorporated in provision (see Chapter 13). One long-held view is that computers stifle and minimise children's learning and the socialisation process as activities are described as passive, whereas proponents of digital devices see opportunities for thinking and motivation. There is an agreement amongst practitioners that understanding children's prior learning with respect to technological awareness is a good starting point, and providing real-world opportunities to use digital technology within exploratory and imaginative play can be beneficial in developing skill and confidence. Another point all curricula guidance agrees upon is that the use of technologies should be purposeful and an enhancement, not a replacement for an actual experience. Across the four nations the approach to technologies appears to promote the use of digital devices within provision to support and develop different skills in new and emerging diverse learning environments, and there is a recognition that these should reflect real-life situations.

The place of play in learning provision for young children is strengthened through research, and the associated understanding that children's positive emotional connection, through play, to an activity reaps cognitive benefits (Howard & McInnes, 2013; Siraj, 2021; Walsh et al., 2017).

Summary

- Children are naturally curious and playful, and with the support and careful planning by knowing professionals, high-quality learning can be afforded through play.
- Play is a key aspect of the educational provision for young children in all four nations of the United Kingdom.
- Planning for play happens in a variety of ways through an integrated approach.
- Children need opportunities for free-play indoors and outdoors, as well as opportunities for structured play directed towards specific learning outcomes.
- The challenges faced by adults working with young children can be exacerbated by a lack of understanding by policymakers of the advantages and fundamental need for children to play in order to make sense of themselves, their communities and the world they inhabit.

Further Reading

Brock, A., Jarvis, P. and Olusoga, Y. (2018) *Perspectives on Play: Learning for Life*. London: Routledge. This book examines play-based activities from a range of settings and includes case studies, interviews and discussions.

Sicart, M. (2014) *Play Matters*. London: MIT Press. This book explores the way in which play is an expression of understanding and a fundamental part of being human.

Wood, E. and Chesworth, L. (2017) *Play and Pedagogy*. Available at: www.bera.ac.uk/blog/play-and-pedagogy. This article explores the tensions between policy and practice and the vulnerability of play as a purposeful pedagogy.

References

Boyd, D., & Hirst, N. (Eds.) (2016). *Understanding early years education across the UK*. London: Routledge.

Brodie, K. (2014). *Sustained shared thinking in the early years*. London: Routledge.

Cremin, T., & Burnett, C. (2018). *Learning to teach in the primary school*. Abingdon: Routledge.

Early Excellence. (2020). *Early excellence: Inspirational learning*. https://earlyexcellence.com/

Howard, J., & McInnes, K. (2013). *The essence of play: A practice companion for professionals working with children and young people*. London: Routledge.

Play England. (2025). *It all starts with play! Our new 10-year strategy*. Available at: https://www.playengland.org.uk/strategy (Accessed 22 May 2025).

Play Scotland. (2025). *Scotland's play vision statement and action plan 2025-2030*. Available at: https://www.playscotland.org/policy/play-strategy/ (Accessed 22 May 2025).

PlayboardNI. (2020). *The importance of play in schools*. Available at: https://www.playboard.org/what-we-do/play-in-schools/ (Accessed 22 May 2025).

Siraj, I. (2021). Learning without limits – everything connects – movement, play and child development. *Presented at online conference healthy, happy curious children - curriculum development & the revised EYFS (8 January 2021)*. Newham Nursery Schools.

Sylva, K., Melhuish, E., Sammons, P., Siraj-Blatchford, I., & Taggart, B. (2004). *The effective provision of pre-school education (EPPE) project: Final report. A longitudinal study funded by the DfES 1997–2004*. London: Institute of Education, University of London/Department for Education and Skills/Sure Start.

Walsh, G., McMillan, D., & McGuiness, C. (2017). *Playful teaching and learning*. London: Sage.

Welsh Government. (2021). *Curriculum for Wales*. Available at: https://hwb.gov.wales/curriculum-for-wales/ (Accessed 22 May 2025).

15

The Role of the Adult in Supporting Play

Angela Rekers and Mel McCree

Chapter Objectives

This chapter will help you to consider the role of the adult in supporting children's play in terms of the following:

- Joining in: Supporting, extending, initiating, validating, modelling, and intervening.
- Stepping back: Observing, assessing, planning, and reflecting.

Introduction

In child-centred practice, the adult's role is crucial. Our role is a vital feature of the environments that support, sustain, and validate children's holistic development and playful activity. During play, children want to be both free from adult interruptions and have their significant adults to play alongside them. Rather than being contradictory, this highlights the complexity of the adult's role in being responsive to children's play and the many decisions adults face when supporting children's playful activity. The roles and responsibilities of the adult supporting play are as diverse as the children and their play activities. Consider how an adult in each of these scenarios is supporting play: playing 'peek-a-boo!' with an infant, colouring alongside an older child or quietly organising resources while two children argue over a toy.

In this chapter, we address one of the most frequent choices adults make in supporting children's play: to join in or step back? Within the process of play, both players and those in supporting roles make this choice, dynamically and responsively, again and again.

We begin this chapter by drawing attention to the tension between conceptualisations of 'child-initiated' and 'adult-led' play; then, we focus on ways in which adults can move beyond such binary definitions to approach play in response to and in collaboration with children. Although we have attempted to categorise adult behaviours as 'joining in' and 'stepping back', we do so not to create another dichotomy, but to suggest that conscientious adults move fluidly between such spaces, considering their own intentions and in response to children's play.

Tricky Definitions and Concepts: *Child-Initiated, Adult-Led and Free Play*

There is a growing body of critical work that aims to answer the question: 'what is play?', as practitioners from multiple fields try to articulate definitions and conceptualisations. In reality, this is a difficult task, as play is full of paradox and infinite diversity (see Chapter 1). A range of play literature has contributed to conceptualising play and its benefits and purposes, augmented in recent years from evidence within neuroscience, evolutionary biology and zoology, among other disciplines. An in-depth discussion of these concepts is beyond the scope of this chapter. However, here, we draw attention to some key ideas, such as 'free play', and explore how the adult fits into such concepts. 'Free play' is one expression of our innate play drive, which fulfils evolutionary purposes, particularly in childhood, contributing to healthy growth and development (see Chapter 6), expanding our relationships with ourselves, others and our environments (see Chapters 7, 8, and 10), and aiding our survival (Hughes, 2012). It is therefore extremely beneficial for adults to create and support conditions in which this can happen.

In play-based settings, 'free play' is often used to describe 'child-initiated' opportunities, in which children are allowed an element of autonomous choice. Csikszentmihalyi (1990) calls an autonomous activity one in which individuals have control over their environment and feel freedom from having to ask permission or being judged by their choices. While adults often provide the spaces for play, they should attempt to empower children to have opportunities for such autonomous activity (see Chapter 10). The Playwork Principles define play as a process that is 'freely chosen, self-directed and intrinsically motivated' (Playwork Principles Scrutiny Group, 2005). The element of the player's choice is crucial in 'free play', compared to what is often referred to as 'adult-led' play, where the adult is directing play activity, according to adult agendas.

Often, the term 'structured' play is used to describe that which is 'adult-led'. Yet, children also initiate structure within their 'free play'; for instance, they may decide there are specific rules to follow in a game. These may be founded upon their own observations of adults, but in such circumstances, these structures and rules are directed, negotiated, appropriated, argued, and agreed upon by the children, who have their own motivations for playing or choosing not to play. Therefore, a binary between *free* and *structured* play may not be very helpful as it does not necessarily represent the fluidity of play as a process.

In the seminal text 'The Colorado Paper' by Sturrock and Else (1998/2007), the Play Cycle was introduced as a model for conceptualising the process of play, including how adults can respond *in the moment* to the child's intrinsic motivation and self-direction. Recognition of this process is useful to consider the interrelationships between the adult, child, and environment. A key aspect of the Play Cycle is that it can help adults, who wish to observe children's play and respond thoughtfully, be aware of the potential of the adult to 'adulterate' – dominate and control – the child's play in ways that hinder or halt the Play Cycle. Sturrock and Else (1998/2007) categorised adult interventions as a hierarchy ranging from play maintenance to complex intervention. Critically, interventions are made with conscious consideration of the child's play process in order to support the continuation of the child's self-directed play (see King & Sturrock, 2020).

However, in some early childhood settings, play is not necessarily framed according to the Playwork Principles. This is in part due to a focus on adult-directed 'school-readiness' skills development, as well as an historic lack of prioritisation of play and playwork at a policy level in the United Kingdom. However, increasingly, in response to ratification of the United Nations Convention on the Rights of the Child (UN, 1989), national play strategies and policy guide play provision nationally and regionally in a range of settings. Formal play spaces may be protected by recent changes to UK National Planning Policy Framework guidance (Section 8, para. 104) for local authorities (UK Government, 2024). Guidelines for play in healthcare have been published by the National Health Service (NHS, 2025) in England. Promoting play training for educators is an essential component of Scotland's strategy and action plan (Scottish Government, 2015) to support its curriculum (see also Chapter 14). In Northern Ireland, the Department of Education has proposed an Outdoor Spaces for Play and Learning Special Schools Programme (Davies, 2021). Wales has refreshed its Play Friendly Country statutory guidance (2025), demonstrating the relevance of play across society. Certainly, the pioneering Welsh Play Sufficiency regulation (Welsh Government, 2012) requiring local authorities to assess, secure and enhance play opportunities has been influential across the United Kingdom (see also Chapter 2).

These policy and guidance changes will improve access to high-quality play opportunities and prompt more adults to become aware of important play principles, such as choice or autonomy in children's self-directed play, and how adults mediate play activity.

However, due to diversity in approaches, different provisions offer play opportunities along a spectrum of mediated activity, for example, with intentions for developmental, educational, or therapeutic aims, or for children to have the opportunity to play undisturbed by adults (Howard, 2009). At one end of the spectrum might be adventure play schemes, intentionally creating conditions for autonomy and promoting children's choices along Playwork Principles. At the other end of the spectrum may be a classroom setting, in which the child is expected to follow particular rules, play with items in a particular way or meet certain outcomes in play, as defined by curriculum expectations (see Chapter 14). Across the range of play opportunities and settings, different constraints, as well as opportunities, shape *how* children (are to) play, both with the resources provided and with each other (King & Howard, 2016; Rekers & Waters-Davies, 2021).

Consequently, King and Howard (2016) argue that, from a child's perspective, truly 'free' play may not exist. Indeed, even in playwork practice, provision for children's play is shaped by the resources available, as well as by adult choices and beliefs (see also chapter 11). For these reasons, King and Howard (2016) suggest the term 'adaptable choice', since 'children's perception of choice can fluctuate between having little (or no) choice to having full' or autonomous choice (p. 59). What might best characterise play, then, are the relations of power, choice and agency (see Chapter 2) in any one situation. When we look at play this way, it expands to mean different things to different people.

Children's Perspective

It is worth thinking about what children themselves perceive as *play*. When asked about their play and their play choices, children responded by describing variable 'combination[s] of play space, resources, and participation by other children and adults' (King & Howard, 2016, p. 60; see also Chapter 1). One memorable description of play by a child is cited by Else (2009, p. 6): '[Play is] what I do when everyone else has stopped telling me what to do'. In addition to such choice and autonomy, children may differentiate between what they consider 'play' and 'work' in general within the early childhood setting, based upon whether playful activity takes place on the floor or at a desk, whether adults are involved or not and whether children feel they are expected to produce something.

Although adults may wish that children did not differentiate between 'play' and 'work' in a setting that is committed to 'learning through play', it is interesting to note that in the early years classroom, adults may contribute to such binaries by saying, 'Play time!', during which they only support children when required, and then signal the end of such activity by calling out: 'Tidy up time!' before an adult-led activity will begin. It is not surprising, therefore, that children learn to make differentiations between work and play and often consider play to be that in which adults are only involved when asked or if needed. Importantly, children may enjoy working and play may not always be enjoyable! What children consider work and play can be simultaneous, if there is some freedom within the task. We wish to make the point that children – *and* adults (see Pyle & Danniels, 2017) – sometimes distinguish between work and play based upon the nature of the involvement of adults.

Children may be unaccustomed to seeing adults playing or being play partners. Or, the presence of adults might be a signal that play is about to be stopped! A study by Sandberg (2002) demonstrated how children's perception of teachers' involvement in play differed from adult perceptions of their own involvement: rather than considering the adult as a facilitator or play-mate, or someone who can usefully extend play, children see adults as often interfering and useful in certain contexts only. Viewing play as child-directed, Sandberg (2002) asserts that 'teachers should be sensitive, observant and engaged, but should not control, decide or interrupt play' (p. 21). Yet, Pyle and Danniels (2017) point out that if adults simply see their role as a play *supervisor*, learning opportunities can be lost. Since 'play is necessary for development and learning' (Pyle & Danniels, 2017, p. 275), it can be tricky to create a fluid, holistic play/learning ethos, especially in the classroom.

It can be argued that since adults often provide the resources, guide what is considered acceptable play behaviour in the space and are responsible for timekeeping, children's choices, even when adults intend 'free play', may be more shaped by adult choices than adults intend or recognise. How, then, can we learn to recognise and be mindful of our choices, and reflect on why we made them?

Adult Perspective

As part of reflective practice, adults can consider their intentions and how that affects their provision for play. Certainly, play in an early years setting is an opportunity for adults to observe, to support and to consider the child's motive development, goals and challenges and emerging conceptual knowledge (Fleer, 2010). In this way, theoretical concepts such as scaffolding and the zone of proximal development (see Chapter 5) may be applied to play, whether structured or unstructured, child- or adult-initiated, since Vygotsky viewed play as 'a mechanism propelling development forward' (Bodrova, 2008, p. 359).

Observation of children's individual emotional, social or material interests in play is 'rich with possibility *for* the educational setting if teachers recognise and respond to it', argues Hedges (2007, p. 12, emphasis in original). How the adult responds will be influenced by their intentions, which may be influenced by policy and curricula, and shaped by practice and experience. As mediators of institutional values, expectations and demands, the adult is critical in developing social and material environments that support, sustain, and validate children's play choices (Rekers-Power, 2020). Planning for play environments can include providing material resources that have specific intentions, such as books, tools, paper and so on, as well as resources that may be considered 'loose parts' or those without specific intention and ways of using (see Chapter 11 and 12). It is also worth considering that children may utilise features and artefacts in ways that adults may not anticipate (Rekers, 2022). For instance, a table in a classroom has a specific function for children that is controlled by adults, primarily *sitting at*. Yet, it can also afford *hiding under, crawling onto, lying down upon*! During play, the adult needs to decide if they are willing to not only learn *about* children and their developing competencies but also learn *from* children about play.

The problem in conceptualising play is not in adult-led or child-led notions, but in the perceived dichotomy between them; that is, the perception that these are separate forms of provision, according to Rogoff et al. (1996). They argue that a model based on the notion of a community of players *and* learners is guided by an alternative philosophical approach: adults and children collaborate, children take an active role in learning and when the situation requires, the more knowledgeable teaches the other (which may be the child guiding the adult). The concept of 'playful pedagogies' (Goouch, 2008) recognises that sometimes children are the experts and sometimes adults are more experienced. To best support children, the adult might allow space for moving between positions of joining in and stepping back from play.

Reflection Point 15.1

Before you continue with this chapter, think about provision for play that you have experienced in early childhood education and care (ECEC) settings:

- How common is it to use or hear the terms 'adult-led' activity and 'child-led' activity? The terms 'free play' or 'structured play'?
- What do these terms mean in the settings you have experienced?

Now read the rest of the chapter and then reflect upon how helpful you feel these four terms are when considering provision for play.

In the case study presented below, a young boy is sitting alone watching others play during an outdoor play session. A forest school leader observes the boy, then decides to intervene in his solitary activity. She does so not because she believes that playing should always be social or active, but because she notices he sits alone much of the time and may need some companionship or encouragement to play with others.

Case Study 15.1

During 'free play' at forest school, a 5-year-old boy, Emyr, sits quietly by himself watching two boys play a game involving throwing sticks into a puddle. Having noticed that he often sits alone and that he has been for some time now, the forest school leader wonders if he is happy sitting there alone or if she should do something. Soon, Emyr's attention is drawn to a bumblebee in the bush near where he sits. The leader sees this and uses this moment to approach him and ask him about what he is watching. Emyr points out the bumblebee, and the adult kneels down to look more closely at it. After a few moments, she asks him to teach her the word for bumblebee in Welsh. He tells her *cacwn* and she practises saying it with his help. She then asks Emyr if he would like to use her iPhone to take a photo of it.

Because they are engaged in observing and photographing the bumblebee together, the two boys come over to see what is happening. Soon, all four are watching the bumblebee and talking about it, as well as arguing whether bumblebee in Welsh is *cacwn* or *cachgi bwm*; to divert the arguing, the adult mispronounces *cachgi bwm*, intentionally creating a 'poo joke', then steps back. When the bumblebee flies away, the boys return to their stick game and Emyr joins them.

Reflection Point 15.2

- Would you consider Emyr's initial activity of 'watching' as play? Why or why not?
- How did the adult contribute to Emyr's play experience?
- In what way could we see the adult's actions as validating Emyr's self-directed activity?
- Do you think she was intervening or interfering in this situation? Did she stop or support self-directed play?

A common misconception of sensitive play provision for children is that the adult just stands back and 'lets them get on with it'. However, it is not quite that straightforward. Lester and Russell (2008) note that key aspects of the adult role in play include providing structure, direction and intervention, and understanding behaviour and the importance of relationships. Arguably, joining in may be necessary in all these aspects, but so is standing back. As in the rest of life, timing is everything. Building skills in social and emotional awareness, practical considerations, observing and reflecting helps to develop skilfulness in knowing how and when to be directly or indirectly engaged with children in their play activity.

When children are playing in an education or care setting, it is useful for the adult to be flexible in moving into multiple roles, based upon the needs of the child(ren). Wood (2013) points out that:

> If spontaneous and responsive pedagogies are to be sustained, then educators need to be aware of children's repertoires of choice, specifically the ways in which the freedom to choose may advantage some but disadvantage others. This is not an argument for limiting children's choices and exerting more adult control. However, it is an argument for critical engagement with established discourses about free choice and free play, and the underpinning knowledge bases for practice (p. 16).

The adult in the case study may have felt that the 'free play' situation did not fully provide Emyr with an opportunity to engage with others. Not all children may know how or what to play or be skilled at finding play partners. We discuss this case study and further examples from play to consider two broad categorisations of the adult's role: 'joining in' and 'stepping back'.

Joining in: Being a Play Partner, Initiating, Validating, Modelling, and Intervening

Play leadership includes creating the conditions for play, advocacy for quality provision, providing resources, holding a safe space with opportunities for developmentally appropriate risk-taking and time-keeping to ensure that children's needs are met. Additionally, one aspect of play leadership is knowing when and how to be a 'play partner'. Understanding children's play as a medium through which children assert their agency (see Chapter 2), co-create their own peer cultures and reproduce and negotiate adult cultures can help the adult to participate in ways which recognise and reflect the child's agenda. Respecting children's play choices provides an opportunity for adults to view the world from the child's perspective, responding to the child's direction, rather than in ways that could potentially limit children's play opportunities.

Play partners adopt a playful approach themselves to problem-solving and learning from mistakes. By noticing when children are getting frustrated, the play leader can ask if the child would like some help – not to take over the play, but to model problem-solving. Using questions such as 'What seems to be going wrong? I wonder why this isn't working? What could we try?' in conjunction with an attitude of playfulness (Dewey, 1916/2011) when something does not go 'right' can model problem-solving and experimentation.

The playful adult joins in when asked by the child and could also take a lead in creating a playful atmosphere. This could be by initiating a group game, for instance, to start a session and joining in themselves where appropriate rather than standing back. The playful adult notices the children who may be 'left out' and considers how to intervene to include them in group activity or smaller circles of children, should they wish. In this way, the playful adult does not relinquish the other roles of the adult, such as observation or intervention, but does so with the intention of collaborating with the child at play.

In the case study, the forest school leader notices Emyr sitting alone. Her understanding of play aligns with play principles of being 'freely chosen, personally directed and intrinsically motivated'. Yet, although it may be argued that he is 'playing' even though he is seated alone, the play leader wonders if he needs adult attention. Because she has been observing him over the course of several play sessions, she has noticed that he is often left out or sits on the side-lines. By respectfully approaching him to see what has caught his interest and sharing her iPhone with him so that he can take photographs of the bumblebee, she joins in with his quiet activity. Rather than 'taking over', she expresses interest in what he is watching. In doing so, other children join in, attracted by the adult's and Emyr's shared observation of the bumblebee.

When the leader mispronounces the Welsh word for bumblebee, she does so deliberately, as she knows it is an excrement joke that will make the boys laugh. Thus, the adult has become a play partner building upon Emyr's interest to create a play dyad, which also leads to attracting potential play partners. The adult has both enabled and empowered Emyr to participate in more social play activity, if he chooses. Had he chosen not to join in with the boys, the adult was still able to extend his play by discussing the bee, showing interest in Emyr's interest and sharing her camera/phone. In this way, the adult has intervened sensitively; she has shaped the direction of Emyr's play, but also allowed space for him to choose to shift his play focus or remain in his original flow of activity. She also responds to the opportunity that is created for her to step back when Emyr joins the other boys.

Stepping Back - The Role of Observation for Learning/ Therapeutic Assessment and Critical Planning/ Reflecting

When we use the term 'stepping back', we do not mean 'ignoring'; instead, we consider the term in the way a lifeguard is alert and watching all the swimmers in the pool or at the beach. The lifeguard is aware of the humans in and around the water and is watchful of the environment in which they are playing, e.g. the weather, tides and so on. In play, however, the adult does not need to wait for an emergency to jump in! In the case study, we can see that by watching Emyr's activity from a distance and over time, the adult was able to make some interpretations based upon her observations. These observations, coupled with reflective practice, may feed into her planning of the next session and also allow her to consider what she can do to further support Emyr's social play development. Having observed Emyr's activity over the course of a single session in conjunction with past sessions, the practitioner intervenes with a view to supporting Emyr's social situation of development. By showing interest in what he is doing and creating a dyad with him, other children arrive, curious. This extends his solitary activity into a more social form of play without her deliberate instigation for this to happen. He then chooses to join the other boys for a short time before returning to his sitting spot.

Sometimes the adult may intervene and then realise that they have stopped or changed the flow of play unintentionally. Of course, if the child is going to come to harm, there may be a good – also child-centred – reason to interrupt the play flow. But often adults get involved without intending to change the course of play. In contrast to the case study with Emyr, for example, the same adult observed children excitedly watching a caterpillar on the woodland floor. The children were trying to pick it up using small twigs, so they could carry it around without harming it. When the adult approached to look, the children responded with excitement to tell her what they had discovered. However, when the adult began to take photos and ask questions, some of the children ran off, saying, 'I'm going to play now!'

By documenting and asking questions to engage with the children's play, the adult had '*adult*erated' the natural flow of play for some of the children, to the extent that it stopped being considered 'play' and started to veer towards 'schoolwork'. It seems the children could sense the playwork turning into schoolwork, even before the adult did! Later, the adult used the photographs of the children and caterpillar when back in the classroom to support scientific concept development of the life cycle of a butterfly. In doing so, the adult utilised the children's self-initiated exploration to create a more structured learning activity, in which the whole class could engage. Although the children who had found the caterpillar were pleased by their accomplishment when they saw it being valued in the classroom environment, we can certainly see how the adult had 'taken over'/'taken opportunity of' their discovery for a curriculum-focused agenda.

So, this is why the adult needs to be reflective. From an adult perspective, we can see that the children were already learning something – how to pick up the caterpillar without hurting it, where it lived, what it might eat; yet, the adult saw an opportunity to discuss the concept of 'lifecycles'. In the case study with Emyr, the adult's intention was to support Emyr's social and communication skills development. In both situations, the adult can reflect upon her intentions and whether these seem appropriate, welcome and responsive to the needs of the child/ren. Thus, the adult's role itself continually shifts between 'stepping back' and 'joining in' to both support and appreciate children's play. Crucially, provision for play is enhanced by adults with pedagogical understandings and awareness of their multiple roles, who are willing to reflect on their *own* learning through play.

Reflection Point 15.3

Howard (in King & Sturrock, 2020) asserts that 'play (or playfulness) as a way of "being" is undoubtedly the springboard for its developmental potential, the "becoming"' (p. xiii).

- How could this statement be used to discuss the 'caterpillar play' or the 'bumblebee play' in the case study above?
- What did the adult do differently in the 'caterpillar play' compared to the 'bumblebee play' in the case study?

Summary

- The tensions between child-led and adult-led play activities in the ECEC setting can make the balance between 'interacting and interfering' (Fisher, 2016) challenging to conceptualise and to achieve.
- The fluidity of adult roles can be complicated by the cultural demands and expectations for play provision or their own intentions for outcomes.
- From a socio-cultural perspective, the concept of freely chosen play is troubled: locations, play partners, resources, adult involvement or lack of involvement, plus cultural-historical constraints and affordances all contribute to the argument that play may not be as 'free' as adults claim (King & Howard, 2016; Wood, 2013).
- The responsive adult needs to have a good understanding of play, play principles, and playful pedagogies in order to 'hold the space' and support children's play responsively. 'Joining in' is not the same as 'interfering', although that may be an unintended consequence. The playful practitioner sets up the site; undertakes risk assessment; provides resources and structure; initiates, models and validates play. Sometimes the practitioner may become an active member of play by joining in a game or activity, but with a sense – borne of intuition, experience and practice – of knowing when to 'step back'.
- 'Stepping back' is not the same as 'ignoring'. The practitioner is constantly alert and watching, in order to respond appropriately. This means the practitioner may watch a scuffle between peers or other risky play activity for a short time, to see if intervention is required or if the children sort it out between themselves in ways that support their development. The practitioner actively observes to consider how to further support play and children's holistic development. The 'stepping back' role is critical for summative assessment, forward planning, and reflective practice.

Further Reading

These three readings offer more detail and depth about the adult role in play. The authors explore extensively the notions of free play, choice and the importance of children being enabled and empowered to become engaged in their play activity.

King, P. and Howard, J. (2016) Free choice or adaptable choice: Self-determination theory and play. *American Journal of Play*, 9(1), 56–70.

King, P. and Sturrock, G. (2020) *The play cycle: Theory, research and application.* London: Routledge.

Wood, E. (2013) Free choice and free play in early childhood education: Troubling the discourse. *International Journal of Early Years Education*, 22(1), 4–18. Available at: http://dx.doi.org/10.1080/09669760.2013.830562

References

Bodrova, E. (2008). Make-believe play versus academic skills: A Vygotskian approach to today's dilemma of early childhood education. *European Early Childhood Education Research Journal*, 16(3), 357–369. https://www.tandfonline.com/doi/abs/10.1080/13502930802291777

Csikszentmihalyi, M. (1990). *Flow: The psychology of optimal experience*. New York: Harper and Row.

Davies, G. (2021). *Department of education equality and human rights policy screening for outdoor spaces for play and learning in special schools*. https://www.education-ni.gov.uk/sites/default/files/publications/education/Completed%20Screening%20form%20of%20Outdoor%20Spaces%20for%20Play%20and%20Learning%20Special%20Schools.pdf

Dewey, J. (1916/2011). *Democracy and education*. Hollywood, FL: Simon and Brown.

Else, P. (2009). *The value of play*. London: Bloomsbury.

Fisher, J. (2016). *Interacting or interfering? Improving interactions in the early years*. Maidenhead: Open University Press.

Fleer, M. (2010). *Early learning and development: Cultural-historical concepts in play*. Melbourne: Cambridge University Press.

Goouch, K. (2008) Understanding playful pedagogies, play narratives and play spaces. *Early Years*, 28(1), 93–102. https://doi.org/10.1080/09575140701815136

Hedges, H. D. (2007). *Funds of knowledge in early childhood communities of inquiry* (Unpublished PhD Thesis, Massey University).

Howard, J. (2009). Play and development in early childhood. In T. Maynard, & N. Thomas (Eds.), *An introduction to early childhood studies*. London: Sage.

Hughes, B. (2012). *Evolutionary playwork* (2nd ed.). London: Routledge.

King, P., & Howard, J. (2016). Free choice or adaptable choice: Self-determination theory and play. *American Journal of Play*, 9(1), 56–70.

King, P., & Sturrock, G. (2020). *The play cycle: Theory, research and application*. London: Routledge.

Lester, S., & Russell, W. (2008). *Play for a change: Play, policy and practice – a review of contemporary perspectives*. National Children's Bureau and Play England. www.playengland.org.uk/media/120504/play-for-a-change-chapter-1.pdf

NHS England. (2025). *Play well: Guidelines for commissioning and designing health play services*. Available at: https://www.england.nhs.uk/long-read/play-well-guidelines-for-commissioning-and-designing-health-play-services/

Playwork Principles Scrutiny Group, Cardiff. (2005). *The playwork principles*. Available at: www.playwales.org.uk/eng/playworkprinciples

Pyle, A., & Danniels, E. (2017). A continuum of play-based learning: The role of the teacher in play-based pedagogy and the fear of hijacking play. *Early Education & Development*, 28(3). https://doi.org/10.1080/10409289.2016.1220771

Rekers, A. (2022). Expansive competencies: Using affordance theory to observe children differently. In C.Conn & A.Murphy (Eds.), *Inclusive pedagogies in early childhood education. Respecting and responding to differences in learning*. London: Routledge.

Rekers, A., & Waters-Davies, J. (2021). 'All of the wild': Cultural formation in Wales through outdoor play at forest school. In L. T. Grindheim, H. V. Sørensen, & A. Rekers (Eds.), *Outdoor learning and play: Pedagogical practices and children's cultural formation*. New York: Springer.

Rekers-Power, A. (2020). *'Exploring young children's participation and motive orientation in the classroom and at forest school* (Doctoral Thesis, University of Wales Trinity Saint David). https://repository.uwtsd.ac.uk/id/eprint/1410/

Rogoff, B., Matusov, E., & White, C. (1996). Models of teaching and learning: Participation in a community of learners. In D. R. Olson & N. Torrance (Eds.), *Handbook of education and human development*. Oxford: Blackwell.

Sandberg, A. (2002). Children's concepts of teachers' ways of relating to play. *Australasian Journal of Early Childhood*, 27(4), 18–22. https://doi.org/10.1177/183693910202700405

Scottish Government. (2015). *Play strategy for Scotland: Learning about play - investigating play through relevant qualifications in Scotland*. ISBN 9781785447761. Available at: https://www.gov.scot/publications/play-strategy-scotland-learning-play-investigating-play-through-relevant-qualifications-scotland/pages/3/

Sturrock, G., & Else, P. (1998/2007). 'The Colorado Paper'. The playground as therapeutic space: Playwork as healing. In G. Sturrock, & P. Else (Eds.), *Therapeutic playwork reader one 1995–2000*. Eastleigh: Common Threads Publications.

UK Government. (2024). *National planning policy framework*. Available at: https://www.gov.uk/government/publications/national-planning-policy-framework-2

United Nations. (1989). *Convention on the rights of the child. Ireland and play*. Available at: https://www.ohchr.org/en/instruments-mechanisms/instruments/convention-rights-child

Welsh Government. (2012). *The play sufficiency assessment (Wales) regulations 2012*. Available at: https://www.legislation.gov.uk/wsi/2012/2555/made

Wood, E. (2013). Free choice and free play in early childhood education: Troubling the discourse. *International Journal of Early Years Education*, 22(1), 4–18. https://doi.org/10.1080/09669760.2013.830562

16
Play and Inclusion

Nanna Ryder and Charlotte Greenway

Chapter Objectives

This chapter will help you:

- Understand the concept of inclusion and the need to include all children in play, regardless of individual needs or family background.
- Identify the aims and objectives of inclusive play.
- Understand how practitioners can support individual needs through planning.
- Know what makes a play environment inclusive and accessible.
- Understand the significance of equity and diversity in play for learning and development.

Introduction

An inclusive approach to play places a duty on education and care settings as well as health and community facilities to welcome children of all backgrounds, abilities, and personalities and to provide them with opportunities to access high-quality playful experiences (Casey, 2010; see also Chapter 9). Inclusion as a concept is deeply rooted in the field of sociology. It emphasises children's fundamental human right to be accepted and respected, to belong to their community and take part, to be equal but different (Glazzard et al., 2019). Inclusive provision also includes providing equitable opportunities, not only treating every child in the same way but also modifying support and approaches to enable all children to participate in play.

Terminology in legislation throughout the United Kingdom (UK) regarding children and young people with diverse needs and disabilities varies. Terms include Additional Learning Needs (ALN) in Wales; Additional Support Needs (ASN) in Scotland; Special Educational Needs (SEN) in Northern Ireland and Special Educational Needs and Disabilities (SEND) in England. Generally, these terms refer to children who have physical, emotional, social or neuro-diverse learning difficulties or disabilities – that is, they may require additional help and support that differs from that of their peers. However, in this chapter, we adopt the term 'Special Rights' (SR) for these categories which is the term used in Reggio Emilia pre-school provision (see Chapter 20). This is a more inclusive term, acknowledging that children have rights as well as needs, particularly in the context of play (Edwards et al., 2011). While environmental and family circumstances, e.g., social deprivation and cultural differences, are included in some instances, generally the legislation consists of four broad areas of need.

1 Communication and interaction, e.g., autism, speech, and language difficulties.
2 Cognition and learning, e.g., dyslexia, dyspraxia.
3 Social, emotional and mental health, e.g., ADHD, attachment disorder.
4 Sensory and/or physical needs, e.g., visual or hearing impairment, mobility issues.

(Department of Education, 2022; Department for Education and Department for Health, 2015; Scottish Government, 2017; Welsh Government, 2021)

Additionally, children from different cultural, linguistic and socio-economic backgrounds should also be considered when focusing on inclusion.

Accessing play can sometimes prove challenging for both children and their families as some environments can pose physical, social and institutional barriers to participation. The concept of inclusion transfers attention from the individual to the environment in ensuring access, participation and a sense of belonging for all children. According to the Inclusion Index (Booth et al., 2006), three key principles should be considered when planning inclusive provision.

1 Inclusive cultures – establishing a collaborative, tolerant, motivational, and safe community where each individual is valued.
2 Inclusive policies – ensuring clear strategies for access and participation for all in response to diversity.
3 Inclusive practices – developing and supporting play and learning activities that reflect inclusive policies and cultures, and which ensure everyone can participate within the setting.

Enacting these three dimensions will ensure that all children are empowered to participate in play activities to the best of their abilities and develop a sense of belonging to the community of their setting. The structure and the ethos of the environment, both indoors and outdoors, should be accessible and inclusive as play is fundamental to learning, development and well-being (see Chapter 6), regardless of individual and diverse needs and backgrounds. Access, inclusion and equity reflect the social model of disability, a term that originated in the UK in the 1980s. The social model emphasises that it is society that causes barriers to access and inclusion rather than the child's disability, impairment or needs. The historical 'medical model', on the other hand, views disability as a deficit of the child and so low expectations are established and the child's independence and choice are not considered. All UK governments have adopted the social model of disability encouraging practitioners to remove barriers, attitudes, policies, practice, and actions within their environment that prevent children with disabilities from having equal and equitable opportunities to participate fully in play activities (Booth et al., 2006).

Inclusive Play

Inclusive play is not solely about inclusion and accessibility. It also includes social factors and the value of play opportunities in their own right, where children with or without SR have an opportunity to actively engage in play collaboratively and in their own way, regardless of needs, stages of development or backgrounds (Casey & Harbottle, 2018, see also Chapter 9). It is about establishing a culture of play where every individual is valued and respected and where there is no prejudice, discrimination or barriers regarding language, culture, needs, or other differences.

Inclusive play allows all children to develop:

- Communication and collaboration.
- Positive relationships and friendships.
- An understanding of similarities and differences.
- An ability to respect and value diversity.
- Social and emotional skills to better participate in paired/group activities.
- Positive self-esteem and self-identity.
- An understanding of the world around them.
- A sense of belonging.
- Skills to take risks in a safe and supportive environment.
- An understanding of their right to play.

These factors, promoted through both child-initiated and adult-led play activities (see Chapter 15), contribute to children's development at their own rate as individuals as well as to their overall happiness and well-being. Playwork Principles for Wales (Play Wales, 2020) argue that play is innate, and all children need to be supported in accessing it as it is a:

> biological, psychological, and social necessity [and] a process that is freely chosen, personally directed and intrinsically motivated. That is, children and young people determine and control the content and intent of their play, by following their own instincts, ideas, and interests, in their own way [and] for their own reasons.

Inclusive play is also influenced by the rights agenda in the United Nations Convention on the Rights of the Child (UNCRC) (UNICEF, 2017) (see Chapter 2). As noted by the Committee on the Rights of the Child, 'accessible and inclusive environments and facilities must be made available to children with disabilities to enable them to enjoy their rights under Article 31'. This is further supported by the United Nations Convention on the Rights of Persons with Disabilities (United Nations, 2020). Inclusive play is therefore not only about ensuring all children have access and can participate in valuable, equitable and developmentally appropriate play experiences, but also empowering them to exercise their rights and develop autonomy.

However, 'following their own instincts, ideas, and interests' can be extremely challenging for some children with SR, those who have had limited experiences of play in the home or children with poor communication, social, and emotional skills. They will need support and guidance from a skilled adult to develop their play skills, ideas, and interests, possibly in an alternative way and through different means than the rest of their peers. Those with SR who cannot express themselves through play because they do not possess the skills and have limited access to an appropriate play environment will be unable to express their experiences and feelings. Thus, the inability to engage in independent, self-directed play may create a further disability of play deprivation (Olds et al., 2007). As play involves the child's physical, mental, and emotional self, if any of these are compromised, these children may require specialist support in the form of play therapy. It is important here to point out that the term 'therapy' in 'play therapy' relates to a therapeutic intervention intended to return the child to a normative state (of natural play). Play is not itself a therapy but part of a child's developmental process. However, while the challenges that SR presents to play and development are significant, this chapter does not focus on play therapy or other interventions designed to address these difficulties. For further reading on play therapy and its role in supporting children with SR, see (Ray et al., 2022; Landreth, 2023).

Reflection Point 16.1

- Is inclusive play for all children a moral obligation, a right or both? Consider the rationale for your response.
- If you were unable to access a play activity that all your friends were able to access, how would you feel? What could you do about the situation? Who or what else would help you?

Planning for Inclusion

Careful planning of the environment and resources, as well as thorough knowledge and understanding of play development and barriers to participation, is crucial for effective, high-quality provision (see also Chapter 10). Two main principles need consideration when planning inclusive play - *accessibility* and *inclusion* (Casey & Harbottle, 2018). Accessibility refers to the physical environment and play facilities, while inclusion denotes the social factors, and the range and value of play opportunities offered. The rights of children with SR to access meaningful and high-quality play provision are underpinned with national and international policies and legislation as well as ethical perspectives. However, ensuring inclusive play for all children requires extensive knowledge and careful planning and direction in designing and structuring appropriate provision.

Some children will inevitably face physical, social, cultural or attitudinal barriers that may prevent them from participating fully in play. Therefore, adults need to plan physical, environmental and human resources to reduce those barriers to provide enriching, accessible and inclusive playful experiences. Research indicates that children who are deprived of these experiences because of disability, culture or social class are at a disadvantage regarding their further development and the relationships they develop during childhood and beyond (Whitebread, 2012). Papatheodorou (2010) further advocates that in early years settings, play can be a means of identifying individual needs, enabling adults to plan additional or different activities to fulfil those needs and, in some cases, prevent further difficulties.

Some children may have trouble initiating and self-directing play and will possibly need additional support and encouragement. This reflects the Vygotskian perspective that play promotes learning and that this occurs through social interaction, cooperation and collaboration with a more skilful adult or peer. Through modelling play, or providing instructions or additional resources, adults or more knowledgeable peers can support children's skills and understanding so that they can achieve their zone of proximal development (ZPD, see Chapter 5), that is beyond what they can achieve on their own (Moyles, 2014). The need for support in achieving their ZPD can be particularly relevant for children with social or emotional difficulties, those with autism or children who have experienced trauma, e.g., those with Adverse Childhood Experiences (ACEs), Looked After Children (LAC) or refugees. Knowledge of the child's individual needs and interests will enable practitioners to plan balanced and meaningful activities to support their engagement and ensure further development. The very nature of play itself ensures there is no right or wrong so children with SR and those with various needs 'can be themselves, making their own meaning, gaining their own satisfaction from play in their own way and at their own pace' (Casey, 2010, p. 9). Planning, resourcing and supporting activities where all children have the freedom to play and play together benefits all involved in the process as it develops cooperation, empathy, and understanding of the diverse society in which we live.

An Inclusive Play Environment

All children need to feel a sense of belonging, so the physical environment should reflect the diversity of the children and the families that use those facilities. Resources and displays should celebrate and respect various disabilities, languages and cultures without prejudice and stereotyping. This ensures that all children play in an inclusive atmosphere where they feel they belong and get a breadth of learning experiences. Each child should be valued equally, regardless of their disability, impairment, social background, culture, beliefs, gender, colour of their skin or any other factor. For example, simply including dolls in wheelchairs, and national costumes in the role play corner is a tokenistic approach to inclusion as these are stereotypical views of disability and multi-culturalism. Stereotyping gives a very prejudiced view of diversity and Siraj-Blatchford (2006) even suggests that we should avoid 'celebrating diversity' in early years provision but instead create an awareness that we all have an individual ethnic or racial identity as well as a variety of gender, language and cultural identities. Play can be a vehicle for developing young children's knowledge, understanding and positive attitudes towards diversity. As with all play environments, there should be plenty of opportunities for children to explore by their own means, at their own level of development and understanding, at their own speed, and spaces for child-initiated and adult-led play that engages their interest and encourages awe and wonder. The National Playing Fields

Association (2000, p. 35) suggests that an enriched inclusive play environment should include the following resources and opportunities:

- A varied, interesting, and challenging physical environment.
- Natural elements – earth, water, and fire.
- Movement – running, jumping, rolling, climbing, and balancing.
- Natural and fabricated materials.
- Stimulation of the five senses.
- Experiencing change in the natural and built environment.
- Social interaction.
- Playing with identity.
- Experiencing a range of emotions.

Casey (2010) proposes that it is unrealistic to try to create a play environment where every element is accessible to all children as how they access experiences may be different. Children will use their senses in different ways or may show preference for different spaces within the environment. Health and safety issues also need to be considered, for example gates need to be accessible for children in wheelchairs with latches at a low height, but these could be opened quite easily by young children with autism so latches would need to be out of reach. The environment should also provide opportunities for all children to take risks and challenges both indoors and outdoors within the parameters of health and safety. This is particularly valuable for some children with vulnerabilities or disabilities, as their freedom and opportunities may be limited compared to their more able or more affluent peers, and adults may present barriers by perceiving them as less able and therefore being over-protective regarding risks and uncertainties. Risk and challenge help children build physical skills, self-confidence and resilience, as 'no child will learn about risk if they are wrapped in cotton wool' (Health and Safety Executive, 2012, p. 1).

Case Study 16.1

Dylan is four years of age and has recently been diagnosed with autism. He finds it challenging at times to control his anxiety and to engage in social activities with peers, but staff have noticed that he behaves differently when playing outdoors than indoors. The outdoor area includes tall trees to climb, shallow ponds to explore and a long rope swing to slide down at great speed. Over time, his self-confidence has improved, and he is less anxious when taking risks in this environment under adult supervision. Staff have also noticed that he has started to engage in rough and tumble play and enjoys play fighting with a few peers, and they avoid intervening unless it becomes too aggressive. These experiences have helped Dylan to develop and practise his social skills as well as give him more autonomy and empowerment.

Reflection Point 16.2

- Consider the advantages and disadvantages of providing risk and challenge in this outdoor play environment for:
  ○ A 2-year-old boy with Cerebral Palsy who finds moving around challenging due to poor muscle control, and although he uses a wheelchair, he prefers not to when playing with friends.
- A 5-year-old girl with social and emotional difficulties who finds it difficult to cooperate with peers and to follow simple instructions, e.g., keeping within boundaries.
- How would you overcome these issues and support these children to play?

Enabling and Empowering: Play for Children with SR

All children with SR who experience barriers within the four areas of need as noted in each country's legislation on special or additional needs and disabilities have a right to equal access to high quality and meaningful play experiences. This also includes LAC who have been in the care of their local authority for more than twenty-four hours. Children with SR will have various levels of competency and physical, intellectual, emotional, or social skills as well as different previous experiences of play within the home environment. Although play is crucial for well-being, learning, and holistic development, some children may need more support than others to fully access and participate in different types of play and learning activities.

Being included in positive play experiences provides children with SR opportunities for meaningful interactions with others, as "friendships could facilitate play and play could facilitate friendships" (Spencer-Cavaliere & Watkinson, 2010). This enhances their self-perception and boosts their self-confidence and self-esteem. It also leads to developing physical, emotional, creative, communication, and intellectual skills through exploring their environment with others and engaging in play activities that promote their fine and gross motor skills. Inclusive play reflects the world's diversity and helps develop empathy and understanding towards peers with SR, breaking down barriers and dispelling misconceptions among children, staff members and parents or carers regarding diverse needs and disability (Mathieson, 2015). It also provides them with transferrable skills for the future in interacting and collaborating with people with diverse needs and from different backgrounds.

Barriers may also exist due to differing levels of vocabulary or communication skills, or due to challenges with physical or social skills. For example, some children with neurodiverse needs such as autism might find playing with peers or taking part in sensory play activities challenging (Olsen et al., 2019). This could be due to challenges they experience in interacting with others, in establishing friendships and relationships or their hypersensitivity and/or hyposensitivity in processing sensory information. There might also be environmental obstacles such as inaccessible or unadaptable physical spaces for those children with mobility issues or lack of sensory-friendly spaces for those that need sensory stimulation. Cade (2023) suggests that there may also be barriers to inclusive play at a systemic level due to staff attitudes, training or support or the implementation of national polices in practice. These therefore need to be removed to ensure effective and purposeful inclusive play provision as outlined in the three key principles of the Inclusion Index (Booth et al. 2006) which is underpinned by the Salamanca Statement (UNESCO, 1994) on inclusion ratified by the UK government in 1994.

Staff working with children with SR therefore need to create a welcoming and inclusive atmosphere and culture within their environment, where every child can develop their confidence, independence, and sense of belonging through participation in play and learning activities. Acknowledging children as individuals, encouraging positive interactions, promoting respect for diversity, and adopting a constructivist approach that focuses on child-centred pedagogy and developmentally appropriate practices (Cade, 2023) are key attributes of inclusive practice. Supporting all children to access play to the best of their ability leads to a positive sense of self, enabling them to build on their strengths, abilities, special interests or play preferences. It also provides them with a sense of empowerment as they are accepted for who they are and are valued for their differences. All children need opportunities for exploration, creativity, and social interaction through play, even those with profound and multiple learning difficulties (PMLD) and complex needs (Anderson, 2022).

The practitioner's role in supporting children with SR in play and learning activities is therefore multi-faceted. This can possibly include:

- Facilitating or scaffolding play.
- Making reasonable adjustments by adapting the environment or re-arranging the physical space so that every child can participate fully.
- Selecting appropriate open-ended play materials.
- Providing time and choices.
- Modelling interactions or turn-taking.
- Challenging and supporting individuals.
- Monitoring and observing engagement to identify any barriers and provide additional or different support if needed.
- Encouraging participation (Moore & Zweig, 2022).

In addition, Olsen et al. (2019) suggest that ensuring consistency and routine is key to making children feel more secure and engaged. They also propose that inclusion can be achieved at several distinct levels but is dependent on practitioners' knowledge, understanding and provision of appropriate support. These include children:

- Keeping their distance while others are playing so they are physically present but not actively engaged with their peers, that is, they perceive themselves to be included but without any direct interaction.
- Engaging in parallel play by staying close to their peers, playing alongside but again without any direct interaction. This suggests that they feel part of the group and are beginning to become more comfortable in the company of their peers.

- Actively engaging and interacting with their peers by playing together, sharing toys, and participating in group activities. However, this is dependent on supportive staff and appropriate environments.
- Demonstrating different levels of comfort in engaging and interacting with others which is dependent on the support provided and the inclusivity of the environment.

Providing an inclusive environment both indoors and outdoors is also key in enabling all children to participate in appropriate play and learning activities. They need to be physically accessible and adaptable, for example by installing ramps, moving furniture or by providing adaptive play equipment. The layout of the play environment should be flexible, and space should be modified to meet the changing needs of the children and to support different types of play (Mathieson, 2015). Those with neurodiverse needs may need a quiet space to self-isolate independently if they feel they are overwhelmed during activities. Sensory-friendly areas such as a sensory room or a sensory garden provide sensory stimulation but also cater for different play needs and interests.

To create a welcoming, engaging and enabling environment, practitioners also need to provide a variety of structured and open-ended materials and supporting resources that are adaptive and cater for a diverse range of different abilities and interests. These may include:

- Visual aids such as visual timetables, social stories, and visual cues to reduce anxiety and enhance comprehension for those with communication difficulties or children who are neurodivergent.
- Tactile materials for sensory play such as rainbow rice, beans, sand, and water trays with tools to explore different textures.
- Books and stories with large print, audio books and bean bags or comfortable chairs so that all children, including those with visual or hearing impairments can enjoy reading.
- Assistive technology such as speech recognition and speech generating devices, communication boards and apps to promote communication and expression.
- Toys that respond to touch and sound, digital tools, and virtual reality to provide immersive play experiences for all (Anderson, 2022).
- Interactive tablets, educational software and augmented reality to make play fun and promote learning.
- Musical instruments such as drums, tambourines, maracas, or those made by the children themselves to develop a sense of rhythm, co-ordination, and social interaction (Macintyre, 2010).

Resources such as these will enable children with SR to explore and learn through play in inclusive ways.

Inclusive play ensures that every child has equal access to meaningful and high-quality play experiences, but true inclusivity is only possible when diversity is recognised and celebrated. Diversity acknowledges differences in ethnicity, race, faith, gender, and lived experiences, all of which shape how children interact, learn, and engage in play. By embracing diversity, inclusive play environments foster a sense of belonging and representation, ensuring that all children – whether from ethnic minority backgrounds, Gypsy Traveller communities, gender-diverse identities, or those with SR – feel valued and empowered to participate freely. This highlights the need for play opportunities that reflect varied cultural identities, provide adaptive and culturally relevant resources, and challenge bias and stereotypes that may limit a child's play experiences. The following section outlines some aspects of diversity that affect children's play experiences.

Play Diversity and Inclusion: Enabling Equitable Access for All

Diversity in play is particularly significant in the UK, where minority groups such as Gypsy, Roma and Traveller (GRT) and multicultural communities necessitate play opportunities that reflect varied cultural identities. Including culturally relevant play materials, books and activities fosters a sense of belonging and encourages children to learn about different traditions.

Ethnic and Racial Diversity

Children from diverse ethnic backgrounds may face challenges accessing and enjoying play in their setting. These difficulties can stem from social, cultural and institutional barriers that impact their ability to participate fully. For example, children who speak English as an Additional Language (EAL) may struggle to communicate with peers during play. This can lead to isolation or difficulties engaging in group activities requiring verbal interaction. Similarly, instructions for structured play activities may be hard to understand, making it difficult for these children to join confidently. Some children from ethnic minorities may come from backgrounds where certain types of play are less emphasised or even discouraged. Physical play, such as rough-and-tumble activities, may not be as prevalent in some cultures. Certain play themes, such as fantasy or make-believe scenarios involving specific cultural references (e.g., fairy tales or superheroes), may be unfamiliar, making it more challenging for some children to engage.

As a result, children from minority ethnic backgrounds may experience unintentional or intentional exclusion. Stereotyping or bias from peers or even staff members can lead to feelings of alienation, affecting their willingness to participate in play. Resources such as dolls, books and games, may predominantly reflect Western cultures, leaving children from ethnic minority backgrounds feeling unrepresented. The absence of diverse role models and culturally inclusive activities can make play environments less welcoming. Some religious practices may influence how children participate in play. For instance, children who wear specific religious attire, such as hijabs or turbans, may feel restricted in certain physical activities. Play opportunities involving themes or celebrations contradicting religious beliefs may lead to exclusion or discomfort.

To foster an inclusive play environment for ethnically diverse children, settings can introduce multilingual support in play areas through visual aids and peer assistance to encourage culturally diverse play activities. As well as resources, settings can also educate staff and students about cultural awareness to prevent exclusion and unconscious bias, and offer flexible play options to accommodate different cultural and religious needs while ensuring all children feel included.

Gender

Children who do not conform to traditional gender norms – such as non-binary, gender-fluid, or transgender children – may encounter several challenges when engaging in play. These difficulties stem from societal expectations, peer interactions, and institutional structures that do not always accommodate diverse gender identities (Heywood & Adzajlic, 2023).

Many environments still reinforce traditional gender norms, where certain activities are seen as "for boys" (e.g., football, building blocks) and others as "for girls" (e.g., role-playing with dolls, home corner). For instance, a non-binary child who enjoys both rough-and-tumble play and dressing up may struggle to fit into either traditionally male or female playgroups. Children who wish to engage in activities that do not align with these expectations may experience peer pressure, teasing, bullying or exclusion. Some children may fear being judged or singled out, leading them to withdraw from play altogether, limiting their opportunities for social development.

There is also a lack of representation in play materials and activities that reinforce binary gender roles. A lack of diverse role models in play-related media and settings may contribute to feelings of isolation or confusion about their identity and gendered language in play (e.g., "boys vs. girls" in competitive games), which can make non-binary or gender-fluid children feel excluded. Institutional barriers and adult attitudes also contribute to individuals feeling excluded. Some school staff may unintentionally reinforce gender norms through the way they organise play activities or address children (e.g., grouping children by gender for specific tasks). A lack of staff training on gender inclusivity can result in missed opportunities to support gender-diverse children in play. Parents and caregivers may also have concerns or biases that influence how children are encouraged to play.

Play settings can encourage open-ended play by providing a variety of toys and activities not limited by gender stereotypes to create a more inclusive and welcoming play environment for gender-diverse children. Introducing gender-neutral language, such as using "friends" instead of "boys and girls" to address groups of children, and staff training on gender diversity can facilitate inclusive play and effectively address discrimination or bias. Allowing flexible dress codes that enable all children to move freely and engage in different forms of play can create a play environment where all children – regardless of gender identity – feel valued, included, and free to express themselves.

Gypsy, Roma and Traveller (GRT) Children

Gypsy, Roma and Traveller (GRT) children often experience significant challenges when accessing and engaging in play. These children often face barriers that stem from social stigma, cultural differences and institutional practices that may not fully accommodate their needs or lived experiences.

GRT children frequently face prejudice and discrimination from both peers, parents, and school staff due to a lack of cultural awareness. Negative stereotypes about their background may lead to bullying, name-calling, or exclusion from play groups. Fear of being judged or treated unfairly may cause some GRT children to withdraw from play or avoid settings altogether (Friends, Families & Travellers, 2023). GRT families may have different views on play and education, sometimes prioritising real-world skills over formal schooling. GRT families may have different views on play and education, sometimes prioritising real-world skills over formal schooling. This can impact a child's willingness or confidence in engaging with school-based play. Gender roles in some GRT communities may also shape how children interact in play, with boys encouraged toward physical activities and girls often expected to engage in more domestic or caregiving play.

Many GRT families live a mobile lifestyle, meaning children may experience gaps in schooling or frequently change schools. This can make it difficult for them to form friendships and establish a sense of belonging. A lack of continuity in educational experiences may also limit access to structured play activities, such as sports teams, drama clubs, or after-school programmes (Burchardt et al., 2018). Practitioners may not always take the time to integrate GRT children into play after long absences, and limited representation in the curriculum often leads to feelings of alienation. Most books, toys and educational materials do not reflect Gypsy and Traveller culture, making it harder for GRT children to see themselves positively represented. Similarly, storytelling and role-playing games may reflect mainstream family experiences and home environments but exclude cultural traditions, customs, or nomadic lifestyles central to GRT identities.

To ensure GRT children feel valued and included, practitioners and policymakers must educate staff, parents and children about GRT cultures to challenge stereotypes and reduce discrimination. Encouraging peer support initiatives and developing play activities celebrating diverse traditions. Examples include storytelling, music and crafts from Traveller heritage and providing outdoor and flexible play opportunities that align with the active and hands-on play styles common in GRT communities.

Conclusion

Inclusion and promoting diversity are evolving and never-ending processes of removing barriers to participation and raising achievement for all children (Ainscow et al., 2020). Effective monitoring, and evaluation of existing provision can identify the way forward for removing those barriers beyond adapting the environment or providing appropriate resources. This may include raising awareness to change attitudes by educating peers, staff, and parents regarding the significance of inclusion. Professional learning, adequate training for staff, access to specialised equipment, collaboration with children, families, schools, local authorities, and community organisations to co-design play spaces that reflect community needs ensures that play environments are inclusive and culturally relevant (Olsen et al., 2019). Developing research and evidence-based practices will also ensure that approaches used within play settings are based on the latest national and international research on inclusion (Cade, 2023). Furthermore, broader reforms might be needed to existing legislation at a national level, as well as monitoring and accountability regarding to what extent these policies are implemented in practice to establish high-quality inclusive play provision. This will ensure that all children, regardless of their needs or disabilities, are empowered to achieve through play-based learning activities.

Reflection Point 16.3

How play looks and works across different cultures can impact its use and effectiveness. From what you have learnt about cultural differences in play (see also Chapter 18), how would you support a child from a different cultural background who has recently joined your setting?

Case Study 16.2

Ben, Ousa, Li, Emma, and Akram are playing in the outdoor 'Pots and Plants' role play area. Ousa and Akram are twins from a Syrian refugee family and have only recently started attending the nursery. Akram joins in with the others immediately and is totally engrossed in the role play activity. He puts on his wellies and overalls, starts digging the new flower beds with his spade, plants some of the seedlings, enjoys watering the flowers and joins in selling the plants to his friends at the counter, smiling and talking. Ousa has decided not to join in with the others and sits on her own near the wall where she can still see what's going on. She watches her peers now and again but spends most of her time with her head curled up into her chest and her hands over her ears, not engaging in any form of play.

Miss Davies, one of the nursery staff, notices this, and while she wants to avoid intruding on the group's quality play experiences, she goes over and sits down beside Ousa. She takes over some of the gardening tools and a few of the plants, but Ousa grabs the tools and throws them as far away as possible. However, she does show interest in the plants and starts to feel the leaves and the flowers gently. The sensory nature of the plants and flowers appeal to Ousa and Miss Davies uses this to engage in conversation with her. Ousa then wanders over to the flower beds herself, kneels by the flowers, and starts touching and stroking them.

Reflection Point 16.4

- Consider Ousa and Akram's participation in this activity. Why do you think this is different?
- Consider the role of the adult in ensuring both are included within the activity. Is there anything Miss Davies could have done differently?
- How would you plan to make both feel more included in their new nursery? Consider possible resources and activities.
- Why is it important to support Akram and Ousa in developing a sense of belonging to their new environment? What would be your role as an adult here?

Summary

- All children, regardless of needs, disabilities or family backgrounds, have the right to be included in all play activities to the best of their ability.
- Play helps children with SR to develop physically, socially, and emotionally and helps them understand the world they live in.
- All children, with or without SR benefit from inclusive play experiences.

(Continued)

(Continued)

- Adults support access and inclusion in play settings through careful planning of the environment.
- Providing opportunities for inclusive play activities that meet children's diverse needs and backgrounds enables them to develop a sense of identity and belonging.

Further Reading

Anderson, A. (2022) *Learning through play for children with PMLD and complex needs.* Abingdon: Routledge. This book explores practical strategies and approaches for supporting children with learning differences and disabilities to engage fully in indoor and outdoor play.

Brassington, L. (2022) Gypsies, Roma and Travellers: The ethnic minorities most excluded from UK education. Higher Education Policy Institute. Available at: https://www.hepi.ac.uk/2022/07/07/gypsies-roma-and-travellers-the-ethnic-minorities-most-excluded-from-uk-education/

John, A. and Wheway, R. (2004) *Can play will play – disabled children and access to outdoor playgrounds.* Available at: www.childrensplayadvisoryservice.org.uk/pdf_files/Publications/can_play_will_play-CPASwebsite.pdf. This report discusses disabled children's rights and freedom to play outdoors and makes recommendations regarding improving access to public play areas for those with a disability.

Landreth, G. L. (2023) *Play therapy: The art of the relationship.* New York: Routledge.

Paley, V. G. (2009) *You can't say you can't play.* Boston, MA: Harvard University Press. This book explores a kindergarten teacher's experiences of children's social relationships, including loneliness and rejection, and how she promotes inclusion for all within her setting. This is written from a child's perspective and gives an insight into their world and the effects of exclusion.

Ray, D. C., Ogawa, Y. and Cheng, Y. (2022) *Multicultural play therapy.* New York: Routledge.

SENSE (2019) *Making play inclusive – a toolkit for play settings.* Available at: www.sense.org.uk/get-support/support-for-children/play-toolkits/. SENSE is a charity that advises parents and settings on how to provide effective support for children with complex difficulties and disabilities.

References

Ainscow, M., Chapman, C., & Hadfield, M. (2020). *Changing education systems – a research-based approach.* London: Routledge.

Anderson, A. (2022). *Learning through play for children with PMLD and complex needs.* Abingdon: Routledge.

Booth, T., Ainscow, M., & Kingston, D. (2006). *Index for inclusion – developing play, learning and participation in early years and childcare.* Available at: www.eenet.org.uk/resources/docs/Index%20EY%20English.pdf

Burchardt, T., Obolenskaya, P., Vizard, P., & Battaglini, M. (2018). *Experience of multiple disadvantage among Roma, Gypsy and Traveller children in England and Wales*. Centre for the Analysis of Social Exclusion (CASE), Paper 208.

Cade, J. (2023). Child-centred pedagogy: Guided play-based learning for preschool children with special needs. *Cogent Education*, 10(2), 1–18. https://doi.org/10.1080/2331186X.2023.2276476

Casey, T. (2010). *Inclusive play – practical strategies for children from birth to eight* (2nd ed.). London: Sage.

Casey, T., & Harbottle, H. (2018). *Free to play – a guide to creating accessible and inclusive public play spaces*. Available at: www.playscotland.org/resources/print/Free-to-Play-Guideto-Accessible-and-Inclusive-Play-Spaces-Casey-Harbottle-2018.pdf?plsctml_id=11211

Department for Education and Department for Health. (2015). *Special educational needs and disability code of practice: 0 to 25 years*. Available at: https://assets.publishing.service.gov.uk/media/5a7dcb85ed915d2ac884d995/SEND_Code_of_Practice_January_2015.pdf

Department of Education. (2022). *Draft SEN code of practice*. Available at: https://www.education-ni.gov.uk/consultations/consultation-draft-sen-code-practice

Edwards, C., Gandini, L., & Forman, G. (Eds.). (2011). *The hundred languages of children: The Reggio Emilia experience in transformation* (3rd ed.). London: Ablex Publishing Corporation.

Friends, Families & Travellers. (2023). *Education inequalities facing Gypsies, Roma and Travellers in England*. Available at: https://www.gypsy-traveller.org

Glazzard, J., Stokoe, J., Hughes, A., Netherwood, A., & Neve, L. (2019). *Teaching and supporting children with special educational needs and disabilities in primary schools* (3rd ed.). London: Sage.

Health and Safety Executive. (2012). *Children's play and leisure – promoting a balanced approach*. Available at: www.hse.gov.uk/entertainment/childrens-play-july-2012.pdf

Heywood, S., & Adzajlic, B. (2023). *Challenging gender stereotypes in the early years: Changing the narrative*. Routledge.

Landreth, G. (2023). *Play therapy: The art of the relationship*. London: Taylor and Francis.

Macintyre, C. (2010). *Play for children with special needs* (2nd ed.) London: Routledge.

Mathieson, K. (2015). *Inclusion in the EYFS*. Maidenhead: Open University Press.

Moore, L. & Zweig, E. (2022). Everyone plays! Recapturing play for children with special needs. *Dimensions*, 50(1), 14–18. Available at: https://files.eric.ed.gov/fulltext/EJ1340670.pdf

Moyles, J. (Ed.). (2014). *The excellence of play* (4th ed.). Maidenhead: Open University Press.

National Playing Fields Association (NPFA). (2000). *Best play: What play provision should do for children*. London: NPFA/Children's Play Council/Playlink.

Olds, D. L., Sadler, L., & Kitzman, H. (2007). Programs for parents of infants and toddlers: Recent evidence from randomized trials. *Journal of Child Psychology and Psychiatry*, 48(3–4), 355–391.

Olsen, K., Croydon, A., Olson, M., Jacobsen, K., & Pellicano, E. (2019). Mapping inclusion of a child with autism in a mainstream kindergarten: How can we move towards more inclusive practices? *International Journal of Inclusive Education*, 23(6), 624–638. https://doi.org/10.1080/13603116.2018.1441914

Papatheodorou, T. (2010). Play and the achievement of potential. In J. Moyles (Ed.), *The excellence of play* (3rd ed.). Maidenhead: Open University Press.

Play Wales. (2020). *The playwork principles*. Available at: www.playwales.org.uk/eng/playworkprinciples

Ray, D., Ogawa, Y., & Cheng, Y. (2022). *Multicultural play therapy: Making the most of cultural opportunities with children*. Abingdon: Routledge.

Scottish Government. (2017). *Additional support for learning Scotland act 2004 (as amended) code of practice* (3rd ed.). Available at: https://www.gov.scot/binaries/content/documents/govscot/ publications/advice-and-guidance/2017/12/supporting-childrens-learning-statutory-guidance- education-additional-support-learning-scotland/documents/00529411-pdf/00529411-pdf/govscot% 3Adocument/00529411.pdf

Siraj-Blatchford, I. (2006). Diversity, inclusion and learning in the early years. In G. Pugh & B. Duffy (Eds.), *Contemporary issues in early years education*. London: Sage.

Spencer-Cavaliere, N., & Watkinson, E. (2010). Inclusion understood from the perspectives of children with disability. *Physical Activity Quarterly*, 27, 275–293.

UNESCO. (1994). *The Salamanca statement and framework for action on special needs education*. Available at: https://unesdoc.unesco.org/ark:/48223/pf0000098427

UNICEF. (2017). *A summary of the UN convention on the rights of the child*. Available at: www.unicef.org.uk/rights-respecting-schools/wp-content/uploads/sites/4/2017/01/Summary-of- the-UNCRC.pdf

United Nations. (2020). *The convention in brief*. Available at: www.un.org/development/desa/ disabilities/convention-on-the-rights-of-persons-with-disabilities/the-convention-in-brief.html

Welsh Government. (2021). *The additional learning needs code for Wales 2021*. Available at: https:// www.gov.wales/sites/default/files/publications/2025-01/250124-the-additional-learning-needs-code- for-wales-2021.pdf

Whitebread, D. (2012). *The importance of play*. Available at: www.csap.cam.ac.uk/media/uploads/ files/1/david-whitebread—importance-of-play-report.pdf

17

Intergenerational Play in Practice

Margaret Kernan, Giulia Cortellesi, and Mariana Palazuelos

Chapter Objectives

- Explore the role of home visits by professionals and volunteers in supporting parents play with their children.
- Show how nonformal community-based play provision can challenge stereotypes and break down barriers between families of different backgrounds.
- Introduce theory and practice about intergenerational learning involving young children and older adults playing and building relationships.

Introduction

In this chapter we will be talking about the magic that happens when children, their parents and other older adults such as grandparents come together in play. In the examples we present, which come from a variety of countries, you will see that not only are the children thriving, but whole communities reap the benefits.

You will realise very quickly in your studies about early childhood education and care (ECEC), as well as in your working life as an ECEC professional, that ECEC is not just about working with children. It is also about working with and supporting families. One of the most important messages you want to share with parents is that they have a crucial role as their child's first and most important educator. A big part of this role is being a good play partner.

Linked to this message is the fact that a significant proportion of young children's learning and development takes place in the home and in the everyday spaces where children spend their time in their neighbourhood. The people they meet there of all ages and generations e.g., grandparents and other family members, neighbours, and friends also have a significant role in children's lives.

This means that part of your job as an ECEC professional is to help fathers and mothers understand the power of play in their children's learning and development, enhance their self-esteem as their children's play partner and introduce them to other informal play, cultural and leisure amenities in the community. Ideally, these should include parent and toddler groups, playgrounds, libraries, parks, and other green natural spaces, community arts and cultural centres. All of this, so that mothers, fathers, and other caregivers can enjoy playing together with their children and participate in community life together.

In recent years much more attention has also been paid to the benefits for young children of also having opportunities to play and socialise with grandparents and other older adults, who are not necessarily family members whereby they can have fun together, learn from each other and develop meaningful relationships. There is now an internationally recognised term for this type of learning and interaction. It is referred to as *Intergenerational Learning* or IGL. One of the reasons why IGL is gaining so much attention is because of the realisation that we are learners our whole life, from 'cradle to grave' and every generation can learn and benefit from the wisdom and insights of another generation. Of course, this second point is not a new idea. Children have been educated by 'elders' in societies the world over long before schools ever existed. However, IGL is having a revival currently. This is also because the separation of generations into care homes, retirement housing at the end of life, and daycare centres, ECEC settings, at the beginning of life, is considered artificial, isolating, and actually damaging to the well-being of both the young and the old.

Our focus in this chapter is on play as a unifying language between generations. We will be referring to programmes and initiatives that we have been directly involved in, as well as other good practice examples. We begin by exploring how first-time parents are being helped to play with their babies, toddlers through home visits by professionals, but also by volunteers who may be experienced parents. In the second part of the chapter, we will describe how non-formal play provision can help parents play with their children in a community setting, challenge stereotypes and break down barriers between people of different backgrounds. By non-formal we mean organised, systematic, educational activities delivered outside the formal system. Non-formal ECEC settings are important parts of any community, providing a safe space for play, learning, interaction and communication between all members of a community. In the last part of the chapter, we will introduce you to *intergenerational learning* which sees young children and older adults playing and building relationships in non-formal settings and in public places.

All three parts of the chapter describe different aspects or interpretations of intergenerational play. Common to all is that the adults are being encouraged to literally *get down with the kids* (Bottrill, 2018; see also Further Reading).

Introducing the Power of Play in Home Visits

Let us now explore the power of play in home visits.

What Do We Mean By Home Visiting?

The term home visiting usually refers to social service programmes that use visits to family homes as a core service and where home visitors model positive interactions and play with both parents and children. Home visiting has a long history as a way to deliver prenatal services, parenting support, child maltreatment prevention and ECEC services. Home visits by nurses and teachers can be traced back to nineteenth century England. Today, home visitors are usually trained professionals such as nurses, social workers, or health care workers. They can also be volunteers, or community leaders.

What Function Do Home Visiting Programmes Have Today?

As we mentioned in the introduction to the chapter, family and home life is the most important context for the development of infants and young children. Here, parents and other caregivers provide nurturance. They are also interaction partners in the social and physical world that infants and young children require to grow and thrive.

Many factors can influence the ability of parents and caregivers to meet these basic needs. The age and maturity of the caregivers, their mental and physical health, level of educational attainment and economic status. All of these will shape the environment that children experience. Children also experience their environment via their parents and caregivers' reaction to different situations. Sometimes, the health or development of the child poses caregiving challenges – for instance, when the child has significant health problems or born at low birth weight or has a developmental delay or disability.

Home visiting programmes support families in providing an environment that promotes the healthy growth and development of their children and are most effective in the first months and years of a child's life. Sometimes home visiting begins during pregnancy.

The intimacy of visiting in the home can make parents more comfortable about opening up and identifying their needs. It also helps home visitors to better tailor their support and guidance to the families' needs. Many parents of young children can sometimes feel isolated and home visits can offer a valuable connection to the outside community and the services and amenities available there such as parent and toddler groups, story sessions in the local library and children's farms. Home visiting is also useful for reaching families with young children who might not otherwise seek out support.

Home Visiting and Playful Parenting

In all cultures in the world, children play alone or in groups while they explore their environment. Through play, they discover and test ideas and develop physical and mental skills. However, parents and caregivers are not always aware of just how important play is for their infants and how playing together actually builds and strengthens parent–child relationships.

Play between a parent and young child is, quite literally, life changing for both parties. A long-lasting bond between parent and child can be established through playful interactions, laying the foundation for a positive and healthy relationship.

Home visiting programmes have an important role in supporting parents to talk with and play with their children and help them recognise the power of play for learning and development in their child's first years of life, often referred to as 'the first 1000 days in a child's life'. This is the approximate number of days between conception and the child's second birthday.

Health professionals and ECEC professionals need to work together and home visiting is often an important part of this work.

Modelling Nurturing Care and Parent-Child Play: Home Visiting Programmes in Practice

Let's look at two examples of programmes where the home-visitor models parent-child play interaction, one based in rural Ethiopia, one in the UK.

'Making the First 1000 Days Count!' (https://icdi.nl/projects/making-the-first-1000-days-count) and 'Foundations for the Future' (https://icdi.nl/projects/foundations-for-the-future-a-strong-start-for-every-child-from-birth-to-school-age/), are two programmes designed by International Child Development Initiatives (ICDI) (https://icdi.nl/) about nurturing care, which respectively operate in 16 villages in Amhara and South Gondar in Ethiopia, and in six villages in the region of Busoga in Uganda. They combine home visiting and centre-based ECEC in the form of non-formal community Play Hubs. The Play Hubs are family-friendly centres, located next to Health centres that are run in collaboration with community members, educators, and health home visitors. Here young children can play with toys and join educational activities, and their parents can participate in workshops on child development, education, health, nutrition, and parenting.

We realised early in the planning stages that not all families were participating in centre-based group activities such as ECEC centres, so we developed a home-visiting programme to reach these families and introduce them gradually to the centre-based activities.

In Ethiopia and in Uganda, there are already government supported home visiting programmes focusing on health and nutrition, the so-called health extension programme in Ethiopia and the Village Health Teams in Uganda. The ICDI's programmes supplemented the existing government programmes by providing home visitors with additional training and information about play, learning and development on topics such as how the brain develops through play and interaction, age-appropriate games, and do-it-you-self toys with locally resourced materials, working with parents respectfully and not preaching to them. Other parts of the Home Visiting 'Toolkit' included easy-to-use illustrated laminated play cards with pictures about simple games, action songs and how to make toys on one side and simple instructions in local language on the other side (Figure 17.1).

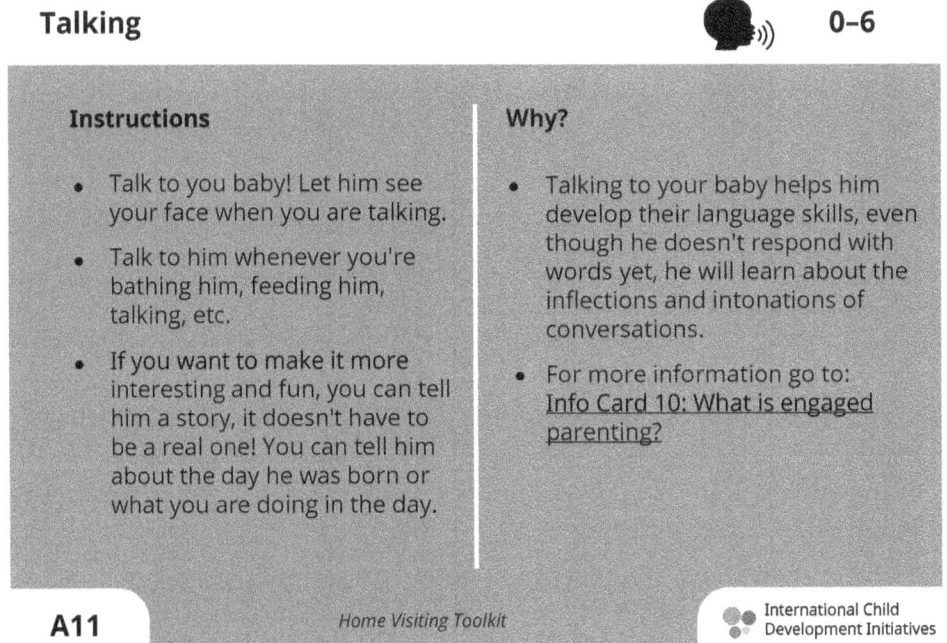

Figure 17.1   Example of an Activity Card From the Home Visiting Toolkit of the 'Making the First 1000 Days Count!' Project

Our experience is that the home visits are alerting parents to the importance of building loving, trusting and supportive relationships with their children. They are also reducing the stress parents and carers may experience in their parenting role by providing a listening ear, calm reassurance, support, and information. Over time, families and home visitors are building strong relationships that lead to lasting benefits for the entire family.

It is important that home visiting programmes are tailored to the needs of the community they are designed to support and build on the knowledge and cultural richness of families. This contrasts with a 'deficit model', which sees parents as lacking expertise and educational knowhow. The next example comes from Peterborough, a city in East Anglia, in the UK, which has high rates of poverty and disadvantage. Those involved in planning the programme wished to find out whether a home-visiting programme called 'Reach Up and Learn', based on the highly successful Jamaican home-visiting programme, would be effective in a city such as Peterborough.

The approach in the 'Reach Up and Learn' is to build the parents' knowledge of child development and their confidence in playing and interacting with their babies through regular visits from a trained home visitor in the first two years of life. Home visitors are provided with quite structured session plans, including outlines of activities and the accompanying resources e.g., toys, songs, and books. Each visit starts with a few minutes of chatting with the parent while the child explores one of the toys that the home visitor has brought. The home visitor then reviews the activities from the previous week, giving the child and parent a chance to show their progress and allowing the home visitor to observe and identify challenges. After that, the home visitor introduces the activities for the visit, in each case giving the child time to explore the toy before doing the activity with him/her and then encouraging the parent to take over. At the end of the visit, the visitor asks the parent to recap the activities for the week and to demonstrate them with the child. Home visitors are encouraged to adapt the curriculum to the needs of the individual child.

As a first step, the developers of the Peterborough pilot found out what they could about already existing services for families and young children and what parents actually needed and wanted. This is what they found out:

- Early years services in the United Kingdom are targeted at children aged three and older. Services that are available for children younger than three years tend to focus on health or safeguarding.
- Parents felt that home visits would help them play and interact with their young children, which is what they wanted. Practitioners recognised that the programme offered something different – which would help them support vulnerable families more effectively.
- Practitioners also reported significant positive changes in parents' behaviours over the course of the short pilot (Grantham-McGregor et al., 2019).

Finding out what parents need, the kind of support they would like in a way that complements and builds on the positives and strengths in their relationship with their young children is important when planning home-visiting programmes. Offering respectful support in the familiar space of the family home focusing on play and interaction between parent and young child is one example of non-formal learning and support. One of the criticisms of formal ECEC provision, such as kindergarten, or pre-school education is that it can be more focused on the institution and assessing children, and not on the rights and needs of children, families and communities. This can unavoidably result in ignoring the capacities of parents, families, or looking upon them as less effective if not incompetent as educators. Furthermore, in many countries formal ECEC settings are often age and culture segregated and are rarely places of multi-generational play, meeting and socialisation.

In the next part of the chapter, we describe an initiative which seeks to challenge such age and culture-segregated approaches to ECEC in favour of an empowering approach, which embraces the role of non-formal and informal ECEC in children's lives, complementing formal ECEC settings. This approach also puts play and community at the heart of learning.

TOY for Inclusion: Social Cohesion Starts With Young Children's Eagerness to Play

The TOY for Inclusion (www.toy4inclusion.eu; TOY stands for *Together Old and Young*) recognises that learning occurs not only within an ECEC or school setting, but in all areas of life, beginning before a child is born and continuing across the entire lifespan. Thus, the focus is on community learning, and community-based ECEC. For a community to reach its full potential with regard to early years provision, it is necessary to recognise the value of all three forms of ECEC (formal, nonformal, and informal), and how they support the well-being of children, families and communities. Part of this involves acknowledging the shared responsibilities communities have for their children and seeing the possibilities for mobilisation around children. This can, for example, involve the active participation of parents, grandparents and service providers in the design and running of ECEC initiatives. This is what our goal was in TOY for Inclusion.

TOY for Inclusion was developed in 2017 by International Child Development Initiatives - ICDI in partnership with NGOs and local authorities in 8 European countries, and is now operating in nine countries. The approach involves different sectors and agencies working together with the community to come up with flexible solutions and responses to the specific needs of young children (0-10 years old) and their families. It provides play, learning and socialising opportunities for children and their parents. It also promotes intergenerational activities which involve grandparents and other older adults living in the neighbourhood. All these activities take place in a Play Hub, which puts TOY for Inclusion at the heart of the communities. These Play Hubs were also the inspiration for the Play Hubs which were opened as part of the 'Making the first 1000 days count!' programme in Ethiopia and Uganda, discussed earlier in this chapter.

In TOY for Inclusion, the Play Hubs are inclusive spaces where:

- children and adults of all ages meet, spend quality time together and play with each other.
- children can borrow toys and educational materials to bring home.
- parents, grandparents and practitioners can informally learn and exchange information about child health, early learning, and development.

Play-based activities are organised to support creativity, increase confidence, develop social, emotional, and verbal skills and unlock each child's potential. This helps children in their transition to formal education. This is particularly relevant for families from a Roma, migrant, or socially disadvantaged background, to whom the Play Hubs give extra attention. In fact, Play Hubs are a flexible solution that offers educational opportunities for all those children who are often excluded from formal educational services.

In the Play Hubs, play is always at the centre of children's and adult's experience. Play is a magnet and a leveller. When children, parents and grandparents, as well as practitioners, play together, they can build trust and overcome stereotypes and fears. Through play, children and families from very different socio-economic and cultural backgrounds can meet, get to know each other, and build a network made of other families and services that can support them in times of need.

The adaptability and flexibility of the TOY for Inclusion approach became evident during the COVID-19 pandemic in 2020–2022 and the refugee crisis caused by the war in Ukraine started in 2022. The Local Action Teams tasked with operating the Play Hubs sprang into action to adjust activities to address community challenges, often in ways formal services weren't able to. Times of crisis (see also chapter 19) shine a light on the essential elements of the TOY for Inclusion project – intersectoral work as a way to address complex issues, innovative and flexible solutions tailored to communities and the development of inclusive and easy to reach services.

Case Study 17.1: A Mobile Play Hub for Children and Families in Rome (Italy)

There are two Play Hubs in the neighbourhood of Tor Bella Monaca in Rome. One is permanent and is located in the Ex Fienile-community centre. The other is a mobile Play Hub i.e. a fully equipped trolley that moves once a week to reach one of the neighbourhood squares. Both are initiatives of Associazione 21 luglio, a TOY for Inclusion partner.

Play Hubs are informal spaces for care and learning, welcoming children aged 0-3 years and their caregivers. The families attending the Play Hubs mostly live in vulnerable socio-economic conditions. The operators strive to build strong relationships with families and foster growth processes for both children and parents.

The permanent Play Hub is open every Monday, Wednesday and Friday from 9:30 a.m. to 12:30 p.m. When the weather is warm, the mobile Play Hub – equipped with chairs, tables, soft mats, games, and books – is set up outdoors in the spacious backyard of the Ex Fienile centre, which includes an educational garden. On these days, outdoor educational activities take place, the garden and plants are tended to, and interactions with nature are encouraged.

On colder days, activities move indoors to the permanent Play Hub. This is a colourful and welcoming space where children and parents, who begin arriving around 9:30 a.m., engage in play and workshops. During the first hour, children are free to explore the environment, with games and books at their disposal. A mid-morning snack, including fruit and often homemade treats prepared by the mothers, is shared while caregivers enjoy a moment of conversation over a hot cup of tea.

(Continued)

(Continued)

After the snack, more structured activities take place, such as creative, sensory and motor-based workshops. These activities encourage creativity, foster autonomy, develop social, emotional, and verbal skills, and support each child's potential, helping prepare them for formal education.

Every Tuesday, the mobile Play Hub moves to Piazza Castano, one of the neighbourhood's busiest squares. Families arrive around 10:00 a.m. and stay until approximately 12:30 p.m. The activities always follow the same routine, with time for free play, a snack and a structured activity.

Both Play Hubs feature toy libraries, where families can borrow high-quality toys and books selected for different age groups. Additionally, weekly Café Labs are organised at the Play Hub – spaces for socialising, sharing skills and engaging with the community. These meetings also feature the participation of specialist professionals supporting parenting, such as midwives, psychologists, and educators.

As you can read in the case study above, grandparents often participate in the activities organised in the Play Hubs. This has been a goal from the very start of TOY for Inclusion and intergenerational learning is one of the key building blocks of the whole approach. In the next section, we will look more in-depth at why bringing young children and older adults together in playful learning experiences benefits both generations and the community at large.

Bringing Older Adults and Children Together Through Play

In the UK, the pioneering television documentary, *Old People's Home for 4 Year Olds*, which was first aired on Channel 4 in Autumn 2017 had a huge role in raising awareness about the benefits of intergenerational learning for both older adults and younger children and their families. The design of the social experiment brought together older adults and 4-year-old children in a 'pop-up' nursery school, which was set up for a six-week period in an older people's retirement home in Bristol. The plan was that both groups would take part in the same kind of activities that the children would have done in their nursery schools i.e., storytelling, going for walks, interacting with nature, singing, craft activities, and playing games.

The resulting 2-part documentary captivated viewers across UK, Ireland and around the world, so much so that the format of *Old People's Home for 4 Year Olds* has since been repeated and translated in Australia, Spain and the Netherlands. The original documentary vividly illustrated how the time spent with the children had changed the lives of the older adults, both physically and mentally. They talked about having more energy and zest for life and having a feeling of being loved and valued. For their part, the 4-year-olds were friendly, inquisitive, accepting, and non-judgemental, full of fun, vitality, and enthusiasm.

According to Rachael Dutton and David Williams, who wrote about the impact of the experiment in *Intergenerational Learning in Practice* (see annotated resources), as the relationships between the children and older adults formed, age became irrelevant; the focus for both groups was fully on the activities and interactions they were having together, and strong friendships grew.

The type of interaction vividly captured in this documentary is typical of international learning (IGL). However, there is much more to IGL as we will now illustrate.

Why Is IGL So Important?

The term IGL is used to capture the way people of all ages can learn together and from each other. It is often linked to the concepts of *lifelong learning* and *lifewide learning*. These describe how we are learners our whole life and that learning can happen anywhere and not confined to educational institutions such as schools, or colleges.

IGL programmes typically take place outside the family home, such as in day or residential care homes for older adults such *Old People's Home for 4 Year Olds*. But they can also take place in early years settings, libraries, museums or parks or 'community play hubs' as described earlier in this chapter.

One reason explaining the growing interest in IGL, is the growing separation of generations because of the way we organise our families and communities. In many countries older adults live in care homes where they rarely see children and many children are spending their days only with their own age group in ECEC centres and schools. Separation can of course be due to migration or family breakdown. Some IGL programmes are designed to recreate multi-generational living together in the same house or community. The benefits of regular contact between grandparents and grandchildren, and family members of all ages came into sharp focus when we realised what was being missed – social interaction, affection, hugs and shared laughter and play – due to the physical distancing imposed during the global COVID-19 pandemic.

Together Old and Young Programme

In 2011, a group of researchers, educators, NGOs, and local authorities in Europe came together to research and develop good practice in intergenerational learning specifically involving children under 8 years and older adults with support of the European Union. By 2021 the project, titled Together Old and Young or TOY has become a programme which includes innovation, professional development and quality assessment components (www.toyproject.net). The vision statement of the TOY Programme, which emerged from the initial TOY fact-finding research about IGL involving young children and older adults in seven countries, captures the affection, joy, and playfulness of their encounters:

> *The Together Old and Young (TOY) approach to IGL brings young children and older adults together to share experiences, have fun, learn from each other and develop meaningful relationships. Intergenerational Learning activities in TOY are friendly and informal social encounters, where children and adults can equally partake as the learner and the teacher.*

The TOY approach also recognises and gives value to the distinctive rhythm and pace that many older adult and young child friendships benefit from. This is a leisurely pace with plenty of time to stop and ponder on rambling walks together, when chatting while eating or playing a board game together. This contrasts with the often rushed, or highly structured rhythm in regular ECEC or in the hurried times of stressed parents of young children (see also Greg Bottrill's note about time in the resources section at the end of this chapter).

One of the places where the pace of interaction can be relaxed and in tune with the natural rhythm of both young and old is in public space where interaction is not structured or part of a planned programme but shows many of the hallmarks of free play. To conclude this chapter, we will consider spontaneous, everyday IG encounters in public space.

Intergenerational Play in Public Space

One of the factors that unifies children and older adults is their attachment to home and neighbourhood. For both generations, the possibilities to move, to socialise, to feel safe and secure, to actively participate and belong are closely connected to what local the neighbourhood makes possible. The arrangement of the urban built environment is key in this regard. Urban design is more important than ever, because around three-quarters of the population of Europe live in urban areas. However, typically cities have been designed with the working adult in mind. Children and older adults are often shifted to the margins in urban design that provides for separate zones for separate functions and age-groups. Think about public playgrounds or skate parks for children, or designated meeting places, retirement homes and communities or senior citizen playgrounds for older adults.

Play is a means to appropriate space, and in the process develops a sense of belonging to place or neighbourhood (see also Chapters 11 and 12). It is often in the areas not actually planned for play that play takes place e.g., footpaths, or on monuments. An intergenerational approach to urban spatial design would allow different generations to meet informally, interact, and even play together and in doing so develop insight and empathy for the other. These kinds of encounters are made possible by design solutions such as green, walkable pathways through neighbourhoods; seating of different heights and forms in public spaces and placing subtle boundaries around children's playgrounds.

An example of an age-inclusive play and recreation space is the tea house and park in the culturally diverse neighbourhood of Leiden Noord, in the Netherlands. This is a volunteer-led community project, which has resulted in the design of an environmentally friendly building that opens out to a range of natural play spaces and green areas with seating. It has proved to be a very attractive meeting space for all generations. Senior volunteers run the tea house, which also hosts community events and can be rented for small parties; families with young children from all around Leiden come to play in the large sand pit and adventurous natural playground. Older adults from the neighbourhood stroll in the park, sit for a coffee, and interact with the other visitors.

By integrating knowledge and insights coming from intergenerational practice with spatial design we can create age-inclusive spaces and in doing so, improve cities' or neighbourhoods' friendliness and cohesion.

Reflection Point 17.1

1 Play and interaction between children and (older) adults can support child development and learning as well as the creation of respectful parenting behaviours and social cohesion in the community. Can you think of a situation you experienced, or heard or read about where play has helped solve a conflict or overcome a stereotype?

2 Bringing children and adults together in play may not always be beneficial. Can you identify situations when this might be the case? Think also about the needs of all generations for privacy either alone or with same-age peers.

Summary

- Parents have a crucial role in their young children's learning and development. A big part of this role is being a good play partner.
- Home visiting programmes support families in providing an environment that promotes the healthy growth and development of their children, including attention to play.
- Nonformal play provision such as community 'play hubs' provide an important bridge between the home and formal school.
- Play is a magnet and a leveller. Everyone, no matter their cultural background, their socio-economic situation or their age or gender or ability, is equal in play and can participate given the right conditions.
- All ages benefit from intergenerational play which can take place at home, in ECEC settings and in public space.

Further Reading

Bottrill, G. (2018) *Can i go & play now? Rethinking the early years*. London: Sage Publications. This book is an important reminder of the energy, creativity and freedom of play. Greg Bottrill's message is that young children need adults (parents and early years professionals) to listen, to watch and sometimes participate in or talk about play by 'getting down with the kids' and making time for 'child chit chat', while all the time remembering that play should be from the child and owned by the child.

ICDI (2023) *Mobile play hubs: operating guidelines and activity cards*. Leiden: ICDI. This Toolkit is intended for organisations wishing to set up and run Mobile Play Hubs for children aged 0-10 years old. It is also useful to regular Play Hubs and other non-formal ECEC settings that want to make (outdoor) play more accessible to children of all ages and their families. It consists of two parts: the Operating Guidelines, and the Activity Cards to be used by practitioners in the Play Hubs and any other non-formal service to promote outdoor play for young children.

https://www.reyn.eu/wp-content/uploads/2023/08/English-MPH-Operating-New_compressed.pdf

https://www.reyn.eu/wp-content/uploads/2023/08/English-MPH-Activity-Cards_compressed.pdf

Kernan, M. and Cortellesi, G. (Eds.) (2020) *Intergenerational learning in practice: Together old and young*. Abington: Routledge.
This is a book for practitioners and leaders in ECEC and primary education, as well as those working in social care and community development. In it you will find up-to-date theory and research about intergenerational learning, information about the changing relationships between young children and older adults, along with tools and resources to help you develop and improve your own intergenerational practice. It includes contributions from Europe, North America, and Australia and from experts in pedagogy, IG learning, practice, and urban design.

Reference
Grantham-Mc Gregor, S., Fulton, E., Fitzsimons, E., Farquharson, C., Cattan, S., Attanasio, O., & Armstrong, A. (2019). *A home-visiting programme for disadvantaged young children: Final report for the feasibility study.* https://doi.org/10.1920/re.ifs.2019.0159

Part IV
International Perspectives

18
Cultural Framing of Expectations for Play

Angela Rekers and Jane Waters-Davies

Chapter Objectives

This chapter will help you:

- Understand that cultural context informs 'taken for granted' practices including play.
- Understand ways in which cultural context shapes opportunities and provision for children's play.
- Recognise how play might reveal cultural value conflicts between the home context and nursery/school setting.

Culture

Culture is generally understood to be the values and beliefs that contribute to group or institutional expectations and demands, traditions, acceptable behaviours and social interactions, and even the design of physical spaces or material environments. Culture can be observed as the ways of *being* and *doing* within particular communities that are based upon shared set(s) of values. In education and play research, we often see the term 'socio-cultural context', which refers to these values, traditions, patterns of behaviour, communication and artefacts such as toys and materials.

Pierre Bourdieu (1977) said that individuals internalise acquired dispositions or *habitus* by participating in culturally based practices and activities. He argued that these dispositions are grounded in cultural institutions, such as family and school. Bourdieu's theory argues that our sense of belonging – or not – is often rooted in how well we fit into or understand the 'rules' of the social situation. Because cultural expectations, understandings and behaviours can be so ingrained, people can take these for granted or mistake habitus as inherent rather than culturally developed. This can lead to reinforcement of social inequality, since people can assume their own way of doing things is how "everyone does/see things", is "natural", or "better" than the way others do things. Part of the purpose of this chapter is to help us recognise the cultural factors that can shape our practices as educators and children's participation in education settings so that we might strive to ensure equity, inclusion and belonging. After exploring further what is meant by 'culture', this chapter examines the ways in which play and play provision can reflect aspects of culture. We focus upon two key themes, gender and risk, to explore examples of how culture not only shapes play itself, but can frame our understanding of play activity. In doing so, we also highlight how an awareness of the concept of culture, as well as cultural conflict, may encourage us to reconsider what we 'take for granted' about children's play.

The theorist Lev Vygotsky (1978) argued that cultural values may be reflected in the everyday social interactions and the material resources with which children engage. Building upon Vygotsky's (1978) theory of children's development as a transformative interaction between the child and their social and material environment, Barbara Rogoff, a leading sociocultural theorist, researches extensively on how children's learning and development is supported by the process of *guided participation* in cultural activities (Rogoff, 2003). Rather than just the transmitting and receiving of information adult to child, the theory of guided participation argues that there is a collaborative process in which learners are 'apprentices', guided by more knowledgeable others. Learning takes place by observing, listening, asking questions and collaborative activity. Guided participation takes place within cultural context, underpinned by cultural and social values inherent in the interactions between the child and their social partners (adults, family and peers) and the material resources that shape development.

The work of Bourdieu, Rogoff and Vygotsky, among others, helps us to understand that play does not sit outside the context in which it takes place; it is shaped by that context and the values, expectations and demands that are associated with it. This is very important when we think about how we provide for, support, and understand children's play across different cultural contexts. It is important when we compare provision across different countries to remember that the cultural context of different countries, regions, and subcultures will frame the expectations of families, practitioners and the children themselves, and that this will shape play provision and participation. This means that we cannot replicate provision in one context and expect it to have the same outcomes in another context. Sometimes, when policymakers or advisors recommend that 'best practice' is copied from one context to another, we need to question whether the practice is only 'best' in specific contexts or for specific children.

When we work with children and families from different backgrounds to our own, it is essential to remember our own *habitus* may be different from that of others and to respect different social and cultural practices. As practitioners, we are often expected to support children to achieve particular aims or outcomes that are valued by the society in which we are working. Yet, if these are in contrast to a child's home culture this may create conflict for us as practitioners and/or for children as they transition between home and school, care or play provision. Recognising cultural context, and being aware of potential cultural conflicts, can help practitioners to understand how best to understand and support children in their play.

Reflection Point 18.1

Consider this short scenario:

Dafydd is 4 $\frac{1}{2}$ years old and the youngest child in a family of three boys; he has joined the reception class, having not attended any pre-school provision. Dafydd's two brothers (now 11 and 13) were considered 'difficult to manage' when they were younger and in primary school, as they both used to be involved in fights in the playground. Dafydd's dad manages the local gym and teaches boxing. Since both brothers started boxing lessons with him, they have won prizes at local competitions for their boxing skills. Neither of them engage in fighting outside of the boxing ring now, except for play fighting with Dafydd, which they do at home.

- How might Dafydd engage in or back away from 'risky play', such as play fighting, when he joins school?
- How might Dafydd understand the school rules about 'no fighting' and the underlying message that 'fighting is bad'?
- How might the practitioners ease any cultural conflict that Dafydd experiences between play that is acceptable at home and that which is acceptable at school?

Culture and Play

The work of socio-cultural theorists can help us understand that development is shaped by both biological and cultural processes; indeed, Rogoff (2003, p. 63) describes humans as being 'biologically cultural'. Playfulness is biologically inherent in many animal species that engage in social play, such as wrestling and chasing, object play, and solitary/rotational play among other forms (Burghardt et al., 2024). These types of play seem to be culturally and historically universal; even prehistoric children's play and play object use has been studied from a cultural evolutionary perspective (Riede et al., 2021). An interdisciplinary approach to play brings theories from developmental psychology, cultural anthropology, archaeology, sociology and human geography together to consider how children play, with whom, with what, and where. Research demonstrates how we can understand play as a way in which children 'act out' cultural relationships that are found within their social and material environments, combining elements from their lived experience with imaginative activity (e.g. Corsaro, 2012; Evaldsson & Corsaro, 1998). Although play is not always imaginative, Vygotsky (1978) asserts that in what may be characterised as imaginative play, children can take risks with transgressing social norms as well as adopting them. By observing children's play, we can see how they actively 'co-construct' culture. Their play behaviour may show appropriation (adoption) of cultural normative behaviours, but it may also display negotiation with or even rejection of cultural norms.

> ## Reflection Point 18.2
>
> Consider games that you played as a child. Were they 'traditional' games, such as a form of tag that you were taught by others or an adaptation of a traditional game in which you made up new rules? Were there specific toys that 'everyone' wanted? Did you imagine yourself to be an adult, playing shopkeeper, parenting a doll, being a teacher, building a bridge out of blocks? As you reflect on your childhood play, did it seem to reflect gender-specific roles or relate to your particular cultural context?

We now examine the way in which play and play provision can be framed by culture, both intentionally or unintentionally. By focusing on two key themes, gender and risk, we offer some examples to demonstrate how play is impacted by cultural context. As stated in the introductory section, we also highlight how cultural conflict may encourage us to reconsider what we might 'take for granted' about children's play.

Gender

Play studies demonstrate there is often a binary gender delineation (girls/boys) in children's play that reflects the cultural significance of adult roles, peer influence, and the available resources, as well as the child's own agency. It is perhaps unsurprising that across cultures when children engage in dramatic or role play, it is typically themed around what children observe and experience in daily life, and most often exemplifies adult roles and the objects or tools that are used in adult work. Fouts et al. (2016), in their study of play in Central Africa's foraging and farming communities, call such play work-themed play. In this study of small-scale societies, the authors explain how young children's play is shaped by the expectations of their respective society in relation to the work of that society. In work-themed play, children utilise aspects of adult-life such as tool use. Often the objects they chose or were given to play with were real or replica/smaller versions of a tool an adult would use, such as small baskets used for 'play' foraging. Fouts et al. (2016) found that cultural occupations of the families, whether farmers or foragers, had a significant impact on play patterns; traditional gender roles within those occupations, too, influenced play activities.

Cultural behaviours and beliefs often lead to 'gender cues' about what is or is not 'acceptable' play behaviour and what is valued by others in regards to what girls do and what boys do. Both adults and children's peers may consciously or subconsciously reinforce certain gender-based play activities and play resources. Brito et al. (2021) argue that this creates stereotypical gender-based roles that can be limiting for children's development. Providing equitable and inclusive resources and opportunities for everyone, however, ensures that all children are supported to reach their full potential creatively, socio-emotionally, physically and cognitively.

Even with deliberate facilitation by teaching staff to ensure gender equity or support non-binary identity formation, the resources that are available to children in a play setting may contribute to gender stereotyping. In a Canadian study of six children between the ages of four and five from a variety of cultural, racial and ethnic backgrounds, Ali (2020) found that certain play materials, such as puzzles and art supplies, were considered more gender-neutral than specific toys, such as cars or Lego. Even by kindergarten, children were negotiating with 'what constitutes "appropriate" or "inappropriate" play... in relation to gender propriety' (Ali, 2020, p. 89). In order to address equitable outcomes, especially encouraging girls in Science, Technology, Engineering and Mathematics (STEM), providing more gender-neutral resources is essential.

Often marketing strategies by toy companies will package and market toys differently to attract particular gender; Lego, for example, has been criticised for marketing gender-differentiated construction sets, e.g., Lego City and Lego Friends (see Reich et al., 2018). While it may seem that marketing strategies, even if marketing to girls and to boys separately, that encourage girls to more STEM play is a good thing, it may be that the binary aspect is difficult to avoid. For instance, Coyle and Liben (2020) found that mothers played differently with their sons than with their daughters when engaging with similar STEM toys packaged and marketed differently for boys and girls (Coyle & Liben, 2020).

Providing a range of open-ended, gender-neutral resources to allow children greater opportunities for play that is not restricted by cultural gender norms is important for academic outcomes, greater participation and skills development across all developmental domains. Having a flexible approach in play that allows children to explore multiple roles with fluidity provides play opportunities that echo the definition of play as freely chosen, personally directed and intrinsically motivated. Particularly for children whose gender identity may not be the same as their sex assigned at birth, or those who have a gender-diverse identity, creating opportunities for children to play in an exploratory, fluid manner. Creating space for children to feel accepted for who they are creates a culture of belonging. For more about this see the American Academic of Paediatrics link in Further Reading.

Certainly, traditional gender roles in society can be reinforced or challenged by play behaviours, activities, resources and spaces. Waller (2010) has argued that outdoor play settings may have the potential to offer more opportunities for gender-neutral play, primarily due to the lack of gender-specific toys, more free-flowing activity, and expectations from outdoor learning staff. Activities such as swings, climbing, mud play and 'bug hunts' are available and may be encouraged by staff as appropriate for everyone. However, there is still the potential for the physical space, as well as gender-beliefs of both adults (parents and teachers) and children to influence play behaviour outside (See Erdan & Alpslan, 2017; Isci & Hasirci, 2023 in Further Reading). The case study below, taken from the first author's doctoral study (Rekers-Power, 2020), provides an example of how children's understandings about builders in 'real-life' influenced their approach to the outdoor play activity described.

Case Study 18.1

At a forest school session in the woods, two 5-year-old boys, Bence and Lee, were mixing mud and water, using sticks and mixing bowls, to make 'cement'. Bence approached me (the researcher) to ask for their work to be filmed with my iPhone. A girl named Chloe, standing nearby, asked if she could join in. Bence looked at me, then said she could reluctantly. He handed her a stick and told her how the mud should be stirred to make

(Continued)

(Continued)

cement. Soon another girl tried to join in, by picking up sticks to help stir the mud. Bence pushed her arm away and said, 'No, Shannon! We are making a cement circle!' Lee told Shannon more gently, 'Cause this is our builder thing, just boys allowed'. Then he glanced at Chloe, who had already started mixing: 'And girls', he added doubtfully.

Bence said, 'No more girls! Just boys!' Nodding, Lee suggested, 'Just one more'. But Bence insisted: 'No! Only boys!' Then Lee said to Shannon, 'See, there's a sign there that says "No girls"', and pointed vaguely off to the trees. Shannon looked around in confusion for the non-existent sign. Then she found another container and a stick and asked, 'Can I do this one?' Bence looked over and said, 'No… I mean yes. You can help with that one. Good job'. Another girl also joined in with the task, and Bence supervised the work.

Later, when I interviewed Bence and his mother, using the video recording of the episode to instigate discussion, I asked him about it: 'Can girls be builders too?' He laughed and said, 'No, girls aren't builders.' I reminded him that one of the forest school leaders was building her own house, and he tilted his head to the side and looked thoughtful: 'I didn't know that girls could build houses.'

In this example, both Bence and Lee can be seen to struggle a little to allow the girls to join their play, based upon their existing perceptions of gender as criteria for who can join in the 'builders' play. The girls, on the other hand, did not consider this activity 'off limits' for them. However, the boys also can be seen to understand that at school and at forest school, there are cultural expectations to not exclude others in their play. The intersection of cultural values can trigger conflict, which can be a transformative learning opportunity. While the episode shows how the girls wanting to make cement presented a conflict with the boys' understandings of gender-related work, both boys were willing to be flexible to be good playmates. Bence's thoughtfulness in the interview can be interpreted as his ongoing willingness to reconsider some of his preconceived notions of gender roles in response to adult inquiry.

Adults in play and education settings can have an important role in sensitively challenging children's cultural formation of gender stereotypes, as the case study above demonstrates. Equally, it is important to recognise that children's home culture may have different values to the education, play or care setting. Sadownik (2021) studied immigrant Polish parents' perceptions of outdoor provision in Norwegian early childhood education institutions from a cultural formation perspective. She notes that those parents with more traditional gender-related value positions, in line with mainstream Polish culture, found it difficult to understand their daughters taking part in non-gender-specific outdoor play. However, this is considered mainstream provision in Norway where kindergartens are based upon egalitarian values, including promoting non-gender-specific play (Sadownik, 2021). With the conversational support of the researcher, the parents began to re-consider some of their beliefs around gender and play activities.

Another example of how cultural values can be reflected in relation to gender-specific play behaviour is Levinson's (2005) study of play behaviour in Gypsy communities. Levinson observed that girls and boys were more likely to participate in play along binary lines that reflected the roles of adult men and women within the Gypsy culture. He attributes this to the intergenerational and multi-age free play groups that he observed, in which children were encouraged to replicate traditional gender activities as preparation for adult life, with its specific expectations. He also noted that the resources available for play contributed to how the children played and replicated adult activities. Rather than playing with toy cars, for instance, boys in the study had opportunities to play with real car parts from a scrapped vehicle. Similarly, girls were playing with and taking care of younger siblings and babies in the community, which they felt was more grown up and thus preferable to playing with dolls. Levinson concluded that from an early age, Gypsy children appear to be 'apprenticed' into adult life and gendered roles.

Education, care and play practitioners have the capacity to support children negotiating and transgressing traditional gender boundaries by encouraging equitable access to toys, ensuring that resources and opportunities are open-ended, and responding thoughtfully to stereotypical activity in play, while doing so with respect for diverse cultural motivations. The practitioner's self-awareness is also important: teachers and play workers, parents and carers can reinforce gender stereotyping if they do not recognise their own biases (Lynch, 2015). It is valuable for the practitioner to have an understanding of the developmental importance of ensuring children have a wide variety of equitable play opportunities (see Chapters 6–10 in part II of this book).

Reflection Point 18.3

- Do toys within your setting (or a setting you are familiar with) allow for open-ended, non-gender specific play?
- Observe some children at play in a setting: what gender roles do you see enacted? Where does this take place? How do you feel about this? Are there examples where children reject traditional gender roles? How has this been facilitated?
- How could binary boundaries between what girls play and what boys play impact on children's development?
- What do you think about companies like Lego creating toys 'aimed' at girls? Does it support their STEM play?

Risk

Here, we think about how cultural perceptions of *risk* shapes outdoor play provision, specifically, by comparing approaches in Sweden, Singapore and the United Kingdom. Risk is a noun (a thing) and also a verb (an action). Risk is described in the Cambridge online dictionary as *the possibility of something bad happening* (the noun) and *to do something although there is a chance of a bad result* (the verb). Sandseter (2009) claims that risk characteristics of children's play can be categorised broadly into environmental features of the play environment and the child's own approach to the play. Both of these categories can be viewed through a socio-cultural lens. Risk, as a noun or a verb, is therefore not fixed; this means it is understood differently in different contexts. Here we explore practice in different countries and notice how cultural attitudes and values regarding risk can frame outdoor play practice.

In Sweden, it is traditionally accepted that young children play in natural outdoor environments in which 'risky play', such as tree climbing, is customary. Historically, acknowledging that children sometimes fall and hurt themselves, and that a short-term injury is part of growing up, characterises the cultural approach to play. A culturally-held view that a healthy childhood includes learning to manage risk and being in the fresh air is common across the Nordic countries (see Einarsdóttir, 2006 for a great summary about this), and underpins early childhood policies and curricula. This means that histori-cally practitioners have not feared retribution if a child is hurt during risky play; their practice is framed by culturally shared beliefs and values about strong and capable children, who need opportunities to be able to challenge themselves in their early childhood play in order to thrive academically. Of course, these practitioners would stop any behaviour that was seriously hazardous, but they prioritise children being competent, capable and able to manage reasonable risk, from a young age (see also Chapter 12).

In other countries, there can be different cultural expectations regarding provision for children's outdoor play. Using Singapore as an example, these are driven, in part, by cultural understandings of the child being vulnerable and in need of protection from an environment that can be harmful. In Singapore, there are environmental conditions that impact upon the behaviours of everyone – the climate is often hot and humid, which can be uncomfortable, even for those who are used to it, and sometimes the air quality is poor. Indoor environments are often air conditioned, and much more comfortable; therefore, people tend to spend much more time indoors than outside. The warm and humid conditions mean that infectious diseases are perceived to be transmitted easily and hygiene in educare settings is a very high priority; children and the spaces they play in are kept very clean.

Additionally, Singapore values are focused upon academic achievement; traditionally, therefore there has been an expectation that young children's early childhood provision will be academically focused. Such conditions have created a culture in which outdoor play in ECEC has been restricted and framed through the lenses of safety and risk-aversion, as well as an emphasis on academic orientation. In the past decade the education department associated with ECEC in Singapore has sought to challenge these approaches and promote access to outdoor environments in which young children can take risks that are carefully managed. Take a look at the national guidance for outdoor learning in ECEC in Singapore (ECDA, 2019) and consider how the guidance ensures carefully managed risk taking during outdoor activity in ECEC settings.

Importantly, within countries there are multiple cultural contexts across geographies, commu-nities, and families. In this sense, not all societal values or expectations may align with what might be considered mainstream. In addition, cultures are not static; cultural understandings and values can shift and develop over time. For instance, in the United Kingdom (UK), risky play outdoors has been considered mainstream *and* alternative over the past 60 years or so. In the 1960s and 1970s children were expected to play outdoors, often unsupervised, and it was generally accepted that bruised knees and scraped arms were an inevitable part of childhood, according to Gill (2007). Over time, however, attitudes – and subsequently, legislation – shifted towards risk-awareness and risk-aversion. In turn, children's play spaces became increasingly restricted, supervised and controlled (Gill, 2007). Thus, *adventure play provision* or risky outdoor play became less commonplace and an alternative to mainstream play/playground provision, largely sitting within the domain of playwork and urban play schemes (Russell, 2018).

Recently, there is a growing awareness of some of the negative impacts on children's development from their lack of outdoor play, as well as lack of opportunity to roam and play without overly restrictive adult supervision. Additionally, there is more research evidence to underscore the benefits and opportunities for learning and development provided by developmentally appropriate risky play. This has led to increased interest in adventure play schemes and forest school provision in the UK. Rather than a lack of supervision or overly restrictive supervision, in best practice, the adult undertakes a risk/benefit analysis (see Chapter 12), in which developmentally appropriate risks are considered in relation to their benefits for the child, as well as controls to minimise unnecessary or severe risk. This demonstrates how the cultures of play, education, and care can be aligned, and also that cultural values, here in relation to risk aversion and risk management, can change over time.

Reflection Point 18.4

- How risk-averse are you? Why? How does the environment in which you grow up inform your idea of what is risky?
- How might this impact upon your approach to risky play in an ECEC setting?
- What are the benefits of being aware of the way in which your own framing of risk might enhance or restrict young children's play?

Conclusion

There can be cultural differences in approaches to play within or between countries and communities that may create conflict for children, parents/carers, and practitioners. For example, in Levinson's (2005) study described earlier, he asserts that the ways in which the Gypsy community children played at school created a conflict for the teachers in the study. Because Gypsy children were more likely to play at home within marginalised spaces, such as wasteland, their play patterns at home included the real-life environment of horses, car parts and scrap materials rather than traditional, representational toys or safety-regulated playground equipment. The study noted that when the children played with traditional toys in the school setting, they were more likely to take them apart, discard them after a short time or consider games and toys 'babyish'. This highlights how our definitions of play, appropriate resources and even notions of age-appropriate play are also culturally based, and have the potential to be challenged when cultures integrate. Understanding cultural contexts can support us in responding sensitively to children's play activity and experience.

Factors such as time devoted to play can also be considered a cultural construct in relation to play. We can reflect on different cultural approaches to organising children's play in the family and community, outside of ECEC and school settings, as a good example. In some cultures, specific times are set aside for 'play dates' or playtime with friends, and these may be orchestrated by the adults in the family. In other cultures, however, children play as they get the chance within the day to day activities of the family and community. These children's play may include imitating or joining adults and other children engaged in the work of the family; young children mimic older siblings who help them to take part in daily tasks such as feeding animals and washing. The activity is playful, but also potentially useful; the youngest children are finding their place within their busy community through playful engagement (see Gaskins, 2013 in Brooker & Woodhead, 2013). Being aware of the way in which play is variously shaped through culture globally helps us remember that even the most established understandings are open for question and negotiation.

Institutional practices, resources and social relationships can support or hinder the ways in which children explore their environments, as well as explore their roles in both children's cultures and their roles within wider culture. As we reinforce throughout this book, play is a complex concept without universal agreement. Since adults have the power to plan and implement early years policy, curriculum, daily schedule, activities, school regulations and rules, children's times and spaces, and so on, adult understandings of play may enhance or limit children's ability to (re) produce play culture as an important developmental tool. Adults who reflect upon children's home cultures and consider possible tensions for children and families with the practices of the ECEC setting or school are more likely to be able to support *all* children to engage in play and reap the benefits that such engagement brings.

Reflection Point 18.5

Read the Brooker and Woodhead (2013) material indicated in Further Reading.

- What is the purpose of play from different cultural perspectives?
- What does this mean for your practice in ECEC?

Summary

- Culture shapes the activity and values of communities; this includes understandings of, and approaches to, play.
- Play is a universal activity of children, but it takes different forms, and assumes different kinds of importance, in the diverse contexts of childhood (Gaskins, 2013 in Brooker & Woodhead, 2013).
- Through their play, children explore and co-create culture.
- Children, families and practitioners can experience tension, or 'cultural conflict', when cultural values are not aligned between the home community and the ECEC setting.

Further Reading

Brooker, L. and Woodhead, M. (Eds.) (2013) *The right to play: Early childhood in focus.* Milton Keynes: The Open University with the support of Bernard van Leer Foundation. Available at: https://oro.open.ac.uk/38679/. Read especially the section on play and culture by Suzanne Gaskins and Liz Brooker (pp. 6-10) to unpack further the shaping nature of culture on how we understand the value of play.

Erden, F. T. and Alpaslan, Z. G. (2017) Gender issues in outdoor play. In Waller et al. (Eds.), *Sage handbook of outdoor play and learning.* London: Sage. http://dx.doi.org/10.4135/9781526402028.n23. This chapter provides a detailed insight into gender issues in outdoor play generally, contextualised specifically in Turkey; it also introduces the theoretical frames available to understand the issues.

American Academic of Paediatrics (n.d.) *Gender identity development in children.* Available at: www.healthychildren.org/English/ages-stages/gradeschool/Pages/Gender-Identity-and-Gender-Confusion-In-Children.aspx. This article and the links from it provide an accessible overview of gender identity in young children.

Isci, B. and Hasirci, D. (2023) Designing gender-neutral playgrounds: The impact of natural environments on children's behaviors. *Journal of Design and Built Environment.* 23(3), 45-66. https://doi.org/10.22452/jdbe.vol23no3.3

Little, H., Sandseter, E. B. H. and Wyver, S. (2012) Early childhood teachers' beliefs about children's risky play in Australia and Norway. *Contemporary Issues in Early Childhood,* 13(4), 300-316. http://dx.doi.org/10.2304/ciec.2012.13.4.300. This paper provides an insight into different culturally framed beliefs about risky play.

References

Ali, A. (2020). "Girls don't like cars, they like 'girl' cars": Kindergarten children's conceptions of gender and play materials. *Jeunesse: Young People, Texts, Cultures,* 12(1), 63-96. https://dx.doi.org/10.1353/jeu.2020.0005

Bourdieu, P. (1977). *Outline of a theory of practice.* Cambridge: Cambridge University Press.

Brito, S., Carneiro, N. S., & Nogueira, C. (2021). Playing gender(s): The re/construction of a suspect "gender identity" through play. *Ethnography and Education,* 16(4), 384-401. https://doi.org/10.1080/17457823.2021.1922927

Brooker, L., & Woodhead, M. (Eds.). (2013). *The right to play: Early childhood in focus.* Milton Keynes: The Open University with the support of Bernard van Leer Foundation. Available at: http://oro.open.ac.uk/38679/1/ecif9the%20right%20to%20play.pdf

Burghardt, G. M., Pellis, S. M., Schank, J. C., Smaldino, P. E., Vanderschuren, L. J. M. J., & Palagi, E. (2024). Animal play and evolution: Seven timely research issues about enigmatic phenomena. *Neuroscience & Biobehavioral Reviews,* 160, 105617. ISSN 0149-7634. https://doi.org/10.1016/j.neubiorev.2024.105617

Corsaro, W. A. (2012). Interpretative reproduction in children's play. *American Journal of Play,* 4(4), 488-504.

Coyle, E. F., & Liben, L. S. (2020). Gendered packaging of a STEM toy influences children's play, mechanical learning, and mothers' play guidance. *Child Development,* 91(1), 43-62. https://doi.org/10.1111/cdev.13139

ECDA (Early Childhood Development Agency). (2019). *Outdoor learning: A national guide for early childhood educators. The education committee.* Singapore: ECDA. https://www.ecda.gov.sg/docs/default-source/default-document-library/early-childhood-educator/outdoor-learning-a-national-guide-for-early-childhood-educators.pdf

Einarsdóttir, J. (2006). Between two continents, between two traditions: Education and care in Icelandic preschools. In J. Einarsdóttir and J. T. Wagner (Eds.), *Nordic childhoods and early education: Philosophy, research, policy and practice in Denmark, Finland, Iceland, Norway, and Sweden.* Charlotte, NC: Information Age Publishing.

Evaldsson, A.-C., & Corsaro, W. A. (1998). Play and games in the peer cultures of preschool and preadolescent children: An interpretative approach. *Childhood: A Global Journal of Child Research,* 5(4), 377–402. https://doi.org/10.1177/0907568298005004003

Fouts, H. N., Neitzel, C. L., & Bader, L. R. (2016). Work-themed play among young children in foraging and farming communities in Central Africa. *Behaviour,* 153(6/7), 663–691. https://www.jstor.org/stable/43955731

Gill, T. (2007). *No fear: Growing up in a risk averse society.* London: Calouste Gulbenkian Foundation.

Levinson, M. P. (2005). The role of play in the formation and maintenance of cultural identity: Gypsy children in home and school contexts. *Journal of Contemporary Ethnography,* 34(5), 499–532. http://dx.doi.org/10.1177/0891241605279018

Lynch, M. (2015). Guys and dolls: A qualitative study of teachers' views of gendered play in kindergarten. *Early Child Development and Care,* 185(5), 679–693. https://doi.org/10.1080/030044

Reich, S. M., Black, R. W., & Foliaki, T. (2018). Constructing difference: LEGO® set narratives promote stereotypic gender roles and play. *Sex Roles,* 79, 285–298. https://doi.org/10.1007/s11199-017-0868-2

Riede, F., Walsh, M. J., Nowell, A., Langley, M. C., & Johannsen, N. N. (2021). Children and innovation: play, play objects and object play in cultural evolution. *Evolutionary Human Sciences,* 3, e11. https://doi.org/10.1017/ehs.2021.7

Rekers-Power, A. (2020). *Exploring young children's participation and motive orientation in the classroom and at forest school* (Doctoral Thesis, University of Wales Trinity Saint David). https://repository.uwtsd.ac.uk/id/eprint/1410/

Rogoff, B. (2003). *The cultural nature of human development.* Oxford: Oxford University Press.

Russell, W. (2018). Nonsense, caring and everyday hope: Rethinking the value of playwork. In B. Hughes & F. Brown (Eds.), *Aspects of playwork: Play and culture studies.* Lanham, MD: Hamilton Books, Rowman and Littlefield.

Sadownik, A. (2021). Princesses (don't) run in the mud. Tracing child's perspectives in parental perception of cultural formation through outdoor activities in Norwegian ECEs. In L. T. Grindheim, H. V. Sørensen & A. Rekers (Eds.), *Outdoor learning and play: Pedagogical practice and children's cultural formation.* Cham: Springer.

Sandseter, E. B. H. (2009). Characteristics of risky play. *Journal of Adventure Education and Outdoor Learning,* 9(1), 3–21. http://doi.org/10.1080/14729670802702762

Vygotsky, L. S. (1978). *Mind in society: The development of higher psychological processes.* Cambridge, MA: Harvard University Press.

Waller, T. (2010). 'Let's throw that big stick in the river': An exploration of gender in the construction of shared narratives around outdoor spaces. *European Early Childhood Education Research Journal,* 18(4), 527–542. https://doi.org/10.1080/1350293X.2010.525953

19

Play in Extremis

Debra Laxton, Linda Cooper,
and Sarah Ndlovu

Chapter Objectives

This chapter will help you to:

- Identify challenges in the development of play-based learning programmes in emergency settings.
- Explore the benefits of play-based learning programmes.
- Reflect on the importance of play in meeting children's educational, health, and psychosocial needs.

Introduction

This book has established the link between early interactions, stimulation and brain development for laying foundations that impact on children's future outcomes. It has been highlighted that play is globally acknowledged as vital for early childhood development and as such has become a fundamental right of every child around the world. This chapter builds on these concepts whilst considering the role of play *in extremis*. In this chapter, the term 'play in extremis' is used to describe play-based learning programmes developed to support children living in extreme circumstances, e.g., refugees from conflict zones and natural disasters. Children's lived experiences and the challenges of access to play in situations of global crisis are discussed. The chapter provides an overview of the complexities of humanitarian crisis and the challenges faced by communities living in extreme circumstances. The importance of play in promoting mental well-being and holistic development for young children in crisis is highlighted, whilst exploring the value placed on play by families and communities often struggling to cope in unique and diverse circumstances where they have little power to control their own lives. The chapter introduces the Sustainable Development Goals (SDG) and discusses these in relation to play provision with an emphasis on

SDG4, Education for all as a fundamental right. A case study, based on a project to provide an Early Education for Displaced Children in Myanmar, explains how organisations can work collaboratively with communities to develop effective play-based learning that benefits all those involved.

Sustainable Development Goals

In 2015, the United Nations demonstrated their continued commitment to global development by introducing the Sustainable Development Goals (United Nations, 2015a, 2015b). The goals address social, economic and environmental factors related to sustainable development and aim to achieve a better and more sustainable world for all:

Goal 1: No poverty
Goal 2: Zero hunger
Goal 3: Good health and well-being
Goal 4: Quality education
Goal 5: Gender equality
Goal 6: Clean water and sanitation
Goal 7: Affordable and clean energy
Goal 8: Decent work and economic growth
Goal 9: Industry, innovation and infrastructure
Goal 10: Reduced inequalities
Goal 11: Sustainable cities and communities
Goal 12: Responsible consumption and production
Goal 13: Climate action
Goal 14: Life below water
Goal 15: Life on land
Goal 16: Peace, justice and strong institutions
Goal 17: Partnerships for the goals

The global targets clearly prioritise early childhood development recognising the impact it can have on fulfilling potential and combatting inequalities by increasing length of school attendance, academic achievement and adult income. The goals intend to protect lives, promote mental and physical health and ensure dignity. These factors are pivotal in improving the lives of children living in extremis.

SDG4 to 'ensure inclusive and equitable quality education and promote lifelong learning opportunities for all' is particularly relevant to the subject of play-based early learning. Target 4.2 emphasises this further; the aim is to ensure all girls and boys have equal access to quality pre-primary education and that by 2030 all children should have access to quality early childhood education programmes before formal learning begins. The target has two indicators:

• The proportion of children aged 24–59 months who are developing as expected for their age in terms of health, learning and psychosocial well-being.
• Children attend early childhood education programmes in the year before formal education.

The significance of a focus on early childhood needs to be clear; in the past children under five received minimal attention in terms of humanitarian assistance. The SDG 2030 agenda should ensure governments and non-government organisations (NGO) include actions for the early phases of life in humanitarian response plans. Investing in early childhood development is a cost-effective strategy to promoting global sustainable economic growth.

Context: Living in Extremis

The number of children affected by crises around the world should not be underestimated. Whilst children account for 30% of the global population, they make up a disproportionate 40% of all forcibly displaced people and are some of the most vulnerable populations in the world. The United Nations High Commissioner for Refugees (UNHCR) estimate that at the end of 2023 an enormous 117.3 million people were displaced (IDAC, 2024). Between 2010 and 2023, the global number of children displaced due to conflict and violence more than doubled, from around 18.8 million to 47.2 million, "this trend shows no signs of slowing down" (IDAC, 2024, p. 6). Over two million children were born as refugees from 2018 to 2023 (UNICEF, 2024; para 2). It may be surprising to learn that 73% of refugees originate from just five countries; Syria (6.3 million), Venezuela (6.2 million), Ukraine (6.1 million), Afghanistan (6.1 million), and Sudan (3.5 million) and that 75% of refugees are hosted by low and middle income countries (UNHCR, 2024). The precarious nature of being a refugee alongside living in low resource countries limits access to education generally for children who are five times more likely to be out of education than non-refugee children. Figures on numbers of children accessing early childhood education (ECE) are sparse but research finds that the barriers to ECE are exacerbated for refugee families even with their right to education. Ereky-Stevens et al. (2023) highlight barriers including:

- Lack of available provision.
- Lack of information about provision that is available.
- ECE may incur basic costs e.g., small fees, food, and clothes that are unaffordable.
- Working families are unable to manage ECE hours.

Enrolment may require documents that families do not have, e.g., birth certificates.

- Parent mental state prevents capacity to plan for ECE.
- Parental concerns about safety in travelling to the ECE provision and treatment in the provision.
- The culture within the family may be that young children do not access ECE.

Girls, women and children with special needs and disabilities (SEND) are often marginalised, treated as less significant and excluded, and emergency situations often increase vulnerabilities, e.g., fewer girls attending school, no education for children with SEND, gender-based violence. These marginalised groups often lack a voice within communities and are powerless to control their lives as other organisations lead support without listening to or responding to their needs and viewpoints.

Before going further, it is important to understand the term *humanitarian crisis*. Crisis settings and emergency settings are terms often used interchangeably to describe those living in extremely challenging circumstances. It is recognised that there are three types of humanitarian crisis:

1 Man-made, e.g., armed conflict zones.
2 Natural disasters:
   ○ Geophysical, e.g., earthquake, tsunami.
   ○ Biological, e.g., epidemics like Ebola and cholera.
   ○ Climatological, e.g., droughts and famine.
3 Complex emergency situations created by a combination of man-made and natural crises, e.g. refugees.

These varied man-made and natural disasters, often traumatic, create diverse communities and each community has its own needs. Differences arise from living in different cultural, spiritual, political and economic situations. For example, different languages and dialects may be spoken between refugees fleeing from one country and these often differ again to the country hosting the refugees. Community needs are based on the crisis experience and current living conditions although there are often common themes, e.g., protection, sanitation, shelter, food, and education. Individual families have unique needs based on personal life experiences and how they respond to the emergency experience.

The Cost of Living in Extremis to Child Development

As previously explained in this book, well planned, stimulating play experiences have a positive impact on children's holistic development and subsequently long-term academic and social outcomes. The impact of play on learning is most significant when it is supported by responsive adults who interact effectively to promote creative and critical thinking. The challenge of providing resources and safe spaces for quality play in emergency situations is very real and children whose lives are disrupted by crises are much less likely to receive early stimulation or access to pre-school education because of their varied and complex circumstances.

Bouchane (2018) argues that babies and young children in crisis settings are the most vulnerable people in the world. She explains that children from birth to five years have the highest illness and death rates of any age group. Those who survive, experience prolonged deprivation and increased stress levels that impact negatively on cognitive, social and emotional development, not only in the short term but impacting on future learning capability and educational opportunity (Bouchane, 2018). Malnutrition, poor health, poverty and inadequate early stimulation and learning opportunities are all factors that impinge on developmental progress (e.g. Hurley et al. 2016).

The Hierarchy of Needs in Figure 19.1 shows five levels that Maslow (1943) proposed humans are motivated to satisfy. He claimed that the most basic needs must be satisfied before motivation to satisfy the next level of need can occur. This continues to level five, 'self-actualisation', where the individual is striving to meet their potential.

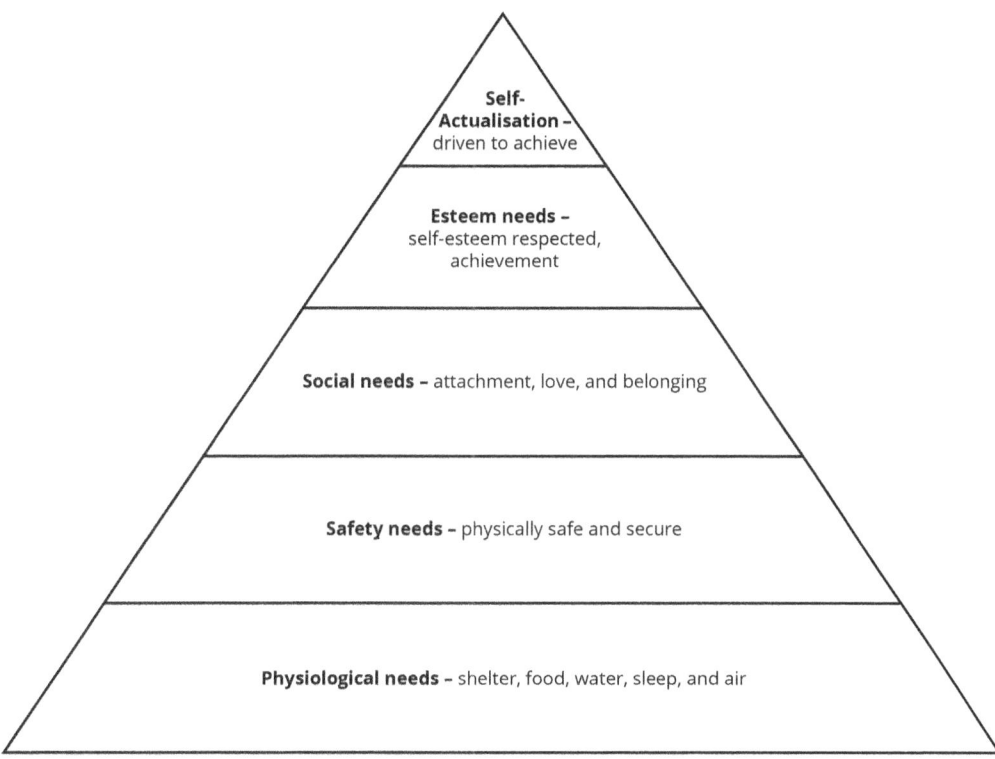

Figure 19.1 Maslow's Hierarchy of Needs
Source: Adapted from Maslow, 1943.

Reflection Point 19.1

- Using Maslow's Hierarchy of Needs, consider how children living in an emergency situation, e.g., a refugee camp or war zone, can be supported to satisfy each level of need.
- What are the potential barriers and opportunities at each level?

Play-Based Early Childhood Programmes: Community Engagement

The following section sets out the context in which play-based early childhood programmes exist, the benefits they can offer, aspects of implementing them and the concept of safe play spaces.

Context

NGOs are not for profit charities, e.g., UNICEF, Children on the Edge and Save the Children, who work to combat social injustice and promote human rights across the globe.

They commonly provide humanitarian responses for those living in extremis. Humanitarian response includes being prepared for expected disasters, the response during an emergency and supporting initial recovery stages that aim to save and sustain lives (INEE, 2024). In recent years, education has become a key part of crisis recovery, seen as the fourth pillar in humanitarian response, 'Quality education can help learners and their families assert their dignity and build the life and the future they aspire to. It also can contribute directly to the social, economic, and political stability of a society' (INNE, 2024, p. 11). Following the 2015 SDGs, early childhood education is being prioritised, as the importance of early brain development for laying future foundations before the age of 5 is fully acknowledged and acted upon. Providing early stimulation and learning at the pre-school stage is seen as critical in enabling young children to be ready to start school and supporting future school achievement (UNESCO, 2024).

Benefits of Play-Based Learning Programmes

Play-based learning programmes developed for young children need to view any crisis response holistically and consider a range of solutions to support children and families that focus on education, play and intellectual development. When funding allows, programmes can provide the opportunity for collaboration with other services so that children, families and the community can improve their health, nutrition, psychosocial and emotional well-being by accessing support at programme centres. In addition, there is an opportunity to communicate with parents and caregivers in relation to a wide range of needs, e.g., health, nutrition, supportive adult/child interactions, play and learning (Ereky-Stevens et al., 2023). Older girls, who often care for younger siblings, can also be supported in accessing school themselves. Encouraging collaboration and integrating services in play-based learning programmes increases the potential impact for children, communities, and subsequently society.

Such programmes are intentionally inclusive and target marginalised members of the community. To ensure equity in provision, marginalised groups, including children with additional needs and girls, are often targeted for support and attendance. Programmes can empower women by offering them opportunities for education on a range of topics that impact on health and psychosocial well-being. In some play-based learning programmes women and older girls in communities are trained to run and lead play sessions. This can enable status and power within the community as they act as local recruiters and advocates of play-based learning. Not only are educator roles significant to the women involved at the time but the impact is far-reaching. The precedent of empowering women, often excluded in society, creates an agenda for future change where those who were marginalised gain a voice in decision-making.

Planning and implementing programmes in crisis settings is clearly complex and there are numerous challenges (see below); however, the benefits are multiple and can be life-changing. Play-based learning programmes offer hope for children and communities and provide opportunities for holistic child development preparing children for future learning journeys. Play can enable children to freely explore their experiences and feelings so that they can make sense of what they have been through and what is happening in the present. Having the time and space to explore challenging and often traumatic experiences in this way promotes mental well-being and can enable a child to thrive through playful learning opportunities. Through play, children are able to exert control and make choices in a world where such normal human behaviours are often beyond reach and where they can lack agency.

To protect the right to play in crisis settings it is essential to source emotionally and physically safe, secure spaces for children and families to access. Ereky-stevens et al. (2023, p. 4) stress that "safe, predictable learning environments with a reliable structure, stable and clear routines and rules can be of particular importance for refugee children in creating a sense of normality and restoring a sense of safety and control".

Implementing and Accessing Safe Spaces for Play-Based Learning

The challenges to planning and implementing effective early childhood programmes that are accessible to vulnerable children are many, varied and often significant; these include:

- The time taken and bureaucracy required to work collaboratively with host countries to run programmes.
- Inadequate safe spaces for early childhood education programmes.
- Access to basic services, e.g., sanitation.
- Access to basic nutrition.
- Access to resources to provide stimulating experiences.
- Differing perspectives of the concept of play from organisations, caregivers and communities.
- Lack of emotional availability by caregiver due to other priorities, e.g., food and shelter.
- High stress levels caused by living conditions.
- Separation from/loss of family members.
- Psychological distress from past and present traumatic experiences.
- Educators' psychological distress prevents capacity to tune into the child's needs.
- Resources are insufficient for the numbers of children attending.

Safe Play Spaces

Emergency settings can be dangerous places to live, especially for children who are vulnerable to exploitation, violence, and neglect. Protected environments provide a place for parents and carers to leave their children knowing they are safe and supervised. Safe spaces for early childhood education vary significantly depending on the environment e.g., tented homes in refugee camps, outside spaces in small communities, spaces created within school buildings. In attending, children have the opportunity to play and learn away from family pressures, responsibilities, chores, e.g., sick or distressed family members, caring for younger siblings, collecting water. Attending safe, play-based learning programmes provides structure and routine within what can be disrupted communities. Structure and routine help children to feel safer and more secure as they provide certainty, familiarity, and normalcy.

- Safe play spaces are crucial; the opportunity to use play to explore and express feelings and experiences alongside sensitive and responsive adults fosters children's resilience and can help them to come to terms with, and adapt to, new situations. Providing play-based learning and emotional support gives children the chance to thrive and develop despite adverse and often unpredictable circumstances they find themselves in.

Snider and Ager (2018) explain how child friendly spaces can address three essential objectives:

- Protection from risk by providing safety and structure in humanitarian settings.
- Promotion of psychosocial well-being by building resilience through play-based learning that allows children to explore feelings and be supported by caring adults and peers in a protected space.
- Strengthening of community child protection capacities by complementing wider work as part of community-based child protection strategies.

Sustainable Play-Based Learning Programmes

To be sustainable and support children for as long as necessary in any safe space, play-based programmes need to consider a variety of factors in the context of each unique situation. Key factors include the value and understanding of play as a tool for learning through the training of adults to become educators within communities who plan and promote quality play and interactions and provide sustainable play resources. Sustainable play-based programmes contribute to global sustainable development; pre-primary education impacts positively on school readiness, academic achievement, health outcomes and economic independence of at-risk groups in crisis settings (Bouchane, 2018).

Value of Play

In some regions and communities play can hold limited value for its learning potential because personal educational experience and knowledge has created differing cultural perspectives. Didactic teaching, where children are instructed and adults impart knowledge to children who listen and repeat by rote, is common and often the cultural norm, and as such is recognised as the format for effective learning. Play can be viewed as something light-hearted that children engage in to amuse themselves. In such contexts parents expect rote learning, workbooks and testing (UNICEF, 2018). Stakeholders, from policymakers to community leaders, both religious and political, teachers, parents and children, can underestimate the power of play as a tool for holistic development, building foundations for future learning.

Recognising child-centred, play-based learning programmes as essential elements of early childhood education is key for enabling policy change, gaining permission to plan and implement programmes. Working collaboratively to develop a shared vision for play-based learning is an effective way to develop public support and demand for more playful learning opportunities. A global shortage of teachers, particularly in emergency situations, could be a barrier to programming. However, sourcing and training community members to become educators who understand the research and practice behind a playful pedagogy provides a meaningful solution. This enables a genuine belief in play pedagogy and teachers become advocates, inspired to create stimulating playful environments and engage in reflective practice to increase the effectiveness of play experiences. Where play is understood by communities a culturally sensitive play pedagogy can be sustained using local resources. When teachers and volunteer educators become advocates of play-based learning they have the capacity to empower and motivate parents to provide playful learning experiences at home. Parents act as active play partners who may more readily engage in culturally grounded play alongside their children, telling stories, enabling dialogue and teaching life skills through role play (UNICEF, 2018).

Sustainable Resources

Access and provision of play materials within crisis settings is a complex matter that should not be underestimated. Access to resources can be limited due to the availability of materials, equipment and funding. For play-based learning programmes to be sustainable, educators need to be able to adapt play opportunities dependent on their cultural and environmental context. Programme developers and educators need to be creative in their thinking, and whilst some resources, e.g. reading and writing media to promote literacy, can be specifically purchased there are other ways of sourcing materials and equipment. When planning for safe space play, ideally resources should be:

- Developmentally appropriate.
- Culturally appropriate.
- Low-cost or freely available.
- Locally sourced, ideally from natural materials.
- Safe, so children can play and explore.
- Open-ended to increase learning potential, e.g., loose parts.
- Interesting and varied to encourage intrinsically motivated, creative play.
- Appropriate for the physical and emotional needs of the community and individual.
- Sufficient in number for many children.
- Accessible to all.
- For use indoors and outdoors.
- Offering opportunities for risk and challenge within a safe environment.
- Offering sensory opportunities.
- Discovery-based learning materials.
- Created using community skills wherever possible, e.g., cars from plastic bottles and dolls from banana plants.

Block Play

Blocks are excellent examples of sustainable, high-quality play materials that can be made in various ways dependent on the resources available. Blocks can be made from local wood or bamboo which is known for its strength, but where these materials are unavailable blocks can be made from mud mixed with sand, straw or grass and water. Research and practice have demonstrated that blocks can be highly effective in promoting holistic development (Gura, 1992; Tortello, 2024). Block play enables children to be creative and innovate, to problem-solve, and work independently and confidently. Children can control their play agenda, secure in the knowledge that there are no rules; there is no right or wrong way to construct with blocks. Block play encourages children to communicate and collaborate with adults and peers, to think mathematically by considering space and shape. Furthermore, blocks enable fine motor skills to develop as children carefully position and balance blocks. Importantly children can create models that represent their feelings and experiences and from these creations, socio-dramatic play can emerge. Such a low-cost resource readily available to make from local materials offers enormous play and learning potential for children in crisis settings.

Reflection Point 19.2

- Make a list of open-ended resources that might be available in a crisis setting to use for loose-parts play. How might these resources promote holistic development?

Case Study 19.1

Early Education for Displaced Children in Myanmar

Children on the Edge (COTE), a UK based, child-rights organisation, alongside local partners Kachin Development Group (KDG) and Kachin Women's Association (KWA), provide play, education and care for children aged 3-6 years old living in Internally Displaced Person (IDP) camps along the China-Myanmar border in Kachin State, Myanmar.

Caught in the middle of one of the longest running civil wars in the world, more than three million people have been internally displaced due to ongoing conflict between the government and the Kachin Independence Army (KIA). This escalated in 2012, and again in 2021 after a military coup triggered a deadly military crackdown, seeing a shift to more complex airstrikes and bombings purposefully targeting civilians, medical centres and infrastructure.

Consequently, thousands of people fled to relative safety in the mountainous China-border area. Here, families live in cramped shelters, precariously perched along mountain terrain, battling severe weather conditions and the constant threat of bombardment and repeated displacement. Matriarchal households are common as many men serve in the army, some have lost their lives, and others move away in search of work. UN travel to the Kachin Independence Organisation (KIO) controlled areas, where COTE Early Childhood Development (ECD) centres are based, has been blocked since 2016 and local organisations have been accused of breaking the law when delivering aid. Donor funding is over-subscribed and food rations are limited to rice, oil and salt.

Life is complex and challenging and many of the youngest children have only known life in remote displacement camps. They are living through a largely unreported war; cut off from learning and support at a vital time of development. COTE is the only organisation providing ECE in these outlying areas, ensuring quality care through safe, community-managed preschools, where displaced children can learn, play and process trauma.

(Continued)

After working in the region for over a decade, COTE has been able to build relationships with key partners on both sides of the Thai-Myanmar border. This is essential in funding supplies for the hardest to reach areas, which most agencies fail to access.

COTE provides fourteen ECD centres, supported by parents and the wider community, offering refuge from chaos and uncertainty for hundreds of young children scattered across eight IDP camps. Children engage with caregivers and peers in a safe space on a daily basis. They are free to play, rest, and express themselves, and receive critical nutritional support and warm clothing.

The core programme components are:

- Community ownership: through ECD committees, who oversee the centres e.g. finances, logistics, curriculum and pedagogy, safeguarding, engaging parents, attendance and quality assurance. They work to forge close links between the centres and parents.
- Play-based curriculum: using locally available resources and vibrant outdoor spaces which offer intrigue for young children. They are equipped with swings, slides, trampolines and climbing equipment, which support children's physical development and provide plentiful opportunities to develop social, emotional, communication, and language skills.
- Parent engagement: sessions support parents to build strong attachments with their children through self-reflection activities, and opportunities to share experiences through topics e.g. child development, parenting styles and literacy. Efforts are made to actively involve fathers. Feedback has shown positive impacts. One father told us: "I can control myself and be patient since I joined this session. I was very aggressive with my family before" (A father offering feedback in 2023).
- Provision of building supplies and equipment to ensure the buildings are safe and fully functional. This includes installing toilets, water tanks and warm flooring, repairing roads, fences, roofs and outdoor areas and providing kitchen equipment, medical bags and supplies. Integral to the programme is the provision of a daily, hot and nutritious meal – often the only meal children have, appropriate clothing for the cold climate and the opportunity for a daily nap in a safe space.
- Caregiver training led by local partners KWA: Consists of initial and ongoing training and refresher courses covering a range of ECE themes e.g. child development, play-based learning, lesson planning, storytelling, first aid, inclusion. Additional creative sessions include music, movement, dance and drawing, encouraging educators to share activities with parents. Fifteen of the most experienced educators became Trainers of Teachers (ToTs) who provide additional training and support for caregivers. One teacher at Maga Yang centre, a mother of two, told us: "I learnt about child rights and child development whilst working as a teacher, which changed my perspective. In my opinion, opening the ECD centre where we live means a safer environment for every child."

(Continued)

(Continued)

Over ten years COTE has educated 2,851 children, trained 35 caregivers and 15 ToTs. Local partners report that communities have an increased sense of ownership and are actively engaged, renovating centres, creating play materials and providing food. Educators report increased parental interest in their children's education and development, leading to noticeable improvements in child behaviour, self-esteem and happiness. Educators have witnessed an improvement in the culture of listening to children's thoughts and feelings.

   Child A is a student from Maga Yang ECD centre. She is four years old and part of the junior class. Her mother says, "In my view, all of the teachers at my daughter's centre are very active and very good at teaching. My child is becoming skilful at singing and dancing, which she shows me every day when she comes home. She has also improved her personal hygiene not because of what I have done, but what she has learned at the centre. I'm very proud of my child for her learning at this centre." Child A said: "When I am at school, I sing and dance together with my friends. I have a good meal and a snack every day, and we always have a sleep at noon. I am very happy to have received new warm clothes and toys to play with."

Reflection Point 19.3

Re-read the scenario and consider the following:

- How many, and what type of, organisations collaborated to create this play-based provision?
- What elements of the programme work together to create a holistic approach to ECE?
- What challenges did you notice and how were these overcome?

Summary

- Investment and prioritising play-based learning programmes within crisis settings is vital as recognised by SDG4.
- Attending pre-school education can provide normality and hope for children and wider communities in times of trauma.

- Inclusive play-based learning programmes prepare children for school. Play promotes holistic development and provides all children with the opportunity to learn and develop.
- Children can navigate traumatic experiences through play and explore and express their feelings supported by trained, sensitive educators.
- Through the integration of other services, play-based learning programmes have a wider purpose that increases impact and importance.

Further Reading

Bouchane, K. (2018) *Early childhood development and early learning for children in crisis and conflict.* Paris: UNESCO. This background paper outlines complex factors and issues related to young children living in crisis and conflict. The paper highlights how refugee and humanitarian response plans rarely include early childhood education actions and provides strong arguments for changing this mindset

Children on the Edge (2025) *Supporting children to thrive in the toughest situations.* https://www.childrenontheedge.org/ Children on the Edge is a child rights organisation created to support the world's most marginalised children, living in some of the toughest situations. The charity currently work with more than 20,000 children in Bangladesh, India, Uganda, Myanmar, and Lebanon. Visit the website to read further case studies about their work.

Laxton, D., Cooper, L., Shrestha, P. and Younie, S. (2020) Translational research to support early childhood education in crisis settings: A different case study that considers collaborative working with Rohingya refugees in Cox's Bazar. *Education, 3–13.* https://doi.org/10.1080/03004279.2020.1813186. It demonstrates how using a relational volunteer model of training empowered a marginalised community to enhance children's learning. In this article refugees are fleeing from Myanmar rather than to Myanmar which makes an interesting contrast and reflection point.

UNICEF (2018) *Learning through play: Strengthening learning.* New York: UNICEF. As well as providing clear evidence to support the importance and value of play-based learning, this document outlines the barriers to early years provision in countries and contexts where play is not recognised as being fundamental to learning and development.

References

Bouchane, K. (2018). *Early childhood development and early learning for children in crisis and conflict.* Paris: UNESCO.

Ereky-Stevens, K., Siraj, I., & Kong, K. (2023). A critical review of the research evidence on early childhood education and care in refugee contexts in low- and middle-income countries. *International Journal of Child Care and Education Policy,* 17(7), 1–23. https://doi.org/10.1186/s40723-023-00109-4

Hurley, K. M., Yousafzai, A. K., Lopez-Boo, F. (2016). Early child development and nutrition: A review of the benefits and challenges of implementing integrated interventions. *Advances in Nutrition*, 7(2), 357-363. https://doi.org/10.3945/an.115.010363. PMID: 26980819; PMCID: PMC4785470.

Gura, P. (1992). *Exploring learning: Young children and blockplay*. London: Paul Chapman.

IDAC. (2024). *International data alliance for children on the move, 9 facts about children on the move: 2024 update*. New York: United Nations Children's Fund.

INEE. (2024). *Minimum standards for education: Preparedness, response, recovery*. International Network for Education in Emergencies. Available at: https://inee.org/sites/default/files/resources/INEE%20Minimum%20Standards%202024%20v2.7%20Web.pdf

Maslow, A. H. (1943). A theory of human motivation. *Psychological Review*, 50(4), 370–396.

Snider, L., & Ager, W. (2018). *Operational guidance for child friendly spaces in humanitarian settings*. Copenhagen: World Vision International& IFRC Reference Centre for Psychosocial Support.

Tortello, R. (2024). *Harnessing the power of play with building blocks*. Available at: https://www.unicefusa.org/stories/harnessing-power-play-building-blocks#:~:text=Block%20play%20may%20look%20simple,skills%2C%20along%20with%20spatial%20awareness

UNESCO. (2024). *Global report on early childhood care and education: The right to a strong foundation*. Available at: https://unesdoc.unesco.org/ark:/48223/pf0000378078

UNHCR. (2024). *Refugee data finder - key indicators*.

UNICEF. (2018). *Learning through play: Strengthening learning*. New York: UNICEF.

UNICEF. (2024). *Child displacement*. Available at: https://data.unicef.org/topic/child-migration-and-displacement/displacement/

United Nations. (2015a). *Resolution adopted by the general assembly on 25 september 2015. Transforming our world: The 2030 agenda for sustainable development*. Available at: www.un.org/ga/search/view_doc.asp?symbol=A/RES/70/1&Lang=E

United Nations. (2015b). *Why should you care about the sustainable development goals?* Available at: www.un.org/sustainabledevelopment/blog/2015/09/why-should-you-care-about-the-sustainable-development-goals/

20
Playful Learning Around the World

Sarah Chicken and Sarah Whitehouse

Chapter Objectives

This chapter will help you to understand three different approaches to playful learning drawn from the following international contexts:

- Reggio Emilia, Italy.
- HighScope, USA.
- Te Whāriki, New Zealand.

Introduction

The chapter begins by contextualising each approach before exploring how play is harnessed within the schools of Reggio Emilia, HighScope, and Te Whāriki and is structured around the key themes considered of significance to each perspective. These studies contribute to a deeper understanding of how international early childhood education frameworks can inform and enrich practices within the UK, highlighting both the opportunities and challenges of integrating diverse educational philosophies. These debates will be useful for early years practitioners with the four nations of the United Kingdom; Scotland, Wales, England, and Northern Ireland. The latter sections compare how play is utilised differently across the three perspectives but always with the central aim of offering meaningful learning opportunities to young children.

What is Reggio Emilia?

The Reggio Emilia approach is named after the Italian city where Loris Malaguzzi, a teacher and psychologist, was instrumental in developing a progressive pedagogy which is now valued globally.

After the Second World War, parents in this traditionally socialist part of Italy reflected upon the rise of fascism and sought to create an education for children where respect for differing opinions was vital. These skills were considered to be essential in rebuilding and creating a democratic society with the fundamental aim of supporting children to become active citizens. Discussions and debate between children are therefore central to this approach underpinned by the view that children will often hold differing yet valid viewpoints. This can be seen in pre-school settings in the area for children who are under the age of six.

The Social and Curious Child

Central to Reggio pedagogy is an explicit belief that children are born with unlimited potential and a sense of wonder, possessing an innate curiosity to make sense of their own worlds through their natural desire to be playful (Malaguzzi, 1998). In line with the views of key theorists such as Vygotsky and Bruner, both play and learning are viewed as social processes which involve other people. Gandini (2011) has argued that there is 'a deep trust in the richness of children's desire to learn with pleasure and also the ability children have to acquire initiatives and inventions that come from their shared relationships' (p. 7). Through our interactions with others, we are supported in learning about the world around us whilst building relationships, developing language skills, and grappling with deep-level thinking through playful problem-solving. This means that play and learning are intrinsically intertwined and viewed as an active and social process. As children participate in play with others, they also are offered experiences through which they relate to various aspects of interest including art, maths and science. In this way children are active agents in their own learning as they 'research' the world around them (Rinaldi, 2011). This also leads to a view of the teacher as a 'partner in the learning process', who is a fellow researcher rather than an 'expert' who possesses more knowledge than the children.

Planning for Playful Learning

Drawing on their natural curiosity and playful nature, educators utilise children's interests and fascinations through *progettazione* or project work to plan playful learning opportunities (see Rinaldi, 2006, 2011 for a deeper insight into this aspect of Reggio pedagogy). These projects are different from the project and topic approaches which can often be seen within provision for younger children in the United Kingdom in terms of both content and planning. This is because in Reggio Emilia the process of engaging in learning takes priority over any final product, and planning is ongoing with limited pre-specified outcomes. There is no cross referencing with pre-defined medium- and long-term planning documents as we might find in the United Kingdom (see Chapter 11); instead the children's developing questions steer the course of the project. As Rinaldi has said: 'The potential of the child is stunted when the endpoint of their learning is formulated in advance' (Rinaldi, 1998, p. 104). Instead, during regular meetings, educators explore together how children are making sense of their worlds to create an emergent or negotiated curriculum. This could involve educators examining children's drawings and artwork, transcripts of conversations, and notes and videos of play observations. These documents are used to explore questions such as:

- Do groups of children have emerging interests, fascinations or complex questions?
- What is being represented through creative media or playful interactions?
- What do representations tell us about how children are thinking or feeling?

After group reflection on questions like this, teachers will plan provision to develop identified areas of exploration, which will often involve children in in-depth collaborative problem-solving.

Play and Art

Through Reggio-style projects children develop deep-level thinking as they represent their understanding through the metaphorical 'hundred languages of children', such as drawing, painting, photography and shadow work (Vecchi & Gandini, 2011). This is a central feature of Reggio Emilia and children are provided a rich range of opportunities to explore their thinking through playful activities involving different media, including painting, clay work and sculpture. This is because children are viewed as 'creative meaning-makers' who explore and represent their worlds in many ways which are not always verbal. Through these playful opportunities, the developing ideas of children are supported, enriched and confronted. Loris Malaguzzi has discussed how this way of working aims to nurture the innate creativity that young children possess (see Malaguzzi, 1998, pp. 73–77 for a detailed discussion of this).

The Role of the Environment in Reggio Settings

The learning environment is referred to as the 'third teacher' and is used by teachers to set up playful 'provocations' to draw on the child's natural disposition to be playful and curious. A range of open-ended materials are also always available for children to choose from aimed at developing independence, creative thinking and problem-solving. This has been referred to as creating 'possibility-rich environments' (Gandini, 2011, p. 6).

All settings have an *atelier* or art studio at the centre with a trained artist who supports children in utilising non-verbal symbolic languages such as painting, drawing, sculpture and clay work to communicate thoughts and feelings in relation to particular project areas whilst simultaneously developing their thinking. Echoing Italian architecture, each setting also has a piazza, the central meeting place where children from all round the school share play and conversations. Many mirrors can be found at different heights and locations within the Reggio environment; this is in keeping with the central philosophy of 'seeing oneself' and of constructing one's own identity.

Case Study 20.1

Some of the children (4 and 5 years old) seemed to be interested in the traffic after watching the busy road outside of the school. The teachers discussed this observation and the children were offered a range of creative media to represent their developing interests. When these were analysed by teachers it was noted that the children were not merely representing vehicles but appeared to be interested in the conceptual idea of what made a 'traffic jam'. This was noted in artwork (drawings and paintings), play observations

(Continued)

(Continued)

and conversations; as one child said, 'a traffic jam is a squash of cars and wheels, all mixed together'.

Some children began to create traffic jams with lots of toy cars whilst others became curious asking if 'jams' might be created with other items. Some children tried to create a 'jam' by squeezing beads and other different sized objects through different size funnels. This prompted a child to share a memory of a different sort of 'jam', during a time when she had gone to a busy local market. She described how 'all the people were tangled up'; this prompted the use of clay for children who, supported by the artist, represented their version of a 'people jam' by making clay models of different sizes and squashing them closely together. In follow-up conversations children and teachers discussed what this might look like from the perspective of a child who might only be able to see up to the knees of adults, 'a muddle of knees and legs!'

During this project, in whole group time, some children wondered if you could create a 'jam of children'. On one morning the teachers from the different classes sent children out at the same time which led to a lot of congestion. This caused great amusement but during follow-up discussions, teachers noted that the children were also pleased that they had been able to answer their own question. Returning to the term 'traffic jam', one child said that this was like jam on toast because the jam was made of strawberries squished together. Another child added, 'A jam is like a squash and a squeeze all mooshed together with no room to move for cars or people or strawberries!'

Towards the end of the project a teacher who was new to the team commented that in her previous practice, the theme of traffic would have been used to plan for a half term of activities aimed at covering pre-specified areas of learning. This might have included tallies of the types of cars passing the school and science work about how things move. She was surprised at the unexpected direction that the children's interests had taken their learning and added that she recognised the significance of the children having their own ideas, questions and theories taken seriously.

Pedagogical Documentation: A Tool for Listening and Assessment

Reggio provision is often referred to as 'a pedagogy of listening' (Rinaldi, 2006). In line with the emphasis placed upon symbolic languages, this is a metaphor that refers to adults being attuned to all aspects of the child as an active and social meaning-maker. Teachers will document the learning process of different groups of children involved in projects through photographs, drawings, and transcripts of conversations. These are displayed on documentation boards which aim to make the playful learning process tangible. In this way, a great deal of attention is given to making visible the learning and thinking of children including detailed observations. This process of pedagogical documentation has been referred to as 'researching children, researching their worlds' (Bancroft et al., 2008) through close exploration of episodes of children's meaning-making used to consider how they are thinking and feeling. This can also be considered as a type of formative assessment since it attempts to make visible how children are thinking in relation to a project area and to then offer follow-up learning opportunities to extend, consolidate or confront this thinking (Maynard & Chicken, 2010). At the same time, it must be noted that there is no attempt to assess children against pre-specified developmental markers or steps.

Parents and the Wider Community

Reggio schools might be described as a system built on relationships, with the child at the centre working with teachers, parents and parts of the wider community. This strong emphasis upon relationships is in line with a social-constructivist approach and the pedagogical practices centre on developing a secure sense of belonging for all children, teachers and families. Such a sense of security is believed to be essential in enabling children to fulfil their potential and to actively contribute to the life of the school. In line with this, project activities are often undertaken by children and teachers in different parts of the city, including the Reggio piazza, where the community can look on and participate. In this way, children begin to view themselves as citizens who are part of a wider community. Parents are often also invited to participate within projects and may add to the pedagogical documentation boards that are displayed within settings and aim to make the thinking of children within projects visible to others.

Reflection Point 20.1

Children are viewed in a particular way by educators in Reggio Emilia; as curious, capable and social 'meaning-makers'.

• How does this shape the pedagogical approach seen within settings?

What is HighScope?

The HighScope Approach began in the early 1960s in the Perry Preschool Project in Michigan, USA. The study aimed to improve the cognitive skills of 123 African American children perceived as being at risk of failing high school. Families with 3–4-year-old children were randomly assigned to two different groups, an intervention group and a control group. Over a two-year period, the intervention group of 58 children attended a HighScope setting for two and a half hours per day where they engaged in activities aimed at developing cognition. During the same time period, the teachers would also regularly visit their homes to build relationships with families. The group of 65 children in the control group did not go through the programme. Longitudinal data suggested that children in the intervention group were more likely to graduate from high school and less likely to become engaged in crime than their counterparts within the control group (Miller & Pound, 2010). Drawing on these findings, it was claimed that every 'tax dollar' invested in high-quality early childhood education would eventually save at least seven dollars for taxpayers in the longer term as it would reduce the chances of children growing up without qualifications and aspirations.

Constructions of the Child

The view of the child within HighScope settings was originally shaped by the thinking of Piaget and Inhelder (1969), who described children as little scientists curious to explore the world around them. In this view, learning is understood as an active process of construction which involves 'hands-on experiences' and the investigation of materials. Children's thinking is understood to be expanded by engaging and exploring a range of diverse materials. However, as the HighScope pedagogy has developed, more emphasis has been placed upon a Vygotskian perspective of learning as a social process with the adult scaffolding the child within the zone of proximal development (see Chapter 5). This was underpinned by an understanding that children's development occurs within sociocultural settings (Epstein et al., 2011).

Planning for Playful Learning

Central to HighScope pedagogy is the need to recognise the interests of children; learning is described as 'play-based' with emphasis placed upon 'hands-on' active learning which offers levels of child agency and choice for children to direct their own learning. This is because children are positioned as capable of making their own decisions. At the beginning of sessions children are supported in first planning what materials they want to work with, what they want to do and whom they want to do work with. Following engagement in their chosen activity, the children reflect upon what they did. This process is known as 'plan-do-review' and is at the heart of HighScope provision. This is viewed as important because adults are able to plan activities that build upon children's interests, therefore expanding their critical thinking. Involving children in this planning process ensures that both adults and children take responsibility for children's learning (Epstein et al., 2011). This can be viewed as active participatory learning where children and adults are partners in shaping children's learning experiences. This process supports the social context of learning.

HighScope Environment

The HighScope approach to education for young children aims to develop a range of skills such as independence, curiosity, resilience and problem-solving; as such the classroom environment can be developed in such a way that it supports children's learning. Epstein et al. (2011) state that there are five essential features of active participatory learning which feature in a HighScope classroom:

- The **use of materials** which are usually open ended and used to stimulate children's experiences and thoughts.
- **Manipulation** where children are able to make discoveries through direct hands-on learning.
- **Choice** is an important consideration in children's learning and children have the opportunity to choose their materials and who they play with.

- **Language** is a key feature of a HighScope classroom, where children are encouraged to communicate their thoughts and feelings through a range of interactions.
- These essential features are supported by adult scaffolding; adults will have a strong understanding of how children learn, and this supports their interactions with children through a range of activities.

The classroom environment is set out in specific areas of interest and usually includes a home corner area, an art area and block play and other materials which aim to acknowledge the developing interests of children. Areas are labelled and well-resourced with a range of diverse materials which reflect the home cultures of the children within that setting. Materials are readily available and accessible to children and this encourages children to be responsible and take control of their learning experiences. The classroom routine provides a variety of experiences; individual and group play is encouraged as is participating in small and large group activities. Epstein et al. (2011) comment that the classroom routine is centred on children's choices, that they are free to choose how they spend their time and that outdoor learning is encouraged. Children are encouraged to join in with tidying up, to socialise with peers at lunchtime and to be responsible for their personal care. Adults in the setting play a key role in developing this approach to encouraging independent learners.

As mentioned earlier in this section the plan-do-review sequence is an essential feature of the HighScope environment, however this approach is best understood through understanding the active learning process constructed by adults and children in their environments. Plan-do-review is both a cognitive and social process, the cognitive elements are best considered in how children can articulate a mental picture of their interests. Case (1985) suggests that their mental tools are an essential component of children's cognitive development. The social element, in Plan-do-review, is evident when children carry out their intentions and, as a result, develop their sense of initiative. These cognitive and social aspects of learning are supported by adults through the plan-do-review process.

Assessment of Children within Highscope

Epstein et al. (2011) state that quality of HighScope settings is measured by considering how well adults support children's learning and how well children learn. Several stakeholders, forming a team, are involved in formative and summative assessment of children's learning which includes parents, children and adults. The team is responsible for the cycle of assessment which includes formal and informal observations, anecdotal evidence, recording and sharing of planning. Children's learning is documented through HighScope's Key Development Indicators which are used to assess children's development (Wiltshire, 2012). The development indicators cover eight areas of learning: Approaches to Learning; Social and Emotional Development; Physical Development and Health; Language, Literacy and Communication; Mathematics; Creative Arts; Science and Technology; and Social Studies.

While HighScope offers an interesting approach to play-based learning, it will only be successful if its approach is applied consistently and reflections by adults on children's learning are part of this process. Training of adults working in HighScope is seen as essential and there is a comprehensive training package that all staff need to undertake to embed this approach within their practice.

Reflection Point 20.2

- What are the similarities and differences between the way playful learning is planned for and assessed within Reggio Emilia and HighScope provision?
- To what extent are these reflective of the construction of the child underpinning the approaches?

What is Te Whāriki?

Te Whāriki is the name for the National Curriculum for children aged birth to 5 in New Zealand developed in 1996 and updated in 2017 and in 2024. It aims to promote an inclusive approach based upon reciprocal relationships with the Māori community, and in so doing values the diverse cultural heritage of children and families within New Zealand (Smith, 1999, p. 6). It embraces the perspectives of Māori, and Pākehā (non-Māori) who are often European immigrants, but also includes populations from Pacific Islands and migrants from Asia. The name 'Te Whāriki' stems from the Māori language and means 'woven mat'. Te Whāriki draws upon real-life experiences of flax weaving which is a central area of learning within traditional Māori culture. The woven mat can be understood as a metaphor in which the central principles of holistic development, empowerment, relationships, and families and community are interwoven in learning situations (Carr & May 2000). The curriculum is founded on the following aspirations for children in New Zealand:

> To grow up as competent and confident learners and communicators, healthy in mind, body, and spirit, secure in their sense of belonging and in the knowledge that they make a valued contribution to the world. (Ministry of Education, 1996, p. 9)

The update curriculum framework expands the legal curriculum to include all four components: principles, strands, goals and learning outcomes. It introduces three distinct pathways.

The Social and Confident Child

Te Whāriki is rooted in a construction of children who are confident and capable learners and communicators. Consequently, significance is placed upon social and cultural learning and upon relationships for young children within their local communities. In this way it is congruent with sociocultural theories since learning is viewed as an active process involving other people. This is expressed explicitly within key government documentation:

> This curriculum emphasises the critical role of socially and culturally mediated learning and of reciprocal and responsive relationships for children with people, places and things. Children learn through collaboration with adults and peers, through guided participation and observation of others, as well as through individual exploration and reflection. (Ministry of Education, 1996, p. 9)

A Complex Curriculum

The curriculum has been described as non-prescriptive and complex (Nuttall, 2003) with learning and development represented as woven from the principles, strands and goals. In each setting there is a need for teachers and children to 'weave' their own curriculum mats reflective of their communities and based around the four principles (empowerment, relationships, family and community, and holistic development) and five strands (well-being, belonging, communication, contribution, and exploration) (Ministry of Education, 1996, pp. 15–16). This leads to a curriculum which can be 'dynamic and responsive' (Hedges, 2014) and reflective of the interests of children and their cultural beliefs. The curriculum is underpinned by the child-centred, sociocultural, bicultural vision of the New Zealand child.

Nurturing Learning Dispositions

The conceptualisation of the curriculum around empowering aims is viewed as a progressive shift and at odds with more traditional ways of working with young children which are often mapped against rigid domains of learning such as physical, intellectual, and social and emotional development (Smith, 2007). Drawing on the first principle, Empowerment (Whakamana), there is a focus on developing 'learning dispositions' which are viewed as characteristics of effective learning. This means that rather than focusing on *what* young children should learn, there is instead a focus on helping children to *develop* positive attitudes within the learning process. Desirable dispositions include courage and curiosity (taking an interest), trust and playfulness (being involved), perseverance (persisting with difficulty, challenge and uncertainty), confidence (expressing a point of view or feeling) and responsibility (taking responsibility) (Smith, 2011).

The second principle, Holistic Development (Kotahitanga) is integrated with the focus on dispositions and leads to the planning of play-based integrated learning with an emphasis on working theories or thinking skills. Hedges and Jones (2012, p. 36) argue that working theories are 'the tentative, evolving ideas and understandings (of) children (as they) formulate... and engage with others to think, ponder, wonder and make sense of the world'. As they are encouraged to engage in play-based opportunities which focus on the collaborative exploration of personal theories of their lived experiences, children are encouraged to persevere with difficulties, overcome challenges and to become autonomous and independent learners (Carr, 1997).

Assessment through 'Learning Stories'

The Te Whāriki curriculum does not aim to assess children's learning and development against pre-specified targets. Instead, 'learning stories', described as 'significant learning moments in a child's day to day experiences', (Carr et al., p. 189), have been developed to capture holistic assessment. Assessment through learning stories does not usually assess specific skills or isolated observations; rather, teachers aim to look at the learning dispositions that align to the goals of the curriculum – persisting where there are difficulties, expressing a point of view, finding something of interest and taking responsibility. Learning stories, which are shared with family members, can include handwritten stories, digital photographs, handwritten notes and short-term reviews, and allow others to see the world from the perspective of the child. Children's voices are an essential aspect of learning stories that allow children to take ownership of their learning, reflecting a positive construction of children's competencies.

Reflection Point 20.3

- How do the three approaches to play-based learning described in this chapter reflect wider social and cultural ideas of children and childhoods?
- How does the construction of the child underpinning each approach relate to its pedagogy?

Summary

The chapter has described three different approaches to structuring learning for young children underpinned by play-based pedagogy. Whilst there are some differences, which have been outlined within this chapter, each approach shares some broad principles around provision for young children. These include:

- A construction of children as curious meaning-makers possessing an innate disposition to be playful.
- Resonance with sociocultural theories in which learning is viewed as an active and social process.
- Recognition that play and learning are intertwined.
- Play being positioned as a vehicle for different types of development.
- Recognition that through playful pedagogies children learn that their own thinking is valued whilst they are being supported in developing independence.
- Use of assessment tools that aim to capture holistic development and make visible the learning of children as opposed to cross referencing with pre-specified targets, steps and outcomes.

In each approach there is also recognition of the important role that families and the wider community play in provision for children and the need for children to be supported in constructing positive self-identities as global citizens. These broad principles related to play are useful reflection points for practitioners who are utilising play-based approaches within the boundaries of different curricular models within the four nations of the United Kingdom.

Further Reading

Learning and Teaching Scotland (2006) The Reggio Emilia approach to early childhood education (Updated ed.). Dundee: Learning and Teaching Scotland. Retrieved from https://education.gov.scot/improvement/documents/elc/elc35_reggioemilia/elc35_reggioaug06.pdf. This short booklet gives a really accessible overview of all of the key aspects of the Reggio approach and would be very useful for anyone who has an initial interest in Reggio Emilia pedagogy.

Edwards, C., Gandini, L. and Forman, G. (2011) *The hundred languages of children: The Reggio Emilia approach – advanced reflections* (3rd ed.). Greenwich, CT: Ablex. This is a seminal book for anyone who is interested in developing their understanding of the different aspects of the Reggio Emilia approach.

Epstein, A. S., Johnson, S. and Lafferty, P. (2011) The HighScope approach. In L. Miller, nd L. Pound (Eds.), *Theories and approaches to learning in the early years*. London: Sage. This chapter gives a really clear overview of the key aspects of the HighScope approach.

Lee, W., Carr, M., Soutar, B. and Mitchell, L. (2013) *Understanding the Te Whāriki approach: Early years education in practice*. London: Routledge. This text provides a clear overview of the Te Whāriki approach with chapters on each of the key principles.

References

Bancroft, S., Fawcett, M., & Hay, P. (2008). *Researching children researching the world*. Stoke on Trent: Trentham Books.

Carr, M. (1997). *Learning stories. Position paper 5, project for assessing children's experiences*. Hamilton: Department of Early Childhood Studies, University of Waikato.

Carr, M., Hatherley, A., Lee, W., & Ramsey, K. (2005). Te Whāriki and assessment: A case study of teacher change. In J. Nuttall (Ed.), *Weaving Te Whāriki: Aotearoa New Zealand's early childhood curriculum document in theory and practice*. Palmerston North: Dunmore Press.

Carr, M., & May, H. (2000). Te Whāriki: Curriculum voices. In H. Penn (Ed.), *Early childhood services: Theory, policy and practice*. Milton Keynes: Open University Press.

Case, R. (1985). *Intellectual development: Birth to adulthood*. Orlando, FL: Academic Press.

Epstein, A. S., Johnson, S. , & Lafferty, P. (2011). The HighScope approach. In L. Miller, & L. Pound (Eds.), *Theories and approaches to learning in the early years*. London: Sage.

Gandini, L. (2011). Play and the hundred languages of children: An interview with Lella Gandini. *American Journal of Play*, 4(1), 1-18.

Hedges, H. (2014). Young children's 'working theories': Building and connecting understandings. *Journal of Early Childhood Research*, 12(1), 35-49.

Hedges, H., & Jones, S. (2012). Children's working theories: The neglected sibling of Te Whāriki's learning outcomes. *Early Childhood Folio*, 16(1), 34-39.

Malaguzzi, L. (1998). History, ideas and basic philosophy. In C. Edwards, L. Gandini, & G. Forman (Eds.), *The hundred languages of children: The Reggio Emilia approach – advanced reflections* (2nd ed.). Greenwich, CT: Ablex.

Maynard, T., & Chicken, S. (2010). Through a different lens: Exploring Reggio Emilia in a Welsh context. *Early Years: An International Journal of Research and Development*, 30(1), 29-39.

Miller, L., & Pound, L. (2010). Taking a critical perspective. In L. Miller & L. Pound (Eds.), *Theories and approaches to learning in the early years*. London: Sage.

Ministry of Education. (1996). *Te Whāriki: He whāriki mātauranga mō ngā mokopuna o Aotearoa. Early childhood curriculum.* Wellington: Learning Media.

Nuttall, J. G. (2003). *Weaving Te Whariki: Aotearoa New Zealand's early childhood curriculum document in theory and practice* (1st ed.) New Zealand Council for Educational Research.

Piaget, J., & Inhelder, B. (1969). *The psychology of the child.* New York: Basic Books.

Rinaldi, C. (1998). Projected curriculum constructed through documentation - progettazione: An interview with Lella Gandini. In C. Edwards, L. Gandini, & G. Forman (Eds.), *The hundred languages of children: The Reggio Emilia approach advanced reflections.* Norwood: Ablex.

Rinaldi, C. (2006). *In dialogue with Reggio Emilia: Listening, researching and learning.* Abingdon: Routledge.

Rinaldi, C. (2011). The pedagogy of listening: The listening perspective from Reggio Emilia. In C. Edwards, L. Gandini, & G. Forman (Eds.), *The hundred languages of children: The Reggio Emilia experience in transformation* (3rd ed.). Santa Barbara, CA: Praeger.

Smith, A. B. (1999). The role of an early childhood curriculum: Promoting diversity versus uniformity. *Paper presented at enhancing quality in the early years conference, Dublin, 19-20 November.*

Smith, A. B. (2007). Children and young people's participation rights in education. *The International Journal of Children's Rights,* 15, 147-164.

Smith, A. B. (2011). Relationships with people, places and things - Te Whāriki. In L. Miller, & P. Pound (Eds.), *Theories and approaches to learning in the early years.* London: Sage.

Vecchi, V., & Gandini, L. (2011). The atelier: A conversation with Vea Vecchi. In C. Edwards, L. Gandini, & G. Forman (Eds.), *The hundred languages of children: The Reggio Emilia experience in transformation* (3rd ed.). Santa Barbara, CA: Praeger.

Wiltshire, M. (2012). *Understanding the HighScope approach: Early years education in practice.* London: Routledge.

Index

United Kingdom (UK), 23, 49, 52, 185, 188, 211–212
  Children on the Edge (COTE), 262
  children's right to play, 26
  curriculum provision for children 0–8 years, 186–187
  Early Years environments, 128–129
  emotional well-being, 104
  four-stage model of creativity, 109–110
  mental health concerns, 104
  Old People's Home for 4 Year Olds, 234
  outdoor play, 168–169
  risky play outdoors, 248–249
  well-being, policies, 104
United Nations (UN), 19, 22
  Sustainable Development Goals, 65, 254–255
United Nations Convention on the Rights of Persons with Disabilities, 213
United Nations Convention on the Rights of the Child (UNCRC), 13, 201
  Article 31 of, 7–8, 19–21, 34, 213
  inclusive play, 213
  play, definition of, 8
  play sufficiency, 26
  the three Ps, 19
United Nations High Commissioner for Refugees (UNHCR), 255
Unoccupied play, 31–32
Upstairs brain, 64

V
Value of play, 260–261
Village Health Teams in Uganda, 230
Visual aids, 219
Vygotsky, L., 11–12, 14, 77–78, 81, 110–111, 118, 215, 242–244, 268, 272

W
Wales, 20, 185–186
  Additional Learning Needs (ALN), 211–212
  Area of Learning and Experience, 104
  case study, 194
  Curriculum for Wales (CfW), 109, 188
  Play Friendly Country statutory guidance, 201
  Play policy (2019), 186
  Play Sufficiency Duty, 26
  Well-Being of Future Generations Act (2015), 104
Wallas, G., 108–110
Waller, T., 245–246
Well-being, 9, 37, 81, 187
  definitions, 103–104
  emotional, 12–13, 51, 104
  free play, 41
  importance of, 104
  measuring, 107
  media practices, protection, 178
  mental, 253–254
  play and, 104–105
  promoting, 105–107
  social-emotional, 78
  subjective, 103–104
Well-Being of Future Generations Act (2015), 104
Westby, C., 120
Whale, L., 2
Whitehouse, S., 4
Williams, D., 235
Wilson, E. O., 169–170
Wood, E., 205
Word of warning, 140–141

Z
Zone of proximal development (ZPD), 77–78, 81, 202–203, 215